A BEGINNER'S GUIDE TO STRUCTURAL EQUATION MODELING

Second Edition

Randall E. Schumacker
University of North Texas

Richard G. Lomax
The University of Alabama

2004

LAWRENCE ERLBAUM ASSOCIATES, PUBLISHERS

Mahwah, New Jersey   London

Psychology Press
Taylor & Francis Group
270 Madison Avenue
New York, NY 10016

Psychology Press
Taylor & Francis Group
27 Church Road
Hove, East Sussex BN3 2FA

© 2004 by Taylor & Francis Group, LLC
Psychology Press is an imprint of Taylor & Francis Group, an Informa business

Printed in the United States of America on acid-free paper
15 14 13 12 11 10 9 8 7 6
IInternational Standard Book Number-13: 978-0-8058-4018-6 (Softcover)
Library of Congress catalog number: 2004003497
Cover Design: Kathryn Houghtaling Lacey

Library of Congress Cataloging-in-Publication Data

Schumacker, Randall E.
  A beginner's guide to structural equation modeling/Randall E. Schumacker. Richard G. Lomax.—2nd ed.
     p. cm.
  Includes bibliographical references and index.
  ISBN 0-8058-4017-6 (case :alk. paper)—ISBN 0-8058-4108-4 (pbk. :alk. paper)
    1. Multivariate analysis. 2. Social sciences—Statistical methods.
I. Lomax, Richard G. II. Title.
QA278.S36   2004
519.5'35—dc22

2004003497

Visit the Taylor & Francis Web site at
http://www.taylorandfrancis.com

and the Psychology Press Web site at
http://www.psypress.com

A BEGINNER'S GUIDE TO STRUCTURAL EQUATION MODELING

Dedicated to Our Families

Joanne, Rachel, and Jamie

and

Lea and Kristen

Contents

PREFACE

APPROACH

This book provides a basic introduction to structural equation modeling (SEM). We first review the concepts of correlation and covariance, then discuss multiple regression, path, and factor analyses to give a better understanding of the building blocks of SEM. We describe a basic structural equation model and then present several different types of structural equation models. Our approach is both conceptual and application oriented. Each chapter covers basic concepts, principles, and practice, and then utilizes SEM software to provide meaningful examples. Most chapters follow the conceptual sequence of SEM steps known as model specification, identification, estimation, testing, and modification. Model validation techniques are covered in a separate chapter. The text includes numerous SEM examples using the Amos, EQS, and LISREL computer programs. We use the latest versions available at time of printing, namely Amos 5.0, EQS 6.1, and LISREL 8.54. Given the advances in SEM software over the past decade, the reader should expect updates of these software packages and therefore become familiar with any new features as well as explore their excellent library and help materials. The SEM software packages are easy-to-use Windows-based programs with pull-down menus, dialog boxes, and drawing tools. The SEM model examples do not require complicated programming skills nor does the reader need an advanced understanding of statistics and matrix algebra to understand the model applications. We provide a chapter on the matrix approach to SEM as well as an appendix on matrix operations for the interested reader. We encourage the understanding of the matrices used in SEM models, especially for some of the more advanced SEM models.

GOALS AND CONTENT COVERAGE

Our main goal is for the reader to be able to conduct his or her own SEM model analyses as well as understand and critique published SEM research. These goals are supported by the conceptual and applied examples contained in the book. We also include a SEM checklist to guide model analysis according to the basic steps a researcher needs to take.

The text begins with an introduction to SEM (what it is, some history, why it should be conducted, and what software we use in the book), followed by chapters on data entry and editing issues and correlation. These early chapters are critical to understanding how missing data, nonnormality, scale of measurement, nonlinearity, outliers, and restriction of range in scores affect SEM analysis. Chapter 4 lays out the basic steps of model specification, identification, estimation, testing, and modification. Chapter 5 covers issues related to model fit indices. Chapters 6 through 10 follow the basic SEM steps of modeling, with examples from different disciplines, using regression, path, confirmatory factor, and structural equation models. Chapter 11 presents information about reporting SEM research and includes a SEM checklist to guide decision making. Chapter 12 presents several approaches to model validation, an important final step after obtaining an acceptable theoretical model. Chapters 13 and 14 provide SEM examples to introduce some of the different types of SEM model applications. The final chapter, chapter 15, describes the matrix approach to structural equation modeling by using examples from the previous chapters.

Theoretical models are present in every discipline, and therefore can be formulated and tested. This second edition expands SEM models and applications to provide researchers in medicine, political science, sociology, education, psychology, business, and the biological sciences the basic concepts, principles, and practice necessary to test their theoretical models. We hope the reader will be more familiar with structural equation modeling after reading the book and use SEM in his or her research.

NEW TO THE SECOND EDITION

The first edition of this book was one of the first textbooks published on SEM. Since that time we have had considerable experience utilizing the book in class with our students. As a result of those experiences the second edition represents a more usable textbook for teaching SEM. We include more examples with computer programs and output integrated into the text, additional chapters, and chapter exercises to further illustrate chapter contents. We believe this second edition can be used to teach a full course in SEM. Several new chapters are added and other chapters are updated and enhanced with additional material. The updated chapters include an introduction to SEM (chap. 1), correlation (chap. 3), model fit (chap. 5), developing structural equation models (chaps. 9 and 10), model validation (chap. 12), and the matrix approach to SEM (chap. 15). These chapters contain substantial revisions over the first edition. Chapter 1 describes structural equation modeling, provides a brief history of its development over the last several decades, and provides updated information for accessing student versions of the software. Chapter 3 includes more information about factors that affect correlation, namely level of measurement, linearity, missing data, outliers, correction for attenuation, and non-positive definite matrices. Chapter 5 is expanded to cover the four-step approach to structural equation modeling and further discusses hypothesis testing, significance, power, and sample size issues. Chapters 9 and 10 include chapter exercises and also follow the five basic steps in structural equation modeling, namely model specification, model identification, model estimation, model testing, and model modification. Chapter 12 is expanded to include multiple-sample models for replication of study findings and updated program examples for cross-validation, simulation, bootstrap, and jackknife methods. Chapter 15 is updated to include matrix notation examples and programs from advanced SEM models discussed in previous chapters. The other chapters in the book are new to the second edition; thus, the second edition is a significant revision with the teacher and researcher at the forefront of our thinking. Chapter 2, for example, shows how to import data into Amos, EQS, and LISREL, and discusses issues related to data editing, including the measurement scale of variables, the restriction of range in the data, missing data, outliers, linearity, and nonnormality. Chapter 4 presents the five basic steps in structural equation modeling, which are used in the new Chapters 6 through 8 to illustrate regression models, path models, and confirmatory factor models, respectively. Chapter 11 provides guidance on how to report SEM research and discusses critical issues related to conducting SEM analyses. Chapters 13 and 14 are new chapters illustrating several recent SEM applications: multiple indicators–multiple causes, multiple groups, multilevels, mixtures, structured means, multitrait–multimethod models and correlated uniqueness, second-order factor models, interaction models, latent growth curve models, and dynamic factor models. We made every attempt to ensure that the programs and applications in these chapters are correct, and any errors or omissions are ours.

We also include two new sets of materials that should help in teaching a course in SEM: an introduction to matrix notation and a CD. The introduction to matrix notation illustrates how matrix calculations are computed and is included in the Appendix. The CD includes the Amos, EQS, and LISREL programs and data sets presented in the text. This will make it easier to run the program examples in the chapters without having to spend burdensome time retyping the programs or entering the data. Having these materials available will be especially helpful with Amos because it contains diagrams linked to data sets rather than the program syntax per se.

ACKNOWLEDGMENTS

The second edition of this book represents more than 20 years of interacting with our colleagues and students who use structural equation modeling. As before, we are most grateful to the pioneers in the field of structural equation modeling, particularly Karl Jöreskog, Dag Sörbom, Peter Bentler, and James Arbuckle. These individuals developed and shaped the field as well as the content of this text by providing Amos, EQS, and LISREL software programs. We are also grateful to Eric Wu, Werner Wothke, Gerhard Mels, and Stephen du Toit, who answered our questions about the SEM programming exercises in the text. Finally, we give special thanks to George Marcoulides, whose collaboration with the first author on new developments and techniques in SEM greatly enhanced the applications presented in this book.

This book was made possible through the wonderful support and encouragement of Lawrence Erlbaum. His remarkable belief in our book, understanding, patience, and guidance are deeply respected and appreciated. We also thank Debra Riegert and Art Lizza for helping us through the difficult process of dealing with revisions and galleys and getting the book into print. They once again put forth a tremendous effort on our behalf.

—*Randall E. Schumacker*
—*Richard G. Lomax*

A BEGINNER'S GUIDE TO STRUCTURAL EQUATION MODELING

1

INTRODUCTION

Chapter Outline

Key Concepts

Latent and observed variables
Independent and dependent variables
Types of structural equation models
   Regression
   Path
   Confirmatory factor
   Structural equation
History of structural equation modeling
Structural equation modeling software programs

Structural equation modeling can be easily understood if the researcher has an understanding of basic statistics, correlations, and regression analysis. The first three chapters provide a brief introduction to structural equation modeling (SEM), basic data entry and editing issues in statistics, and concepts related to the use of correlation coefficients in structural equation modeling. Chapter 4 covers the basic concepts of SEM: model specification, identification, estimation, testing, and modification. This basic understanding provides the framework for understanding the material presented in chapters 5 through 8 on model fit indices and regression analysis, path analysis, and confirmatory factor analysis models (measurement models), which form the basis for understanding the structural equation models (latent variable models) presented in chapters 9 and 10. Chapter 11 provides guidance on reporting structural equation modeling research. Chapter 12 addresses techniques used to establish model validity and generalization of findings. Chapters 13 and 14 present basic SEM applications using Amos, EQS, and LISREL SEM software. The final chapter, chapter 15, presents matrix notation for some of these SEM applications and covers the eight matrices used in various structural equation models. We include an introduction to matrix operations in the Appendix for readers who want a more mathematical understanding of matrix operations.

To start our journey of understanding, we ask what is structural equation modeling, then give a brief history of SEM, discuss the importance of SEM, and note the availability of the software programs used in the book.

1.1 WHAT IS STRUCTURAL EQUATION MODELING?

Structural equation modeling (SEM) uses various types of models to depict relationships among observed variables, with the same basic goal of providing a quantitative test of a theoretical model hypothesized by a researcher. More specifically, various theoretical models can be tested in SEM that hypothesize how sets of variables define constructs and how these constructs are related to each other. For example, an educational researcher might hypothesize that a student's home environment influences her later achievement in school. A marketing researcher may hypothesize that consumer trust in a corporation leads to increased product sales for that corporation. A health care professional might believe that a good diet and regular exercise reduce the risk of a heart attack.

In each example, the researcher believes, based on theory and empirical research, that sets of variables define the constructs that are hypothesized to be related in a certain way. The goal of SEM analysis is to determine the extent to which the theoretical model is supported by sample data. If the sample data support the theoretical model, then more complex theoretical models can be hypothesized. If the sample data do not support the theoretical model, then either the original model can be modified and tested or other theoretical models need to be developed and tested. Consequently, SEM tests theoretical models using the scientific method of hypothesis testing to advance our understanding of the complex relationships amongst constructs.

SEM can test various types of theoretical models. Basic models include regression (chap. 6), path (chap. 7), and confirmatory factor (chap. 8) models. Our reason for covering these basic models is that they provide a basis for understanding structural equation models (chaps. 9 and 10). To better understand these basic models, we need to define a few terms. First, there are two major types of variables: *latent variables* and *observed variables*. Latent variables (constructs or factors) are variables that are not directly observable or measured. Latent variables are indirectly observed or measured, and hence are inferred from a set of variables that we do measure using tests, surveys, and so on. For example, intelligence is a latent variable that represents a psychological construct. The confidence of consumers in American business is another latent variable, one representing an economic construct. The physical condition of adults is a third latent variable, one representing a health-related construct.

The observed, measured, or indicator variables are a set of variables that we use to define or infer the latent variable or construct. For example, the Wechsler Intelligence Scale for Children–Revised (WISC–R) is an instrument that produces a measured variable (scores) that one uses to infer the construct of a child's intelligence. Additional indicator variables, that is, intelligence tests, could be used to indicate or define the construct of intelligence (latent variable). The Dow–Jones index is a standard measure of the American corporate economy construct. Other measured variables might include gross national product, retail sales, or export sales. Blood pressure is one of many health-related variables that could indicate a latent variable defined as "fitness." Each of these observed or indicator variables represents one definition of the latent variable. Researchers use sets of indicator variables to define a latent variable; thus, other instruments are used to obtain indicator variables, for example, in the foregoing cases, the Stanford–Binet Intelligence Scale, the NASDAQ index, and an individual's cholesterol level, respectively.

Variables, whether they are observed or latent, can also be defined as either *independent variables* or *dependent variables*. An independent variable is a variable that is not influenced by any other variable in the model. A dependent variable is a variable that is influenced by another variable in the model. Let us return to the foregoing examples and specify the independent and dependent variables. The educational researcher hypothesizes that a student's home environment (independent latent variable) influences school achievement (dependent latent variable). The marketing researcher believes that consumer trust in a corporation (independent latent variable) leads to increased product sales (dependent latent variable). The health care professional wants to determine whether a good diet and regular exercise (two independent latent variables) influence the frequency of heart attacks (dependent latent variable).

The basic SEM models in chapters 6 through 8 illustrate the use of observed variables and latent variables when defined as independent or dependent. A regression model consists solely of observed variables where a single dependent observed variable is predicted or explained by one or more independent observed variables; for example, a parent's education level (independent observed variable) is used to predict his or her child's achievement score (dependent observed variable). A path model is also specified entirely with observed variables, but the flexibility allows for multiple independent observed variables and multiple dependent observed variables; for example, export sales, gross national product, and NASDAQ index influence consumer trust and consumer spending (dependent observed variables). Path models therefore test more complex models than regression models. Confirmatory factor models consist of observed variables that are hypothesized to measure one or more latent variables (independent or dependent); for example, diet, exercise, and physiology are observed measures of the independent latent variable "fitness." An understanding of these basic models will help in understanding structural equation analysis, which combines path- and factor-analytic models. Structural equation models consist of observed variables and latent variables, whether independent or dependent; for example, an independent latent variable (aptitude) influences a dependent latent variable (achievement) where both types of latent variables are measured, defined, or inferred by multiple observed or measured indicator variables.

1.2 HISTORY OF STRUCTURAL EQUATION MODELING

To discuss the history of structural equation modeling, we explain the following four types of related models and their chronological order of development: regression, path, confirmatory factor, and structural equation models.

The first model involves linear regression models that use a correlation coefficient and least squares criterion to compute regression weights. Regression models were made possible due to the creation by Karl Pearson of a formula for the correlation coefficient in 1896 that provides an index for the relationship between two variables (Pearson, 1938). The regression model permits the prediction of dependent observed variable scores (Y) given a linear weighting of a set of independent observed scores (X's) that minimizes the sum of squared residual values. The mathematical basis for the linear regression model is found in basic algebra. Regression analysis provides a test of a theoretical model that may be useful for prediction (e.g., admission to graduate school or budget projections).

Some years later, Charles Spearman (1904, 1927) used the correlation coefficient to determine which items correlated or went together to create the factor model. His basic idea was that if a set of items correlated or went together, individual responses to the set of items could be summed to yield a score that would measure, define, or imply a construct. Spearman was the first to use the term factor analysis in defining a two-factor construct for a theory of intelligence. D. N. Lawley and L. L. Thurstone in 1940 further developed applications of factor models and proposed instruments (sets of items) that yielded observed scores from which constructs could be inferred. Most of the aptitude, achievement, and diagnostic tests, surveys, and inventories in use today were created using factor techniques. The term *confirmatory factor analysis* (CFA) as used today is based in part on work by Howe (1955), Anderson and Rubin (1956), and Lawley (1958). The CFA method was more fully developed by Karl Jöreskog in the 1960s to test whether a set of items defined a construct. Jöreskog completed his dissertation in 1963, published the first article on CFA in 1969, and subsequently helped develop the first CFA software program. Factor analysis has been used for over 100 years to create measurement instruments used in many academic disciplines, while today CFA is used to test the existence of these theoretical constructs.

Sewell Wright (1918, 1921, 1934), a biologist, developed the third type of model, a path model. Path models use correlation coefficients and regression analysis to model more complex relationships among observed variables. The first applications of path analysis dealt with models of animal behavior. Unfortunately, path analysis was largely overlooked until econometricians reconsidered it in the 1950s as a form of simultaneous equation modeling (e.g., H. Wold) and sociologists rediscovered it in the 1960s (e.g., O. D. Duncan and H. M. Blalock). In many respects, path analysis involves solving a set of simultaneous regression equations that theoretically establish the relationship among the observed variables in the path model.

The final model type is structural equation modeling (SEM). SEM models essentially combine path models and confirmatory factor models, that is, SEM models incorporate both latent and observed variables. The early development of SEM models was due to Karl Jöreskog (1973), Ward Keesling (1972), and David Wiley (1973); this approach was initially known as the JKW model, but became known as the linear structural relations model (LISREL) with the development of the first software program, LISREL, in 1973.

Jöreskog and van Thillo originally developed the LISREL software program at the Educational Testing Service (ETS) using a matrix command language (i.e., Greek and matrix notation), which is described in chapter 15. The first publicly available version, LISREL III, was released in 1976. In 1993, LISREL8 was released; it introduced the SIMPLIS (SIMPle LISrel) command language, in which equations are written using variable names. In 1999, the first interactive version of LISREL was released. LISREL8 introduced the dialog box interface, using pull-down menus and point-and-click features to develop models and the path diagram mode, a drawing program to develop models. Cudeck, DuToit, and Sörbom (2001) edited a Festschrift in honor of Jöreskog's contributions to the field of structural equation modeling. Their volume contains chapters by scholars who address the many topics, concerns, and applications in the field of structural equation modeling today, including milestones in factor analysis; measurement models; robustness, reliability, and fit assessment; repeated measurement designs; ordinal data; and interaction models. We cover many of these topics in this book, although not in as great a depth. The field of structural equation modeling across all disciplines has expanded since 1994. Hershberger (2003) found that between 1994 and 2001 the number of journal articles concerned with SEM increased, the number of journals publishing SEM research increased, SEM became a popular choice among multivariate methods, and the journal *Structural Equation Modeling* became the primary source for technical developments in structural equation modeling.

Although the LISREL program was the first SEM software program, other software programs have been developed since the mid-1980s. There are numerous programs available to the SEM researcher, each unique in its own way and each capable of different SEM applications. We use Amos, EQS, and LISREL in this book to demonstrate many different SEM applications including regression models, path models, factor models, multiple causes–multiple indicators models, multiple group models, multilevel models, mixture models, multitrait–multimethod models, interaction models, latent growth curve models, and dynamic models.

1.3 WHY CONDUCT STRUCTURAL EQUATION MODELING?

Why is structural equation modeling popular? There are at least four major reasons for the popularity of SEM. The first reason suggests that researchers are becoming more aware of the need to use multiple observed variables to better understand their area of scientific inquiry. Basic statistical methods only utilize a limited number of variables, which are not capable of dealing with the sophisticated theories being developed. The use of a small number of variables to understand complex phenomena is limiting. For instance, the use of simple bivariate correlations is not sufficient for examining a sophisticated theoretical model. In contrast, structural equation modeling permits complex phenomena to be statistically modeled and tested. SEM techniques are therefore becoming the preferred method for confirming (or disconfirming) theoretical models in a quantitative fashion.

A second reason involves the greater recognition given to the validity and the reliability of observed scores from measurement instruments. Specifically, measurement error has become a major issue in many disciplines, but measurement error and statistical analysis of data have been treated separately. Structural equation modeling techniques explicitly take measurement error into account when statistically analyzing data. As noted in subsequent chapters, SEM analysis includes latent and observed variables as well as measurement error terms in certain SEM models.

A third reason pertains to how structural equation modeling has matured over the last 30 years, especially the ability to analyze more advanced theoretical SEM models. For example, group differences in theoretical models can be assessed through multiple-group SEM models. In addition, collecting educational data at more than one level, for example, from students, teachers, and schools, is now possible using multilevel SEM modeling. As a final example, interaction terms can now be included in an SEM model so that main effects and interaction effects can be tested. These advanced SEM models and techniques have provided many researchers with an increased capability to analyze sophisticated theoretical models of complex phenomena, thus requiring less reliance on basic statistical methods.

Finally, SEM software programs have become increasingly user-friendly. For example, until 1993 LISREL users had to input the program syntax for their models using Greek and matrix notation. At that time, many researchers sought help because of the complex programming requirement and knowledge of the SEM syntax that was needed. Today, most SEM software programs are Windows based and use pull-down menus or drawing programs to generate the program syntax internally. Therefore, the SEM software programs are now easier to use and contain features similar to other Windows based software packages. However, such ease of use necessitates statistical training in SEM modeling and software via courses, workshops, or textbooks to avoid mistakes and errors in analyzing sophisticated theoretical models.

I.4 STRUCTURAL EQUATION MODELING SOFTWARE PROGRAMS

A researcher who is just starting to use structural equation modeling software will find several new, user-friendly, Windows based, personal computer programs to choose from. Many of the new versions provide statistical analysis of raw data (means, correlations, missing data conventions, etc.), provide routines for handling missing data and detecting outliers, generate the program's syntax language, diagram the model, and provide for import and export of data and figures of the theoretical model(s). Also, many of the programs come with sets of data and program examples that are clearly explained in their user guides. Many of these software packages have been reviewed in the *Structural Equation Modeling* journal.

The pricing information for SEM software varies depending on individual, group, or site license arrangements; corporate versus educational settings; and even whether one is a student or faculty member. Furthermore, newer versions and updates necessitate changes in pricing. Most programs will run in the Windows environment; some run on MacIntosh personal computers (e.g., EQS). We are often asked to recommend a software package to a beginning SEM researcher; however, given the different individual needs of researchers and the multitude of different features available in these programs (which also change with each version), we are not able to make such a recommendation. Ultimately the decision depends upon the researcher's needs and preferences. Consequently, with so many software packages, we felt it important to narrow our examples in the book to three: Amos, EQS, and LISREL. These three SEM software packages are available as follows:

- **Amos (SPSS interface)**
  Developed by
     Dr. James Arbuckle
     Department of Psychology

Temple University
Philadelphia, PA 19122
Distributed by
SPSS Inc.
Corporate Headquarters
233 S. Wacker Drive, 11th floor
Chicago, IL 60606-6307
Telephone: (312) 651-3000
Fax: (312) 651-3668
Internet: http://www.spss.com
or
Lawrence Erlbaum Associates, Inc.
10 Industrial Avenue
Mahwah, NJ 07430-2262
Telephone: (201) 258-2200
Fax: (201) 236-0072
Orders: (800) 926-6579
E-mail: orders@erlbaum.com
Internet: http://www.erlbaum.com

- **EQS**
Developed by
Dr. Peter M. Bentler
Department of Psychology
University of California, Los Angeles
Los Angeles, CA 90025
Distributed by
Multivariate Software, Inc.
15720 Ventura Blvd.
Suite 306
Encino, CA 91436-2989
Telephone: (818) 906-0740
Fax: (818) 906-8205
Orders: (800) 301-4456
E-mail: sales@mvsoft.com
Internet: http://www.mvsoft.com
- **LISREL–SIMPLIS, LISREL–PRELIS, Interactive LISREL**
Developed by
Karl Jöreskog and Dag Sörbom
Department of Statistics
Uppsala University
P.O. Box 513
S-751 20 Uppsala
Sweden

Distributed by
    Scientific Software International, Inc.
    7383 N. Lincoln Ave., Suite 100
    Lincolnwood, IL 60712-1704
    Telephone: (847) 675-0720
    Fax: (847) 675-2140
    Orders: (800) 247-6113
    E-mail: info@ssicentral.com
    Internet: http://www.ssicentral.com
or

    Lawrence Erlbaum Associates, Inc.
    10 Industrial Avenue
    Mahwah, NJ 07430-2262
    Telephone: (201) 258-2200
    Fax: (201) 236-0072
    Orders: (800) 926-6579
    E-mail: orders@erlbaum.com
    Internet: http://www.erlbaum.com

1.5   SUMMARY

In this chapter we introduced structural equation modeling by describing basic types of variables—latent, observed, independent, and
dependent—and basic types of SEM models—regression, path, confirmatory factor, and structural equation models. In addition, we gave a
brief history of structural equation modeling and a discussion of the importance of SEM. The chapter concluded with information about where
to obtain the structural equation modeling software programs used in
the book. In chapter 2 we consider the importance of examining data for
issues related to measurement level (nominal, ordinal, interval, or ratio),
restriction of range (fewer than 15 categories), missing data, outliers (extreme values), linearity or nonlinearity, and normality or nonnormality,
which affect all statistical methods, and especially SEM applications.

EXERCISES

1. Define the following terms:
   a. Latent variable
   b. Observed variable
   c. Dependent variable
   d. Independent variable
2. Explain the difference between a dependent latent variable and a dependent observed
   variable.

3. Explain the difference between an independent latent variable and an independent observed variable.
4. List the reasons why a researcher would conduct structural equation modeling.
5. Download the student versions of Amos, EQS, and LISREL from the websites given in this chapter.

REFERENCES

Anderson, T. W., & Rubin, H. (1956). Statistical inference in factor analysis. In J. Neyman (Ed.), *Proceedings of the third Berkeley symposium on mathematical statistics and probability, Vol. V* (pp. 111–150). Berkeley: University of California Press.

Cudeck, R., Du Toit, S., & Sörbom, D. (2001) (Eds). *Structural equation modeling: Present and future. A Festschrift in honor of Karl Jöreskog.* Lincolnwood, IL: Scientific Software International.

Hershberger, S. L. (2003). The growth of structural equation modeling: 1994–2001. *Structural Equation Modeling, 10*(1), 35–46.

Howe, W. G. (1955). *Some contributions to factor analysis* (Report No. ORNL-1919). Oak Ridge National Laboratory, Oak Ridge, TN.

Jöreskog, K. G. (1963). *Statistical estimation in factor analysis: A new technique and its foundation.* Stockholm: Almqvist & Wiksell.

Jöreskog, K. G. (1969). A general approach to confirmatory maximum likelihood factor analysis. *Psychometrika, 34*, 183–202.

Jöreskog, K. G. (1973). A general method for estimating a linear structural equation system. In A. S. Goldberger & O. D. Duncan (Eds.), *Structural equation models in the social sciences* (pp. 85–112). New York: Seminar.

Keesling, J. W. (1972). *Maximum likelihood approaches to causal flow analysis.* Unpublished doctoral dissertation, University of Chicago.

Lawley, D. N. (1958). Estimation in factor analysis under various initial assumptions. *British Journal of Statistical Psychology, 11*, 1–12.

Pearson, E. S. (1938). Karl Pearson. An appreciation of some aspects of his life and work. *Biometrika, 29*, 1–248.

Spearman, C. (1904). The proof and measurement of association between two things. *American Journal of Psychology, 15*, 72–101.

Spearman, C. (1927). *The abilities of man.* New York: Macmillan.

Wiley, D. E. (1973). The identification problem for structural equation models with unmeasured variables. In A. S. Goldberger & O. D. Duncan (Eds.), *Structural equation models in the social sciences* (pp. 69–83). New York: Seminar.

Wright, S. (1918). On the nature of size factors. *Genetics, 3*, 367–374.

Wright, S. (1921). Correlation and causation. *Journal of Agricultural Research, 20*, 557–585.

Wright, S. (1934). The method of path coefficients. *Annals of Mathematical Statistics, 5*, 161–215.

ANSWERS TO EXERCISES

1. Define the following terms:
   a. Latent variable: an unobserved variable that is not directly measured, but is computed using multiple observed variables.

   b. Observed variable: a raw score obtained from a test or measurement instrument on a trait of interest.
   c. Dependent variable: a variable that is measured and related to outcomes, performance, or criterion.
   d. Independent variable: a variable that defines mutually exclusive categories (e.g., gender, region, or grade level) or, as a continuous variable, influences a dependent variable.
2. Explain the difference between a dependent latent variable and a dependent observed variable: A dependent latent variable is not directly measured, but is computed using multiple dependent observed variables. A dependent observed variable is a raw score obtained from a measurement instrument or assigned to a criterion variable.
3. Explain the difference between an independent latent variable and an independent observed variable: An independent latent variable is not directly measured, but is computed using multiple independent observed variables. An independent observed variable is a raw score obtained from a measurement instrument or assigned to an attribute variable.
4. List the reasons why a researcher would conduct structural equation modeling.
   a. Researchers are becoming more aware of the need to use multiple observed variables to better understand their area of scientific inquiry.
   b. More recognition is given to the validity and reliability of observed scores from measurement instruments.
   c. Structural equation modeling has improved recently, especially the ability to analyze more advanced statistical models.
   d. SEM software programs have become increasingly user-friendly.
5. Download the student versions of Amos, EQS, and LISREL from the websites given in this chapter.
   a. Amos: http://www.smallwaters.com/
   b. EQS: http://www.mvsoft.com/
   c. LISREL: http://www.ssicentral.com/

CHAPTER

2

DATA ENTRY AND DATA EDITING ISSUES

Chapter Outline

Key Concepts

ASCII data file
Importing data file
System file
Measurement scale
Restriction of range
Missing data
Outliers
Linearity
Nonnormality

An important first step in using SEM software programs is to be able to enter raw data and/or import data, especially between different software programs. Other important steps involve being able to use the SEM software programs' saved file (system file), and output and save files that contain the variance–covariance matrix, the correlation matrix, means, and standard deviations of variables so they can be input into command syntax programs, for example, EQS and SIMPLIS. The three SEM programs (Amos, EQS, and LISREL) will be briefly explained in this chapter to demonstrate how each handles raw data entry, importing of data from other programs, and the output of saved files.

There are several key issues in the field of statistics that impact our analyses once data have been imported into a software program. These data issues are commonly referred to as the measurement scale of variables, restriction in the range of data, missing data values, outliers, linearity, and nonnormality. Each of these data issues will be discussed because they not only affect traditional statistics, but present additional problems and concerns in structural equation modeling.

We use Amos, EQS, and LISREL software throughout the book, so you will need to use their software programs and become familiar with their websites, and should have downloaded a free student version of their software. We also use some of the data and model examples available in their free student versions to illustrate SEM applications. The free student versions of the software have user guides, library and help functions, and tutorials. The websites also contain important research, documentation, and information about structural equation modeling. However, be aware that the free student versions of the software do not contain the full capabilities for importing data, data analysis, and computer output available in their full product versions.

2.1   DATA ENTRY

Amos

The first thing you will notice when running Amos is the impressive toolbox with numerous icons. If you hold the mouse over any of the toolbox icons it will provide a basic description of what it does. Data files are imported by using the **File** option on the pull-down menu.

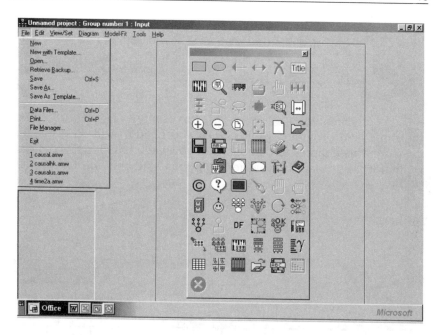

Clicking on the **Data Files** under the **File** pull-down menu reveals the **Data Files** dialog box. Now click on **File Name** to open the second dialog box to browse for a data file. SPSS saved data files are indicated here, but other programs can also be accessed, for example, dBase, Excel, Lotus, and ASCII data. Amos interfaces with SPSS to make it easier to enter raw data and label variable names and variable values for file input into Amos.

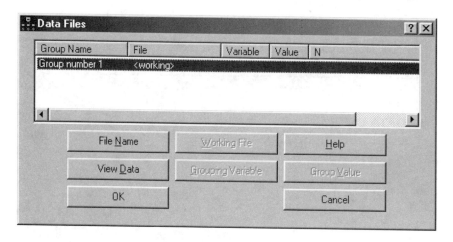

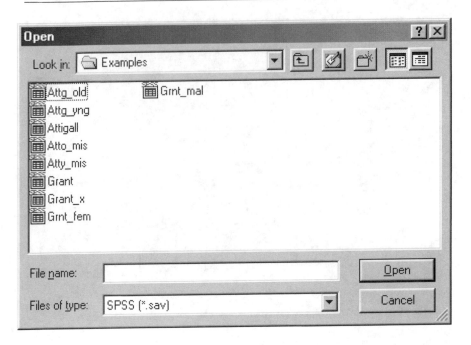

The SPSS saved file *Attigall.sav* is selected, and the Amos dialog box indicates the file name and number of subjects. Clicking on **View Data** opens the SPSS software program so that the raw data can be viewed. SPSS can also be used to edit data for missing values, outliers, linearity, and nonnormality of variable values as discussed in this chapter.

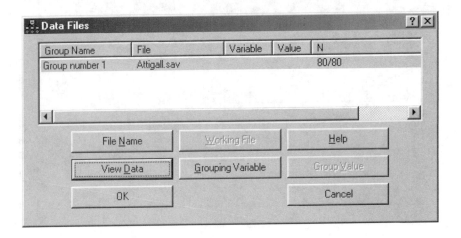

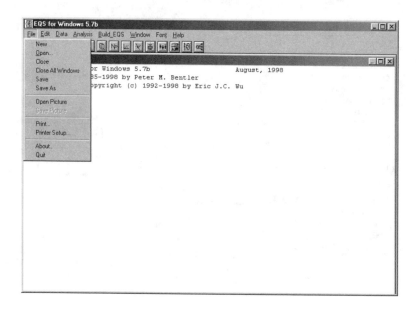

EQS

The EQS software program permits the inputting of ASCII data and the importing of data files from other software programs, for example, dBase, Excel, Lotus, and SPSS, and text-formatted files using the **File** menu option; click on **New** for ASCII data or **Open** to import a data file.

When clicking on **New** to input ASCII data or create an EQS system file, it is important to know how many variables and cases are being input, otherwise you will not be able to input raw data into an ASCII file or create an EQS spreadsheet-style system file. It is recommended that raw data be input and saved as an EQS system file for future use; and also be saved as an SPSS save file for input into another program.

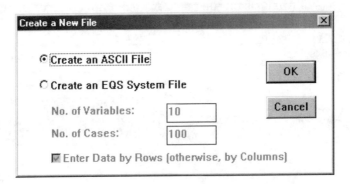

When clicking on **Open**, you can browse to find either a saved EQS system file, for example, *airpoll.ess*, or saved files from other programs.

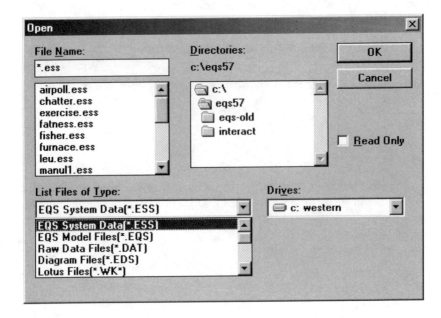

EQS also includes additional program features that permit statistical analysis of data, for example, frequency, crosstabs, *t* test, analysis of variance, factor analysis, correlation, and regression. EQS uses a spreadsheet when viewing data, creates and saves its own system files, and offers menu options for editing data, handling missing values, identifying outliers, checking linearity, and testing for nonnormality in data values. For example, the EQS system file *airpoll.ess* is opened to permit the use of **Analysis** on the pull-down menu to conduct a statistical analysis.

LISREL–PRELIS

The LISREL software program interfaces with PRELIS, a preprocessor of data program prior to running LISREL (matrix command language) or SIMPLIS (easier-to-use variable syntax) programs. The newer Interactive LISREL uses a spreadsheet format for data with pull-down menu options. LISREL offers several different options for inputting ASCII data and importing files from numerous other programs. The **New, Open, Import Data in Free Format**, and **Import External Data in Other Formats** provide maximum flexibility for inputting data.

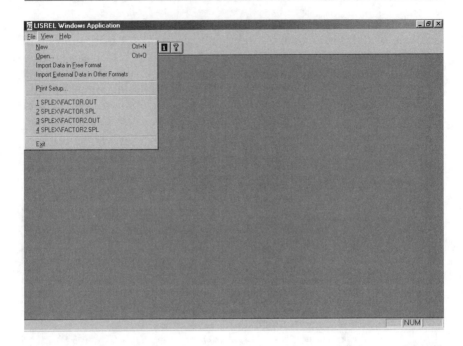

The **New** option permits the creation of a command syntax language program (PRELIS, LISREL, or SIMPLIS) to read in a PRELIS data file or open SIMPLIS and LISREL saved projects as well as a previously saved path diagram.

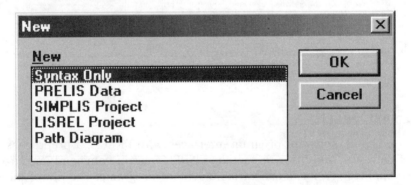

The **Open** option permits you to browse and locate previously saved PRELIS (.pr2), LISREL (.ls8), or SIMPLIS (.spl) programs. The student version has distinct folders containing several program examples, for example, LISREL (ls8ex folder), PRELIS (pr2ex folder), and SIMPLIS (splex folder).

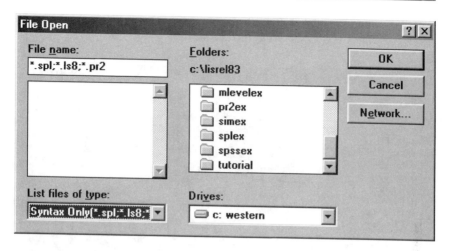

The **Import Data in Free Format** option permits inputting raw data files or SPSS saved files. The raw data file *lsat6.dat* is in the PRELIS folder (pr2ex). When selecting this file, you will need to know the number of variables in the file.

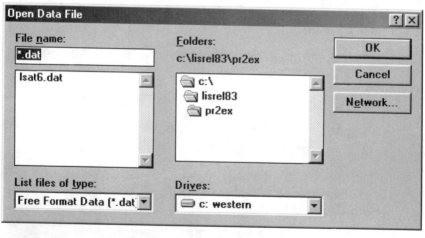

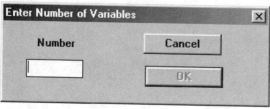

An SPSS saved file, *data100.sav*, is in the SPSS folder (spssex). Once you open this file, a PRELIS system file is created.

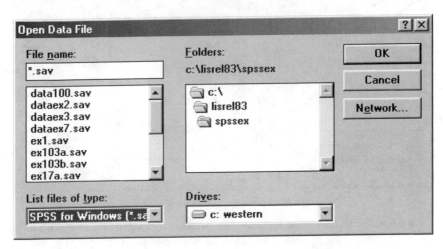

Once the PRELIS system file becomes active it is automatically saved for future use. The PRELIS system file (.psf) activates a new pull-down menu that permits data editing features, data transformations, statistical analysis of data, graphical display of data, multilevel modeling, and many other related features.

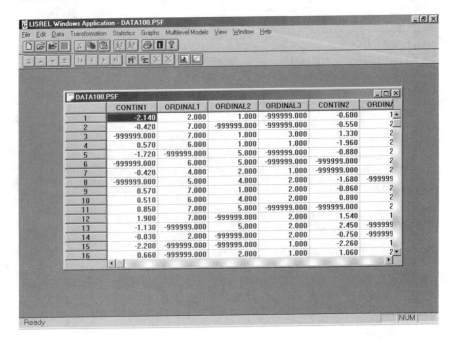

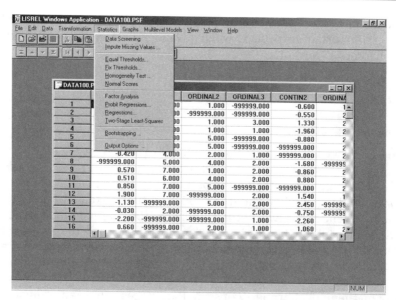

The statistical analysis of data includes factor analysis, probit regression, least squares regression, and two-stage least squares methods. Other important data editing features include imputing missing values, a homogeneity test, creation of normal scores, bootstrapping, and data output options. The data output options permit saving different types of variance–covariance matrices and descriptive statistics in files for

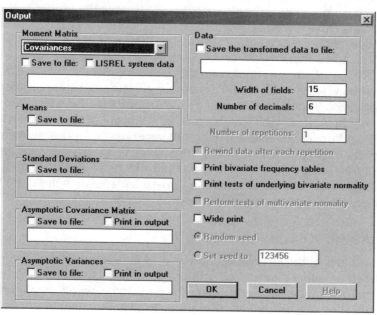

use in LISREL and SIMPLIS command syntax programs. This capability
is very important, especially when advanced SEM models are analyzed
in chapters 13 and 14.

2.2 DATA EDITING ISSUES

Measurement Scale

How variables are measured or scaled influences the type of statistical
analyses we perform (Anderson, 1961; Stevens, 1946). Properties of scale
also guide our understanding of permissible mathematical operations.
For example, a nominal variable implies mutually exclusive groups; for
example, gender has two mutually exclusive groups, male and female. An
individual can only be in one of the groups that define the levels of the
variable. In addition, it would **not** be meaningful to calculate a mean and
a standard deviation on the variable gender. Consequently, the number
or percentage of individuals at each level of the gender variable is the
only mathematical property of scale that makes sense. An ordinal variable, for example, attitude toward school, that is scaled *strongly agree*,
agree, *neutral*, *disagree*, and *strongly disagree* implies mutually exclusive categories that are ordered or ranked. When levels of a variable
have properties of scale that involve mutually exclusive groups that are
ordered, only certain mathematical operations are meaningful, for example, a comparison of ranks between groups. An interval variable, for
example, continuing education credits, possesses the property of scale
implying equal intervals between the data points, but no true zero point.
This property of scale permits the mathematical operation of computing
a mean and a standard deviation. Similarly, a ratio variable, for example,
weight, has the property of scale that implies equal intervals and a true
zero point (weightlessness). Therefore, ratio variables also permit mathematical operations of computing a mean and a standard deviation. Our
use of different variables requires us to be aware of their properties of
scale and what mathematical operations are possible and meaningful, especially in SEM, where variance–covariance (correlation) matrices are
used with means and standard deviations of variables. Different correlations among variables are therefore possible depending upon the level
of measurement, but create unique problems in SEM (see chap. 3).

Restriction of Range

Data values at the interval or ratio level of measurement can be further
defined as being discrete or continuous. For example, the number of
continuing education credits could be reported in whole numbers (discrete). Similarly, the number of children in a family would be considered

a discrete level of measurement (e.g., 5 children). In contrast, a continuous variable is reported using decimal places; for example, a students' grade point average would be reported as 3.75 on a 5-point scale.

Jöreskog and Sörbom (1996) provided a criterion in the PRELIS program based on research that defines whether a variable is ordinal or interval based on the presence of 15 distinct scale points. If a variable has fewer than 15 categories, it is referenced in PRELIS as ordinal (OR), whereas a variable with 15 or more categories is referenced as continuous (CO). This 15-point criterion allows Pearson correlation coefficient values to vary between ±1.0. Variables with fewer distinct scale points restrict the value of the Pearson correlation coefficient such that it may only vary between ±0.5. Other factors that affect the Pearson correlation coefficient are presented in this chapter and discussed further in chapter 3.

Missing Data

The statistical analysis of data is affected by missing data values in variables. It is common practice in statistical packages to have default values for handling missing values. The researcher has the options of deleting subjects who have missing values, replacing the missing data values, and using robust statistical procedures that accommodate for the presence of missing data.

SEM software programs handle missing data differently and have different options for replacing missing data values. Table 2.1 lists the various options for dealing with missing data. These options can dramatically affect the number of subjects available for analysis and the magnitude and the direction of the correlation coefficient, and can create problems if means, standard deviations, and correlations are computed based on different sample sizes. Listwise deletion of cases and pairwise deletion of cases are not always recommended due to the possibility of

TABLE 2.1
Options for Dealing with Missing Data

Listwise	Delete subjects with missing data on any variable
Pairwise	Delete subjects with missing data on only the two variables used
Mean substitution	Substitute the mean for missing values of a variable
Regression imputation	Substitute a predicted value for the missing value of a variable
Maximum likelihood (EM)	Find expected value based on maximum likelihood parameter estimation
Matching response pattern	Match variables with incomplete data to variables with complete data to determine a missing value

losing a large number of subjects, thus dramatically reducing the sample size. Mean substitution works best when only a small number of missing values is present in the data, whereas regression imputation provides a useful approach with a moderate amount of missing data. The maximum likelihood (EM algorithm) approach in EQS or the more recent matching response pattern approach in LISREL–PRELIS is recommended when larger amounts of data are missing at random. Amos uses full information maximum likelihood estimation in the presence of missing data, so it does not impute or replace values for missing data.

LISREL–PRELIS Missing Data Example

Imputation of missing values using the matching response pattern approach is possible for a single variable (Impute Missing Values) or several variables (Multiple Imputation) by selecting **Statistics** from the tool bar menu. The value to be substituted for the missing value of a single case is obtained from another case that has a similar response pattern over a set of matching variables. In multivariable data sets, where missing values occur on more than one variable, one can use multiple imputation of missing values with mean substitution, delete cases, or leave the variables with defined missing values as options in the dialog box. In addition, the multiple imputation procedure implemented in LISREL uses either the expected maximization (EM) algorithm or Monte Carlo Markov chain (MCMC; generating random draws from probability distributions via Markov chains) approaches to replacing missing values across multiple variables.

We present an example from LISREL–PRELIS involving the cholesterol levels for 28 patients treated for heart attacks. We assume the data to be missing at random (MAR) with an underlying multivariate normal distribution. Cholesterol levels were measured after 2 days (VAR1), after 4 days (VAR2), and after 14 days (VAR3), but only for 19 of the 28 patients. The first 18 rows of the data set are shown from the PRELIS system file *chollev.psf*. The PRELIS system file was created by selecting **File**, **Import Data in Free Form**, and selecting the raw data file *chollev.raw* located in the **Tutorial** folder. *We must know the number of variables in the raw data file.* We must also select **Data**, then **Define Variables**, and then select **-9.00** as the missing value for the **VAR3** variable.

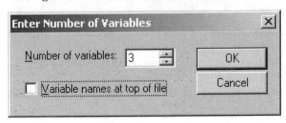

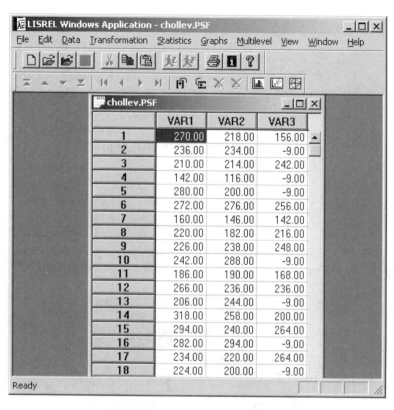

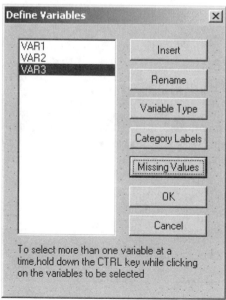

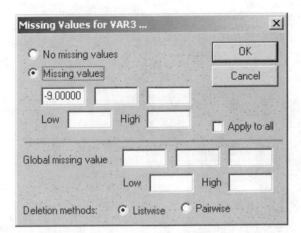

We now click on **Statistics** on the tool bar menu and select either **Impute Missing Values** or **Multiple Imputation** from the pull-down menu.

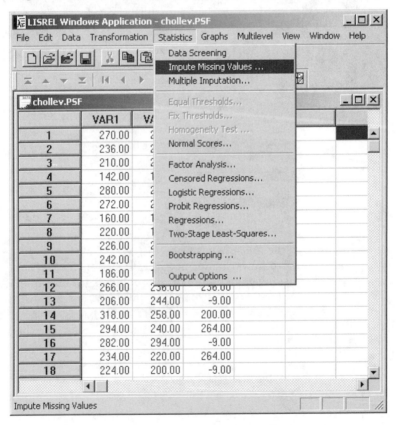

We next select **Output Options** and save the transformed data in a new PRELIS system file, *cholnew.psf*, and output new correlation matrix, mean, and standard deviation files.

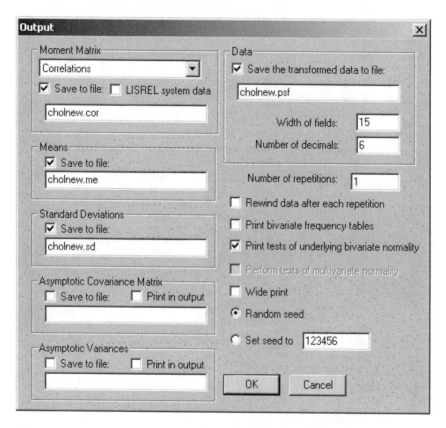

We should examine our data both before (Table 2.2) and after (Table 2.3) imputation of missing values. This provides us with valuable information about the nature of the missing data.

We can also view our new transformed PRELIS system file, *cholnew.psf*, to verify that the missing values were in fact replaced; for example, VAR3 has values replaced for Case 2 = 204, Case 4 = 142, Case 5 = 182, Case 10 = 280, and so on. We also highly recommend comparing SEM analyses before and after the replacement of missing data values to fully understand the impact missing data values have on the parameter estimates and standard errors. A comparison of EM and MCMC is also warranted in multiple imputations to determine the effect of using a different algorithm for the replacement of missing values. We have also noticed that selecting matching variables with a higher correlation to the variable

TABLE 2.2
Data Before Imputation of Missing Values

Number of missing values per variable:

VAR1	VAR2	VAR3
0	0	9

Distribution of missing values:
Total sample size   28
Number of missing values   0   1
Number of cases   19   9

Effective sample sizes
[univariate (in diagonal) and pairwise bivariate (off diagonal)]:

	VAR1	VAR2	VAR3
VAR1	28		
VAR2	28	28	
VAR3	19	19	19

Percentage of missing values
[univariate (in diagonal) and pairwise bivariate (off diagonal)]:

	VAR1	VAR2	VAR3
VAR1	0.00		
VAR2	0.00	0.00	
VAR3	32.14	32.14	32.14

Missing data map:

Frequency	Percent	Pattern
19	67.9	0 0 0
9	32.1	0 0 1

Correlation matrix ($N = 19$):

	VAR1	VAR2	VAR3
VAR1	1.000		
VAR2	0.689	1.000	
VAR3	0.393	0.712	1.000

Means ($N = 19$):

VAR1	VAR2	VAR3
259.474	230.842	221.474

Standard deviations ($N = 19$):

VAR1	VAR2	VAR3
47.948	43.870	43.184

TABLE 2.3
Data After Imputation of Missing Values

Number of missing values per variable:

VAR1	VAR2	VAR3
0	0	9

Imputations for VAR3:
Case 2 imputed with value 204 (variance ratio = 0.000), NM = 1
Case 4 imputed with value 142 (variance ratio = 0.000), NM = 1
Case 5 imputed with value 182 (variance ratio = 0.000), NM = 1
Case 10 imputed with value 280 (variance ratio = 0.000), NM = 1
Case 13 imputed with value 248 (variance ratio = 0.000), NM = 1
Case 16 imputed with value 256 (variance ratio = 0.000), NM = 1
Case 18 imputed with value 216 (variance ratio = 0.000), NM = 1
Case 23 imputed with value 188 (variance ratio = 0.000), NM = 1
Case 25 imputed with value 256 (variance ratio = 0.000), NM = 1

Number of missing values per variable after imputation:

VAR1	VAR2	VAR3
0	0	0

Correlation matrix ($N = 28$):

	VAR1	VAR2	VAR3
VAR1	1.000		
VAR2	0.673	1.000	
VAR3	0.404	0.787	1.000

Means ($N = 28$):

VAR1	VAR2	VAR3
253.929	230.643	220.714

Standard deviations ($N = 28$):

VAR1	VAR2	VAR3
47.710	46.967	42.771

with missing values provides better imputed values for the missing data. LISREL–PRELIS also permits replacement of missing values using the EM approach, which may be practical when matching sets of variables are not possible.

Outliers

Outliers or influential data points can be defined as data values that are extreme or atypical on either the independent (X variables) or

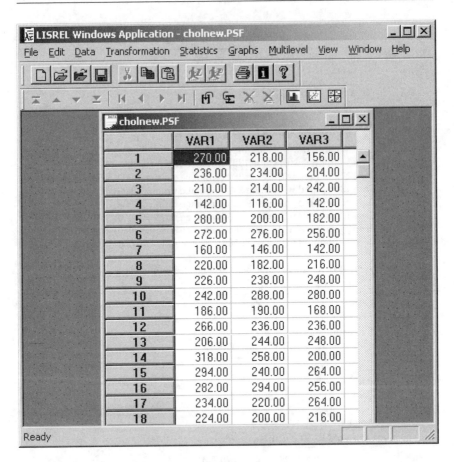

dependent (Y variables) variables or both. Outliers can occur as a result of observation errors, data entry errors, instrument errors based on layout or instructions, or actual extreme values from self-report data. Because outliers affect the mean, the standard deviation, and correlation coefficient values, they must be explained, deleted, or accommodated by using robust statistics (e.g., see EQS robust option). Sometimes, additional data will need to be collected to **fill in** the gap along either the Y or the X axis.

Amos using the SPSS interface, EQS, and LISREL have outlier detection methods available, which include stem and leaf display, box plot display, scatterplot/histogram, frequency distributions, and Cooks D or Mahalanobis statistics. EQS has an interesting feature: a **black hole** into which a researcher can drop an outlier and immediately view the change in parameter estimates. In addition, EQS permits three-dimensional (3D) rotation of factor analysis axes to visualize the pattern of coordinate points.

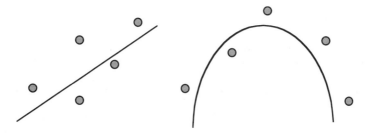

FIG. 2.1.   Left: correlation is linear. Right: correlation is nonlinear.

Linearity

A standard practice is to visualize the coordinate pairs of data points of continuous variables by plotting the data in a scatterplot. These bivariate plots depict whether the data are linearly increasing or decreasing. The presence of curvilinear data reduces the magnitude of the Pearson correlation coefficient, even resulting in the presence of zero correlation. Recall that the Pearson correlation value indicates the magnitude and the direction of the *linear* relationships between pairs of data. Figure 2.1 shows the importance of visually displaying the bivariate data scatterplot.

Nonnormality

Inferential statistics often rely on the assumption that the data are normally distributed. Data that are skewed (lack of symmetry) or more frequently occurring along one part of the measurement scale will affect the variance–covariance among variables. In addition, *kurtosis* (flatness) in data will impact statistics. *Leptokurtic* data values are more peaked than the symmetric normal distribution, whereas *platykurtic* data values are flatter and more dispersed along the X axis, but have a consistent low frequency on the Y axis, that is, the frequency distribution of the data appears rectangular in shape.

Nonnormal data can occur because of the scaling of variables (ordinal rather than interval) or the limited sampling of subjects. Possible solutions for skewness are to resample more participants or perform a permissible linear transformation, for example, square root, reciprocal, logit, or probit. Our experience is that a probit data transformation works best in correcting skewness. Kurtosis in data is more difficult to resolve; however, leptokurtic data can be analyzed using elliptical estimation techniques in EQS. Platykurtic data are the most problematic and require additional sampling of subjects or bootstrap methods available in the SEM software programs.

The presence of skewness and kurtosis can be detected in the SEM software programs using univariate tests, multivariate tests, and measures of skewness and kurtosis that are available in the pull-down menus or output when running programs. A recommended method of handling nonnormal data is to use an asymptotic covariance matrix as input along with the sample covariance matrix in LISREL or SIMPLIS, for example, as follows:

    LISREL
        CM = boy.cov
        AC = boy.acm
    SIMPLIS
        Covariance matrix from file boy.cov
        Asymptotic covariance matrix from file boy.acm

We can use the asymptotic covariance matrix in two different ways: (a) as a weight matrix when specifying the method of optimization as weighted least squares (WLS) and (b) as a weight matrix that adjusts the normal-theory weight matrix to correct for bias in standard errors and fit statistics. The appropriate moment matrix in PRELIS, using OUTPUT OPTIONS, must be selected before requesting the calculation of the asymptotic covariance matrix.

2.3 SUMMARY

Structural equation modeling is a correlation research method; therefore the measurement scale, restriction of range in the data values, missing data, outliers, nonlinearity, and nonnormality of data affect the variance–covariance among variables and thus affect the SEM analysis. The factor loading matrices must be full rank and have no rows with zeros in them to be able to compute structure coefficients, that is the variance–covariance matrices must be positive definite (Wothke, 1993). Researchers should use the built-in menu options to examine, graph, and test for any of these problems in the data prior to conducting any SEM model analysis. Basically, researchers should know their data characteristics. Data screening is a very important first step in structural equation modeling.

The next chapter illustrates in more detail issues related to the use of correlation and variance–covariance in SEM models. We provide specific examples to illustrate the importance of topics covered in this chapter.

EXERCISES

1. Amos uses which command to import data sets?
   a. **File**, then **Data Files**
   b. **File**, then **Open**
   c. **File**, then **Import External Data in Other Formats**
   d. **File**, then **New**
2. EQS uses which command to import data sets?
   a. **File**, then **Data Files**
   b. **File**, then **Open**
   c. **File**, then **Import External Data in Other Formats**
   d. **File**, then **New**
3. LISREL uses which command to import data sets?
   a. **File**, then **Data Files**
   b. **File**, then **Open**
   c. **File**, then **Import External Data in Other Formats**
   d. **File**, then **New**
4. Define the following levels of measurement.
   a. Nominal
   b. Ordinal
   c. Interval
   d. Ratio
5. Mark each of the following statements true (T) or false (F).
   a. Amos can compute descriptive statistics.
   b. EQS can compute descriptive statistics.
   c. LISREL can compute descriptive statistics.
   d. PRELIS can compute descriptive statistics.
6. Explain how each of the following affects statistics:
   a. Restriction of range
   b. Missing data
   c. Outliers
   d. Nonlinearity
   e. Nonnormality

REFERENCES

Anderson, N. H. (1961). Scales and statistics: Parametric and non-parametric. *Psychological Bulletin, 58*, 305–316.

Jöreskog, K., & Sörbom, D. (1996). *PRELIS2: User's reference guide*. Lincolnwood, IL: Scientific Software International.

Stevens, S. S. (1946). On the theory of scales of measurement. *Science, 103*, 677–680.

Wothke, W. (1993). Nonpositive definite matrices in structural equation modeling. In K. A. Bollen & S. J. Long (Eds.), *Testing structural equation models* (pp. 256–293). Newbury Park, CA: Sage.

ANSWERS TO EXERCISES

1. Amos uses which command to import data sets?
   a. **File**, then **Data Files**
2. EQS uses which command to import data sets?
   a. **File**, then **Open**
3. LISREL uses which command to import data sets?
   a. **File**, then **Import External Data in Other Formats**
4. Define the following levels of measurement.
   a. Nominal: mutually exclusive groups or categories with number or percentage indicated.
   b. Ordinal: mutually exclusive groups or categories that are ordered with a ranking indicated.
   c. Interval: continuous data with arbitrary zero point, permitting a mean and a standard deviation.
   d. Ratio: continuous data with a true zero point, permitting a mean and a standard deviation.
5. Mark each of the following statements true (T) or false (F).
   a. Amos can compute descriptive statistics.   F
   b. EQS can compute descriptive statistics.   T
   c. LISREL can compute descriptive statistics.   F
   d. PRELIS can compute descriptive statistics.   T
6. Explain how each of the following affects statistics:
   a. Restriction of range: A set of scores that are restricted in range implies reduced variability. Variance and covariance are important in statistics, especially correlation.
   b. Missing data: A set of scores with missing data can affect the estimate of the mean and standard deviation. It is important to determine whether the missing data are due to data entry error, are missing at random, or are missing systematically due to some other variable (e.g., gender).
   c. Outliers: A set of scores with an outlier (extreme score) can affect the estimate of the mean and standard deviation. It is important to determine whether the outlier is an incorrect data value due to data entry error, represents another group of persons, or potentially requires the researcher to gather more data to fill in between the range of data.
   d. Nonlinearity: Researchers have generally analyzed relationships in data assuming linearity. Linearity is a requirement for the Pearson correlation coefficient. Consequently, a lack of linearity that is not included in the statistical model would yield misleading results.
   e. Nonnormality: Skewness, or lack of symmetry in the frequency distribution, and kurtosis, the departure from a normal distribution, affect inferential statistics, especially the mean, the standard deviation, and correlation coefficient estimates. Data transformations, especially a probit transformation, can help to yield a more normally distributed set of scores.

3

CORRELATION

———◇◆◇———

Chapter Outline

Key Concepts

Types of correlation coefficients
Factors affecting correlation
Correction for attenuation
Non-positive definite matrices

Bivariate, part, and partial correlation
Suppressor variable
Covariance and causation

3.1   TYPES OF CORRELATION COEFFICIENTS

Sir Francis Galton conceptualized the correlation and regression procedure for examining covariance in two or more traits, and Karl Pearson
(1896) developed the statistical formula for the correlation coefficient
and regression based on his suggestion (Crocker & Algina, 1986; Ferguson & Takane, 1989; Tankard, 1984). Shortly thereafter, Charles Spearman (1904) used the correlation procedure to develop a factor analysis
technique. The correlation, regression, and factor analysis techniques
have for many decades formed the basis for generating tests and defining constructs. Today, researchers are expanding their understanding of
the roles that correlation, regression, and factor analysis play in theory
and construct definition to include latent variable, covariance structure,
and confirmatory factor measurement models.

The relationships and contributions of Galton, Pearson, and Spearman to the field of statistics, especially correlation, regression, and factor analysis, are quite interesting (Tankard, 1984). In fact, the basis of
association between two variables, that is, correlation or covariance,
has played a major role in statistics. The Pearson correlation coefficient
provides the basis for point estimation (test of significance), explanation (variance accounted for in a dependent variable by an independent
variable), prediction (of a dependent variable from an independent variable through linear regression), reliability estimates (test–retest, equivalence), and validity (factorial, predictive, concurrent).

The Pearson correlation coefficient also provides the basis for establishing and testing models among measured and/or latent variables. The
partial and part correlations further permit the identification of specific
bivariate relationships between variables that allow for the specification of unique variance shared between two variables while controlling for the influence of other variables. Partial and part correlations
can be tested for significance, similar to the Pearson correlation coefficient, by simply using the degrees of freedom, $n - 2$, in the standard
correlation table of significance values or an F test in multiple regression that tests the difference in R^2 values between full and restricted
models (see Tables A.3 and A.5, pp. 475 and 478, respectively).

Although the Pearson correlation coefficient has had a major impact
in the field of statistics, other correlation coefficients have emerged
depending upon the level of variable measurement. Stevens (1968)

TABLE 3.1
Types of Correlation Coefficients

Correlation coefficient	Level of measurement
Pearson product–moment	Both variables interval
Spearman rank, Kendall's tau	Both variables ordinal
Phi	Both variables nominal
Point-biserial	One variable interval, one variable dichotomous
Gamma, rank biserial	One variable ordinal, one variable nominal
Contingency	Both variables nominal
Biserial	One variable interval, one variable artificial*
Polyserial	One variable interval, one variable ordinal with underlying continuity
Tetrachoric	Both variables dichotomous (nominal-artificial)
Polychoric	Both variables ordinal with underlying continuities

*Artificial refers to recoding variable values into a dichotomy.

provided the properties of scales of measurement that have become known as nominal, ordinal, interval, and ratio. The types of correlation coefficients developed for these various levels of measurement are categorized in Table 3.1.

Many popular computer programs, for example, SAS and SPSS, typically do not compute all of these correlation types. Therefore, you may need to check a popular statistics book or look around for a computer program that will compute the type of correlation coefficient you need, for example, the phi or the point-biserial coefficient. In SEM analyses, the Pearson coefficient, tetrachoric (or polychoric for several ordinal variable pairs) coefficient, and biserial (or polyserial for several continuous and ordinal variable pairs) coefficient are typically used (see PRELIS for the use of Kendall's tau-c or tau-b, and canonical correlation). The SEM software programs permit *mixture models*, which use variables with ordinal and interval-ratio levels of measurement (see chap. 13). Although SEM software programs are now demonstrating how mixture models can be analyzed, the use of variables with different levels of measurement has traditionally been a problem in the field of statistics (e.g., multiple regression and multivariate statistics).

In this chapter we describe the important role that correlation (covariance) plays in structural equation modeling. We also include a discussion of factors that affect correlation coefficients and the assumptions and limitations of correlation methods in structural equation modeling.

3.2   FACTORS AFFECTING CORRELATION COEFFICIENTS

Given the important role that correlation plays in structural equation modeling, we need to understand the factors that affect establishing relationships among multivariable data points. The key factors are the level of measurement, restriction of range in data values (variability, skewness, kurtosis), missing data, nonlinearity, outliers, correction for attenuation, and issues related to sampling variation, confidence interval, effect size, significance, and power addressed in bootstrap estimates.

Level of Measurement and Range of Values

Four types or levels of measurement typically define whether the characteristic or scale interpretation of a variable is nominal, ordinal, interval, or ratio (Stevens, 1968). In structural equation modeling, each of these types of scaled variables can be used. However, it is not recommended that they be included together or mixed in a correlation (covariance) matrix. Instead, the PRELIS data output option should be used to save an asymptotic covariance matrix for input along with the sample variance–covariance matrix into a LISREL or SIMPLIS program.

Until recently, SEM required variables measured at the interval or ratio level of measurement, so the Pearson product–moment correlation coefficient was used in regression, path, factor, and structural equation modeling. The interval or ratio scaled variable values should also have a sufficient range of score values to introduce variance. If the range of scores is restricted, the magnitude of the correlation value is decreased. Basically, as a group of subjects becomes more homogeneous, score variance decreases, reducing the correlation value between the variables. This points out an interesting concern, namely, that there must be enough variation in scores to allow a correlation relationship to manifest itself between variables. Variables with fewer than 15 categories are treated as ordinal variables in LISREL–PRELIS, so if you are assuming continuous interval-level data, you will need to check whether the variables meet this assumption. Also, the use of the same scale values for variables helps in the interpretation of results and/or relative comparison among variables. The meaningfulness of a correlation relationship will depend on the variables employed; hence, your theoretical perspective is very important. You may recall from your basic statistics course that a spurious correlation is possible when two sets of scores correlate significantly but are not meaningful or substantive in nature.

If the distributions of variables are widely divergent, correlation can also be affected, so several permissible data transformations are suggested by Ferguson and Takane (1989) to provide a closer approximation to a normal, homogeneous variance for skewed or kurtotic data. Some possible transformations are the square root transformation (sqrt X), the logarithmic transformation (log X), the reciprocal transformation $(1/X)$, and the arcsine transformation (arcsin X). The probit transformation appears to be most effective in handling univariate skewed data.

Consequently, the type of scale used and the range of values for the measured variables can have profound affects on your statistical analysis (in particular, on the mean, variance, and correlation). The scale and range of a variable's numerical values affect statistical methods, and this is no different in structural equation modeling. The PRELIS program is available to provide tests of normality, skewness, and kurtosis on variables and to compute an asymptotic covariance matrix for input into LISREL if required. Other statistical packages, such as EQS and Amos using the SPSS interface, are also available for checking the skewness and kurtosis of scores.

Nonlinearity

The Pearson correlation coefficient indicates the degree of linear relationship between two variables. It is possible that two variables can indicate no correlation if they have a curvilinear relationship. Thus, the extent to which the variables deviate from the assumption of a linear relationship will affect the size of the correlation coefficient. It is therefore important to check for linearity of the scores; the common method is to graph the coordinate data points. The linearity assumption should not be confused with recent advances in testing interaction in structural equation models discussed in chapter 14. You should also be familiar with the *eta* coefficient as an index of nonlinear relationship between two variables and with the testing of linear, quadratic, and cubic effects. Consult an intermediate statistics text (e.g., Lomax, 2001) to review these basic concepts.

The heuristic data set in Table 3.2 demonstrates the dramatic effect a lack of linearity has on the Pearson correlation coefficient value. In the first data set, the Y values increase from 1 to 10 and the X values increase from 1 to 5, then decrease from 5 to 1 (nonlinear). The result is a Pearson correlation coefficient of $r = 0$; although a relationship does exist in the data, it is not indicated by the Pearson correlation coefficient. The restriction of range in values can be demonstrated using the fourth heuristic data set in Table 3.2. The Y values only range between

TABLE 3.2
Heuristic Data Sets

Nonlinear data		Complete data		Missing data		Range of data		Sampling effect	
Y	X	Y	X	Y	X	Y	X	Y	X
1.00	1.00	8.00	6.00	8.00	—	3.00	1.00	8.00	3.00
2.00	2.00	7.00	5.00	7.00	5.00	3.00	2.00	9.00	2.00
3.00	3.00	8.00	4.00	8.00	—	4.00	3.00	10.00	1.00
4.00	4.00	5.00	2.00	5.00	2.00	4.00	4.00		
5.00	5.00	4.00	3.00	4.00	3.00	5.00	1.00		
6.00	5.00	5.00	2.00	5.00	2.00	5.00	2.00		
7.00	4.00	3.00	3.00	3.00	3.00	6.00	3.00		
8.00	3.00	5.00	4.00	5.00	—	6.00	4.00		
9.00	2.00	3.00	1.00	3.00	1.00	7.00	1.00		
10.00	1.00	2.00	2.00	2.00	2.00	7.00	2.00		

3 and 7 and the X values only range from 1 to 4. The Pearson correlation coefficient is also $r = 0$ for these data. The fifth data set indicates how limited sampling can affect the Pearson coefficient. In these sample data, only three pairs of data are sampled, and the Pearson correlation is $r = -1.0$, or perfectly negatively correlated.

Missing Data

A complete data set is also given in Table 3.2 where the Pearson correlation coefficient is $r = .782$, $p = .007$, for $n = 10$ pairs of scores. If missing data were present, the Pearson correlation coefficient would drop to $r = .659$, $p = .108$, for $n = 7$ pairs of scores. The Pearson correlation coefficient changes from statistically significant to not statistically significant. More importantly, in a correlation matrix with several variables, the various correlation coefficients could be computed on different sample sizes. If we used *listwise* deletion of cases, then any variable in the data set with a missing value would cause a subject to be deleted, possibly causing a substantial reduction in our sample size, whereas *pairwise* deletion of cases would result in different sample sizes for our correlation coefficients in the correlation matrix.

Researchers have examined various aspects of how to handle or treat missing data beyond our introductory example using a small heuristic data set. One basic approach is to eliminate any observations where some of the data are missing, *listwise deletion*. Listwise deletion is not recommended, because of the loss of information on other variables, statistical estimates based on differing sample sizes, and a possible large reduction in the sample size. *Pairwise deletion* excludes data only when they are missing on the variables selected for analysis. However, this could lead to different sample sizes for the correlations and related statistical estimates. A third approach, *data imputation*, replaces missing values with an estimate, for example, the mean value on a variable for all subjects who did not report any data for that variable (Beale & Little, 1975; also see chap. 2).

Missing data can arise in different ways (Little & Rubin, 1987, 1990). *Missing completely at random* (MCAR) implies that data are missing unrelated statistically to the values that would have been observed. *Missing at random* (MAR) implies that data values are missing conditional on other variables or a stratifying variable. A third situation, *nonignorable* data, implies probabilistic information about the values that would have been observed. Rather than use data imputation methods, the researcher can use *full information maximum likelihood* (FIML) estimation in the presence of missing data in Amos (Arbuckle & Wothke, 1999). For MCAR data, mean substitution yields biased variance and covariance estimates, whereas FIML and listwise and pairwise deletion methods yield consistent solutions. For MAR data, FIML yields estimates that are consistent and efficient, whereas mean substitution and listwise and pairwise deletion methods produce biased results. When missing data are nonignorable, all approaches yield biased results; however, FIML estimates tend to be less biased. It would be prudent for the researcher to investigate how parameter estimates are affected by the use or nonuse of a data imputation method. Basically, FIML is the recommended parameter estimation method when data are missing in structural equation model analyses. For a more detailed understanding of FIML and the handling of missing data see Arbuckle (1996) and Wothke (2000).

Outliers

The Pearson correlation coefficient is drastically effected by a single outlier on X or Y. For example, the two data sets in Table 3.3 indicate a $Y = 27$ value (Set A) versus a $Y = 2$ value (Set B) for the last subject. In the first set of data, $r = .524$, $p = .37$, whereas in the second set of data, $r = -.994$, $p = .001$. Is the $Y = 27$ data value an outlier based on limited sampling or is it a data entry error?

A large body of research has been undertaken to examine how different outliers on X, Y, or both X and Y affect correlation relationships and how to better analyze the data using robust statistics (Anderson & Schumacker, 2003; Ho & Naugher, 2000; Huber, 1981; Rousseeuw & Leroy, 1987; Staudte & Sheather, 1990).

TABLE 3.3
Outlier Data Sets

Set A		Set B	
X	Y	X	Y
1	9	1	9
2	7	2	7
3	5	3	5
4	3	4	3
5	27	5	2

An EQS example will illustrate the unique feature of the *black hole* in quickly identifying the impact of a single outlier on a parameter estimate. In EQS, open the data set *manul7.ess*, next click on **Data Plot** in the main menu, then select **Scatter Plot**, and enter V1 for the *Y* axis and V2 for the *X* axis.

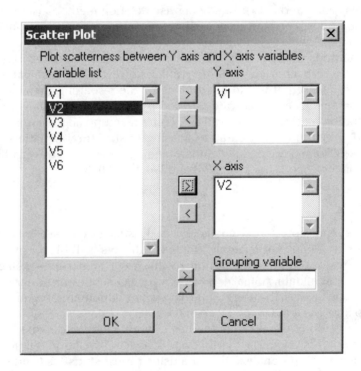

After clicking **OK**, one sees the following scatterplot:

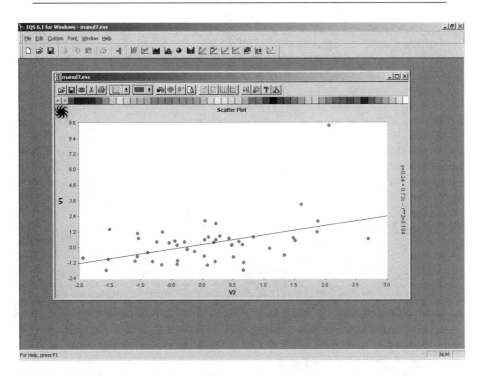

The scatterplot of V1 with V2 indicates an R^2 value of .194. Notice the outlier data point in the upper right-hand corner at the top of the scatterplot.
To identify which data value this is, simply double click on the data
point to reveal V2 = 2.07 and V1 = 9.39. If we *brush* this data point and
then drop it in the black hole in the upper left corner, our regression
calculations are automatically updated without this outlier data point.
To brush the outlier data point, use the left mouse button and drag from
the upper left to the lower right as if forming a rectangle. The outlier
data point should turn red once you release the left mouse button, as
indicated in the first diagram.

   To drag the outlier data point to the black hole, place the mouse
pointer on the data point, depress the left mouse button, and drag the
outlier data point to the black hole. Once you release the left mouse button, the outlier data point should drop into the black hole, as indicated
in the second diagram.

   The regression equation is automatically updated with an R^2 value
of .137. This indicates the impact of a single outlier data point. Other
outlier data points can be brushed and dragged to the black hole to see
cumulative effects of other outlier data points. To re-enter the data point

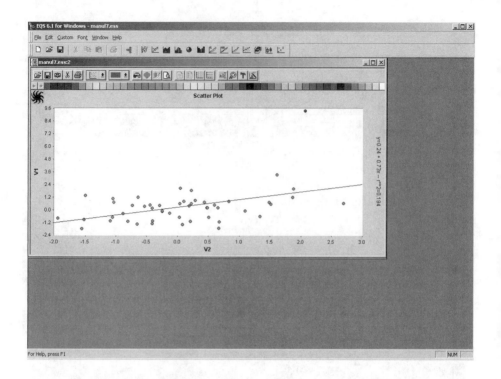

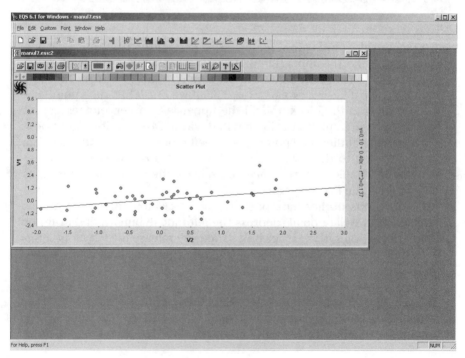

in the scatterplot, simply double click the black hole and the data value will instantly reappear.

Correction for Attenuation

A basic assumption in psychometric theory is that observed data contain measurement error. A test score (observed data) is a function of a true score and measurement error. A Pearson correlation coefficient has different values depending on whether it is computed with observed scores or the true scores where measurement error has been removed. The Pearson correlation coefficient can be corrected for attenuation or unreliable measurement error in scores, thus yielding a true score correlation; however, the corrected correlation coefficient can become greater than 1.0! Low reliability in the independent and/or dependent variables coupled with a high correlation between the independent and dependent variable can result in correlations greater than 1.0. For example, given a correlation of $r = .90$ between the observed scores on X and Y, the Cronbach alpha reliability coefficient of .60 for X scores, and the Cronbach alpha reliability coefficient of .70 for Y scores, the Pearson correlation coefficient, corrected for attenuation is greater than 1.0:

$$r_{xy}^* = \frac{r_{xy}}{\sqrt{r_{xx}r_{yy}}} = \frac{.90}{\sqrt{.60(.70)}} = \frac{.90}{.648} = 1.39.$$

When this happens, either a condition code or a non-positive definite error message occurs stopping the structural equation software program.

Non-Positive Definite Matrices

Correlation coefficients greater than 1.0 in a correlation matrix cause the correlation matrix to be *non-positive definite*. In other words, the solution is not admissible, indicating that parameter estimates cannot be computed. Correction for attenuation is not the only situation that causes non-positive definite matrices to occur (Wothke, 1993). Sometimes the ratio of covariance to the product of variable variance yields correlations greater than 1.0. The following variance–covariance matrix is non-positive definite because it contains a correlation coefficient greater than 1.0 between relations and attribute latent variables (denoted by an asterisk):

Variance–covariance matrix
Task	1.043			
Relations	.994	1.079		
Management	.892	.905	.924	
Attribute	1.065	1.111	.969	1.12

Correlation matrix
Task	1.000			
Relations	.937	1.000		
Management	.908	.906	1.000	
Attribute	.985	1.010*	.951	1.000

Non-positive definite covariance matrices occur when the determinant of the matrix is zero or the inverse of the matrix is not possible. This can be caused by correlations greater than 1.0, linear dependence among observed variables, collinearity among the observed variables, a variable that is a linear combination of other variables, a sample size less than the number of variables, the presence of negative or zero variance (*Heywood case*), variance–covariance (correlation) outside the permissible range (±1.0), and bad *start values* in the user-specified model. A Heywood case also occurs when the communality estimate is greater than 1.0. Possible solutions to resolve this error are to reduce communality or fix communality to less than 1.0, extract a different number of factors (possibly by dropping paths), rescale observed variables to create a more linear relationship, and eliminate a *bad* observed variable that indicates linear dependence or multicollinearity.

Regression, path, factor, and structural equation models mathematically solve a set of simultaneous equations typically using ordinary least squares (OLS) estimates as initial estimates of coefficients in the model. However, these initial estimates or coefficients are sometimes distorted or too different from the final admissible solution. When this happens, more reasonable *start values* need to be chosen. It is easy to see from the basic regression coefficient formula that the correlation coefficient value and the standard deviation values of the two variables affect the initial OLS estimates:

$$b = r_{xy} \frac{S_y}{S_x}.$$

Sample Size

A common formula used to determine sample size when estimating means of variables was given by McCall (1982): $n = (Z\sigma/\epsilon)^2$, where n

is the sample size needed for the desired level of precision, ϵ is the effect size, Z is the confidence level, and σ is the population standard deviation of scores (σ can be estimated from prior research studies, test norms, or the range of scores divided by 6). For example, given a random sample of ACT scores from a defined population with a standard deviation of 100, a desired confidence level of 1.96 (which corresponds to a .05 level of significance), and an effect size of 20 (difference between sampled ACT mean and population ACT mean), the sample size needed is $[100(1.96)/20)]^2 = 96$.

In structural equation modeling, however, the researcher often requires a much larger sample size to maintain power and obtain stable parameter estimates and standard errors. The need for larger sample sizes is also due in part to the program requirements and the multiple observed indicator variables used to define latent variables. Hoelter (1983) proposed the *critical N* statistic, which indicates the sample size that would make the obtained chi-square from a structural equation model significant at the stated level of significance. This sample size provides a reasonable indication of whether a researcher's sample size is sufficient to estimate parameters and determine model fit given the researcher's specific theoretical relationships among the latent variables. SEM software programs estimate coefficients based on the user-specified theoretical model, or *implied model*, but also must work with the saturated and independence models. A *saturated model* is the model with all parameters indicated, whereas the *independence model* is the null model or model with no parameters estimated. A saturated model with p variables has $p(p+3)/2$ free parameters. For example, with 10 observed variables, $10(10+3)/2 = 65$ free parameters. If the sample size is small, then there is not information to estimate parameters in the saturated model for a large number of variables. Consequently, the chi-square fit statistic and derived statistics such as Akaike's information criterion (AIC) and the root-mean-square error of approximation (RMSEA) cannot be computed. In addition, the fit of the independence model is required to calculate other fit indices such as the comparative fit index (CFI) and the normal fit index (NFI).

Ding, Velicer, and Harlow (1995) found numerous studies (e.g., Anderson & Gerbing, 1988) that were in agreement that 100 to 150 subjects is the *minimum* satisfactory sample size when constructing structural equation models. Boomsma (1982, 1983) recommended 400, and Hu, Bentler, and Kano (1992) indicated that in some cases 5,000 is insufficient! Many of us may recall rules of thumb in our statistics texts, for example, 10 subjects per variable or 20 subjects per variable. In our examination of the published research, we found that many articles used from 250 to 500 subjects, although the greater the sample size, the more likely it is that one can validate the model using cross-validation (see chap. 12). For example, Bentler and Chou (1987) suggested that a ratio as low as 5 subjects per variable would be sufficient for normal and elliptical distributions when the latent variables have multiple indicators and that a ratio of at least 10 subjects per variable would be sufficient for other distributions.

3.3 BIVARIATE, PART, AND PARTIAL CORRELATIONS

The types of correlations indicated in Table 3.1 are considered bivariate correlations, or associations between two variables. Cohen and Cohen (1983), in describing correlation research, further presented the correlation between two variables controlling for the influence of a third. These correlations are referred to as *part* and *partial* correlations, depending upon how variables are controlled or partialed out. Some of the various ways in which three variables can be depicted are illustrated in Fig. 3.1. The diagrams illustrate different situations among variables where (a) all the variables are uncorrelated (Case 1), (b) only one pair of variables is correlated (Cases 2 and 3), (c) two pairs of variables are correlated (Cases 4 and 5), and (d) all of the variables are correlated (Case 6). It is obvious that with more than three variables the possibilities become overwhelming. It is therefore important to have a theoretical perspective to suggest why certain variables are correlated and/or controlled in a study. A theoretical perspective is essential in specifying a model and forms the basis for testing a structural equation model.

The *partial correlation coefficient* measures the association between two variables while controlling for a third, for example, the association between age and comprehension, controlling for reading level. Controlling for reading level in the correlation between age and comprehension partials out the correlation of reading level with age and the correlation of reading level with comprehension. *Part correlation*, in contrast, is the correlation between age and comprehension level with reading level controlled for, where only the correlation between comprehension level and reading level is removed before age is correlated with comprehension level.

Whether a part or partial correlation is used depends on the specific model or research question. Convenient notation helps distinguish these two types of correlations (1 = age, 2 = comprehension, 3 = reading level): partial correlation, $r_{12.3}$; part correlation, $r_{1(2.3)}$ or $r_{2(1.3)}$. Different correlation values are computed depending on which variables

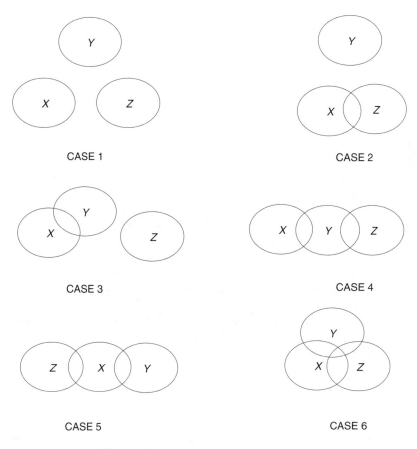

FIG. 3.1. Possible three-variable relationships.

are controlled or partialed out. For example, using the correlations in Table 3.4, we can compute the partial correlation coefficient $r_{12.3}$ (correlation between age and comprehension, controlling for reading level) as

$$r_{12.3} = \frac{r_{12} - r_{13}r_{23}}{\sqrt{(1 - r_{13}^2)(1 - r_{23}^2)}}$$

$$= \frac{.45 - (.25)(.80)}{\sqrt{[1 - (.25)^2][1 - (.80)^2]}} = .43.$$

Notice that the partial correlation coefficient should be smaller in magnitude than the Pearson product–moment correlation between age and comprehension, which is $r_{12} = .45$. If the partial correlation coefficient

TABLE 3.4
Correlation Matrix ($n = 100$)

Variable	Age	Comprehension	Reading level
1. Age	1.00		
2. Comprehension	.45	1.00	
3. Reading level	.25	.80	1.00

is not smaller than the Pearson product–moment correlation, then a *suppressor variable* may be present (Pedhazur, 1997). A suppressor variable correlates near zero with a dependent variable but correlates significantly with other predictor variables. This correlation situation serves to control for variance shared with predictor variables and not the dependent variable. The partial correlation coefficient increases once this effect is removed from the correlation between two predictor variables with a criterion. Partial correlations will be greater in magnitude than part correlations, except when independent variables are zero correlated with the dependent variable; then, part correlations are equal to partial correlations.

The part correlation coefficient $r_{1(2.3)}$, or correlation between age and comprehension where reading level is controlled for in comprehension only, is computed as

$$r_{1(2.3)} = \frac{r_{12} - r_{13}r_{23}}{\sqrt{(1 - r_{23}^2)}} = \frac{.45 - (.25)(.80)}{\sqrt{1 - .80^2}} = .42,$$

or, in the case of correlating comprehension with age where reading level is controlled for age only,

$$r_{2(1.3)} = \frac{r_{12} - r_{13}r_{23}}{\sqrt{1 - r_{13}^2}} = \frac{.45 - (.25)(.80)}{\sqrt{1 - .25^2}} = .26.$$

The correlation, whether zero order (bivariate), part, or partial, can be tested for significance, interpreted as variance accounted for by squaring each coefficient, and diagramed using Venn or Ballentine figures to conceptualize their relationships. In our example, the zero-order relationships among the three variables can be diagramed as in Fig. 3.2. However, the partial correlation of age with comprehension level controlling for reading level is $r_{12.3} = .43$, or area a divided by the combined area of a and e $[a/(a + e)]$; see Fig. 3.3. A part correlation of age with comprehension level while controlling for the correlation between reading level and comprehension level is $r_{1(2.3)} = .42$, or just area a; see Fig. 3.4.

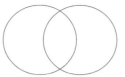

Age and Comprehension

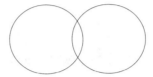

Age and Reading

Reading and Comprehension

FIG. 3.2. Bivariate correlations.

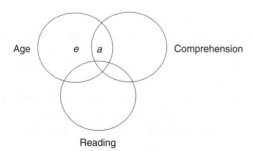

FIG. 3.3. Partial correlation area.

These examples consider only controlling for one variable when correlating two other variables (partial), or controlling for the impact of one variable on another before correlating with a third variable (part). Other higher order part correlations and partial correlations are possible (e.g., $r_{12.34}, r_{12(3.4)}$), but are beyond the scope of this book. Readers should refer to the references at the end of the chapter for a more detailed discussion of part and partial correlation.

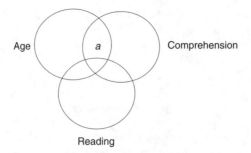

FIG. 3.4.   Part correlation area.

3.4   CORRELATION VERSUS COVARIANCE

The type of data matrix typically used for computations in struc-tural equation modeling programs is a variance–covariance matrix. A variance–covariance matrix is made up of variance terms on the diag-onal and covariance terms on the off-diagonal. If a correlation matrix is used as the input data matrix, most of the computer programs con-vert it to a variance–covariance matrix using the standard deviations of the variables, unless specified otherwise. The researcher has the option to input raw data, a correlation matrix, or a variance–covariance ma-trix. The SEM software defaults to using a variance–covariance matrix. The correlation matrix provides the option of using standardized or un-standardized variables for analysis purposes. If a correlation matrix is input with a row of variable means and a row of standard deviations, then a variance–covariance matrix is used with unstandardized output. If only a correlation matrix is input, the means and standard deviations, by default, are set at 0 and 1, respectively, and standardized output is printed. When raw data are input, a variance–covariance matrix is computed.

The number of distinct elements in a variance–covariance matrix S is $p(p+1)/2$, where p is the number of observed variables. For example, the variance–covariance matrix for the three variables X, Y, and Z, is

$$
S = \begin{array}{c} X \\ Y \\ Z \end{array} \begin{bmatrix} 15.80 & & \\ 10.16 & 11.02 & \\ 12.43 & 9.23 & 15.37 \end{bmatrix} .
$$

It has $3(3+1)/2 = 6$ distinct values: 3 variances and 3 covariances.

Correlation is computed using the variance and covariance among the bivariate variables using the following formula:

$$r = \frac{s^2_{XY}}{\sqrt{s^2_X * s^2_Y}}.$$

Dividing the covariance between two variables (covariance is the off-diagonal values in the matrix) by the square root of the product of the two variable variances (variances of variables are on the diagonal of the matrix) yields the correlations among the three variables:

$$r_{xy} = 10.16/(15.80 * 11.02)^{1/2} = .77$$
$$r_{xz} = 12.43/(15.80 * 15.37)^{1/2} = .80$$
$$r_{yz} = 9.23/(11.02 * 15.37)^{1/2} = .71.$$

Structural equation software uses the variance–covariance matrix rather than the correlation matrix because Boomsma (1983) found that the analysis of correlation matrices led to imprecise parameter estimates and standard errors of the parameter estimates in a structural equation model. In SEM, incorrect estimation of the standard errors for the parameter estimates could lead to statistically significant parameter estimates and an incorrect interpretation of the model, that is, the parameter divided by the standard error indicates a critical ratio statistic or t-value (see Table A.2, p. 474). Browne (1982), Jennrich and Thayer (1973), and Lawley and Maxwell (1971) suggested corrections for the standard errors when correlations or standardized coefficients are used in SEM. However, only one structural equation modeling program, SEPATH in the program *Statistica*, permits correlation matrix input with the analysis computing the correct standard errors. In general, a variance–covariance matrix should be used in structural equation modeling, although some SEM models require variable means (e.g., structured means; see chap. 13).

3.5 VARIABLE METRICS (STANDARDIZED VS. UNSTANDARDIZED)

Researchers have debated the use of unstandardized or standardized variables (Lomax, 2001). The standardized coefficients are thought to be sample specific and not stable across different samples because of changes in the variance of the variables. The unstandardized coefficients permit an examination of change across different samples. The standardized coefficients are useful, however, in determining the relative importance of each variable to other variables for a given sample. Other reasons for using standardized variables are that variables are on the same scale of measurement, are more easily interpreted, and can easily be converted back to the raw scale metric. In SIMPLIS, the command *LISREL OUTPUT SS SC* provides a standardized solution. The Amos and EQS programs routinely provide both unstandardized and standardized solutions.

3.6   CAUSATION ASSUMPTIONS AND LIMITATIONS

As previously discussed, the Pearson correlation coefficient is limited by the range of score values and the assumption of linearity, among other things. Even if the assumptions and limitations of using the Pearson correlation coefficient are met, a cause-and-effect relationship still has not been established. The following conditions are necessary for cause and effect to be inferred between variables X and Y (Tracz, 1992): (a) temporal order (X precedes Y in time), (b) existence of covariance or correlation between X and Y, and (c) control for other causes, for example, partial *Z out of X and Y*.

These three conditions may not be present in the research design setting, and in such a case, only association rather than causation can be inferred. However, if *manipulative* variables are used in the study, then a researcher could change or manipulate one variable in the study and examine subsequent effects on other variables, thereby determining cause-and-effect relationships (Resta & Baker, 1972). In structural equation modeling, the amount of influence rather than a cause-and-effect relationship is assumed and interpreted by direct, indirect, and total effects among variables, which are explained later in a structural equation model example.

Philosophical and theoretical differences exist between assuming causal versus inference relationships among variables, and the resolution of these issues requires a sound theoretical perspective. Bullock, Harlow, and Mulaik (1994) provided an in-depth discussion of causation issues related to structural equation modeling research; see their article for a more elaborate discussion. We feel that structural equation models will evolve beyond model fit into the domain of model testing. Model testing involves the use of manipulative variables, which, when changed, affect the model outcome values, and whose effects can hence be assessed. This approach, we believe, best depicts a causal assumption. In addition, structural models in longitudinal research can depict changes in latent variables over time (Collins & Horn, 1992).

3.7 SUMMARY

In this chapter, we have described some of the basic correlation concepts underlying structural equation modeling. This discussion included various types of bivariate correlation coefficients, part and partial correlation, variable metrics, and the assumptions and limitations of causation in models.

Most computer programs do not compute all the types of correlation coefficients used in statistics, so the reader should refer to a standard statistics textbook for computational formulas and understanding (Hinkle, Weirsma, & Jurs, 2003). Structural equation modeling programs typically use a variance–covariance matrix and include features to output the type of matrices they use. In SEM, categorical and/or ordinal variables with underlying continuous latent-variable attributes have been used with tetrachoric or polychoric correlations (Muthén, 1982, 1983, 1984; Muthén & Kaplan, 1985). PRELIS has been developed to permit a correlation matrix of various types of correlations to be conditioned or converted into an asymptotic covariance matrix for input into structural equation modeling programs (Jöreskog & Sörbom, 1993). The use of various correlation coefficients and subsequent conversion into a variance–covariance matrix will continue to play a major role in structural equation modeling, especially given mixture models (see chap. 13).

The chapter also presented numerous factors that affect the Pearson correlation coefficient, for example, restriction of range in the scores, outliers, skewness, and nonnormality. SEM software also converts correlation matrices with means and standard deviations into a variance–covariance matrix, but if attenuated correlations are greater than 1.0, a non-positive definite error message will occur because of an inadmissible solution. Non-positive definite error messages are all too common among beginners because they do not screen the data, thinking instead that structural equation modeling will be unaffected. Another major concern is when OLS initial estimates lead to bad start values for the coefficients in a model; however, changing the number of default iterations sometimes solves this problem.

EXERCISES

1. Given the Pearson correlation coefficients $r_{12} = .6$, $r_{13} = .7$, and $r_{23} = .4$, compute the part and partial correlations $r_{12.3}$ and $r_{1(2.3)}$.

2. Compare the variance explained in the bivariate, partial, and part correlations of Exercise 1.
3. Explain causation and provide examples of when a cause-and-effect relationship could exist.
4. Given the following variance–covariance matrix, compute the Pearson correlation coefficients r_{XY}, r_{XZ}, and r_{YZ}:

$$
\begin{array}{c c c c}
 & X & Y & Z \\
X & \left[\begin{array}{c} 15.80 \end{array}\right. & & \\
Y & 10.16 & 11.02 & \\
Z & \left. 12.43 & 9.23 & 15.37 \end{array}\right]
\end{array}.
$$

REFERENCES

Anderson, J. C., & Gerbing, D. W. (1988). Structural equation modeling in practice: A review and recommended two step approach. *Psychological Bulletin, 103*, 411–423.

Anderson, C., & Schumacker, R. E. (2003). A comparison of five robust regression methods with ordinary least squares regression: Relative efficiency, bias, and test of the null hypothesis. *Understanding Statistics, 2*, 77–101.

Arbuckle, J. L. (1996). Full information estimation in the presence of incomplete data. In G. A. Marcoulides & R. E. Schumacker (Eds.), *Advanced structural equation modeling* (pp. 243–277). Mahwah, NJ: Lawrence Erlbaum Associates, Inc.

Arbuckle, J. L., & Wothke, W. (1999). *Amos 4.0 users guide*. Chicago: Smallwaters.

Beale, E. M. L., & Little, R. J. (1975). Missing values in multivariate analysis. *Journal of the Royal Statistical Society Series B, 37*, 129–145.

Bentler, P. M., & Chou, C. (1987). Practical issues in structural equation modeling. *Sociological Methods and Research, 16*, 78–117.

Boomsma, A. (1982). The robustness of LISREL against small sample sizes in factor analysis models. In K. G. Jöreskog & H. Wold (Eds.), *Systems under indirect observation: Causality, structure, prediction (Part I)* (pp. 149–173). Amsterdam: North-Holland.

Boomsma, A. (1983). *On the robustness of LISREL against small sample size and nonnormality*. Amsterdam: Sociometric Research Foundation.

Browne, M. W. (1982). Covariance structures. In D. M. Hawkins (Ed.), *Topics in applied multivariate analysis* (pp. 72–141). Cambridge: Cambridge University Press.

Bullock, H. E., Harlow, L. L., & Mulaik, S. A. (1994). Causation issues in structural equation modeling. *Structural Equation Modeling: A Multidisciplinary Journal, 1*, 253–267.

Cohen, J., & Cohen, P. (1983). *Applied multiple regression/correlation analysis for the behavioral sciences* (2nd ed.). Hillsdale, NJ: Lawrence Erlbaum Associates, Inc.

Collins, L. M., & Horn, J. L. (Eds.). (1992). *Best methods for the analysis of change: Recent advances, unanswered questions, future directions*. Washington, DC: American Psychological Association.

Crocker, L., & Algina, J. (1986). *Introduction to classical and modern test theory*. New York: Holt, Rinehart & Winston.

Ding, L., Velicer, W. F., & Harlow, L. L. (1995). Effects of estimation methods, number of indicators per factor, and improper solutions on structural equation modeling fit indices. *Structural Equation Modeling: A Multidisciplinary Journal, 2*, 119–143.

Ferguson, G. A., & Takane, Y. (1989). *Statistical analysis in psychology and education* (6th ed.). New York: McGraw-Hill.

Hinkle, D. E., Wiersma, W., & Jurs, S. G. (2003). *Applied statistics for the behavioral sciences* (5th ed.). Boston: Houghton Mifflin.

Ho, K., & Naugher, J. R. (2000). Outliers lie: An illustrative example of identifying outliers and applying robust methods. *Multiple Linear Regression Viewpoints, 26*(2), 2–6.

Hoelter, J. W. (1983). The analysis of covariance structures: Goodness-of-fit indices. *Sociological Methods and Research, 11*, 325–344.

Hu, L., Bentler, P. M., & Kano, Y. (1992). Can test statistics in covariance structure analysis be trusted? *Psychological Bulletin, 112*, 351–362.

Huber, P. J. (1981). *Robust statistics.* New York: Wiley.

Jennrich, R. I., & Thayer, D. T. (1973). A note on Lawley's formula for standard errors in maximum likelihood factor analysis. *Psychometrika, 38*, 571–580.

Jöreskog, K. G., & Sörbom, D. (1993). *PRELIS2 user's reference guide.* Chicago: Scientific Software International.

Lawley, D. N., & Maxwell, A. E. (1971). *Factor analysis as a statistical method.* London: Butterworth.

Little, R. J. A., & Rubin, D. B. (1987). Statistical analysis with missing data. New York: Wiley.

Little, R. J., & Rubin, D. B. (1990). The analysis of social science data with missing values. *Sociological Methods and Research, 18*, 292–326.

Lomax, R. G. (2001). *Statistical concepts: A second course for education and the behavioral sciences* (2nd ed.). Mahwah, NJ: Lawrence Erlbaum Associates, Inc.

McCall, C. H., Jr. (1982). *Sampling statistics handbook for research.* Ames: Iowa State University Press.

Muthén, B. (1982). A structural probit model with latent variables. *Journal of the American Statistical Association, 74*, 807–811.

Muthén, B. (1983). Latent variable structural equation modeling with categorical data. *Journal of Econometrics, 22*, 43–65.

Muthén, B. (1984). A general structural equation model with dichotomous, ordered categorical, and continuous latent variable indicators. *Psychometrika, 49*, 115–132.

Muthén, B., & Kaplan, D. (1985). A comparison of some methodologies for the factor analysis of non-normal Likert variables. *British Journal of Mathematical and Statistical Psychology, 38*, 171–189.

Pearson, K. (1896). Mathematical contributions to the theory of evolution. Part 3. Regression, heredity and panmixia. *Philosophical Transactions, A, 187*, 253–318.

Pedhazur, E. J. (1997). *Multiple regression in behavioral research: Explanation and prediction* (3rd ed.). Fort Worth, TX: Harcourt Brace.

Resta, P. E., & Baker, R. L. (1972). *Selecting variables for educational research.* Inglewood, CA: Southwest Regional Laboratory for Educational Research and Development.

Rousseeuw, P. J., & Leroy, A. M. (1987). *Robust regression and outlier detection.* New York: Wiley.

Spearman, C. (1904). The proof and measurement of association between two things. *American Journal of Psychology, 15*, 72–101.

Staudte, R. G., & Sheather, S. J. (1990). *Robust estimation and testing.* New York: Wiley.

Stevens, S. S. (1968). Measurement, statistics, and the schempiric view. *Science, 101*, 849–856.

Tankard, J. W., Jr. (1984). *The statistical pioneers.* Cambridge, MA: Schenkman.

Tracz, S. M. (1992). The interpretation of beta weights in path analysis. *Multiple Linear Regression Viewpoints, 19*(1), 7–15.

Wothke, W. (1993). *Nonpositive definite matrices in structural equation modeling.* In K. A. Bollen & S. J. Long (Eds.), *Testing structural equation models* (pp. 256–293). Newbury Park, CA: Sage.

Wothke, W. (2000). Longitudinal and multi-group modeling with missing data. In T. D. Little, K. U. Schnabel, and J. Baumert (Eds.), *Modeling longitudinal and multiple group data: Practical issues, applied approaches and specific examples* (pp. 1–24). Mahwah, NJ: Lawrence Erlbaum Associates, Inc.

ANSWERS TO EXERCISES

1. Partial and part correlations:

$$r_{12.3} = \frac{.6 - (.7)(.4)}{\sqrt{[1 - (.7)^2][1 - (.4)^2]}} = .49$$

$$r_{1(2.3)} = \frac{.6 - (.7)(.4)}{\sqrt{[1 - (.4)^2]}} = .35.$$

2. Bivariate = area $(a + c) = (.6)^2 = 36\%$.
     Partial = area $[a/(a + e)] = (.49)^2 = 24\%$.
        Part = area $a = (.35)^2 = 12\%$.
3. A meaningful theoretical relationship should be plausible given that:
   a. Variables logically precede each other in time.
   b. Variables covary or correlate together as expected.
   c. Other influences or "causes" are controlled.
   d. Variables should be measured on at least an interval level.
   e. Changes in a preceding variable should affect variables that follow, either directly or
      indirectly.
4. The formula for calculating the Pearson correlation coefficient r_{XY} from the covariance
   and variance of variables is

$$r_{XY} = \frac{s_{XY}^2}{\sqrt{s_X^2 * s_Y^2}}.$$

Therefore

$$r_{XY} = \frac{10.16}{\sqrt{(15.80)(11.02)}} = .77$$

$$r_{XZ} = \frac{12.43}{\sqrt{(15.80)(15.37)}} = .80$$

$$r_{YZ} = \frac{9.23}{\sqrt{(11.02)(15.37)}} = .71.$$

4

SEM Basics

Chapter Outline

Key Concepts

Model specification and specification error
Fixed, free, and constrained parameters
Under-, just-, and overidentified models
Recursive versus nonrecursive models
Indeterminancy
Different methods of estimation
Specification search

In this chapter we introduce the basic building blocks of all SEM analyses, which follow a logical sequence of five steps or processes: model specification, model identification, model estimation, model testing, and model modification. In subsequent chapters, we further illustrate these five steps. These basic building blocks are absolutely essential to all SEM models.

4.1   MODEL SPECIFICATION

Model specification involves using all of the available relevant theory, research, and information and developing a theoretical model. Thus, prior to any data collection or analysis, the researcher specifies a specific model that should be confirmed with variance–covariance data. In other words, available information is used to decide which variables to include in the theoretical model (which implicitly also involves which variables not to include in the model) and how these variables are related. *Model specification* involves determining every relationship and parameter in the model that is of interest to the researcher. Cooley (1978) stated that this was the hardest part of structural equation modeling.

A given model is properly specified when the true population model is deemed consistent with the implied theoretical model being tested, that is, the sample covariance matrix S is sufficiently reproduced by the implied theoretical model. The goal of the applied researcher is therefore to determine the best possible model that generates the sample covariance matrix. The sample covariance matrix implies some underlying, yet unknown theoretical model or structure (known as the covariance structure), and the researcher's goal is to find the model that most closely fits that variable covariance structure. Take the simple example of a two-variable situation involving observed variables X and Y. We know from prior research that X and Y are highly correlated, but why? What theoretical relationship is responsible for this correlation? Does X influence Y, does Y influence X, or does a third variable Z influence both X and Y? These are among the many possible reasons why X and Y are related in a particular fashion. The researcher needs prior research and theories to choose among plausible explanations and specify a model, that is, develop an implied theoretical model (model specification).

Ultimately, an applied researcher wants to know the extent to which the true model that generated the data deviates from the implied theoretical model. If the true model is not consistent with the implied theoretical model, then the implied theoretical model is *misspecified*. The difference between the true model and the implied model may be due to errors of omission and/or inclusion of any variable or parameter. For example, an important parameter may have been omitted from the model tested (e.g., it neglected to allow X and Y to be related) or an important variable may have been omitted (e.g., an important variable, such as amount of education or training, was not included in the model). Likewise, an unimportant parameter and/or unimportant variable may have been unfortunately included in the model, that is, there is an error of inclusion.

The exclusion or inclusion of unimportant variables will produce implied models that are misspecified. Why should we be concerned about this? The problem is that a misspecified model may result in biased parameter estimates, in other words, estimates that are systematically different from what they really are in the true model. This bias is known as *specification error*. In the presence of specification error, it is likely that one's theoretical model may not fit the data and be deemed statistically unacceptable (see *model testing* in sect. 4.4). There are a number of procedures available for the detection of specification error so that a more properly specified model may be evaluated. The *model modification* procedures are described in section 4.5.

4.2   MODEL IDENTIFICATION

In structural equation modeling, it is crucial that the researcher resolve the *identification problem* prior to the estimation of parameters. In the identification problem, we ask the following question: On the basis of the sample data contained in the sample covariance matrix S and the theoretical model implied by the population covariance matrix Σ, can a unique set of parameter estimates be found? For example, the theoretical model might suggest that $X + Y =$ some value, the data might indicate that $X + Y = 10$, and yet it may be that no unique solution for X and Y exists. One solution is that $X = 5$ and $Y = 5$, another is that $X = 2$ and $Y = 8$, and so on, because there is an infinite number of possible solutions for this problem, that is, there is *indeterminacy*, or the possibility that the data fit more than one implied theoretical model equally well. The problem is that there are not enough constraints on the model and the data to obtain unique estimates of X and Y. Therefore, if we wish to solve this problem, we need to impose some constraints. One such constraint might be to fix the value of X to 1; then Y would have to be 9. We have solved the identification problem in this instance by imposing one constraint. However, except for simplistic models, the solution to the identification problem in structural equation modeling is not so easy (although algebraically one can typically solve the problem).

Each potential parameter in a model must be specified to be either a free parameter, a fixed parameter, or a constrained parameter. A *free* parameter is a parameter that is unknown and therefore needs to be estimated. A *fixed* parameter is a parameter that is not free, but is fixed to a specified value, typically either 0 or 1. A *constrained* parameter is a parameter that is unknown, but is constrained to equal one or more other parameters.

Model identification depends on the designation of parameters as fixed, free, or constrained. Once the model is specified and the parameter specifications are indicated, the parameters are combined to form one and only one Σ (model-implied variance–covariance matrix). The problem still exists, however, in that there may be several sets of parameter values that can form the same Σ. If two or more sets of parameter values generate the same Σ, then they are *equivalent*, that is, yield equivalent models (Lee & Hershberger, 1990; MacCallum, Wegener, Uchino, & Fabrigar, 1993; Raykov & Penev, 2001). If a parameter has the same value in all equivalent sets, then the parameter is identified. If all of the parameters of a model are identified, then the entire model is identified. If one or more of the parameters are not identified, then the entire model is not identified.

Traditionally, there have been three levels of model identification. They depend on the amount of information in the sample variance–covariance matrix S necessary for uniquely estimating the parameters of the model. The three levels of model identification are as follows:

1. A model is *underidentified* (or not identified) if one or more parameters may not be uniquely determined because there is not enough information in the matrix S.
2. A model is *just-identified* if all of the parameters are uniquely determined because there is just enough information in the matrix S.
3. A model is *overidentified* when there is more than one way of estimating a parameter (or parameters) because there is more than enough information in the matrix S.

If a model is either just- or overidentified, then the model is identified. If a model is underidentified, then the parameter estimates are not to be trusted, that is, the degrees of freedom for the model are zero or negative. However, such a model may become identified if additional constraints are imposed, that is, the degrees of freedom equal 1 or greater.

There are several conditions for establishing the identification of a model. A necessary, but not the only sufficient condition for identification is the *order condition*, under which the number of free parameters to be estimated must be less than or equal to the number of distinct values in the matrix S, that is, only the diagonal variances and one set of off-diagonal covariances are counted. For example, because $s_{12} = s_{21}$ in the off-diagonal of the matrix, only one of these covariances is counted. The number of distinct values in the matrix S is equal to $p(p+1)/2$, where

p is the number of observed variables. A saturated model (all paths) with p variables has $p(p+3)/2$ free parameters. For a sample matrix S with three observed variables, there are 6 distinct values $[3(3+1)/2 = 6]$ and 9 free (independent) parameters $[3(3+3)/2]$ that can be estimated. Consequently, the number of free parameters estimated in any theoretical implied model must be less than or equal to the number of distinct values in the S matrix. However, this is only one necessary condition for model identification; it does not by itself imply that the model is identified. For example, if the sample size is small ($n = 10$) relative to the number of variables ($p = 20$), then not enough information is available to estimate parameters in a saturated model.

Whereas the order condition is easy to assess, other sufficient conditions are not, for example, the rank condition. The *rank condition* requires an algebraic determination of whether each parameter in the model can be estimated from the covariance matrix S. Unfortunately, proof of this rank condition is often problematic in practice, particularly for the applied researcher. However, there are some procedures that the applied researcher can use. For a more detailed discussion on the rank condition, refer to Bollen (1989) or Jöreskog and Sörbom (1988). The basic concepts and a set of procedures to handle problems in model identification are discussed next and in subsequent chapters.

Three different methods for avoiding identification problems are available. The first method is necessary in the measurement model, where we decide which observed variables measure each latent variable. Either one indicator for each latent variable must have a factor loading fixed to 1 or the variance of each latent variable must be fixed to 1. The reason for imposing these constraints is to set the measurement scale for each latent variable, primarily because of *indeterminacy* between the variance of the latent variable and the loadings of the observed variables on that latent variable. Utilizing either of these methods will eliminate the scale indeterminacy problem, but not necessarily the identification problem, and so additional constraints may be necessary.

The second method comes into play where reciprocal or nonrecursive structural models are used; such models are sometimes a source of the identification problem. A structural model is *recursive* when all of the structural relationships are unidirectional (two latent variables are not reciprocally related), that is, they are such that no feedback loops exist whereby a latent variable feeds back upon itself. *Nonrecursive* structural models include a reciprocal or bidirectional relationship, so that there is feedback, for example, models that allow product attitude and product interest to influence one another. For a nonrecursive model, ordinary least squares (OLS; see *model estimation* in sect. 4.3) is not an appropriate method of estimation.

The third method is to begin with a parsimonious (simple) model with a minimum number of parameters. The model should only include variables (parameters) considered to be absolutely crucial. If this model is identified, then one can consider including other parameters in subsequent models.

A second set of procedures involves methods for checking on the identification of a model. One method is Wald's (1950) rank test, provided in the EQS computer program. A second, related method is described by Wiley (1973), Keesling (1972), and Jöreskog and Sörbom (1988). This test has to do with the inverse of the information matrix and is computed by programs such as LISREL and EQS. Unfortunately, these methods are not 100% reliable, and there is no general necessary-and-sufficient test available for the applied researcher to use. Our advice is to use whatever methods are available for identification. If you still suspect that there is an identification problem, follow the recommendation of Jöreskog and Sörbom (1988). The first step is to analyze the sample covariance matrix S and save the estimated population matrix Σ. The second step is to analyze the estimated population matrix Σ. If the model is identified, then the estimates from both analyses should be identical. Another option, often recommended, is to use different starting values in separate analyses. If the model is identified, then the estimates should be identical.

4.3 MODEL ESTIMATION

In this section we examine different methods for estimating the parameters, that is, estimates of the population parameters, in a structural equation model. We want to obtain estimates for each of the parameters specified in the model that produce the implied matrix Σ, such that the parameter values yield a matrix as close as possible to S, our sample covariance matrix of the observed or indicator variables. When elements in the matrix S minus the elements in the matrix Σ equal zero ($S - \Sigma = 0$), then $\chi^2 = 0$, that is, one has a perfect model fit to the data.

The estimation process involves the use of a particular *fitting function* to minimize the difference between Σ and S. Several fitting functions or estimation procedures are available. Some of the earlier methods include unweighted or ordinary least squares (ULS or OLS), generalized least squares (GLS), and maximum likelihood (ML).

The ULS estimates are consistent, have no distributional assumptions or associated statistical tests, and are scale dependent, that is, changes in observed variable scale yield different solutions or sets of estimates. In fact, of all the estimators described here, only the ULS estimation method is scale dependent. The GLS and ML methods are scale free, which means that if we transform the scale of one or more of our observed variables, the untransformed and transformed variables will yield estimates that are properly related, that is, that differ by the transformation. The GLS procedure involves a weight matrix W such as S^{-1}, the inverse of the sample covariance matrix. Both GLS and ML estimation methods have desirable asymptotic properties, that is, large sample properties, such as minimum variance and unbiasedness. Also, both GLS and ML estimation methods assume multivariate normality of the observed variables (the sufficient conditions are that the observations are independent and identically distributed and that kurtosis is zero). The weighted-least squares (WLS) estimation method generally requires a large sample size and as a result is considered an asymptotically distribution-free (ADF) estimator, which does not depend upon the normality assumption. Raykov and Widaman (1995) further discussed the use of ADF estimators.

If standardization of the latent variables is desired, one may obtain a standardized solution (and thereby standardized estimates) where the variances of the latent variables are fixed at 1. A separate but related issue is standardization of the observed variables. When the unit of measurement for the indicator variables is of no particular interest to the researcher, that is, is arbitrary or irrelevant, then only an analysis of the correlation matrix is typically of interest. The analysis of correlations usually gives correct chi-square goodness-of-fit values, but estimates standard errors incorrectly. There are ways to specify a model, analyze a correlation matrix, and obtain correct standard errors. For example, the SEPATH structural equation modeling program by Steiger (1995) does permit correlation matrix input and computes the correct standard errors. Because the correlation matrix involves a standardized scaling among the observed variables, the parameters estimated for the measurement model, for example, the factor loadings, will be of the same order of magnitude, that is, on the same scale. When the same indicator variables are measured either over time (i.e., longitudinal analysis) for multiple samples or when equality constraints are imposed on two or more parameters, an analysis of the covariance matrix is appropriate and recommended so as to capitalize on the metric similarities of the variables (Lomax, 1982).

More recently, other estimation procedures have been developed for the analysis of covariance structure models. Beginning with LISREL, automatic starting values have been provided for all of the parameter estimates. These are referred to as *initial estimates* and involve a fast, noniterative procedure (unlike other methods such as ML, which is iterative). The initial estimates involve the instrumental variables and least-squares methods (ULS and the two-stage least-squares method, TSLS) developed by Hagglund (1982). Often, the user may wish to obtain only the initial estimates (for cost efficiency) or use them as starting values in subsequent analyses. The initial estimates are consistent and rather efficient relative to the ML estimator and have been shown, as in the case of the centroid method, to be considerably faster, especially in large-scale measurement models (Gerbing & Hamilton, 1994).

If one can assume multivariate normality of the observed variables, then moments beyond the second, that is, skewness and kurtosis, can be ignored. When the normality assumption is violated, parameter estimates and standard errors are suspect. One alternative is to use GLS, which assumes multivariate normality and stipulates that kurtosis be zero (Browne, 1974). Browne (1982, 1984) later recognized that the weight matrix of GLS may be modified to yield ADF or WLS estimates, standard errors, and test statistics. Others (Bentler, 1983; Shapiro, 1983) developed more general classes of ADF estimators. All of these methods are based on the GLS method and specify that the weight matrix be of a certain form; for EQS, they include both distribution-specific and distribution-free estimates, although none of these methods takes multivariate kurtosis into account. Research by Browne (1984) suggested that goodness-of-fit indices and standard errors of parameter estimates derived under the assumption of multivariate normality should not be employed if the distribution of the observed variables has a nonzero value for kurtosis. In this case, one of the methods mentioned earlier should be utilized.

An implicit assumption of ML estimators is that information contained in the first- and second-order moments (location–mean and dispersion–variance, respectively) of the observed variables is sufficient so that information contained in higher order moments (skewness and kurtosis) can be ignored. If the observed variables are interval scaled and multivariate normal, then the ML estimates, standard errors, and chi-square test are appropriate. However, if the observed variables are ordinal scaled and/or extremely skewed or peaked (nonnormally distributed), then the ML estimates, standard errors, and chi-square test are not robust.

The use of binary and ordinal response variables in structural equation modeling was pioneered by Muthén (1983, 1984). Muthén proposed a three-stage limited-information GLS estimator that provides a large-sample chi-square test of the model and large-sample standard errors. The Muthén categorical variable methodology (CVM) approach is believed to produce more suitable coefficients of association than the ordinary Pearson product–moment correlations and covariances applied to ordered categorical variables (Muthén, 1983). This is particularly so with markedly skewed categorical variables, where correlations must be adjusted to assume values throughout the -1 to $+1$ range, as is done in the PRELIS computer program.

The PRELIS computer program handles ordinal variables by computing a polychoric correlation for two ordinal variables (Olsson, 1979) and a polyserial correlation for an ordinal and an interval variable (Olsson, Drasgow, & Dorans, 1982), where the ordinal variables are assumed to have an underlying bivariate normal distribution, which is not necessary with the Muthén approach. All correlations (Pearson, polychoric, and polyserial) are then used by PRELIS to create an asymptotic covariance matrix for input into LISREL. The reader is cautioned to *not directly* use mixed types of correlation matrices or covariance matrices in EQS or LISREL–SIMPLIS programs, but instead use an asymptotic variance–covariance matrix produced by PRELIS along with the sample variance–covariance matrix as input in a LISREL–SIMPLIS or LISREL matrix program.

During the last 15 or 20 years, we have seen considerable research on the behavior of methods of estimation under various conditions. The most crucial conditions are characterized by a lack of multivariate normality and interval-level variables. When the data are generated from nonnormally distributed populations and/or represent discrete variables, the normal theory estimators of standard errors and model fit indices discussed in chapter 5 are suspect. According to theoretical and simulation research investigating nonnormality, one of the distribution-free or weighted procedures (e.g., ADF, WLS, GLS) should be used (Lomax, 1989). In dealing with noninterval variables, the research indicates that only when categorical data show small skewness and kurtosis values (in the range of -1 to $+1$, or -1.5 to $+1.5$) should normal theory be used. When these conditions are not met, several options already mentioned are recommended. These include the use of tetrachoric, polyserial, and polychoric correlations rather than Pearson product–moment correlations, or the use of distribution-free or weighted procedures available in the SEM software. Considerable research remains to be conducted to determine what the optimal estimation procedure is for a given set of conditions.

4.4 MODEL TESTING

Once the parameter estimates are obtained for a specified SEM model, the applied researcher should determine how well the data fit the model. In other words, to what extent is the theoretical model supported by the obtained sample data? There are two ways to think about model fit. The first is to consider some global-type omnibus test of the fit of the entire model. The second is to examine the fit of individual parameters of the model.

We first consider the global tests in SEM known as model fit criteria. Unlike many statistical procedures that have a single, most powerful fit index (e.g., F test in ANOVA), in SEM there is an increasingly large number of model fit indices. Many of these measures are based on a comparison of the model-implied covariance matrix Σ to the sample covariance matrix S. If Σ and S are similar in some fashion, then one may say that the data fit the theoretical model. If Σ and S are quite different, then one may say that the data do not fit the theoretical model. We further explain several model fit indices in chapter 5.

Second, we consider the individual parameters of the model. Three main features of the individual parameters can be considered. One feature is whether a free parameter is significantly different from zero. Once parameter estimates are obtained, standard errors for each estimate are also computed. A ratio of the parameter estimate to the estimated standard error can be formed as a *critical value*, which is assumed normally distributed (unit normal distribution), that is, critical value equals parameter estimate divided by standard error of the parameter estimate. If the *critical value* exceeds the expected value at a specified α level (e.g., 1.96 for a two-tailed test at the .05 level), then that parameter is significantly different from zero. The parameter estimate, standard error, and critical value are routinely provided in the computer output for a model. A second feature is whether the sign of the parameter agrees with what is expected from the theoretical model. For example, if the expectation is that more education will yield a higher income level, then an estimate with a positive sign would support that expectation. A third feature is that parameter estimates should make sense, that is, they should be within an expected range of values. For instance, variances should not have negative values and correlations should not exceed 1. Thus, all free parameters should be in the expected direction, be statistically different from zero, and make practical sense.

4.5 MODEL MODIFICATION

If the fit of the implied theoretical model is not as strong as one would like (which is typically the case with an initial model), then the next step is to modify the model and subsequently evaluate the new modified model. In order to determine how to modify the model, there are a number of procedures available for the detection of specification errors so that more properly specified subsequent models may be evaluated (during respecification). In general, these procedures are used for performing what is called a *specification search* (Leamer, 1978). The purpose of a specification search is to alter the original model in the search for a model that is better fitting in some sense and yields parameters having practical significance and substantive meaning. If a parameter has no substantive meaning to the applied researcher, then it should never be included in a model. Substantive interest must be the guiding force in a specification search; otherwise, the resultant model will not have practical value or importance. There are procedures designed to detect and correct for specification errors. Typically, applications of structural equation modeling include some type of specification search, informal or formal, although the search process may not always be explicitly stated in a research report.

An obvious intuitive method is to consider the statistical significance of each parameter estimated in the model. One specification strategy would be to fix parameters that are not statistically significant, that is, have small *critical values,* to 0 in a subsequent model. Care should be taken, however, because statistical significance is related to sample size; parameters may not be significant with small samples but significant with larger samples. Also, substantive theoretical interests must be considered. If a parameter is not significant but is of sufficient substantive interest, then the parameter should probably remain in the model. The guiding rule should be that the parameter estimates make sense to you. If an estimate makes no sense to you, how are you going to explain it, how is it going to be of substantive value or meaningful?

Another intuitive method of examining misspecification is to examine the residual matrix, that is, the differences between the observed covariance matrix S and the model-implied covariance matrix Σ; these are referred to as fitted residuals in the LISREL program output. These values should be small in magnitude and should not be larger for one variable than another. Large values overall indicate serious general model misspecification, whereas large values for a single variable indicate misspecification for that variable only, probably in the structural model (Bentler, 1989). Standardized or normalized residuals can also be examined. Theoretically these can be treated like standardized z scores, and hence problems can be more easily detected from the standardized residual matrix than from the unstandardized residual matrix. Large standardized residuals (larger than, say, 1.96 or 2.58) indicate that a particular covariance is not well explained by the model. The model should be examined to determine ways in which this particular covariance could be explained, for example, by freeing some parameters.

Sörbom (1975) considered misspecification of correlated measurement error terms in the analysis of longitudinal data. Sörbom proposed considering the first-order partial derivatives, which have values of zero for free parameters and nonzero values for fixed parameters. The largest value, in absolute terms, indicates the fixed parameter most likely to improve model fit. A second model, with this parameter now free, is then estimated and goodness of fit assessed. Sörbom defined an acceptable fit as occurring when the difference between two models' successive chi-square values is not significant. The derivatives of the second model are examined and the process continues until an acceptable fit is achieved. This procedure, however, is restricted to the derivatives of the observed variables and provides indications of misspecification only in terms of correlated measurement error.

More recently, other procedures have been developed to examine model specification. In the LISREL–SIMPLIS program, modification indices are reported for all nonfree parameters. These indices were developed by Sörbom (1986) and represent an improvement over the first-order partial derivatives already described. A modification index for a particular nonfree parameter indicates that if this parameter were allowed to become free in a subsequent model, then the chi-square goodness-of-fit value would be predicted to decrease by at least the value of the index. In other words, if the value of the modification index for a nonfree parameter is 50, then when this parameter is allowed to be free in a subsequent model, the value of chi-square will decrease by at least 50. Thus, large modification indices would suggest ways that the model might be altered by allowing the corresponding parameters to become free and the researcher might arrive at a better fitting model. As reported in an earlier LISREL manual (Jöreskog & Sörbom, 1988), "This procedure seems to work well in practice" (p. 44), although there is little research on these indices.

The LISREL program also provides squared multiple correlations for each observed variable separately. These values indicate how well the observed variables serve as measures of the latent variables and are scaled from 0 to 1. Squared multiple correlations are also given for each structural equation separately. These values serve as an indication of the strength of the structural relationships and are also scaled from 0 to 1.

Some relatively new indices are the *expected parameter change, Lagrange multiplier,* and *Wald statistics.* The expected parameter change (EPC) statistic in the LISREL and EQS programs indicates the estimated change in the magnitude and direction of each nonfree parameter if it were to become free (rather than the predicted change in the goodness-of-fit test as with the modification indices). This could be useful, for example, if the sign of the potential free parameter is not in the expected direction (e.g., positive instead of negative). This would suggest that such a parameter should remain fixed. The Lagrange multiplier and Wald statistics are provided in the EQS program. The Lagrange multiplier

(LM) statistic allows one to evaluate the effect of freeing a set of fixed parameters in a subsequent model [referred to by Bentler (1986) as a *forward search*]. Because the Lagrange multiplier statistic can consider a set of parameters, it is considered the multivariate analogue of the modification index. The Wald (W) statistic is used to evaluate whether the free parameters in a model are necessary in a statistical sense. It indicates which parameters in a model should be dropped and was referred to by Bentler (1986) as a *backward search*. Because the Wald statistic can consider a set of parameters, it is considered the multivariate analogue of the *individual critical values*.

Empirical research suggests that specification searches are most successful when the model tested is very similar to the model that generated the data. More specifically, these studies begin with a known true model from which sample data are generated. The true model is then misspecified. The goal of the specification search is to begin with the misspecified model and determine whether the true model can be located as a result of the search. If the misspecified model is more than two or three parameters different from the true model, then the true model cannot typically be located. Unfortunately, in these studies the true model was almost never located through the specification search, regardless of the search procedure or combination of procedures used (e.g., Baldwin & Lomax, 1990; Gallini, 1983; Gallini & Mandeville, 1984; MacCallum, 1986; Saris & Stronkhorst, 1984; Tippets, 1992).

What is clear is that there is no single procedure sufficient for finding a properly specified model. As a result, there has been a flurry of research in recent years to determine what combination of procedures is most likely to yield a properly specified model (e.g., Chou & Bentler, 1990; Herting & Costner, 1985; Kaplan, 1988, 1989, 1990; MacCallum, 1986; Saris, Satorra, & Sörbom, 1987; Satorra & Saris, 1985; Silvia & MacCallum, 1988). No optimal strategy has been found. A computer program known as TETRAD was developed by Glymour, Scheines, Spirtes, and Kelly (1987), and the new version, TETRAD II (Spirtes, Scheines, Meek, & Glymour, 1994), thoughtfully reviewed by Wood (1995), offers new search procedures. A new specification search procedure, known as Tabu, was recently developed by Marcoulides, Drezner, and Schumacker (1998). The newest version of Amos also includes a specification search, which produces plausible models to choose from once optional paths in the model are indicated. If one selected all of the paths in the Amos model as optional, then all possible models would be listed; for example, a multiple regression equation with 17 independent variables and 1 dependent variable would yield 2^{17} or 131,072 regression models, not all of which would be theoretically meaningful. Selection of the "best" equation would require the use of some fit criteria for comparing models

(Marcoulides, Drezner, & Schumacker, 1998). Current modeling software permits the formulation of all possible models; however, the outcome of any specification search should still be guided by theory and practical considerations (e.g., the time and cost of acquiring the data).

Given our lengthy discussion about specification search procedures, some practical advice is warranted for the applied researcher. The following is our suggested eight-step procedure for a specification search:

1. Let substantive theory and prior research guide your model spec- ification.
2. When you are satisfied that Rule 1 has been met, test your implied theoretical model and move to Rule 3.
3. Conduct a specification search, first on the measurement model and then on the structural model.
4. For each model tested, look to see if the parameters are of the ex- pected magnitude and direction, and examine several appropriate goodness-of-fit indices.

Steps 5 through 7 can be followed in an iterative fashion. For example, you might go from Step 5 to Step 6, and successively on to Steps 7, 6, 5, and so on.

5. Examine the statistical significance of the nonfixed parameters, and possibly the Wald statistic. Look to see if any nonfixed parameters should be fixed in a subsequent model.
6. Examine the modification indices, expected parameter change statistics, and possibly the Lagrange multiplier statistic. Look to see if any fixed parameters should be freed in a subsequent model.
7. Consider examining the standardized residual matrix to see if any- thing suspicious is occurring (e.g., larger values for a particular observed variable).
8. Once you test a final acceptable model, cross-validate it with a new sample, or use half of the sample to find a properly specified model and the other half to check it (cross-validation index, CVI), or report a single-sample cross-validation index (ECVI) for alterna- tive models (Cudeck & Browne, 1983; Kroonenberg & Lewis, 1982). Cross-validation procedures are discussed in chapter 12.

4.6 SUMMARY

In this chapter we considered the basics of structural equation mod- eling. The chapter began with a look at model specification (fixed, free, and constrained parameters) and then moved on to model identification (under-, just-, and overidentified models). Next, we discussed the various types of estimation procedures. Here we considered each estimation method, its underlying assumptions, and some general guidelines as to when each is appropriate. We then moved on to a general discussion of model testing, where the fit of a given model is assessed. Finally, we described the specification search process, where information is used to arrive at a more properly specified model that is theoretically meaningful.

In chapter 5, we discuss the numerous goodness-of-fit indices available in structural equation modeling software to determine whether a model is parsimonious and which competing or alternative models are better, and to examine submodels (i.e., nested models). We classify the model fit indices according to whether a researcher is testing model fit, seeking a more parsimonious model (complex to simple), or comparing nested models. In addition, we discuss hypothesis testing, parameter significance, power, and sample size as these affect our interpretation of global model fit.

EXERCISES

1. Define model specification.
2. Define model identification.
3. Define model estimation.
4. Define model testing.
5. Define model modification.
6. Determine the number of distinct values (variances and covariances) in the variance–covariance matrix S:

$$S = \begin{bmatrix} 1.0 & & \\ .25 & 1.0 & \\ .35 & .45 & 1.00 \end{bmatrix}$$

7. How many distinct values are in a variance–covariance matrix for the following variables {hint: $[p(p+1)/2]$}?
   a. Five variables
   b. Ten variables
8. A saturated model with p variables has $p(p+3)/2$ free parameters. Determine the number of free parameters for the following number of variables in a model:
   a. Three observed variables
   b. Five observed variables
   c. Ten observed variables

REFERENCES

Baldwin, B., & Lomax, R. G. (1990). *Measurement model specification error in LISREL structural equation models.* Paper presented at the annual meeting of the American Educational Research Association, Boston.

Bentler, P. M. (1983). Some contributions to efficient statistics in structural models: Specification and estimation of moment structures. *Psychometrika, 48,* 493–517.

Bentler, P. M. (1986). *Lagrange multiplier and Wald tests for EQS and EQS/PC.* Unpublished manuscript, BMDP Statistical Software, Los Angeles.

Bentler, P. M. (1989). *Theory and implementation of EQS: A structural equations program.* Los Angeles: BMDP Statistical Software.

Bollen, K. A. (1989). *Structural equations with latent variables.* New York: Wiley.

Browne, M. W. (1974). Generalized least-squares estimators in the analysis of covariance structures. *South African Statistical Journal, 8,* 1–24.

Browne, M. W. (1982). Covariance structures. In D. M. Hawkins (Ed.), *Topics in applied multivariate analysis* (pp. 72–141). Cambridge: Cambridge University Press.

Browne, M. W. (1984). Asymptotically distribution-free methods for the analysis of covariance structures. *British Journal of Mathematical and Statistical Psychology, 37,* 62–83.

Chou, C.-P., & Bentler, P. M. (1990, April). *Power of the likelihood ratio, Lagrange multiplier, and Wald tests for model modification in covariance structure analysis.* Paper presented at the annual meeting of the American Educational Research Association. Boston: MA.

Cooley, W. W. (1978). Explanatory observational studies. *Educational Researcher, 7*(9), 9–15.

Cudeck, R., & Browne, M. W. (1983). Cross-validation of covariance structures. *Multivariate Behavioral Research, 18,* 147–167.

Gallini, J. K. (1983). Misspecifications that can result in path analysis structures. *Applied Psychological Measurement, 7,* 125–137.

Gallini, J. K., & Mandeville, G. K. (1984). An investigation of the effect of sample size and specification error on the fit of structural equation models. *Journal of Experimental Education, 53,* 9–19.

Gerbing, D. W., & Hamilton, J. G. (1994). The surprising viability of a simple alternate estimation procedure for construction of large-scale structural equation measurement models. *Structural Equation Modeling: A Multidisciplinary Journal, 1,* 103–115.

Glymour, C. R., Scheines, R., Spirtes, P., & Kelly, K. (1987). *Discovering causal structure.* Orlando, FL: Academic.

Hagglund, G. (1982). Factor analysis by instrumental variable methods. *Psychometrika, 47,* 209–222.

Herting, J. R., & Costner, H. L. (1985). Respecification in multiple indicator models. In H. M. Blalock, Jr. (Ed.), *Causal models in the social sciences* (2nd ed., pp. 321–393). New York: Aldine.

Jöreskog, K. G., & Sörbom, D. (1988). *LISREL 7: A guide to the program and applications.* Chicago: SPSS.

Kaplan, D. (1988). The impact of specification error on the estimation, testing, and improvement of structural equation models. *Multivariate Behavioral Research, 23,* 69–86.

Kaplan, D. (1989). Model modification in covariance structure analysis: Application of the parameter change statistic. *Multivariate Behavioral Research, 24,* 285–305.

Kaplan, D. (1990). Evaluating and modifying covariance structure models: A review and recommendation. *Multivariate Behavioral Research, 25,* 137–155.

Keesling, J. W. (1972). *Maximum likelihood approaches to causal flow analysis.* Unpublished dissertation, University of Chicago, Department of Education.

Kroonenberg, P. M., & Lewis, C. (1982). Methodological issues in the search for a factor model: Exploration through confirmation. *Journal of Educational Statistics, 7,* 69–89.

Leamer, E. E. (1978). *Specification searches.* New York: Wiley.

Lee, S., & Hershberger, S. (1990). A simple rule for generating equivalent models in covariance structure modeling. *Multivariate Behavioral Research, 25,* 313–334.

Lomax, R. G. (1982). A guide to LISREL-type structural equation modeling. *Behavior Research Methods and Instrumentation, 14,* 1–8.

Lomax, R. G. (1989). Covariance structure analysis: Extensions and developments. In B. Thompson (Ed.), *Advances in social science methodology* (Vol. 1, pp. 171–204). Greenwich, CT: JAI.

MacCallum, R. C. (1986). Specification searches in covariance structure modeling. *Psychological Bulletin, 100*, 107–120.

MacCallum, R. C., Wegener, D. T., Uchino, B. N., & Fabrigar, L. R. (1993). The problem of equivalent models in applications of covariance structure analysis. *Psychological Bulletin, 114*, 185–199.

Marcoulides, G. A., Drezner, Z., & Schumacker, R. E. (1998). Model specification searches in structural equation modeling using Tabu search. *Structural Equation Modeling: A Multidisciplinary Journal, 5*, 365–376.

Muthén, B. (1983). Latent variable structural equation modeling with categorical data. *Journal of Econometrics, 22*, 43–65.

Muthén, B. (1984). A general structural equation model with dichotomous, ordered categorical, and continuous latent variable indicators. *Psychometrika, 49*, 115–132.

Olsson, U. (1979). Maximum likelihood estimation of the polychoric correlation coefficient. *Psychometrika, 44*, 443–460.

Olsson, U., Drasgow, F., & Dorans, N. J. (1982). The polyserial correlation coefficient. *Psychometrika, 47*, 337–347.

Raykov, T., & Penev, S. (2001). The problem of equivalent structural equation models: An individual residual perspective. In G. A. Marcoulides & R. E. Schumacker (Eds.), *New developments and techniques in structural equation modeling* (pp. 297–321). Mahwah, NJ: Lawrence Erlbaum Associates, Inc.

Raykov, T., & Widaman, K. F. (1995). Issues in applied structural equation modeling research. *Structural Equation Modeling: A Multidisciplinary Journal, 2*, 289–318.

Saris, W. E., & Stronkhorst, L. H. (1984). *Causal modeling in nonexperimental research: An introduction to the LISREL approach.* Amsterdam: Sociometric Research Foundation.

Saris, W. E., Satorra, A., & Sörbom, D. (1987). The detection and correction of specification errors in structural equation models. In C. C. Clogg (Ed.), *Sociological methodology* (pp. 105–130). Washington, DC: American Sociological Association.

Satorra, A., & Saris, W. E. (1985). Power of the likelihood ratio test in covariance structure analysis. *Psychometrika, 50*, 83–90.

Shapiro, A. (1983). Asymptotic distribution theory in the analysis of covariance structures (a unified approach). *South African Statistical Journal, 17*, 33–81.

Silvia, E. S. M., & MacCallum, R. (1988). Some factors affecting the success of specification searches in covariance structure modeling. *Multivariate Behavioral Research, 23*, 297–326.

Sörbom, D. (1975). Detection of correlated errors in longitudinal data. *British Journal of Mathematical and Statistical Psychology, 27*, 229–239.

Sörbom, D. (1986). *Model modification* (Research Report 86-3). University of Uppsala, Department of Statistics, Uppsala, Sweden.

Spirtes, P., Scheines, R., Meek, C., & Glymour, C. (1994). *TETRAD II: Tools for causal modeling.* Hillsdale, NJ: Lawrence Erlbaum Associates, Inc.

Steiger, J. H. (1995). SEPATH. In *STATISTICA 5.0.* Tulsa, OK: StatSoft.

Tippets, E. (1992). *A comparison of methods for evaluating and modifying covariance structure models.* Paper presented at the annual meeting of the American Educational Research Association, San Francisco.

Wald, A. (1950). A note on the identification of economic relations. In T. C. Koopmans (Ed.), *Statistical inference in dynamic economic models* (pp. 238–244). New York: Wiley.

Wiley, D. E. (1973). The identification problem for structural equation models with unmea-
    sured variables. In A. S. Goldberger & O. D. Duncan (Eds.), *Structural equation models
    in the social sciences* (pp. 69–83). New York: Seminar.
Wood, P. K. (1995). Toward a more critical examination of structural equation models.
    Structural Equation Modeling: A Multidisciplinary Journal, 2, 277–287.

ANSWERS TO EXERCISES

1. *Model specification*: developing a theoretical model to test based on all of the relevant
   theory, research, and information available.
2. *Model identification*: determining whether a unique set of parameter estimates can be
   computed given the sample data contained in the sample covariance matrix S and the
   theoretical model that produced the implied population covariance matrix Σ.
3. *Model estimation*: obtaining estimates for each of the parameters specified in the model
   that produced the implied population covariance matrix Σ. The intent is to obtain parameter estimates that yield a matrix Σ as close as possible to S, our sample covariance
   matrix of the observed or indicator variables. When elements in the matrix S minus the
   elements in the matrix Σ equal zero $(S - \Sigma = 0)$, then $\chi^2 = 0$, indicating a perfect model
   fit to the data and all values in S are equal to values in Σ.
4. *Model testing*: determining how well the sample data fit the theoretical model. In other
   words, to what extent is the theoretical model supported by the obtained sample data?
   Global omnibus tests of the fit of the model are available as well as the fit of individual
   parameters in the model.
5. *Model modification*: changing the initial implied model and retesting the global fit and
   individual parameters in the new, respecified model. To determine how to modify the
   model, there are a number of procedures available to guide the adding or dropping of
   paths in the model so that alternative models can be tested.
6. The correlation matrix S has three variances in the diagonal and three covariances in
   the off-diagonal of the matrix, so there are six distinct values for the three observed
   variables.
7. How many distinct values are in a variance–covariance matrix for the following variables
   {hint: $[p(p + 1)/2]$}?
   a. Five variables = 15 distinct values
   b. Ten variables = 55 distinct values
8. A saturated model with p variables has $p(p + 3)/2$ free parameters. Determine the number of free parameters for the following number of variables in a model:
   a. Three observed variables = 9 free parameters
   b. Five observed variables = 20 free parameters
   c. Ten observed variables = 65 free parameters

5

MODEL FIT

Chapter Outline

Key Concepts

Confirmatory models, alternative models, model generating
Specification search
Saturated models and independence models
Model fit, model comparison, and model parsimony fit indices
Measurement model versus structural model interpretation
Parameter and model significance tests
Sample size, power, and parameter significance

In the previous chapter we considered the basic building blocks of SEM, namely *model specification, model identification, model estimation, model testing, and model modification*. These five steps fall into three main approaches for going from theory to a SEM model in which the covariance structure among variables is analyzed. In the *confirmatory approach* a researcher hypothesizes a specific theoretical model, gathers data, and then tests whether the data fit the model. In this approach, the theoretical model is either accepted or rejected based on a chi-square statistical test of significance and/or meeting acceptable model fit criteria. In the second approach, using *alternative models*, the researcher creates a limited number of theoretically different models to determine which model the data fit best. When these models use the same data set, they are referred to as *nested* models. The alternative approach conducts a chi-square difference test to compare each of the alternative models. The third approach, *model generating*, specifies an initial model (implied or theoretical model), but usually the data do not fit this initial model at an acceptable model fit criterion level, so modification indices (Lagrange or Wald test in EQS) are used to add or delete paths in the model to arrive at a final best model. The goal in model generating is to find a model that the data fit well statistically, but that also has practical and substantive theoretical meaning. The process of finding the best-fitting model is also referred to as a *specification search*, implying that if an initially specified model does not fit the data, then the model is modified in an effort to improve the fit (Marcoulides & Drezner, 2001, 2003). Recent advances in *Tabu search* algorithms have permitted the generation of a set of models that data fit equally well, with a final determination by the researcher of which model to accept (Marcoulides, Drezner, & Schumacker, 1998). Amos has an *exploratory SEM specification search*, which generates alternative models by specifying optional and/or required paths in a model. A researcher can then explore other substantive meaningful theoretical models and choose from a set of plausible models rather than use modification indices individually to generate and test successive models by adding or deleting paths.

5.1   TYPES OF MODEL FIT CRITERIA

Finding a statistically significant theoretical model that also has practical and substantive meaning is the primary goal of using structural equation modeling to test theories. A researcher typically uses the following three criteria in judging the statistical significance and substantive meaning of a theoretical model:

1. The first criterion is the non-statistical significance of the chi-square test and the root-mean-square error of approximation (RMSEA) values, which are global fit measures. A non-statistically significant chi-square value indicates that the sample covariance matrix and the reproduced model-implied covariance matrix are similar. A RMSEA value less than or equal to .05 is considered acceptable.
2. The second criterion is the statistical significance of individual parameter estimates for the paths in the model, which are critical values computed by dividing the parameter estimates by their respective standard errors. This is referred to as a *t* value or a critical value and is typically compared to a tabled *t* value of 1.96 at the .05 level of significance.
3. The third criterion considers the magnitude and the direction of the parameter estimates, paying particular attention to whether a positive or a negative coefficient makes sense for the parameter estimate. For example, it would not be theoretically meaningful to have a negative parameter (coefficient) between number of hours spent studying and grade point average.

We now describe the numerous criteria for assessing model fit and offer suggestions on how and when these criteria might be used. Determining model fit is complicated because several model fit criteria have been developed to assist in interpreting structural equation models under different model-building assumptions. In addition, the determination of model fit in structural equation modeling is not as straightforward as it is in other statistical approaches in multivariable procedures such as the analysis of variance, multiple regression, path analysis, discriminant analysis, and canonical analysis. These multivariable methods use observed variables that are assumed to be measured without error and have statistical tests with known distributions. SEM fit indices have no single statistical test of significance that identifies a correct model given the sample data, especially since *equivalent models* or *alternative* models can exist that yield exactly the same data-to-model fit.

TABLE 5.1
Model Fit Criteria and Acceptable Fit Interpretation

Model fit criterion	Acceptable level	Interpretation
Chi-square	Tabled χ^2 value	Compares obtained χ^2 value with tabled value for given df
Goodness-of-fit (GFI)	0 (no fit) to 1 (perfect fit)	Value close to .95 reflects a good fit
Adjusted GFI (AGFI)	0 (no fit) to 1 (perfect fit)	Value adjusted for df, with .95 a good model fit
Root-mean-square residual (RMR)	Researcher defines level	Indicates the closeness of Σ to S matrix
Root-mean-square error of approximation (RMSEA)	<.05	Value less than .05 indicates a good model fit
Tucker–Lewis index	0 (no fit) to 1 (perfect fit)	Value close to .95 reflects a good model fit
Normed fit index	0 (no fit) to 1 (perfect fit)	Value close to .95 reflects a good model fit
Normed chi-square	1.0–5.0	Less than 1.0 is a poor model fit; more than 5.0 reflects a need for improvement
Parsimonious fit index	0 (no fit) to 1 (perfect fit)	Compares values in alternative models
Akaike information criterion	0 (perfect fit) to negative value (poor fit)	Compares values in alternative models

Chi-square (χ^2) is the only statistical test of significance for testing the theoretical model (see Table 5.1 for fit indices and their interpretation). The chi-square value ranges from zero for a saturated model with all paths included to a maximum for the independence model with no paths included. The theoretical implied model chi-square value lies somewhere between these two extremes. This can be visualized as follows:

Saturated model $\longleftrightarrow$ Independence model
(all paths in model)   (no paths in model)
$\chi^2 = 0$ $\chi^2 = $ maximum value

A chi-square value of zero indicates a perfect fit, or no difference between values in the sample covariance matrix S and the reproduced implied covariance matrix Σ that was created based on the specified theoretical model. Obviously, a theoretical model in SEM with all paths specified is of limited interest (saturated model). The goal in structural equation modeling is to achieve a parsimonious model with a few substantive meaningful paths and a nonsignificant chi-square value close to this saturated model value, thus indicating little difference between the sample variance–covariance matrix and the reproduced implied covariance matrix. The difference between these two covariance matrices is contained in a residual matrix. When the chi-square value is nonsignificant (close to zero), residual values in the residual matrix are close to zero, indicating that the theoretical specified model fits the sample data, hence there is little difference between the sample variance–covariance matrix and the model-implied reproduced variance–covariance matrix.

Many of the model fit criteria are computed based on knowledge of the saturated model, independence model, sample size, degrees of freedom, and/or the chi-square values to formulate an index of model fit that ranges in value from 0 (no fit) to 1 (perfect fit). These various model fit indices, however, are subjectively assessed as to what is an acceptable model fit. Some researchers suggested that a structural equation model with a model fit value of .95 or higher is acceptable (Baldwin, 1989; Bentler & Bonett, 1980), whereas more recently a noncentrality parameter close to zero [NCP = max $(0, \chi^2 - df)$] has been suggested (Browne & Cudeck, 1993; Steiger, 1990). The various structural equation modeling programs report a variety of model fit criteria, but only those output by Amos, EQS, and LISREL are reported in this chapter. Because other structural equation modeling software programs may have different model fit indices, it would be prudent to check the other software programs for any additional indices they output. It is recommended that various model fit criteria be used in combination to assess *model fit, model comparison,* and *model parsimony* as global fit measures (Hair, Anderson, Tatham, & Black, 1992).

Some of the fit indices are computed given knowledge of the null model χ^2 (independence model, where the covariances are assumed to be zero in the model), null model *df*, hypothesized model χ^2, hypothesized model *df*, number of observed variables in the model, number of free parameters in the model, and sample size. The formulas for the goodness-of-fit index (GFI), normed fit index (NFI), relative fit index (RFI), incremental fit index (IFI), Tucker–Lewis index (TLI), comparative fit index (CFI), model AIC, null AIC, and RMSEA using these values are, respectively,

$$\text{GFI} = 1 - (\chi^2_{\text{model}}/\chi^2_{\text{null}})$$

$$\text{NFI} = (\chi^2_{\text{null}} - \chi^2_{\text{model}})/\chi^2_{\text{null}}$$

$$\text{RFI} = 1 - [(\chi^2_{\text{model}}/df_{\text{model}})/(\chi^2_{\text{null}}/df_{\text{null}})]$$

$$\text{IFI} = (\chi^2_{\text{null}} - \chi^2_{\text{model}})/(\chi^2_{\text{null}} - df_{\text{model}})$$

$$\text{TLI} = [(\chi^2_{\text{null}}/df_{\text{null}}) - (\chi^2_{\text{model}}/df_{\text{model}})]/[(\chi^2_{\text{null}}/df_{\text{null}}) - 1]$$

$$\text{CFI} = 1 - [(\chi^2_{\text{model}} - df_{\text{model}})/(\chi^2_{\text{null}} - df_{\text{null}})]$$

$$\text{Model AIC} = \chi^2_{\text{model}} + 2q \text{ (number of free parameters)}$$

$$\text{Null AIC} = \chi^2_{\text{null}} + 2q \text{ (number of free parameters)}$$

$$\text{RMSEA} = \sqrt{[\chi^2_M - df_M]/[(N - 1)df_M]}.$$

These model fit statistics can also be expressed in terms of the noncentrality parameter (NCP), designated λ. The estimate of NCP (λ) using the maximum likelihood chi-square is $\chi^2 - df$. A simple substitution reexpresses these model fit statistics using NCP. For example, CFI, TLI, and RMSEA are

$$\text{CFI} = 1 - (\lambda_M/\lambda_N)$$

$$\text{TLI} = 1 - [(\lambda_M/df_M)/[(\lambda_N/df_N)]$$

$$\text{RMSEA} = \sqrt{\lambda_M/[(N - 1)df_M]}.$$

Bollen and Long (1993) as well as Hu and Bentler (1995) have thoroughly discussed several issues related to model fit, and we recommend reading their assessments of how model fit indices are affected by small sample bias, estimation methods, violation of normality and independence, and model complexity, and for an overall discussion of model fit indices.

Amos, EQS, and LISREL Program Outputs

Our purpose in this chapter is to better understand the model fit criteria output by Amos, EQS, and LISREL–SIMPLIS. The theoretical model in Fig. 5.1 is analyzed to aid in the understanding of model fit criteria. The theoretical basis for this model is discussed in more detail in chapter 8. The two-factor model is based on data from Holzinger and Swineford (1939), who collected data on 26 psychological tests on 145 seventh- and eighth-grade children in a suburban school district of Chicago. Over the years, different subsamples of the children and different subsets of the variables of this data set have been analyzed and presented in various multivariate statistics textbooks (e.g., Gorsuch, 1983; Harmon, 1976) and SEM software program guides (e.g., Amos: Arbuckle & Wothke, 1999, example 8, p. 186; EQS: Bentler & Wu, 2002, p. 236; LISREL: Jöreskog & Sörbom, 1993, example 5, pp. 23–28). For our analysis, we used data on the first six variables for all 145 subjects (see correlation matrix in LISREL, EX5A.SPL, p. 24). We now give the Amos, EQS, and LISREL–SIMPLIS programs and model fit indices for the theoretical model in Fig. 5.1.

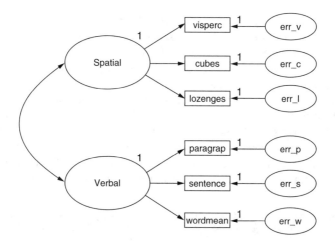

FIG. 5.1.   Amos common factor model (Holzinger & Swineford, 1939).

Amos Program Analysis

In Amos, first draw the diagram of Fig. 5.1 and label the variables using the handy *Toolkit* icons. We then click on **File** and select the **Data
Files** option. When the dialog box opens, click on **File Name** and select
the data set for analysis. For our analysis, we select an SPSS save file,
Grant.sav, which contains the six variables and 145 subjects. If you click
on **View Data**, SPSS opens the data set so you can verify that you have
the correct data with the variable names spelled correctly in the Amos
diagram.

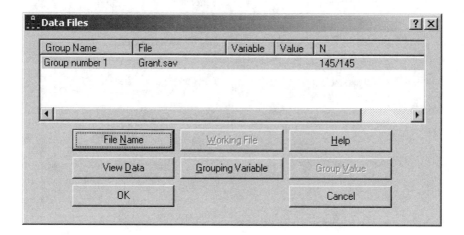

Next, click on **OK** and then select **Model-Fit** from the tool bar menu. To run the analysis, click on **Calculate Estimates** (alternatively, you can click on the *abacus* icon in the *Toolkit*). A dialog box appears, to name and save the Amos diagram before running the analysis. We named our Amos diagram *factor.amw*. To view the computer output with the analysis results and model fit criteria, click on **View/Set**, then click on **Table Output** or **Text Output** (*Note:* the results are different from those in the Amos manual because sample data for both boys and girls were used). You can select different program analysis results by clicking on **View/Set** and selecting **Analysis Properties** from the pull-down menu. Under the **Output** tab, select the type of result you want, for example, modification indices.

Analysis Properties | ? | X

Estimation	Numerical	Bias
Permutations	Random #	Title
Output formatting	Output	Bootstrap

☑ Minimization history   ☐ Indirect, direct & total effects

☑ Standardized estimates   ☐ Factor score weights

☑ Squared multiple correlations ☐ Covariances of estimates

☐ Sample moments   ☐ Correlations of estimates

☐ Implied moments   ☐ Critical ratios for differences

☐ All implied moments   ☐ Tests for normality and outliers

☐ Residual moments   ☐ Observed information matrix

☑ Modification indices   [4] Threshold for modification indices

TABLE 5.2
Amos Fit Measures

Fit measure	Default	Saturated	Independence	Macro
Discrepancy	3.638	0.000	321.320	CMIN
df	8	0	15	DF
P	0.888	0.000		P
Number of parameters	13	21	6	NPAR
Discrepancy/df	0.455	21.421		CMINDF
RMR	0.905	0.000	12.654	RMR
GFI	0.991	1.000	0.525	GFI
Adjusted GFI	0.978		0.335	AGFI
Parsimony-adjusted GFI	0.378		0.375	PGFI
Normed fit index	0.989	1.000	0.000	NFI
Relative fit index	0.979		0.000	RFI
Incremental fit index	1.014	1.000	0.000	IFI
Tucker–Lewis index	1.027		0.000	TLI
Comparative fit index	1.000	1.000	0.000	CFI
Parsimony ratio	0.533	0.000	1.000	PRATIO
Parsimony-adjusted NFI	0.527	0.000	0.000	PNFI
Parsimony-adjusted CFI	0.533	0.000	0.000	PCFI
Noncentrality parameter	0.000	0.000	306.320	NCP
NCP lower bound	0.000	0.000	251.710	NCPLO
NCP upper bound	2.396	0.000	368.361	NCPHI
FMIN	0.025	0.000	2.231	FMIN
F0	0.000	0.000	2.127	F0
F0 lower bound	0.000	0.000	1.748	F0LO
F0 upper bound	0.017	0.000	2.558	F0HI
RMSEA	0.000		0.377	RMSEA
RMSEA lower bound	0.000		0.341	RMSEALO
RMSEA upper bound	0.046		0.413	RMSEAHI
p for test of close fit	0.958		0.000	PCLOSE
Akaike information criterion (AIC)	29.638	42.000	333.320	AIC
Browne–Cudeck criterion	0.966	44.146	333.933	BCC
Bayes information criterion	91.628	142.138	361.931	BIC
Consistent AIC	81.336	125.511	357.181	CAIC
Expected cross-validation index	0.206	0.292	2.315	ECVI
ECVI lower bound	0.236	0.292	1.935	ECVILO
ECVI upper bound	0.253	0.292	2.746	ECVIHI
MECVI	0.215	0.307	2.319	MECVI
Hoelter .05 index	614		12	HFIVE
Hoelter .01 index	796		14	HONE

Amos Model Fit Output. The two-factor model in Fig. 5.1 has $p = 6$ observed variables. The number of distinct values in the variance–covariance matrix is therefore 21 $[p(p+1)/2 = 6(7)/2 = 21]$. A saturated model with all paths would have 27 free parameters that could be estimated $[p(p+3)/2 = 6(9)/2 = 27]$. The number of parameters in Fig. 5.1 that we want to estimate, however, is 13 (1 factor covariance, 6 factor loadings, and 6 variable error covariances). The degrees of freedom for the two-factor model is therefore $df = 21 - 13 = 8$. We can check this by clicking on the **DF** icon in the *Toolkit*. The chi-square value is 3.638 with $df = 8$ and $p = .88$ (nonsignificant), indicating that the two-factor model fits the sample variance–covariance data. The factor loadings (standardized regression weights) are 0.632 (visperc), 0.533 (cubes), 0.732 (lozenges), 0.868 (paragraph), 0.825 (sentence), and 0.828 (wordmean). The two factors spatial and verbal are correlated, $r = .533$. The *Fit Measures* are listed by selecting **Table Output** (see Table 5.2). The selection options include *Fit Measures 1* (portrait format) and *Fit Measures 2* (landscape format). The *Macro* column provides a list of commands that can be used to print the values on the Amos diagram, for example, chi-square $= \backslash$cmin$(df = \backslash df)p = \backslash p$. Appendix C of the *Amos User's Guide* presents the calculation and a discussion of each model fit criterion along with recommending that the following fit indices be reported: CMIN, P, FMIN, F0, PCLOSE, RMSEA, and ECVI or MECVI for most model applications.

EQS Program Analysis

In EQS, the SPSS file *grant.sav*, which contains the six variables and 145 subjects, can be opened by first clicking on the **File** command in the toolbar menu and selecting **Open**. EQS automatically opens the SPSS file and creates an EQS system file (*grant.ess*).

To create an EQS program, select **Build EQS** on the tool bar menu and click on **Title/Specifications**. An *EQS Model Specifications* dialog box appears with basic EQS programming information included. Simply click **OK** and an EQS model file (*.eqx) will appear with the initial EQS program

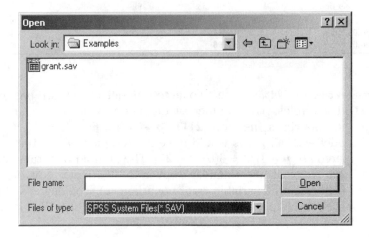

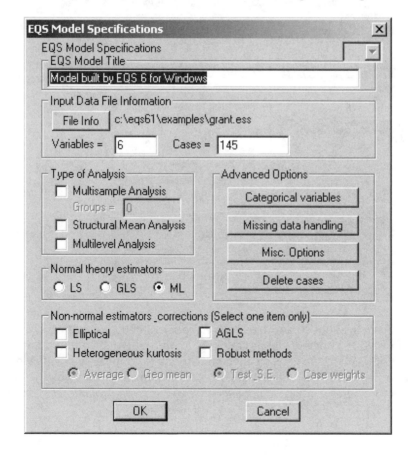

syntax in the file *grant.eqx*. *Note*: The *grant.eqx* model file cannot be edited. *Changes to any model file must be made using the dialog boxes.*

We again click on the **Build EQS** command and all of the other options appear. Select **Equations** and then enter 2 in the *Build Equations* dialog box for the number of factors.

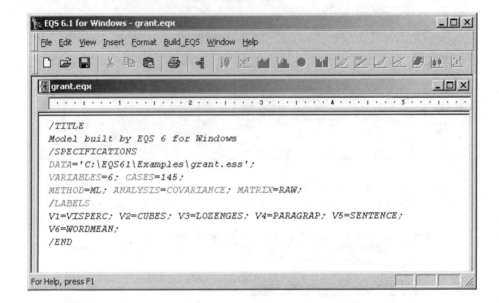

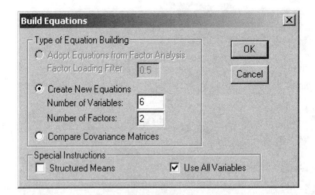

After clicking **OK**, another *Build Equations* dialog box appears, which allows you to specify which variables identify the two common factors. Click in each of the cells to have an asterisk (*) appear to signify which variables identify which factors. Do not click in each cell along the diagonal for each variable. *Do not click in the cells for the common factors* (F1 and F2).

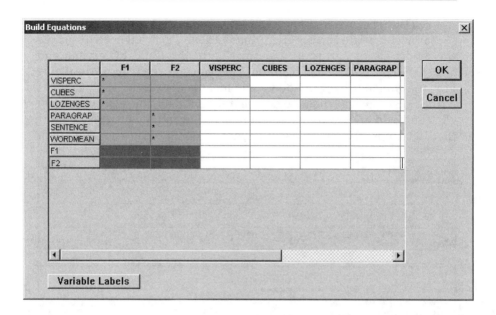

Click **OK**; then the *Build Variances–Covariances* dialog box appears. The *Build Variances/Covariances* dialog box permits specification of covariance (correlation) among the common factors, factor variance, and the specification of error variances for each of the variables used to identify the two common factors.

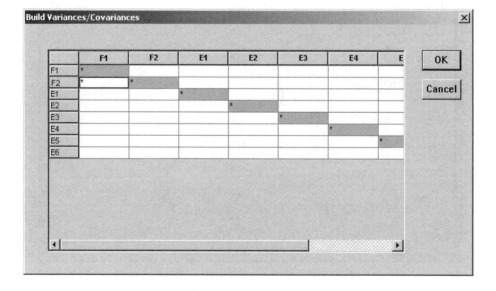

Click **OK**. The *grant.eqx* model file now contains all of the EQS program syntax necessary to run the Fig. 5.1 model analysis. If you need to change the model file or add to it, you must go to the **Build EQS** menu and select the appropriate menu option. After you make changes in the dialog box, the *grant.eqx* file will update and include the changes. All changes to the EQS model file must be done in relevant dialog boxes. Once again click on **Build EQS**, and then select *Run EQS* to run the program. Notice that the Amos diagram in Fig. 5.1 requires one indicator variable path

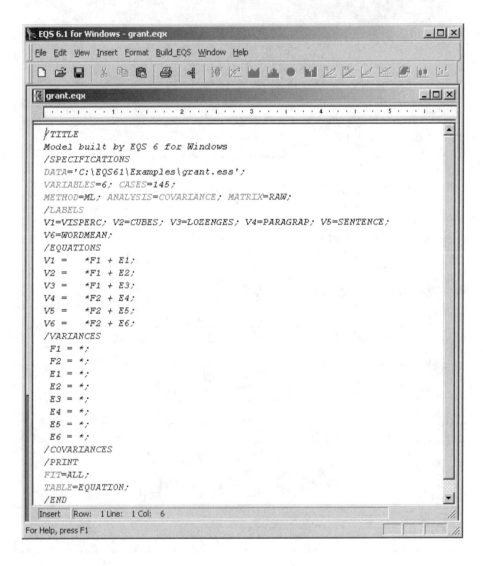

for each latent variable set to 1.0 for model identification, but this is not necessary in the EQS program.

The computer output is placed in an ASCII text file, *grant.out*, so output can be cut and pasted. We look at the model fit criteria output by EQS and how these values compare to the model fit criteria in Amos. The chi-square, degrees of freedom, and *p* values are identical, but EQS lists fewer model fit criteria than Amos. EQS does list a few fit indices that are not output by AMOS, namely the McDonald fit index (MFI) and the root mean-square residual (RMR). The Bentler–Bonett index in EQS is identical in value to the Tucker–Lewis index in Amos. EQS does provide composite reliability indices for congeneric measures (Raykov, 1997) based on a one-factor model (scale score or sum of items that constitute a single factor), but these would not be interpreted in this example (see chap. 8).

EQS Model Fit Output

```
GOODNESS OF FIT SUMMARY FOR METHOD = ML
   INDEPENDENCE MODEL CHI-SQUARE = 321.320 ON 15 DEGREES OF FREEDOM
   INDEPENDENCE AIC = 291.32031 INDEPENDENCE CAIC = 231.66931
         MODEL AIC = -12.36200        MODEL CAIC = -44.17587
CHI-SQUARE =       3.638 BASED ON    8 DEGREES OF FREEDOM
PROBABILITY VALUE FOR THE CHI-SQUARE STATISTIC IS   .88822
THE NORMAL THEORY RLS CHI-SQUARE FOR THIS ML SOLUTION IS 3.704.
FIT INDICES
-----------
BENTLER-BONETT    NORMED FIT INDEX =  .989
BENTLER-BONETT NON-NORMED FIT INDEX = 1.027
COMPARATIVE FIT INDEX (CFI)         = 1.000
BOLLEN   (IFI) FIT INDEX            = 1.014
MCDONALD (MFI) FIT INDEX            = 1.015
LISREL    GFI  FIT INDEX            =  .991
LISREL    AGFI FIT INDEX            =  .978
ROOT MEAN-SQUARE RESIDUAL (RMR)     =  .912
STANDARDIZED RMR                    =  .027
ROOT MEAN-SQUARE ERROR OF APPROXIMATION (RMSEA)= .000
90% CONFIDENCE INTERVAL OF RMSEA (.000,.045)

RELIABILITY COEFFICIENTS
------------------------
  CRONBACH'S ALPHA                   =       .757
  RELIABILITY COEFFICIENT RHO        =       .834
  GREATEST LOWER BOUND RELIABILITY              =       .845
  BENTLER'S DIMENSION-FREE LOWER BOUND RELIABILITY =    .845
  SHAPIRO'S LOWER BOUND RELIABILITY FOR A WEIGHTED COMPOSITE = .866
  WEIGHTS THAT ACHIEVE SHAPIRO'S LOWER BOUND:
  VISPERC   CUBES     LOZENGES  PARAGRAP SENTENCE WORDMEAN
     .262      .151       .312      .454     .472     .618
```

An alternative approach to the analysis of data for the Fig. 5.1 model is to run an EQS command file: Select **File**, then **New**, then **EQS Command File**.

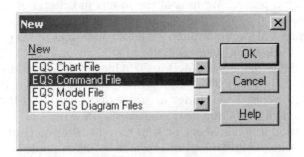

Click **OK** and a dialog box appears that can be renamed, edited, and saved with the EQS program syntax. We entered the following EQS command statements and options in the dialog box, then saved our EQS command file as *grant.eqs*. The EQS program *grant.eqs* contains the following program syntax:

```
/TITLE
 Two Factor Model from Holzinger and Swineford
/SPECIFICATIONS
 VARIABLES= 6; CASES= 145;
 DATAFILE='c:\eqs61\examples\grant.ess ';
 MATRIX=RAW;
 METHOD=ML; ANALYSIS=Covariance;
/LABELS
 V1=VISPERC;V2=CUBES;V3=LOZENGES;
 V4=PARAGRAP;V5=SENTENCE;V6=WORDMEAN;
/EQUATIONS
 V1=*F1 + E1;
 V2=*F1 + E2;
 V3=*F1 + E3;
 V4=*F2 + E4;
 V5=*F2 + E5;
 V6=*F2 + E6;
/VARIANCES
 F1 TO F2 = 1.0;
 E1 TO E6 = *;
/COVARIANCES
 F2,F1 = *;
/PRINT
 FIT=ALL;
 TABLE=EQUATION;
/END
```

```
EQS 6.1 for Windows - grant.eqs                          _ □ ×

File  Edit  View  Insert  Format  Build_EQS  Window  Help

   □  ☞  ⊟     ✄  ▤  ▣    ⎙    ⛀

   ▨  ⊠  ▰  ▲  ●  ▤  ☒  ☒  ☒  ☒  ▨  ▥  ▦
```

```
grant.eqs                                                _ □ ×

 · · · | · · · 1 · · · | · · · 2 · · · | · · · 3 · · · | · · · 4 ·

/TITLE
   Two Factor Model from Holzinger and Swineford
/SPECIFICATIONS
VARIABLES= 6; CASES= 145;
DATAFILE='c:\eqs61\examples\grant.ess ';
MATRIX=RAW;
METHOD=ML; ANALYSIS=Covariance;
/LABELS
V1=VISPERC;V2=CUBES;V3=LOZENGES;
V4=PARAGRAP;V5=SENTENCE;V6=WORDMEAN;
/EQUATIONS
V1=*F1 + E1;
V2=*F1 + E2;
V3=*F1 + E3;
V4=*F2 + E4;
V5=*F2 + E5;
V6=*F2 + E6;
/VARIANCES
F1 TO F2 = 1.0;
E1 TO E6 = *;
/COVARIANCES
F2,F1 = *;
/PRINT
FIT=ALL;
TABLE=EQUATION;
/END
```

```
For Help, press F1
```

LISREL–SIMPLIS Program Analysis

The LISREL program can easily import many different file types. To import the SPSS data file *grant.sav*, simply click on **File**, then select **Import External Data in Other Formats**. Next select the SPSS file type from the pull-down menu and find the location of the data file.

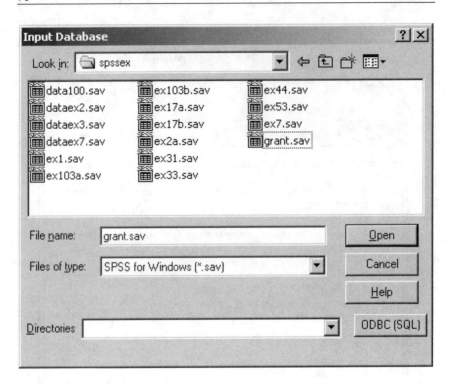

After clicking on **Open**, a *Save As* dialog box appears, to save a PRELIS system file, *grant.psf*.

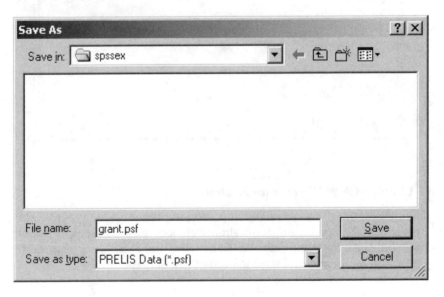

An expanded tool bar menu now appears permitting case selection, data transformation, statistical analysis, graphing, and multilevel analysis along with an added **Export LISREL** *Data* option under the **File** command. You should import data into a PRELIS system file whenever possible to take advantage of data screening, imputing missing values, computation of normal scores, output data options, and many other features in LISREL–PRELIS.

For our purposes we click on **Statistics**, then select the **Output** *Options*. The *Output* dialog box will be used to save a correlation matrix file (*grant.cor*), a means file (*grant.mea*), and a standard deviations file (*grant.sd*) for the variables we will use in our Fig. 5.1 model analysis. The correlation, means, and standard deviation files must be saved (or moved) to the same directory as the LISREL–SIMPLIS program file. Click **OK** and descriptive statistics appear.

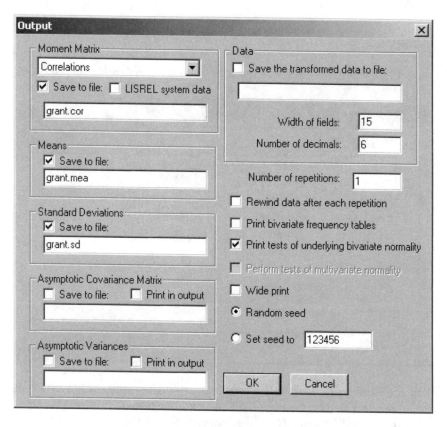

The next step is to create the LISREL–SIMPLIS program syntax file that will specify the model analysis for Fig. 5.1. This is accomplished by selecting **File** on the tool bar, then clicking on **New**, selecting **Syntax Only**, and entering the program syntax. If you forget the SIMPLIS program syntax, refer to the LISREL–SIMPLIS manual or modify an existing program. The LISREL–SIMPLIS program *grant.spl* contains the following program syntax:

```
LISREL Figure 5.1 Program
Observed Variables
    visperc cubes lozenges paragrap sentence wordmean
Correlation matrix from file grant.cor
Means from file grant.mea
Standard deviations from file grant.sd
Sample Size 145
Latent Variables
   Spatial Verbal
Relationships
  visperc - lozenges = Spatial
  paragrap - wordmean = Verbal
End of Problem
```

Select **File**, then **Save As**, to save the file as *grant.spl* (SIMPLIS file type).

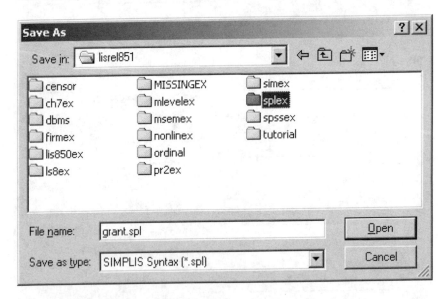

You are now ready to run the analysis using the *grant.spl* file you just created. Click on the running **L** on the tool bar menu and the ASCII text file *grant.out* will appear. The chi-square, degrees of freedom, and *p* value are the same in Amos, EQS, and LISREL (rounded to two decimal places). The LISREL command programs (*grant.ls8*) report both the minimum fit function chi-square (C1) and the normal theory weighted least-squares fit function (C2), but use C2 in all model fit indices including the chi-square independence model (C1 = 321.32 and C2 = 391.16 in our example). Consequently, some of the Amos and EQS model fit indices differ (see the Appendix to this chapter for a more detailed explanation).

LISREL–SIMPLIS Model Fit Output

```
Goodness of Fit Statistics
                        Degrees of Freedom = 8
              Minimum Fit Function Chi-Square = 3.638 (P = 0.888)
 Normal Theory Weighted Least Squares Chi-Square = 3.704 (P = 0. 883)
              Estimated Non-centrality Parameter (NCP) = 0.0
           90 Percent Confidence Interval for NCP = (0.0 ; 2.556)

                    Minimum Fit Function Value = 0.0253
             Population Discrepancy Function Value (F0) = 0.0
           90 Percent Confidence Interval for F0 = (0.0 ; 0.0178)
           Root Mean Square Error of Approximation (RMSEA) = 0.0
           90 Percent Confidence Interval for RMSEA = (0.0 ; 0.0471)
              P-Value for Test of Close Fit (RMSEA < 0.05) = 0.955

              Expected Cross-Validation Index (ECVI) = 0.236
           90 Percent Confidence Interval for ECVI = (0.236 ; 0.254)
                    ECVI for Saturated Model = 0.292
                    ECVI for Independence Model = 2.315

   Chi-Square for Independence Model with 15 Degrees of Freedom = 321.320
                    Independence AIC = 333.320
                         Model AIC = 29.704
                      Saturated AIC = 42.000
                 Independence CAIC = 357.181
                       Model CAIC = 81.402
                    Saturated CAIC = 125.511

                 Normed Fit Index (NFI) = 0.989
                 Non-Normed Fit Index (NNFI) = 1.027
            Parsimony Normed Fit Index (PNFI) = 0.527
            Comparative Fit Index (CFI) = 1.000
            Incremental Fit Index (IFI) = 1.014
              Relative Fit Index (RFI) = 0.979

                 Critical N (CN) = 796.245

            Root Mean Square Residual (RMR) = 0.912
                 Standardized RMR = 0.0271
            Goodness of Fit Index (GFI) = 0.991
       Adjusted Goodness of Fit Index (AGFI) = 0.978
   Parsimony Goodness of Fit Index (PGFI) = 0.378
```

The chi-square statistic is nonsignificant, indicating a good model fit to the sample variance–covariance matrix ($\chi^2 = 3.638$, $df = 8$, $p = .88$). Several of the other model fit indices for the theoretical model in Fig. 5.1 indicate a good data-to-model fit, thus confirming our model (e.g., GFI = .99, RMSEA = 0.0, NCP = 0.0, and NFI = .99). Overall, the fit indices fall into three main categories of *model fit, model comparison*, and *model parsimony* fit indices. We discuss the fit indices in these three categories next to understand their development and recommended applications. Extensive comparisons and discussions of many of these fit indices can be found in recent issues of the journals *Structural Equation Modeling: A Multidisciplinary Journal, Psychological Bulletin, Psychological Methods,* and *Multivariate Behavioral Research.*

5.2 MODEL FIT

Model fit determines the degree to which the sample variance–covariance data fit the structural equation model. Model fit criteria commonly used are chi-square (χ^2), the goodness-of-fit index (GFI), the adjusted goodness-of-fit index (AGFI), and the root-mean-square residual (RMR) (Jöreskog & Sörbom, 1989). These criteria are based on differences between the observed (original, S) matrix and the model-implied (reproduced, Σ) variance–covariance matrix.

Chi-Square (χ^2)

A significant χ^2 value relative to the degrees of freedom indicates that the observed and implied (estimated) variance–covariance matrices differ. Statistical significance indicates the probability that this difference is due to sampling variation. A nonsignificant χ^2 value indicates that the two matrices are similar, indicating that the implied theoretical model significantly reproduces the sample variance–covariance relationships in the matrix. The researcher is interested in obtaining a nonsignificant χ^2 value with associated degrees of freedom.

The chi-square test of model fit can lead to erroneous conclusions regarding analysis outcomes. The χ^2 model fit criterion is sensitive to sample size because as sample size increases (generally above 200), the χ^2 statistic has a tendency to indicate a significant probability level. In contrast, as sample size decreases (generally below 100), the χ^2 statistic indicates nonsignificant probability levels. The chi-square statistic is therefore affected by sample size, as shown by its calculation from $\chi^2 = (n-1)F_{\mathrm{ML}}$, where F_{ML} is the maximum likelihood fit function. The χ^2 statistic is also sensitive to departures from multivariate normality of the observed variables.

Three estimation methods are commonly used to calculate χ^2 in latent-variable models (Loehlin, 1987): maximum likelihood (ML), generalized least squares (GLS), and unweighted least squares (ULS). Each approach estimates a best-fitting solution and evaluates the model fit. The ML estimates are consistent, unbiased, efficient, scale invariant, scale free, and normally distributed if the observed variables meet the multivariate normality assumption. The GLS estimates have the same properties as the ML approach under a less stringent multivariate normality assumption and provide an approximate chi-square test of model fit to the data. The ULS estimates do not depend on a normality distribution assumption; however, the estimates are not as efficient, nor are they scale invariant or scale free. The ML χ^2 statistic is $\chi^2 = (n-1)F_{ML}$, the GLS χ^2 statistic is $\chi^2 = (n-1)F_{GLS}$, and the ULS χ^2 statistic is $\chi^2 = (n-1)F_{ULS}$, where

$$F_{ML} = \text{tr}(S\Sigma^{-1}) - p + \ln|\Sigma| - \ln|S|$$
$$F_{GLS} = .5\,\text{tr}[(S-\Sigma)S^{-1}]^2$$
$$F_{ULS} = .5\,\text{tr}[(S-\Sigma)^2]$$
$$df = .5(p)(p+1) - t.$$

Here, t is the total number of independent parameters estimated, n is the number of observations, p is the number of observed variables analyzed, and tr indicates the trace of the matrix (sum of the diagonal elements of the matrix).

In our model analysis, we chose the maximum likelihood chi-square estimation method. The ML χ^2 statistic is $\chi^2 = (n-1)F_{ML}$, where n is the sample size and F_{ML} is the minimum fit function. The Amos (FMIN) and LISREL (Minimum Fit Function Value) computer outputs provide the minimum fit function as .025. The chi-square statistic for our model is therefore calculated as $\chi^2 = (145-1)\cdot 0253 = 3.6$.

Goodness-of-Fit Index (GFI) and Adjusted Goodness-of-Fit Index (AGFI)

The goodness-of-fit index (GFI) is based on the ratio of the sum of the squared differences between the observed and reproduced matrices to the observed variances, thus allowing for scale. The GFI measures the amount of variance and covariance in S that is predicted by the reproduced matrix Σ. In our model, GFI $= .99$, so 99% of the S matrix is predicted by the reproduced matrix Σ.

The GFI index can be computed for ML, GLS, or ULS estimates (Bollen, 1989). For example, given the original covariance matrix

$$S = \begin{bmatrix} .507 & & \\ .480 & .224 & \\ .275 & .062 & .577 \end{bmatrix}$$

and the reproduced (implied) covariance matrix Σ based on a single-factor model

$$\Sigma = \begin{bmatrix} .271 & & \\ .541 & .321 & \\ .361 & .215 & .427 \end{bmatrix},$$

the GFI using the unweighted least squares approach (ULS) can be computed as

$$\begin{aligned} \text{GFI} &= 1 - .5 \, \text{tr}(S - \Sigma)^2 \\ &= 1 - .5[(1.308 - 1.019)^2] \\ &= 1 - .0417 \\ &= .9583. \end{aligned}$$

The values 1.308 and 1.019 are the traces of the two matrixes computed as the sums of the diagonal elements (values) in the respective covariance matrices. The GFI indicates that 96% of the variance covariance in S is predicted by the reproduced (implied) matrix Σ, given the one-factor model.

The adjusted goodness-of-fit (AGFI) index is adjusted for the degrees of freedom of a model relative to the number of variables. The AGFI index is computed as $1 - [(k/df)(1 - \text{GFI})]$, where k is the number of unique distinct values in S, $p(p+1)/2$, and df is the number of degrees of freedom in the model. The GFI index in our model analysis is .9915; therefore the AGFI index is

$$\begin{aligned} 1 - [(k/df)(1 - \text{GFI})] &= 1 - [(21/8)(1 - .9915)] \\ &= 1 - [2.625(.0085)] \\ &= 1 - .022 = .978. \end{aligned}$$

The GFI and AGFI indices can be used to compare the fit of two different models with the same data or compare the fit of a single model using different data, such as separate data sets for males and females (e.g., test for measurement invariance in a factor).

Root-Mean-Square Residual Index (RMR)

The RMR index uses the square root of the mean-squared differences between matrix elements in S and Σ. It is used to compare the fit of two different models with the same data. The RMR index is computed as

$$\text{RMR} = \left[(1/k) \quad \sum_{ij} (S_{ij} - \sigma_{ij})^2 \right]^{1/2}.$$

The EQS computer program outputs the residual covariance matrix, which is used to compute RMR. This can be requested in LISREL–SIMPLIS by adding the *Print Residuals* command. In Amos, RMR $= .905$.

5.3 MODEL COMPARISON

Given the role chi-square has in the model fit of latent-variable models, three other indices have emerged as variants for comparing alternative models: the Tucker–Lewis index (TLI) or Bentler–Bonett nonnormed fit index (NNFI), the Bentler–Bonett normed fit index (NFI) (Bentler & Bonett, 1980; Loehlin, 1987), and the comparative fit index (CFI). These criteria typically compare a proposed model with a null model (independence model). In Amos, EQS, and LISREL, the null model is indicated by the independence-model chi-square value. The null model could also be any model that establishes a base from which one could expect other alternative models to be different.

Tucker–Lewis Index (TLI)

Tucker and Lewis (1973) initially developed the TLI for factor analysis but later extended it to structural equation modeling. The measure can be used to compare alternative models or a proposed model against a null model. The TLI is computed using the χ^2 statistic as

$$\text{TLI} = [(\chi^2_{\text{null}}/df_{\text{null}}) - (\chi^2_{\text{proposed}}/df_{\text{proposed}})]/[(\chi^2_{\text{null}}/df_{\text{null}}) - 1].$$

It is scaled from 0 (no fit) to 1 (perfect fit). In our analysis, the TLI in Amos, the NNFI in EQS, and the NNFI in LISREL were computed as

$$[(\chi^2_{\text{null}}/df_{\text{null}}) - (\chi^2_{\text{proposed}}/df_{\text{proposed}})]/[(\chi^2_{\text{null}}/df_{\text{null}}) - 1]$$

$$= [(321.32/15) - (3.638/8)]/[(321.32/15) - 1]$$

$$= (21.421 - .455)/(21.421 - 1)$$

$$= 1.027.$$

Normed Fit Index (NFI) and Comparative Fit Index (CFI)

The NFI is a measure that rescales chi-square into a 0 (no fit) to 1.0 (perfect fit) range (Bentler & Bonett, 1980). It is used to compare a restricted model with a full model using a baseline null model as follows: $(\chi^2_{null} - \chi^2_{model})/\chi^2_{null}$. In our model analysis this was computed as NFI $= (321.32 - 3.638)/321.32 = .99$.

Bentler (1990) developed a new coefficient of comparative fit within the context of specifying a population parameter and distribution, such as a population comparative fit index, to overcome the deficiencies in NFI for nested models. The rationale for assessment of comparative fit in the nested-model approach involves a series of models that range from least restrictive (M_i) to saturated (M_s). Corresponding to this sequence of nested models is a sequence of model fit statistics with associated degrees of freedom. The new comparative fit index (CFI) measures the improvement in noncentrality in going from model M_i to M_k and uses the noncentral $\chi^2(d_k)$ distribution with noncentrality parameter λ_k to define comparative fit as $(\lambda_i - \lambda_k)/\lambda_i$. In the EQS output, CFI $= 1.0$

McDonald and Marsh (1990) further explored the noncentrality and model fit issue by examining nine fit indices as functions of noncentrality and sample size. They concluded that only the Tucker–Lewis index and their relative noncentrality index (RNI) were unbiased in finite samples and recommended them for testing null or alternative models. For absolute measures of fit that do not test null or alternative models, they recommended d_k (Steiger & Lind, 1980) because it is a linear function of χ^2, or a normed measure of centrality m_k (McDonald, 1989), because neither of these varies systematically with sample size. The model fit measures of centrality are useful when selecting among a few competing models based on theoretical considerations.

5.4 MODEL PARSIMONY

Parsimony refers to the number of estimated parameters required to achieve a specific level of fit. Basically, an overidentified model is compared with a restricted model. The AGFI measure discussed previously also provides an index of model parsimony. Others indices that indicate model parsimony are normed chi-square (NC), the parsimonious fit index (PNFI or PCFI), and the Akaike information criterion (AIC). Parsimony-based fit indices for multiple indicator models were reviewed by Williams and Holahan (1994). They found that the AIC performed the best (see their article for more details on additional current indices and related references). The model parsimony goodness-of-fit indices take into account the number of parameters required to achieve a given value for chi-square.

Normed Chi-Square (NC)

Jöreskog (1969) proposed that χ^2 be adjusted by the degrees of freedom to assess model fit. The NC measure can identify two kinds of inappropriate models: (a) a model that is overidentified and capitalizes on chance and (b) a model that does not fit the observed data and needs improvement. The NC measure, like many others, is affected by sample size. It is calculated as NC = (χ^2/df) and indicated in the Amos output as discrepancy/df = 3.638/8 = .455 for the default model (implied model) and 321.32/15 = 21.421 for the independence model. **Note**: These two NC values are used in computing the TLI and NNFI.

Parsimonious Fit Index (PFI)

The PFI measure is a modification of the NFI measure (James, Muliak, & Brett, 1982). The PFI, however, takes into account the number of degrees of freedom used to obtain a given level of fit. Parsimony is achieved with a high degree of fit for fewer degrees of freedom in specifying coefficients to be estimated. The PFI is used to compare models with different degrees of freedom and is calculated as PFI = $(df_{\text{proposed}}/df_{\text{null}}) \cdot$ NFI. In our model analysis, Amos gave PNFI = (8/15) · 989 = .527 and PCFI = (8/15) · 1.0 = .533, whereas LISREL only gave PNFI = (8/15) · 1.0 = .533.

Akaike Information Criterion (AIC)

The AIC measure is used to compare models with differing numbers of latent variables, much as the PNFI is used (Akaike, 1987). The AIC can be calculated in two different ways: as $\chi^2 + 2q$, where q is the number of parameters in the model, or as $\chi^2 - 2df$. The first AIC is positive and the second AIC is negative, but either AIC value close to zero indicates a more parsimonious model. The AIC indicates model fit (S and Σ elements similar) and model parsimony (overidentified model). In Amos, the AIC measure is calculated as $\chi^2 + 2q$, where q is the number of parameters in the model. In our analysis, Amos gave separate AIC values for the default model (implied), saturated model, and independence model [AIC default model = 3.638 + 2 (13) = 29.638; AIC saturated model = 0 + 2 (21) = 42; and AIC independence model = 321.32 + 2 (6) = 333.32; same results in LISREL]. In EQS, AIC is computed as $\chi^2 - 2df$, where df is the degrees of freedom, so AIC values are different.

Summary

Mulaik et al. (1989) evaluated the χ^2, NFI, GFI, AGFI, and AIC goodness-of-fit indices. They concluded that these indices fail to assess parsimony and are insensitive to misspecification of structural relationships. See their definitive work for additional information. This outcome should not be surprising because it has been suggested that a *good* fit index is one that is independent of sample size, accurately reflects differences in fit, imposes a penalty for inclusion of additional parameters (Marsh, Balla, & McDonald, 1988), and supports the choice of the true model when it is known (McDonald & Marsh, 1990). *No model fit criterion can actually meet all of these criteria.*

We presented several model fit indices that are used to assess model fit, model comparison, and model parsimony. In addition, we calculated many of these based on the model analyzed in this chapter. Amos and LISREL programs output the most model fit criteria. The Amos and LISREL user guides also provide an excellent discussion of the model fit indices in their programs. We recommend that once you feel comfortable using these fit indices for your specific model applications, you check the references cited for additional information on their usefulness and/or limitations. Following their initial description, there has been much controversy and discussion on their subjective interpretation and appropriateness under specific modeling conditions [see Marsh, Balla, & Hau (1996) for further discussion]. Further research and discussion will surely follow; for example, Kenny and McCoach (2003) indicated that RMSEA improves as more variables are added to a model, whereas TLI and CFI both decline in correctly specified models as more variables are added.

5.5 TWO-STEP VERSUS FOUR-STEP APPROACH TO MODELING

Anderson and Gerbing (1988) proposed a two-step model-building approach that emphasized the analysis of two conceptually distinct models: a measurement model followed by the structural model. The *measurement* model, or factor model, specifies the relationships among measured (observed) variables underlying the latent variables. The *structural* model specifies relationships among the latent variables as posited by theory. The measurement model provides an assessment of convergent and discriminant validity, and the structural model provides an assessment of nomological validity.

Mulaik et al. (1989) expanded the idea of model fit by assessing the relative fit of the structural equation model among latent variables independently of assessing the fit of the indicator variables in the measurement model. The relative normed fit index (RNFI) makes the following adjustment to separately estimate the effects of the structural model from the measurement model: $\text{RNFI}_j = (F_u - F_j)/[F_u - F_m - (df_j - df_m)]$, where $F_u = \chi^2$ of the full model, $F_j = \chi^2$ of the structural equation model, $F_m = \chi^2$ of the measurement model, df_j is the degrees of freedom for the structural equation model, and df_m is the degrees of freedom for the measurement model. A corresponding relative parsimony ratio (RP) is given by $\text{RP}_j = (df_j - df_m)/(df_u - df_m)$, where df_j is the degrees of freedom for the structural equation model, df_m is the degrees of freedom for the measurement model, and df_u is the degrees of freedom for the null model. In comparing different models for fit, Mulaik et al. multiplied RP_j by RNFI_j to obtain a relative parsimonious fit index appropriate for assessing how well and to what degree the models explained both relationships in the measurement of latent variables and the structural relationship among the latent variables by themselves. McDonald and Marsh (1990), however, doubted whether model parsimony and goodness of fit could be captured by this multiplicative form because it is not a monotonic increasing function of model complexity. Obviously, further research will be needed to clarify these issues.

Mulaik and Millsap (2000) also presented a four-step approach to testing a nested sequence of SEM models. Step 1 pertains to specifying an unrestricted measurement model, namely conducting an exploratory common factor analysis to determine the number of factors (latent variables) that fit the variance–covariance matrix of the observed variables. Step 2 involves a confirmatory factor analysis model that tests hypotheses about certain relations among indicator variables and latent variables. Basically, certain factor loadings are set to zero in an attempt to have only a single nonzero factor loading for each indicator variable of a latent variable. Sometimes this leads to a lack of measurement model fit because an indicator variable may have a relation with another latent variable. We discuss this further in chapter 11 when presenting pattern and structure coefficients. Step 3 involves specifying relations among the latent variables in a structural model. Certain relations among the latent variables are set to zero so some latent variables are not dependent on other latent variables. One continues to Step 4 if an acceptable fit of the structural model is achieved, that is, CFI > .95 and RMSEA < .05. In Step 4, the researcher tests planned hypotheses about free parameters in the model. Several approaches are possible: (a) Perform simultaneous test in which free parameters are fixed based on theory or estimates obtained from other research studies; (b) impose fixed parameter values on free parameters in a nested sequence of models until a misspecified model is achieved (misspecified parameter); or (c) perform a sequence of confidence-interval tests around free parameters using the standard errors of the estimated parameters.

We agree with the basic Mulaik and Millsap (2000) approach and recommend that the measurement models for latent variables be established first and then structural models establishing relationships among the latent independent and dependent variables be formed. It is in the formulation of measurement models that most of the model modifications occur to obtain acceptable data to model fit. In fact, a researcher could begin model generation by using exploratory factor analysis (EFA) on a sample of data to find the number and type of latent variables in a plausible model. Once a plausible model is identified, another sample of data could be used to confirm or test the model, that is, confirmatory factor analysis (CFA). Exploratory factor analysis is even recommended as a precursor to confirmatory factor analysis when the researcher does not have a substantive theoretical model.

Measurement invariance is also important to examine, which refers to considering similar measurement models across different groups; for example, does the factor (latent variable) mean the same thing to boys and girls? This usually involves adding between-group constraints in the measurement model. If measurement invariance cannot be established, then the finding of a between-group difference is questionable (Cheung & Rensvold, 2002). Cheung and Rensvold (2002) also recommended that the comparative fit index (CFI), gamma hat, and McDonald noncentrality index (NCI) be used for testing between-group measurement invariance of CFA models rather than the goodness-of-fit index (GFI) or the likelihood ratio test (LR), also known as the chi-square difference test.

5.6 PARAMETER FIT DETERMINATION

Individual parameter estimates in a model can be meaningless even though model fit criteria indicate an acceptable measurement or structural model. Therefore, interpretation of parameter estimates in any model analysis is essential. The following steps are therefore recommended:

1. Examine the parameter estimates to determine whether they have the correct sign (either plus or minus).
2. Examine parameter estimates (standardized coefficients) to determine whether they are out of bounds or exceed an expected range of values.
3. Examine the parameter estimates for statistical significance (critical value = parameter/standard error of parameter).
4. Test for measurement invariance by setting parameter estimates equal (constraints) in different groups (e.g., girls and boys), then make relative comparisons among the parameter estimates.

An examination of initial parameter estimates can also help in identifying a faulty or misspecified model. In this instance, initial parameter estimates serve as start values, for example, initial two-stage least-squares (TSLS) estimates in LISREL. The researcher then replaces the TSLS estimate with a user-defined start value. Sometimes parameter estimates take on impossible values, as in the case of a correlation between two variables that exceeds $r > 1.0$. Sometimes negative variance is encountered (known as a *Heywood* case). Also, if the error variance for a variable is near zero, the indicator variable implies an almost perfect measure of the latent variable, which may not be the case. Outliers can also influence parameter estimates. Use of sufficient sample size ($n > 150$) and several indicators per latent variable (four is recommended based on the TETRAD approach) has also been recommended to produce reasonable and stable parameter estimates (Anderson & Gerbing, 1984).

Once these issues have been taken into consideration, the interpretation of modification indices (Lagrange and Wald tests) and subsequent changes in model fit indices can begin, but there is still a need for guidance provided by a theoretical model and the researcher's expertise. Researchers should use the indices as potential indicators of misfit when respecifying or modifying a model. Cross-validation or replication using another independent sample, once an acceptable model is achieved, is always recommended to ensure stability of parameter estimates and validity of the model (Cliff, 1983). Bootstrap procedures also afford a resampling method, given a single sample, to determine the efficiency and precision of sample estimates (Lunneborg, 1987). These model validation topics are discussed further in chapter 12.

Significance Tests of Parameter Estimates

Significance tests of parameter estimates for nested models include the likelihood ratio (LR), Lagrange multiplier (LM), and Wald (W) tests. Each will be briefly explained, but first we clarify the concept of nested models. In a *nested model* a sample variance–covariance matrix with an initial model is compared with a restricted model in which a parameter estimate has been set equal to zero. This is analogous to testing full and restricted models in multiple regression. In structural equation modeling, the intent is to determine the significance of the decrease in the χ^2 value for the full model. For GLS, ML, and WLS estimation methods, this involves determining the significance of χ^2 with one degree of freedom ($\chi^2 > 3.84, df = 1$) for a single-parameter estimate, thus determining the significance of the reduction in χ^2 that should equal or exceed the modification index value for the parameter estimate set equal to zero.

A likelihood ratio (LR) test is possible between alternative models to examine the difference in χ^2 values between the initial (full) model and the restricted (modified) model where a parameter estimate has been set equal to zero. The LR test is calculated as $\chi^2_{full} - \chi^2_{restricted}$, with degrees of freedom equal to $df_{full} - df_{restricted}$. For example, for an initial model with $\chi^2 = 46$, $df = 20$, and for a restricted model with $\chi^2 = 26$, $df = 19$; then LR $= 20$ with $df = 1$, which is statistically significant ($\chi^2 > 3.84$, $df = 1$, $\alpha = .05$).

In Amos, nested models are compared by first selecting **Model Fit** from the tool bar and clicking on **Calculate Estimates** to obtain the model fit indices and parameter estimates for an initial implied model. A nested model could be compared to this initial implied model by once again selecting **Model Fit**, but now with **Specification Search** selected. A toolbox appears with *dashed* arrows to indicate optional paths and *straight* arrows to indicate required paths in a model. A nested model would have an additional path as optional or required.

Click on ▶ to run the analysis, and a dialog box appears with all of the models listed given the optional and/or required paths specified in the model. The best-fitting model has model fit criteria underlined: the number of parameters, degrees of freedom, chi-square (C), noncentrality parameter (NCP $= C - df$), Browne–Cudeck fit criteria, chi-square divided by degrees of freedom, and significance level (*p* value). If you highlight the model of interest and click on the solid monitor icon (■■), you can view the model in a path diagram. If we made every path optional in a model, then all possible models would be generated; for example, multiple regression with 17 predictor variables would have 2^{17} or 131,072 regression models. The following results are from an illustration of the Amos specification search in chapter 11:

Specification Search

Model	Params	df	C	C - df	BCC_0	BIC_0	C / df	p	Notes
1	12	9	38.769	29.769	28.715	26.640	4.308	0.000	
2	13	8	7.838	-0.162	0.000	0.000	0.980	0.449	
3	13	8	26.345	18.345	18.506	18.506	3.293	0.001	
4	14	7	7.141	0.141	1.518	3.593	1.020	0.414	
Sat	21	0	0.000	0.000	9.885	26.485			

In EQS, the Lagrange multiplier (LM) test compares the fit of the restricted model with lesser restricted models given the same sample variance–covariance matrix. It has the benefit of requiring only estimation of the restricted model. The LM distribution is a chi-square variate with *df* equal to the difference in degrees of freedom between the restricted models that are compared.

In EQS, the Wald (W) test establishes an $r \times 1$ vector, $r(\theta)$, of constraints (parameters chosen by the researcher to be set to zero). If an examination of this vector yields values greater than zero, then the restricted model is not valid, and the researcher must go back to the interpretation of the initial model. The W statistic is also a chi-square distribution with *df* equal to the number of constraints in $r(\theta)$. Both LM and W do not require separate estimations of initial (full) and modified (restricted) models as in the case of LR. The LM statistic, however, tests whether restrictions can be deleted. The W statistic tests whether restrictions imposed on a model are valid.

A researcher using EQS examines either the LM statistic or the W statistic. The LM test indicates parameters that need to be *added* or *included* in the model. The LM test therefore indicates potential missing parameters in a model. A researcher selects the variable listed with the largest reduction in the chi-square estimate, thereby including it in the model. This process is repeated in subsequent models until an acceptable model fit is achieved. EQS permits the testing of *all* significant parameters in a subsequent model by using the following command:

```
/PRINT
   RETEST = >MODEL2.EQS=; LMTEST=YES;
```

The **RETEST** subcommand specifies the file MODEL2.EQS =, which contains the revised model setup for a subsequent model analysis. This model setup includes all the parameters found to be statistically significant in the multivariate LM test for the initial model. The newly added parameters do not have start values indicated for them, but all other parameter estimates have their initial model estimates indicated as start values. The researcher should understand that this method may cause meaningless parameters (paths) to be included in a subsequent model. We therefore recommend that the *MODEL2.EQS* file be examined and any parameters that are not meaningful be deleted. In some models, it may be prudent to select only one significant parameter to add to a subsequent model analysis. Afterward, if warranted, add another, and retest the new model.

This process of adding one significant parameter at a time and retesting the newer model has its own rewards, the testing of alternative nested models. A researcher would obviously not use the **RETEST** subcommand in this instance.

The W test indicates parameters that might need to be *deleted* in a model. The W test therefore indicates parameters that are nonsignificant in a model, and therefore if deleted in a subsequent model might improve model fit. The deletion of *all* nonsignificant parameters (paths) in the initial model is accomplished by the following command:

```
/PRINT
    RETEST = >MODEL2.EQS=; WTEST=YES;
```

The deletion of all nonsignificant parameter estimates is indicated in the new model setup contained in the file *MODEL2.EQS =*. All parameter estimates in the file with a zero (0) in front of them are not included in a subsequent model analysis. Obviously, they could be edited out of the file, but this is not necessary. Once again, we caution the researcher that such automatic model respecification can cause problems. For example, residual variances may be nonsignificant, causing parameters to be dropped. We suggest editing the file and including a start value followed by an asterisk for any meaningful variable parameters.

In LISREL–SIMPLIS, the researcher will most likely be guided by the modification indices with their associated change (decrease) in chi-square when respecifying a model. Sample output from a later model analysis illustrates how to interpret the modification indices:

```
THE MODIFICATION INDICES SUGGEST TO ADD THE
PATH TO   FROM    DECREASE IN CHI-SQUARE   NEW ESTIMATE

  FAMINC  ABILITY          35.5                  0.51
  MOED    ABILITY           9.8                 -0.24

THE MODIFICATION INDICES SUGGEST TO ADD AN ERROR COVARIANCE
BETWEEN   AND    DECREASE IN CHI-SQUARE   NEW ESTIMATE

FAED    FAMINC             7.9             -0.09
MOED    FAMINC            10.5             -0.10
MOED    FAED              40.2              0.21
```

On the basis of these LISREL–SIMPLIS modification indices, we *add* an error covariance for the variables MoEd and FaEd (mother's education and father's education, respectively) in our subsequent model analysis because it gives us the largest *decrease* in our chi-square value (see chap. 10 for a complete explanation).

5.7 HYPOTHESIS TESTING, SIGNIFICANCE, POWER, AND SAMPLE SIZE

Hypothesis testing involves confirming that a theoretical specified model fits sample variance–covariance data, testing structural coefficients for significance, or testing whether coefficients are equal between groups. These hypothesis-testing methods should involve constrained models with fewer parameters than the initial model. The initial (full) model represents the null hypothesis (H_o) and the alternative (constrained) model with fewer parameters is denoted H_a. Each model generates a χ^2 goodness-of-fit measure, and the difference between the models for significance testing is computed as $D^2 = \chi_o^2 - \chi_a^2$, with $df_d = df_o - df_a$. The D^2 statistic is tested for significance at a specified alpha level (probability of Type I error), where H_o is rejected if D^2 exceeds the critical tabled χ^2 value with df_d degrees of freedom (Table A.4, p. 476). The chi-square difference test or likelihood ratio test is used with GLS, ML, and WLS estimation methods.

The *significance* of parameter estimates that do not require two separate models to yield separate χ^2 values includes (a) generating a two-sided t value for the parameter estimate ($t = $ parameter estimate divided by standard error of the parameter estimate), and (b) interpreting the modification index directly for the parameter estimate as a χ^2 with one degree of freedom. The relationship is simply $t^2 = D^2 = $ MI (modification index) for large sample sizes. Gonzalez and Griffin (2001), however, indicated that the standard errors of the parameter estimates are sensitive to how the model is identified, that is, alternative ways of identifying a model may yield different standard errors, and hence different t-test values for the statistical significance of a parameter estimate. This lack of invariance due to model identification could result in different conclusions about a parameter's significance level from different, yet equivalent, models on the same data. The authors recommended that parameter estimates be tested for significance using the likelihood ratio (LR) test because it is invariant to model identification, rather than the t test (or z test) (Table A.1 and A.2, pp. 473 and 474).

The *power* for hypothesis testing, or the probability of rejecting H_o when H_a is true, depends on the true population model, significance level, degrees of freedom, and sample size (MacCullum, Browne, & Sugawara, 1996). Kaplan (1995) also pointed out that power in SEM is affected by the size of the misspecified parameter, sample size, and location of the parameter in the model. Specification errors induce bias in the standard errors and parameter estimates, and thus affect power. These factors also affect power in other parametric statistical tests (Cohen, 1988). Saris and Sattora (1993) pointed out that the larger the noncentrality parameter, the greater is the power of the test, that is, an evaluation of the power of the test is an evaluation of the noncentrality parameter. Methods for generating D^2 and power using LISPOWER are also outlined in the *LISREL 7 User's Reference Guide* (Jöreskog and Sörbom, 1989). Muthén and Muthén (2002) recently outlined how Monte Carlo methods can be used to decide on the power for a given specified model using the *Mplus* program. Power is indicated as the percentage (%) of significant coefficients or the proportion of replications for which the null hypothesis that a parameter is equal to zero is rejected at the .05 level of significance, two-tailed test, with a critical value of 1.96. The authors suggested that power equal or exceed the traditional .80 level for determining the probability of rejecting the null hypothesis when it is false.

Power values for modification index values can be computed using SAS because the modification index (MI) obtained from the Lagrange multiplier test in EQS is a noncentrality parameter (NCP). The power of a MI value is computed in SAS using the probability of chi-square argument as follows:

```
Data;
Input MI;
Power = 1 - probchi (3.841, 1, MI);
Cards;
.80
Proc Print; Var MI Power;
```

Power values for parameter estimates can also be computed using SAS because a squared *t* value for parameter estimates in the Wald test is asymptotically distributed as a noncentral chi-square. The power of a squared *t* value for a parameter estimate is computed in SAS using the probability of chi-square argument as follows:

```
Data;
Input T;
NCP = T**2;
Power = 1 - probchi (3.841, 1, NCP);
Cards;
8.20
Proc Print; Var T NCP Power;
```

The other model fit indices (GFI, AGFI, NFI, IFI, CFI, etc.) do not have a test of statistical significance and therefore do not involve power calculations.

Muthén and Muthén (2002) also used *Mplus* to determine appropriate sample sizes in the presence of model complexity, distribution of variables, missing data, reliability, and variance–covariance of variables. For example, given a two-factor CFA model and 10 indicator variables with normally distributed nonmissing data, a sample size of 150 is indicated with power = .81. In the presence of missing data, sample size increases to $n = 175$. Given nonnormal missing data, sample size increases to $n = 315$.

Research suggests that certain model fit indices are less susceptible to sample size than others. We have already learned that χ^2 is affected by sample size, that is, $\chi^2 = (n - 1)F_{\mathrm{ML}}$, where F_{ML} is the maximum likelihood fit function for a specified model, and therefore χ^2 increases in direct relation to $n - 1$ (Bollen, 1989). Marsh et al. (1988, 1996) examined the influence of sample size on 30 different model fit indices and found that the Tucker–Lewis index (Tucker & Lewis, 1973) and four new indices based on the Tucker–Lewis index were the only ones relatively independent of sample size. Bollen (1990) argued that the claims regarding which model fit indices were affected by sample size needed further clarification. There are actually two sample size effects that are confounded: (a) whether sample size enters into the calculation of the model fit index and (b) whether the means of the sampling distribution of the model fit index are associated with sample size. Sample size was shown not to affect the calculation of NFI, TL, GFI, AGFI, and CN, but the means of the sampling distribution of these model fit indices were associated with sample size. Bollen concluded that, given a lack of consensus on the best measure of fit, it is prudent to report multiple measures rather than rely on a single choice.

Finally, one should beware of claims of sample size influence on fit measures that do not distinguish the type of sample size effect (Satorra & Bentler, 1994). Cudeck and Henly (1991) also argued that a uniformly negative view of the effects of sample size in model selection is unwarranted. They focused instead on the predictive validity of models in the sense of cross-validation in future samples while acknowledging that sample size issues are a problem in other statistical decisions and unavoidable in structural equation modeling. One way to determine an appropriate sample size is to compute the critical N (CN) statistic (Hoelter, 1983), which is given by $CN = (\chi^2/F_{\mathrm{ML}}) + 1$. *CN gives the sample size at which the F_{ML} value leads to a rejection of H_o.* The CN statistic is output by the Amos and LISREL–SIMPLIS programs. For a further discussion of this statistic, see Bollen and Liang (1988) and Bollen (1989). In our model analysis of Fig. 5.1, the sample size was small ($n = 145$), but afforded several good model fit indices and a nonsignificant chi-square, so the CN = 796 (.01 level) recommended sample size cutoff for testing the model was more than satisfied.

5.8 SUMMARY

In this chapter, we began by discussing three approaches a researcher could take in structural equation modeling: confirmatory models, alternative models, and model generation. We then considered categories of model fit indices, namely model fit, model comparison, and model parsimony. In addition, current and new innovative approaches to specification searches were mentioned for the assessment of model fit in structural equation modeling. We examined in detail the different categories of model fit criteria because different fit indices have been developed depending upon the type of specified model tested. Generally, no single model fit index is sufficient for testing a hypothesized structural model. An ideal fit index just does not exist. This is not surprising because it has been suggested that an ideal fit index is one that is independent of sample size, accurately reflects differences in fit, imposes a penalty for inclusion of additional parameters (Marsh et al., 1988), and supports the choice of a true model when it is known (McDonald & Marsh, 1990). Current model-fitting practice involves the use of optional paths in Amos, modification indices in LISREL–SIMPLIS, and the use of Lagrange multiplier (LM) and Wald (W) tests in EQS, with other advances in specification search techniques (Tabu and optimization algorithms) identifying the best model given sample data.

A two-factor confirmatory model was analyzed using Amos, EQS, and LISREL computer programs with model fit output to enhance our understanding of the many different model fit criteria. We concluded in this chapter with a discussion of the two-step and four-step approaches to SEM modeling, the significance of parameters in a model, power, and sample size. An understanding of model fit criteria will help your understanding of the examples presented in the remaining chapters of the book.

APPENDIX: STANDARD ERRORS AND CHI-SQUARES IN LISREL

LISREL computes two different sets of standard errors for parameter estimates and up to four different chi-squares for testing overall fit of the model. These new standard errors and chi-squares can be obtained for single-group problems as well as multiple-group problems using variance–covariance matrices with or without means.

Which standard errors and which chi-squares will be reported depend on whether an asymptotic covariance matrix is provided and which method of estimation is used to fit the model (ULS, GLS, ML, WLS, DWLS).

The asymptotic covariance matrix is a consistent estimate of N times the asymptotic covariance matrix of the sample matrix being analyzed.

Standard Errors

Standard errors are estimated under nonnormality if an asymptotic co-variance matrix is used. Standard errors are estimated under multivariate normality if no asymptotic covariance matrix is used.

Chi-Squares

Four different chi-squares are reported below and denoted as C1, C2, C3, and C4, where the x indicates if it is reported for any of the five estimation methods. The asterisk indicates that the chi-square value is reported only if the asymptotic covariance matrix is used.

Asymptotic covariance matrix not provided:

	ULS	GLS	ML	WLS	DWLS
C1	—	x	x	—	—
C2	x	x	x	—	*
C3	—	—	—	—	—
C4	—	—	—	—	—

Asymptotic covariance matrix provided:

	ULS	GLS	ML	WLS	DWLS
C1	—	x	x	x	—
C2	x	x	x	—	x
C3	x	x	x	—	x
C4	x	x	x	—	x

Note 1. C1 is $n - 1$ times the minimum value of the fit function; C2 is $n - 1$ times the minimum of the WLS fit function using a weight matrix estimated under multivariate normality; C3 is the Satorra–Bentler scaled chi-square statistic or its generalization to mean and covariance structures and multiple groups (Satorra & Bentler, 1994); and C4 is computed from equations in Browne (1984) or Satorra (1993) using the asymptotic covariance matrix.

The corresponding chi-squares are now given in the output as follows:

C1. Minimum fit function chi-square
C2. Normal theory weighted least squares chi-square

C3. Satorra–Bentler scaled chi-square

C4. Chi-square corrected for nonnormality

Note 2. Under multivariate normality of the observed variables, C1 and C2 are asymptotically equivalent and have an asymptotic chi-square distribution if the model holds exactly and an asymptotic noncentral chi-square distribution if the model holds approximately. Under normality and nonnormality, C2 and C4 are correct asymptotic chi-squares, but may not be the best chi-square in small and moderate samples. Hu, Bentler, and Kano (1992) and Yuan and Bentler (1997) found that C3 performed better given different types of models, sample sizes, and degrees of nonnormality.

EXERCISES

1. Define confirmatory models, alternative models, and model-generating approaches.
2. Define model fit, model comparison, and model parsimony.
3. Calculate the following Amos fit indices for the model output in Fig. 5.1:

$$GFI = 1 - (\chi^2_{model}/\chi^2_{null})$$

$$NFI = (\chi^2_{null} - \chi^2_{model})/\chi^2_{null}$$

$$RFI = 1 - [(\chi^2_{model}/df_{model})/(\chi^2_{null}/df_{null})]$$

$$IFI = (\chi^2_{null} - \chi^2_{model})/(\chi^2_{null} - df_{model})$$

$$TLI = [(\chi^2_{null}/df_{null}) - (\chi^2_{model}/df_{model})]/[(\chi^2_{null}/df_{null}) - 1]$$

$$CFI = 1 - [(\chi^2_{model} - df_{model})/(\chi^2_{null} - df_{null})]$$

$$\text{Model AIC} = \chi^2_{model} + 2q \text{ (number of free parameters)}$$

$$\text{Null AIC} = \chi^2_{null} + 2q \text{ (number of free parameters)}$$

$$RMSEA = \sqrt{(\chi^2_M - df_M)/[(N - 1)df_M]}$$

4. The Lagrange Multiplier (LM) test in EQS indicates what about the parameters in an initial specified model?
5. The Wald (W) test in EQS indicates what about the parameters in an initial specified model?
6. How are modification indices in LISREL–SIMPLIS used?
7. What steps should a researcher take in examining parameter estimates in a model?
8. How should a researcher test for the difference between two alternative models?
9. How are structural equation models affected by sample size and power considerations?
10. Contrast the two-step and four-step approaches in SEM.
11. What new approaches are available to help researchers identify the best model?

REFERENCES

Akaike, H. (1987). Factor analysis and AIC. *Psychometrika, 52,* 317–332.

Anderson, J. C., & Gerbing, D. W. (1984). The effects of sampling error on convergence, improper solutions and goodness-of-fit indices for maximum likelihood confirmatory factor analysis. *Psychometrika, 49,* 155–173.

Anderson, J. C., & Gerbing, D. W. (1988). Structural equation modeling in practice: A review and recommended two-step approach. *Psychological Bulletin, 103,* 411–423.

Arbuckle, J. L., & Wothke, W. (1999). *Amos 4.0 User's Guide.* Chicago, IL: Small Waters Corporation.

Baldwin, B. (1989). A primer in the use and interpretation of structural equation models. *Measurement and Evaluation in Counseling and Development, 22,* 100–112.

Bentler, P. M. (1990). Comparative fit indexes in structural models. *Psychological Bulletin, 107,* 238–246.

Bentler, P. M., & Bonett, D. G. (1980). Significance tests and goodness-of-fit in the analysis of covariance structures. *Psychological Bulletin, 88,* 588–606.

Bentler, P. M., & Wu, E. J. C. (2002). *EQS 6 for Windows User's Guide.* Encino, CA: Multivariate Software, Inc.

Bollen, K. A. (1989). *Structural equations with latent variables.* New York: Wiley.

Bollen, K. A. (1990). Overall fit in covariance structure models: Two types of sample size effects. *Psychological Bulletin, 107,* 256–259.

Bollen, K. A., & Liang, J. (1988). Some properties of Hoelter's CN. *Sociological Methods and Research, 16,* 492–503.

Bollen, K. A., & Long, S. J. (1993). *Testing structural equation models.* Newbury Park, CA: Sage.

Browne, M. W. (1984). Asymptotically distribution-free methods for the analysis of covariance structures. *British Journal of Mathematical and Statistical Psychology, 37,* 62–83.

Browne, M. W., & Cudeck, R. (1993). Alternative ways of assessing model fit. In K. A. Bollen & J. S. Long (Eds.), *Testing structural equation models* (pp. 132–162). Beverly Hills, CA: Sage.

Cheung, G. W., & Rensvold, R. B. (2002). Evaluating goodness-of-fit indexes for testing measurement invariance. *Structural Equation Modeling, 9,* 233–255.

Cliff, N. (1983). Some cautions concerning the application of causal modeling methods. *Multivariate Behavioral Research, 18,* 115–126.

Cohen, J. (1988). *Statistical power analysis for the behavioral sciences* (2nd ed.). Hillsdale, NJ: Lawrence Erlbaum Associates, Inc.

Cudeck, R., & Henly, S. J. (1991). Model selection in covariance structures analysis and the "problem" of sample size: A clarification. *Psychological Bulletin, 109,* 512–519.

Gonzalez, R., & Griffin, D. (2001). Testing parameters in structural equation modeling: Every "one" matters. *Psychological Methods, 6*(3), 258–269.

Gorsuch, R. L. (1983). *Factor analysis* (2nd ed.). Hillsdale, NJ: Lawrence Erlbaum Associates.

Hair, J. F., Jr., Anderson, R. E., Tatham, R. L., & Black, W. C. (1992). *Multivariate data analysis with readings* (3rd ed.). New York: Macmillan.

Harmon, H. H. (1976). *Modern factor analysis* (3rd ed.). Chicago: University of Chicago Press.

Hoelter, J. W. (1983). The analysis of covariance structures: Goodness-of-fit indices. *Sociological Methods and Research, 11,* 325–344.

Holzinger, K. J., & Swineford, F. A. (1939). A study in factor analysis: The stability of a bi-factor solution. Supplementary Educational Monographs, No. 48. Chicago: Univ. of Chicago, Dept. of Education.

Hu, L., & Bentler, P. M. (1995). Evaluating model fit. In R. H. Hoyle (Ed.), *Structural equation modeling: Concepts, issues, and applications* (pp. 76–99). Thousand Oaks, CA: Sage.

Hu, L., Bentler, P. M., & Kano, Y. (1992). Can test statistics in covariance structure analysis be trusted? *Psychological Bulletin, 112*, 351–362.

James, L. R., Mulaik, S. A., & Brett, J. M. (1982). *Causal analysis: Assumptions, models, and data.* Beverly Hills, CA: Sage.

Jöreskog, K. G. (1969). A general approach to confirmatory maximum likelihood factor analysis. *Psychometrika, 34*, 183–202.

Jöreskog, K. G., & Sörbom, D. (1989). *LISREL 7 user's reference guide.* Mooresville, IN: Scientific Software.

Jöreskog, K. G., & Sörbom, D. (1993). *LISREL 8: Structural equation modeling with the SIMPLIS command language.* Hillsdale, NJ: Lawrence Erlbaum Associates.

Kaplan, D. (1995). Statistical power in structural equation modeling. In R. H. Hoyle, (Ed.), *Structural equation modeling: Concepts, issues, and applications* (pp. 100–117). Thousand Oaks, CA: Sage.

Kenny, D. A., & McCoach, D. B. (2003). Effect of the number of variables on measures of fit in structural equation modeling. *Structural Equation Modeling, 10*, 333–351.

Loehlin, J. C. (1987). *Latent variable models: An introduction to factor, path, and structural analysis.* Hillsdale, NJ: Lawrence Erlbaum Associates, Inc.

Lunneborg, C. E. (1987). *Bootstrap applications for the behavioral sciences. Vol. 1.* Seattle: University of Washington, Psychology Department.

MacCallum, R. C., Browne, M. W., & Sugawara, H. M. (1996). Power analysis and determination of sample size for covariance structure modeling. *Psychological Methods, 1*, 130–149.

Marcoulides, G. A., & Drezner, Z. (2001). Specification searches in structural equation modeling with a genetic algorithm. In G. A. Marcoulides & R. E. Schumacker (Eds.), *New developments and techniques in structural equation modeling* (pp. 247–268). Mahwah, NJ: Lawrence Erlbaum Associates, Inc.

Marcoulides, G. A., & Drezner, Z. (2003). Model specification searches using ant colony optimization algorithms. *Structural Equation Modeling, 10*, 154–164.

Marcoulides, G. A., Drezner, Z., & Schumacker, R. E. (1998). Model specification searches in structural equation modeling using Tabu search. *Structural Equation Modeling, 5*, 365–376.

Marsh, H. W., Balla, J. R., & McDonald, R. P. (1988). Goodness-of-fit indexes in confirmatory factor analysis: The effect of sample size. *Psychological Bulletin, 103*, 391–410.

Marsh, H. W., Balla, J. R., & Hau, K.-T. (1996). An evaluation of incremental fit indices: A clarification of mathematical and empirical properties. In G. A. Marcoulides & R. E. Schumacker (Eds.), *Advanced structural equation modeling: Issues and techniques* (pp. 315–353). Mahwah, NJ: Lawrence Erlbaum Associates, Inc.

McDonald, R. P. (1989). An index of goodness-of-fit based on noncentrality. *Journal of Classification, 6*, 97–103.

McDonald, R. P., & Marsh, H. W. (1990). Choosing a multivariate model: Noncentrality and goodness of fit. *Psychological Bulletin, 107*, 247–255.

Mulaik, S. A., & Millsap, R. E. (2000). Doing the four-step right. *Structural Equation Modeling, 7*, 36–73.

Mulaik, S. A., James, L. R., Alstine, J. V., Bennett, N., Lind, S., & Stilwell, C. D. (1989). Evaluation of goodness-of-fit indices for structural equation models. *Psychological Bulletin, 105*, 430–445.

Muthén, B., & Muthén, L. (2002). How to use a Monte Carlo study to decide on sample size and determine power. *Structural Equation Modeling, 9*, 599–620.

Raykov, T. (1997). Estimation of composite reliability for congeneric measures. *Applied Psychological Measurement, 21*, 173–184.

Saris, W. E., & Satorra, A. (1993). Power evaluations in structural equation models. In

K. Bollen & J. S. Long (Eds.), *Testing structural equation models* (pp. 181–204). Newbury Park, CA: Sage.

Satorra, A. (1993). Multi-sample analysis of moment structures: Asymptotic validity of inferences based on second-order moments. In K. Haagen, D. J. Bartholomew, & M. Deistler (Eds.), *Statistical modeling and latent variables* (pp. 283–298). Amsterdam: Elsevier.

Satorra, A., & Bentler, P. M. (1994). Corrections to test statistics and standard errors in covariance structure analysis. In A. Von Eye & C. C. Clogg (Eds.), *Latent variable analysis: Applications for developmental research* (pp. 399–419). Thousands Oaks, CA: Sage.

Steiger, J. H. (1990). Structural model evaluation and modification: An interval estimation approach. *Multivariate Behavioral Research, 25*, 173–180.

Steiger, J. H., & Lind, J. M. (1980, May). *Statistically-based tests for the number of common factors*. Paper presented at Psychometric Society Meeting, Iowa City, IA.

Tucker, L. R., & Lewis, C. (1973). The reliability coefficient for maximum likelihood factor analysis. *Psychometrika, 38*, 1–10.

Williams, L. J., & Holahan, P. J. (1994). Parsimony-based fit indices of multiple indicator models: Do they work? *Structural Equation Modeling: A Multidisciplinary Journal, 1*, 161–189.

Yuan, K. H., & Bentler, P. M. (1997). Mean and covariance structure analysis: Theoretical and practical improvements. *Journal of the American Statistical Association, 92*, 767–774.

ANSWERS TO EXERCISES

1. Define confirmatory models, alternative models, and model-generating approaches.

   In *confirmatory models*, a researcher can hypothesize a specific theoretical model, gather data, and then test whether the data fit the model.

   In *alternative models*, a researcher specifies different models to see which model fits the sample data the best. A researcher usually conducts a chi-square difference test.

   In *model generating*, a researcher specifies an initial model, then uses modification indices to modify and retest the model to obtain a better fit to the sample data.

2. Define model fit, model comparison, and model parsimony.

   Model fit determines the degree to which the sample variance–covariance data fit the structural equation model.

   Model comparison involves comparing an implied model with a null model (independence model). The null model could also be any model that establishes a basis for expecting other alternative models to be different.

   Model parsimony seeks the minimum number of estimated coefficients required to achieve a specific level of model fit. Basically, an overidentified model is compared with a restricted model.

3. Calculate the following Amos fit indices for the model analysis in Fig. 5.1:

$$\text{GFI} = 1 - (\chi^2_{model}/\chi^2_{null}) = .99$$
$$\text{NFI} = (\chi^2_{null} - \chi^2_{model})/\chi^2_{null} = .989$$
$$\text{RFI} = 1 - [(\chi^2_{model}/df_{model})/(\chi^2_{null}/df_{null})] = .979$$
$$\text{IFI} = (\chi^2_{null} - \chi^2_{model})/(\chi^2_{null} - df_{model}) = 1.014$$

$$\mathrm{TLI} \; = \; [(\chi^2_{\text{null}}/df_{\text{null}}) - (\chi^2_{\text{model}}/df_{\text{model}})]/[(\chi^2_{\text{null}}/df_{\text{null}}) - 1] = 1.027$$

$$\mathrm{CFI} \; = \; 1 - [(\chi^2_{\text{model}} - df_{\text{model}})/(\chi^2_{\text{null}} - df_{\text{null}})] = 1.00$$

$$\text{Model AIC} \; = \; \chi^2_{\text{model}} + 2q \; (\text{number of free parameters}) = 29.638$$

$$\text{Null AIC} \; = \; \chi^2_{\text{null}} + 2q \; (\text{number of free parameters}) = 333.32$$

$$\mathrm{RMSEA} \; = \; \sqrt{(\chi^2_{\text{M}} - df_{\text{M}})/[(N-1)df_{\text{M}}]} = 0.0$$

4. The Lagrange multiplier (LM) test in EQS indicates what about the parameters in an initial specified model?
The LM test indicates additional paths that could be added to improve the model-to-data fit.

5. The Wald (W) test in EQS indicates what about the parameters in an initial specified model?
The W test indicates paths that can be deleted to improve the model-to-data fit.

6. How are modification indices in LISREL–SIMPLIS used?
Modification indices in LISREL–SIMPLIS indicate the amount of change in chi-square that would result if a path was added or deleted.

7. What steps should a researcher take in examining parameter estimates in a model?
A researcher should examine the sign of the parameter estimate and whether the value of the parameter estimate is within a reasonable range of values, and test the parameter for significance.

8. How should a researcher test for the difference between two alternative models?
A researcher computes a chi-square difference test (referred to as a likelihood ratio test) by subtracting the base model chi-square value from the constrained-model chi-square value with one degree of freedom. When testing measurement invariance between groups in a specified model, the comparative fit index (CFI) and McDonald's noncentrality index (NCI) are recommended.

9. How are structural equation models affected by sample size and power considerations?
Several factors affect determining the appropriate sample size and power including model complexity, distribution of variables, missing data, reliability, and variance–covariance of variables. If variables are normally distributed with no missing data, samples sizes less than 500 should yield power = .80 and satisfy Hoelter's CN criterion. Monte Carlo methods or other software programs can be used to determine power and sample size.

10. Contrast the two-step and four-step approaches in SEM.
The two-step approach involves first establishing valid and reliable indicators of latent variables in a measurement model and then specifying relationships among the latent variables in a structural model. The four-step approach first uses exploratory factor analysis to establish a meaningful theoretical model. Next, one conducts a confirmatory factor analysis with a new sample of data. Then, one conducts a test of the structural equation model. Finally, one tests planned hypotheses about free parameters in the model.

11. What new approaches are available to help researchers identify the best model?
Amos currently includes a new exploratory specification search, which identifies several models that fit the data. The researcher needs to decide which model can be supported by theory in the research literature. Also, Tabu and optimization algorithms have been proposed to identify the best model fit with the sample variance–covariance matrix.

CHAPTER

6

REGRESSION MODELS

---◆◇◆---

Chapter Outline

Key Concepts

Explanation versus prediction
Standardized partial regression coefficients
Coefficient of determination
Squared multiple correlation coefficient
Full versus restricted models

Confidence intervals around R^2
Measurement error
Additive versus relational model

In this chapter, we consider the use of multiple regression models as a method for modeling multiple observed variables. Multiple regression, a general linear modeling approach to the analysis of data, has become increasingly popular since 1967 (Bashaw & Findley, 1968). In fact, it has become recognized as an approach that bridges the gap between correlation and analysis of variance in answering research hypotheses (McNeil, Kelly, & McNeil, 1975). Many statistical textbooks elaborate the relationship between multiple regression and analysis of variance (Draper & Smith, 1966; Edwards, 1979; Hinkle, Wiersma, & Jurs, 2003; Lomax, 2001).

Graduate students who take an advanced statistics course are typically provided with the multiple linear regression framework for data analysis. Given knowledge of multiple linear regression techniques (one dependent variable), understanding can be extended to various multivariable statistical techniques (Newman, 1988). A basic knowledge of multiple regression concepts is therefore important in further understanding path analysis as presented in chapter 7.

This chapter shows how beta weights (standardized partial regression coefficients) are computed in multiple regression using structural equation modeling software programs. More specifically, we illustrate how the structural equation modeling approach can be used to compute parameter estimates in multiple regression and what model fit criteria are reported. We begin with a brief overview of multiple regression concepts followed by an example that illustrates model specification, model identification, model estimation, model testing, and model modification.

6.1 OVERVIEW

Multiple regression techniques require a basic understanding of sample statistics (n, mean, and variance), standardized variables, correlation (Pedhazur, 1982), and partial correlation (Cohen & Cohen, 1975; Houston & Bolding, 1974). In standard score form (z scores), the simple linear regression equation is

$$\hat{z}_y = \beta z_x,$$

where β is the standardized regression coefficient. The basic rationale for using the standard-score formula is that variables are converted to the same scale of measurement, the z scale. Conversion back to the raw-score scale is easily accomplished by using the raw score, the mean, and the standard deviation.

The relationship connecting the Pearson product–moment correlation coefficient, the unstandardized regression coefficient b and the standardized regression coefficient β is

$$\beta = \frac{\sum z_x z_y}{\sum z_x^2} = b \frac{s_x}{s_y} = r_{xy},$$

where s_x and s_y are the sample standard deviations for variables X and Y, respectively. For two independent variables, the multiple linear regression equation with standard scores is

$$\hat{z}_y = \beta_1 z_1 + \beta_2 z_2$$

and the standardized partial regression coefficients β_1 and β_2 are computed from

$$\beta_1 = \frac{r_{y1} - r_{y2} r_{12}}{1 - r_{12}^2} \quad \text{and} \quad \beta_2 = \frac{r_{y2} - r_{y1} r_{12}}{1 - r_{12}^2}.$$

The correlation between the dependent observed variable Y and the predicted scores $\hat{Y}$ is given the special name *multiple correlation coefficient*. It is written as

$$R_{y\hat{y}} = R_{y.12},$$

where the latter subscripts indicate that the dependent variable Y is being predicted by two independent variables, X_1 and X_2. The *squared multiple correlation coefficient* is computed as

$$R_{y\hat{y}}^2 = R_{y.12}^2 = \beta_1 r_{Y1} + \beta_2 r_{Y2}.$$

The squared multiple correlation coefficient indicates the amount of variance explained, predicted, or accounted for by the set of independent predictor variables. The R^2 value is used as a model fit criterion in multiple regression analysis.

Kerlinger and Pedhazur (1973) showed that multiple regression analysis can play an important role in prediction and explanation. Prediction and explanation reflect different research questions, study designs, inferential approaches, analysis strategies, and reported information. In prediction, the main emphasis is on practical application such that independent variables are chosen by their effectiveness in enhancing

prediction of the dependent variable. In explanation, the main emphasis is on the variability in the dependent variable explained by a theoretically meaningful set of independent variables. Huberty (2003) established a clear distinction between prediction and explanation when
referring to multiple correlation analysis (MCA) and multiple regression
analysis (MRA). In MCA, the parameter of interest is the correlation between the dependent variable Y and a composite of the independent
variables X_N. The adjusted formula using sample size N and the number
of independent predictors p is

$$R^2_{\text{Adj}} = R^2 - \frac{p}{N - p - 1}(1 - R^2).$$

In MRA, regression weights are also estimated to achieve a composite
for the independent variables X_N, but the index of fit R^2 is computed
differently:

$$R^2_{\text{Adj}^*} = R^2 - \frac{2p}{N - p}(1 - R^2).$$

Comparing these two formulas, we see that $R^2_{\text{Adj}^*}$ has a larger adjustment.
For example, given $R^2 = .50$, $p = 10$ predictor variables, and $N = 100$
subjects, these two different fit indices are

$$R^2_{\text{Adj}} = R^2 - \frac{p}{N - p - 1}(1 - R^2) = .50 - .11(.50) = .50 - .055 = .45$$

$$R^2_{\text{Adj}^*} = R^2 - \frac{2p}{N - p}(1 - R^2) = .50 - .22(.50) = .50 - .11 = .39.$$

Hypothesis testing involves using the *expected value* or chance value
of R^2 for testing the null hypothesis, which is $p/(N-1)$, not 0 as typically
indicated. In our example, the expected or chance value for R^2 is $10/99 =$
.10, so the null hypothesis H_o is $\rho^2 = .10$. An F test is used to test the
statistical significance of the R^2 value:

$$F = \frac{R^2/p}{(1 - R^2)/N - p - 1}.$$

In our example,

$$F = \frac{R^2/p}{(1 - R^2)/N - p - 1} = \frac{.50/10}{(1 - .50)/89} = \frac{.05}{.0056} = 8.9,$$

which is statistically significant when compared to the tabled $F = 1.93$, $df = 10, 89, p < .05$ (Table A.5, p. 478). In addition to the statistical significance test, a researcher should calculate *effect sizes* and *confidence intervals* to aid understanding and interpretation.

The *effect size* (ES) is computed as $ES = R^2 - [p/(N - 1)]$. In our example, $ES\ R^2_{Adj} = .45 - .10 = .35$ and $ES\ R^2_{Adj^*} = .39 - .10 = .29$. This indicates a moderate to large effect size according to Cohen (1988), who gave a general reference for effect sizes of F tests (small $= .1$, medium $= .25$, and large $= .4$).

Confidence intervals (CIs) around the R^2 value can also help our interpretation of multiple regression analysis. Steiger and Fouladi (1992) reported an R^2 CI DOS program that computes confidence intervals, power, and sample size. Steiger and Fouladi (1997) and Cumming and Finch (2001) both discussed the importance of converting the central F value (see above) to an estimate of the noncentral F before computing a confidence interval around R^2. Smithson (2001) wrote an R^2 SPSS program to compute confidence intervals. We use the Steiger and Fouladi (1997) R^2 CI DOS program with our hypothetical example. After entering the program, **Option** is selected from the tool bar menu and then **Confidence Interval** is selected from the drop-down menu. To obtain R^2CI, the number of subjects ($N = 100$), the number of variables ($K = 10$), the R^2 value ($R = .35$), and the desired confidence level ($C = .95$) are entered by using the arrow keys (mouse not supported), and then **GO** is selected to compute the values. The 95% confidence interval around $R^2 = .35$ is .133 to .449 at the $p = .0001$ level of significance for a null hypothesis that $R^2 = 0$ in the population.

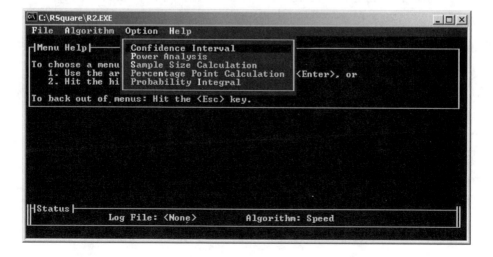

After assessing our initial regression model fit, we might want to determine whether adding or deleting an independent variable would improve the index of fit R^2, but we avoid using stepwise regression methods (Huberty, 1989). We run a second multiple regression equation where a single independent variable is added or deleted to obtain a second R^2 value. We then compute a different F test to determine the statistical significance between the two regression models as follows:

$$ F = \frac{\left(R_F^2 - R_R^2\right)/(p_1 - p_2)}{\left(1 - R_F^2\right)/N - p_1 - 1}, $$

where R_F^2 is the multiple regression equation with the original set of independent variables p_1 and R_R^2 is the multiple regression equation with the reduced set of independent variables p_2. In our heuristic example, we drop a single independent variable and obtain $R_R^2 = .49$ with $p_2 = 9$ predictor variables. The F test is computed as

$$ F = \frac{\left(R_F^2 - R_R^2\right)/(p_1 - p_2)}{\left(1 - R_F^2\right)/N - p_1 - 1} = \frac{(.50 - .49)/(10 - 9)}{(1 - .50)/100 - 10 - 1} = \frac{.01}{.0056} = 1.78. $$

The F value is not significant at the .05 level, so the variable we dropped does not statistically add to the prediction of Y, which supports our dropping the single predictor variable, that is, a 1% decrease in R^2 is not statistically significant. The nine-variable regression model therefore provides a more parsimonious model.

It is important to understand the basic concepts of multiple regression and correlation because they provide a better understanding of path analysis in chapter 7 and structural equation modeling in general. An example is presented next to further clarify these basic multiple regression computations.

6.2 AN EXAMPLE

A multiple linear regression analysis is conducted using a data file from the EQS program (Bentler & Wu, 1995, p. 157; Bentler & Wu, 2002, p. 157). The data set chatter.ess (EQS system file) is saved as an SPSS data file for use in Amos and LISREL (chatter.sav). The data file contains scores from 24 patients on four variables (Var1 = patient's age in years, Var2 = severity of illness, Var3 = level of anxiety, and Var4 = satisfaction level) from Chatterjee and Yilmaz (1992).

Given raw data, two different approaches are possible: (a) system file in EQS and LISREL–PRELIS using regression statistics from the pull-down menu and (b) correlation matrix input in EQS and LISREL–SIMPLIS command syntax files. Amos requires that a path model be drawn and then the data file input, that is, the SPSS file *chatter.sav*.

6.3 MODEL SPECIFICATION

Model specification involves finding relevant theory and prior research to formulate a theoretical regression model. The researcher is interested in specifying a regression model that should be confirmed with sample variance–covariance data, thus yielding a high R^2 value and statistically significant F value. Model specification directly involves deciding which variables to include or not to include in the theoretical regression model.

If the researcher does not select the right variables, then the regression model could be misspecified and lack validity (Tracz, Brown, & Kopriva, 1991). The problem is that a misspecified model may result in biased parameter estimates or estimates that are systematically different from what they really are in the true population model. This bias is known as *specification error*.

The researcher's goal is to determine whether the theoretical regression model fits the sample variance–covariance structure in the data, that is, whether the sample variance–covariance matrix implies some underlying theoretical regression model. The multiple regression model of theoretical interest in our example is to predict the satisfaction level of patients based on patient's age, severity of illness, and level of anxiety (independent variables). This would be characteristic of an *MCA* model because a particular set of variables was selected based on theory. The dependent variable Var4 is therefore predicted by the three independent variables (Var1, Var2, and Var3). The path diagram of the implied regression model is shown in Fig. 6.1.

6.4 MODEL IDENTIFICATION

Once a theoretical regression model is specified, the next concern is model identification. Model identification refers to deciding whether a set of unique parameter estimates can be computed for the regression equation. Algebraically, every free parameter in the multiple regression equation can be estimated from the sample variance–covariance matrix (a *free* parameter is an unknown parameter that you want to estimate).

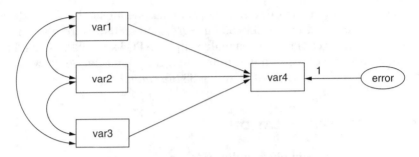

FIG. 6.1.   Satisfaction regression model.

The number of distinct values in the sample variance–covariance matrix equals the number of parameters to be estimated; thus, multiple
regression models are always considered *just-identified* (see chap. 4).
SEM computer output will therefore indicate that regression analyses
are *saturated* models; thus, $\chi^2 = 0$ and degrees of freedom $= 0$.

6.5   MODEL ESTIMATION

Model estimation involves estimating the parameters in the regression
model, that is, computing the sample regression weights for the independent predictor variables. The squared multiple correlation equation
with three predictor variables is

$$R^2_{y.123} = \beta_1 r_{y1} + \beta_2 r_{y2} + \beta_3 r_{y3}.$$

The correlation coefficients are multiplied by their respective standardized partial regression weights and summed to yield the squared multiple
regression coefficient $R^2_{Y.123}$.

We selected EQS for our regression analysis example, although Amos,
LISREL–PRELIS, and LISREL–SIMPLIS regression analyses are presented
at the end of the chapter. In EQS, we select **File, Open,** and pick the
file *chatter.ess* (EQS system file) from the *Examples* folder. Next, select
Analysis from the tool bar menu, and click on **Regressions**.

We select the *Standard Multiple Regression* option and then select
VAR4 as the dependent variable and VAR1 to VAR3 as the independent
variables. We also click on the box to have the regression estimates
(predicted *Y* values) and residuals (error of prediction values) added to
the EQS system file. We can plot these values using the graphical display
features in EQS. The EQS regression output is the most informative:

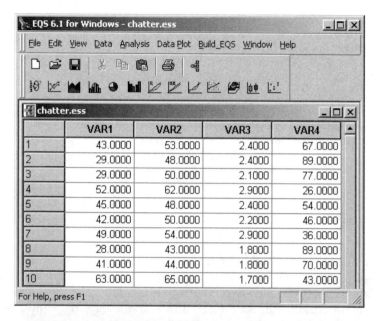

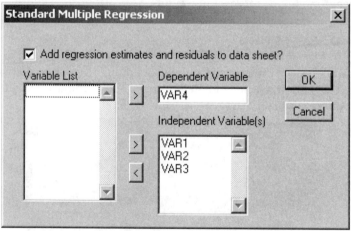

```
                          ANALYSIS OF VARIANCE
                          ====================

Source       SUM OF SQUARES    DF    MEAN SQUARES        F        p

REGRESSION        4433.166      3       1477.722    14.525    0.000
RESIDUAL          2034.667     20        101.733
TOTAL             6467.833     23


Dependent Variable =      VAR4
Number of obs.     =        24
```

```
Multiple R          =    0.8279
R-square            =    0.6854
Adjusted R-square   =    0.6382
F( 3,     20)       =   14.5254
Prob > F            =    0.0000
Std. Error of Est. =   10.0863
Durbin-Watson Stat.=    1.5764
```

```
=======REGRESSION COEFFICIENTS=======
                                  HETERO-
                      ORDINARY   SCEDASTIC
VARIABLE          B  STD. ERROR  STD. ERROR    BETA       t      p
```

VARIABLE	B	ORDINARY STD. ERROR	HETERO-SCEDASTIC STD. ERROR	BETA	t	p
Intercept	156.622	22.605	21.859		7.165	0.000
VAR1	-1.153	0.279	0.296	-0.657	-3.901	0.001
VAR2	-0.265	0.544	0.613	-0.083	-0.433	0.670
VAR3	-15.594	7.243	7.645	-0.294	-2.040	0.055

We are not interested in interpreting any of the model fit indices reported in chapter 5, but compute the appropriate R^2 model fit, F test, confidence interval, and effect size presented in this chapter. EQS output reports the R^2, adjusted R^2, F test, and standardized and unstandardized (intercept included) regression weights.

6.6   MODEL TESTING

EQS can compute the correlation matrix among the variables in the regression equation; we select **Analysis** from the tool bar menu and then select **Correlations**.

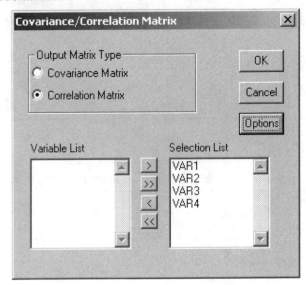

The correlation matrix is output as follows:

	VAR1	VAR2	VAR3	VAR4
VAR1	1.0000			
VAR2	0.6136	1.0000		
VAR3	0.1935	0.3888	1.0000	
VAR4	−0.7649	−0.6002	−0.4530	1.0000

EQS can also compute the descriptive statistics by selecting **Analysis**, then **Descriptive Statistics** (abridged values shown here).

ID	Name	Cases	Mean	Standard deviation
1	VAR1	24	40.583	9.560
2	VAR2	24	51.375	5.224
3	VAR3	24	2.283	.316
4	VAR4	24	60.583	16.769

We can now verify the R^2 value using the standardized regression formula:

$$R^2_{y.123} = \beta_1 r_{y1} + \beta_2 r_{y2} + \beta_3 r_{y3}$$
$$= -.657(-.7649) + -.083(-.60) + -.294(-.4530) = .685.$$

The adjusted R^2 value for the MCA theoretical regression model approach is

$$R^2_{Adj} = R^2 - \frac{p}{N-p-1}(1-R^2) = .685 - .15(.315) = .685 - .047 = .638.$$

The *F test* for the significance of the R^2 value is

$$F = \frac{R^2/p}{(1-R^2)/N-p-1} = \frac{.685/3}{(1-.685)/20} = \frac{.228}{.00157} = 14.52$$

The *effect size* is

$$R^2 - [p/(N-1)] = .685 - (3/23) = .685 - .130 = .554.$$

This is a large effect size. The 95% *confidence interval* around $R^2 = .685$ using the R^2 CI program is (.33, .83).

The results indicate that a patient's age, severity of illness, and level of anxiety make up a statistically significant set of predictors of a patient's satisfaction level. There is a large effect size and the confidence interval reveals the range of R^2 values one can expect in conducting a regression analysis on another sample of data. The negative standardized regression coefficients indicate that as patient age, severity of illness, and anxiety increase, patient satisfaction decreases.

6.7 MODEL MODIFICATION

The theoretical regression model included a set of three independent explanatory variables, which resulted in a statistically significant $R^2 = .685$. This implies that 69% of the patient satisfaction level score variance is explained by knowledge of a patient's age, severity of illness, and level of anxiety. The regression analysis, however, indicated that the standardized regression weight for *Var2* was not statistically significant ($t = -0.433$, $p = .670$).

The theoretical regression model would therefore be modified to produce a two-variable regression equation, thus allowing for the *F* test of the difference between the two regression analysis R^2 values. We repeat the steps for the regression analysis, but this time only including *Var1* and *Var3* in the analysis. The results for the regression equation with these two variables are:

```
                      ANALYSIS OF VARIANCE
                      ====================
```

Source	SUM OF SQUARES	DF	MEAN SQUARES	F	p
REGRESSION	4408.945	2	2204.473	22.485	0.000
RESIDUAL	2058.888	21	98.042		
TOTAL	6467.833	23			

```
Dependent Variable =    VAR4
Number of obs.     =      24
Multiple R         =  0.8256
R-square           =  0.6817
Adjusted R-square  =  0.6514
F(  2,     21)     = 22.4849
Prob > F           =  0.0000
Std. Error of Est. =  9.9016
Durbin-Watson Stat.=  1.6707
```

```
=======REGRESSION COEFFICIENTS=======
```

VARIABLE	B	ORDINARY STD. ERROR	HETERO-SCEDASTIC STD. ERROR	BETA	t	p
Intercept	149.091	16.213	13.802		10.802	0.000
VAR1	-1.234	0.220	0.196	-0.704	-6.309	0.000
VAR3	-16.826	6.664	5.221	-0.317	-3.223	0.004

The F test for the difference between the two models is

$$F = \frac{(R_F^2 - R_R^2)/(p_1 - p_2)}{(1 - R_F^2)/N - p_1 - 1} = \frac{(.6854 - .6817)/(3 - 2)}{(1 - .6854)/24 - 3 - 1} = \frac{.0037}{.0157} = .23.$$

The F test for the difference in the two R^2 values is nonsignificant, indicating that dropping *Var2* does not affect the explanation of a patient's satisfaction level ($R^2 = .6854$ vs. $R^2 = .6817$). We therefore use the more parsimonious two-variable regression model [68% of the variance in a patient's satisfaction level is explained by knowledge of a patient's age and level of anxiety, i.e., 68% of $(16.769)^2 = 191.22$].

Because the R^2 value is not 1.0 (perfect explanation or prediction), additional variables could be added if more recent research indicated that another variable was important in a patient's satisfaction level, for example, the number of psychological assessment visits. Obviously, more variables can be added in the model modification process, but a theoretical basis should be established by the researcher for the additional variables.

6.8 SUMMARY

This chapter illustrated the important statistics to report when conducting a regression analysis. We found that the model fit statistics in chapter 5 do not apply because regression models are saturated just-identified models. However, the selection of independent variables in the regression model (model specification) and the subsequent regression model modification are key issues not easily resolved without a good sound theoretical justification.

The selection of a set of independent variables and the subsequent regression model modification are important issues in multiple regression. How does a researcher determine the best set of independent variables for explanation or prediction? It is highly recommended that a regression model be based on some theoretical framework that can be used to guide the decision of what variables to include. Model specification consists in determining what variables to include in the model and which variables are independent or dependent. A systematic determination of the most important set of variables can then be accomplished by setting the partial regression weight of a single variable to zero, thus testing full and restricted models for a difference in the R^2 values (F test). This approach and other alternative methods were presented by Darlington (1968).

In multiple regression, the selection of a wrong set of variables can yield erroneous and inflated R^2 values. The process of determining which set of variables yields the best prediction, given time, cost, and staffing, is often problematic because several methods and criteria are available to choose from. Recent methodological reviews have indicated that stepwise methods are not preferred, and that an *all-possible-subset* approach is recommended (Huberty, 1989; Thompson, Smith, Miller, & Thomson, 1991). In addition, the Mallows C_P statistic is advocated by some rather than R^2 for selecting the best set of predictors (Mallows, 1966; Schumacker, 1994; Zuccaro, 1992). Overall, which variables are included in a regression equation will determine the validity of the model.

Because multiple regression techniques have been shown to be robust to violations of assumptions (Bohrnstedt & Carter, 1971) and applicable to contrast coding, dichotomous coding, ordinal coding (Lyons, 1971), and criterion scaling (Schumacker, 1993), they have been used in a variety of research designs. In fact, multiple regression equations can be used to address several different types of research questions. The model specification issue, however, is paramount in specifying a valid multiple regression model.

There are other issues related to using the regression method, namely variable measurement error and the additive nature of the equation. These two issues are described next.

Measurement Error

The issue of unreliable variable measurements and their effect on multiple regression has been previously discussed (Cleary, 1969; Cochran, 1968; Fuller & Hidiroglou, 1978; Subkoviak & Levin, 1977; Sutcliffe, 1958). A recommended solution is to multiply the dependent variable reliability and/or average of the independent variable reliabilities by the R^2 value (Cochran, 1968, 1970). The basic equation using only the reliability of the dependent variable is

$$\hat{R}^2_{y.123} = R^2_{y.123} r_{yy},$$

or, including the dependent variable reliability and the average of the independent variable reliabilities,

$$\hat{R}^2_{y.123} = R^2_{y.123} r_{yy} \bar{r}_{xx}.$$

This is not always possible if reliabilities of the dependent and independent variables are unknown. This correction to R^2 for measurement error (unreliability) has intuitive appeal given the definition of classical reliability, namely the proportion of true score variance accounted for given the observed scores. In our previous example, $R^2 = .68$. If the dependent variable reliability is .80, then only 54% of the variance in patient's satisfaction level is true variance, rather than 68%. Similarly, if the average of the two independent variable reliabilities was .90, then multiplying .68 by .80 by .90 yields only 49% variance as true variance. Obviously, unreliable variables (measurement error) can have a dramatic effect on statistics. Werts, Rock, Linn, and Jöreskog (1976) examined correlations, variances, covariances, and regression weights with and without measurement error and developed a program to correct the regression weights for attenuation. Our basic concern is that unreliable measured variables coupled with a potential misspecified model do not represent theory well.

The impact of measurement error on statistical analyses is not new, but is often forgotten by researchers. Fuller (1987) extensively covered structural equation modeling, and especially extended regression analysis to the case where the variables were measured with error. Cochran (1968) studied four different aspects of how measurement error affected statistics: (a) types of mathematical models, (b) standard techniques of analysis that take measurement error into account, (c) effect of errors of measurement in producing bias and reduced precision and what remedial procedures are available, and (d) techniques for studying error of measurement. Cochran (1970) also studied the effects of measurement error on the squared multiple correlation coefficient.

The validity and reliability issues in measurement have traditionally been handled by first examining the validity and reliability of scores on instruments used in a particular research design. Given an acceptable level of score validity and reliability, the scores are then used in a statistical analysis. The traditional statistical analysis of these scores using multiple regression, however, did not adjust for measurement error, so it is not surprising that an approach was developed to incorporate measurement error adjustments into statistical analyses (Loehlin, 1992).

Additive Equation

The multiple regression equation is by definition additive ($Y = X_1 + X_2$) and thus does not permit any other relationships among the variables to be specified. This limits the potential for variables to have direct, indirect, and total effects on each other as described in chapter 7 on path analysis. In fact, a researcher's interest should not be with the Pearson product–moment correlations, but rather with partial or part correlations that reflect the unique additive contribution of each variable, that is, standardized regression weights. Even with this emphasis, the basic problem is that variables are typically added to a regression model, a process that functions ideally only if all independent variables are highly correlated with the dependent variable and uncorrelated among themselves. Path models, in contrast, provide theoretically meaningful relationships in a manner not restricted to an additive model (Schumacker, 1991).

Multiple regression as a general data-analytic technique is widely accepted and used by educational researchers and behavioral scientists. Multiple regression methods basically determine the overall contribution of a set of observed variables to explanation or prediction, test full and restricted models for the significant contribution of a variable in a model, and delineate the best subset of multiple independent predictors. Multiple regression equations also permit the use of nominal, ordinal, effect, contrast, or polynomial coded variables (Pedhazur, 1982; Pedhazur & Schmelkin, 1992). The multiple regression approach, however, is not robust to measurement error and model misspecification (Bohrnstedt & Carter, 1971) and gives an additive model rather than a relational model; this accounts for the important role played by path analysis.

APPENDIX: COMPUTER PROGRAMS

Amos Regression Analysis

In Amos, you will need to first draw Fig. 6.1 making sure you use the variable names in the *chatter.sav* file (**Amos will not run the analysis if the variable names in the data file do not match the variable names in the diagram**) and fixing the error path to unity. Draw the diagram, then select **File** from the tool bar menu and click on **Data Files** in the pull-down menu to associate the SPSS data file *chatter.sav* with the diagram. You can check to make sure the variable names match by clicking on *View Data*.

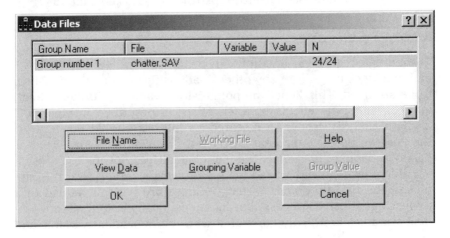

Next, we must fix the error path to unity by selecting **View/Set** and selecting **Object Properties**. Enter a 1 (one) for the error path. This is necessary because we cannot estimate both the error path and the error variance. The next step is to decide what *Output* properties you want reported. Once again select **View/Set**, but this time click on *Analysis Properties* and select the *Output* tab. We choose standardized estimates and squared multiple correlations. Close the dialog to continue.

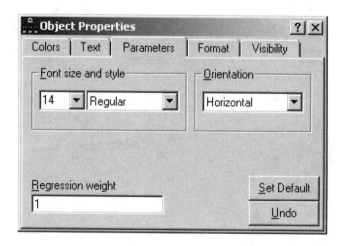

To run the regression analysis, select **Model-Fit** from the tool bar menu and click on **Calculate Estimates**. You can practice these same basic steps in the *Amos 4.0 User's Guide*, pp. 13 through 34, using the Hamilton data file, where SAT scores are predicted by education and income data from 21 different states.

The Amos regression output looks like

```
Computation of degrees of freedom

    Number of distinct sample moments = 10
    Number of distinct parameters to be estimated = 10
    Degrees of freedom = 10 - 10 = 0

Regression Weights
```

	Estimate	S.E.	C.R.	P
var4 <-- var1	-1.153	0.260	-4.430	0.000
var4 <-- var2	-0.265	0.507	-0.523	0.601
var4 <-- var3	-15.594	6.754	-2.309	0.021

```
Covariances

                     Estimate    S.E.      C.R.      P

    var2 <--> var3     0.615     0.354     1.738     0.082
    var1 <--> var2    29.365    11.707     2.508     0.012
    var1 <--> var3     0.560     0.614     0.911     0.362

Variances

                     Estimate    S.E.      C.R.      P

             var1     87.576    25.825     3.391     0.001
             var2     26.151     7.712     3.391     0.001
             var3      0.096     0.028     3.391     0.001
            error     84.778    25.000     3.391     0.001
```

LISREL–PRELIS and LISREL–SIMPLIS
Regression Analysis

In LISREL–SIMPLIS, we select **File**, select *Import* **External Data in Other Formats**, select file type *SPSS for Windows (*.sav)*, and find the folder where we saved the file *chatter.sav*.

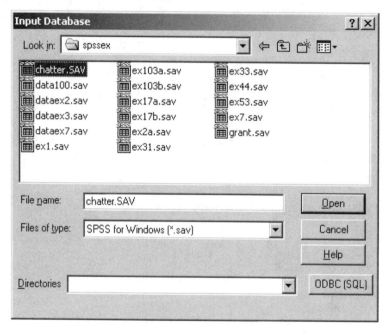

Click on **Open** and save it as a PRELIS system file (*chatter.psf*).

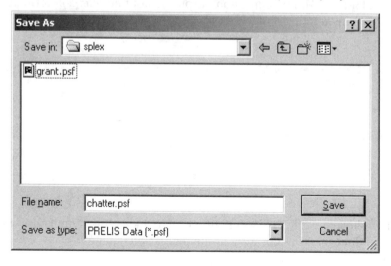

Click on **File**, then **New**, and select *Syntax Only.*

A SIMPLIS command file window appears; then enter the following SIMPLIS commands:

LISREL–SIMPLIS Program (No Intercept Term):

```
Regression Analysis using EQS data file
Raw Data from file chatter.psf
Equation: VAR4 = VAR1 VAR2 VAR3
Path Diagram
End of Problem
```

The LISREL–SIMPLIS regression output without an *intercept* term in the regression equation looks like

```
VAR4 = - 1.15*VAR1 - 0.27*VAR2 - 15.59*VAR3, Errorvar.= 88.46 , R² = 0.69
        (0.28)         (0.54)        (7.24)                  (27.97)
       -4.13          -0.49         -2.15                     3.16

Degrees of Freedom = 0
Minimum Fit Function Chi-Square = 0.0 (P = 1.00)
Normal Theory Weighted Least Squares Chi-Square = 0.00 (P = 1.00)

The Model is Saturated, the Fit is Perfect!
```

The following LISREL–SIMPLIS program includes the command **CONST** to produce an intercept term in the regression equation:

LISREL–SIMPLIS Program (Intercept Term):

```
Regression Analysis using EQS data file
Raw Data from file chatter.psf
Equation: VAR4 = VAR1 VAR2 VAR3 CONST
Path Diagram
End of Problem
```

The LISREL–SIMPLIS output looks like

```
VAR4 = 156.62 - 1.15*VAR1 - 0.27*VAR2 - 15.59*VAR3, Errorvar. = 88.46, R² = 0.69
      (22.61)  (0.28)     (0.54)      (7.24)                       (27.97)
       6.93    -4.13       -0.49       -2.15                         3.16


Degrees of Freedom = 0
Minimum Fit Function Chi-Square = 0.0 (P = 1.00)
Normal Theory Weighted Least Squares Chi-Square = 0.00 (P = 1.00)

The Model is Saturated, the Fit is Perfect!
```

In LISREL–SIMPLIS (Jöreskog & Sörbom, 1993), the program **EX1A. SPL** computes the regression equation *without* an intercept term, whereas the program **EX1B. SPL** computes the regression equation *with* an intercept term. In general, if you include sample means, then an intercept term is included in the equation. These examples are further explained in Jöreskog and Sörbom (1993, pp. 1–6).

EXERCISES

1. Analyze the regression model in LISREL–SIMPLIS using the covariance matrix below with a sample size of 23 as described in Jöreskog and Sörbom (1993, pp. 3–6). The theoretical regression model specifies that the dependent variable, gross national product (GNP), is predicted by labor, capital, and time (three independent variables).

   Covariance matrix

GNP	4256.530			
Labor	449.016	52.984		
Capitol	1535.097	139.449	1114.447	
Time	537.482	53.291	170.024	73.747

2. Is there an alternative regression model that predicts GNP better? Report the F, effect size, and confidence interval for the model.
3. Use the Amos specification search procedure to answer question. The regression model as diagramed in Amos is shown in Fig. 6.2.

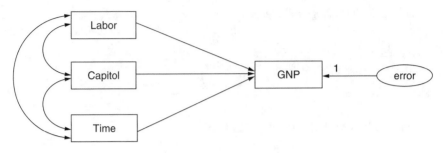

FIG. 6.2.   Amos GNP model.

REFERENCES

Bashaw, W. L., & Findley, W. G. (1968). *Symposium on general linear model approach to the analysis of experimental data in educational research* (Project No. 7-8096). Washington, DC: U.S. Department of Health, Education, and Welfare.

Bentler, P. M., & Wu, E. J. C. (1995). *EQS for Windows user's guide*. Encino, CA: Multivariate Software.

Bentler, P. M., & Wu, E. J. C. (2002). *EQS 6 for Windows user's guide*. Encino, CA: Multivariate Software.

Bohrnstedt, G. W., & Carter, T. M. (1971). Robustness in regression analysis. In H. L. Costner (Ed.), *Sociological methodology* (pp. 118–146). San Francisco: Jossey–Bass.

Chatterjee, S., & Yilmaz, M. (1992). A review of regression diagnostics for behavioral research. *Applied Psychological Measurement, 16*, 209–227.

Cleary, T. A. (1969). Error of measurement and the power of a statistical test. *British Journal of Mathematical and Statistical Psychology, 22*, 49–55.

Cochran, W. G. (1968). Errors of measurement in statistics. *Technometrics, 10*, 637–666.

Cochran, W. G. (1970). Some effects of errors of measurement on multiple correlation. *Journal of the American Statistical Association, 65*, 22–34.

Cohen, J. (1988). *Statistical power analysis for the behavioral sciences* (2nd ed.). Hillsdale, NJ: Lawrence Erlbaum Associates, Inc.

Cohen, J., & Cohen, P. (1975). *Applied multiple regression/correlation analysis for the behavioral sciences*. Hillsdale, NJ: Lawrence Erlbaum Associates, Inc.

Cumming, G., & Finch, S. (2001). A primer on the understanding, use and calculation of confidence intervals that are based on central and noncentral distributions. *Educational and Psychological Measurement, 61*, 532–574.

Darlington, R. B. (1968). Multiple regression in psychological research and practice. *Psychological Bulletin, 69*, 161–182.

Draper, N. R., & Smith, H. (1966). *Applied regression analysis*. New York: Wiley.

Edwards, A. L. (1979). *Multiple regression and the analysis of variance and covariance*. San Francisco: Freeman.

Fuller, W. A. (1987). *Measurement error models*. New York: Wiley.

Fuller, W. A., & Hidiroglou, M. A. (1978). Regression estimates after correcting for attentuation. *Journal of the American Statistical Association, 73*, 99–104.

Hinkle, D. E., Wiersma, W., & Jurs, S. G. (2003). *Applied statistics for the behavioral sciences* (5th ed.). Boston, MA: Houghton Mifflin.

Houston, S. R., & Bolding, J. T., Jr. (1974). Part, partial, and multiple correlation in commonality analysis of multiple regression models. *Multiple Linear Regression Viewpoints, 5*, 36–40.

Huberty, C. J. (1989). Problems with stepwise methods—Better alternatives. In B. Thompson (Ed.), *Advances in social science methodology* (Vol. 1, pp. 43–70). Greenwich, CT: JAI.

Huberty, C. J. (2003). Multiple correlation versus multiple regression. *Educational and Psychological Measurement, 63,* 271–278.

Jöreskog, K., & Sörbom, D. (1993). *LISREL8: Structural equation modeling with the SIMPLIS command language.* Chicago, IL: Scientific Software International.

Kerlinger, F. N., & Pedhazur, E. J. (1973). *Multiple regression in behavioral research.* New York: Holt, Rinehart, & Winston.

Loehlin, J. C. (1992). *Latent variable models: An introduction to factor, path, and structural analysis* (2nd ed.). Mahwah, NJ: Lawrence Erlbaum Associates, Inc.

Lomax, R. G. (2001). *Statistical concepts: A second course for education and the behavioral sciences* (2nd ed.). Mahwah, NJ: Lawrence Erlbaum Associates, Inc.

Lyons, M. (1971). Techniques for using ordinal measures in regression and path analysis. In H. L. Costner (Ed.), *Sociological methodology* (pp. 147–171). San Francisco: Jossey–Bass.

Mallows, C. L. (1966, March). *Choosing a subset regression.* Paper presented at the Joint Meetings of the American Statistical Association, Los Angeles.

McNeil, K. A., Kelly, F. J., & McNeil, J. T. (1975). *Testing research hypotheses using multiple linear regression.* Carbondale: Southern Illinois University Press.

Newman, I. (1988). *There is no such thing as multivariate analysis: All analyses are univariate.* President's address at Mid-Western Educational Research Association, October 15, 1988, Chicago.

Pedhazur, E. J. (1982). *Multiple regression in behavioral research: Explanation and prediction* (2nd ed.). New York: Holt, Rinehart, & Winston.

Pedhazur, E. J., & Schmelkin, L. P. (1992). *Measurement, design, and analysis: An integrated approach.* Hillsdale, NJ: Lawrence Erlbaum Associates, Inc.

Schumacker, R. E. (1991). Relationship between multiple regression, path, factor, and LISREL analyses. *Multiple Linear Regression Viewpoints, 18,* 28–46.

Schumacker, R. E. (1993). Teaching ordinal and criterion scaling in multiple regression. *Multiple Linear Regression Viewpoints, 20,* 25–31.

Schumacker, R. E. (1994). A comparison of the Mallows C_P and principal component regression criteria for best model selection. *Multiple Linear Regression Viewpoints, 21,* 12–22.

Smithson, M. (2001). Correct confidence intervals for various regression effect sizes and parameters: The importance of noncentral distributions in computing intervals. *Educational and Psychological Measurement, 61,* 605–632.

Steiger, J. H., & Fouladi, T. (1992). R2: A computer program for interval estimation, power calculation, and hypothesis testing for the squared multiple correlation. *Behavior Research Methods, Instruments, and Computers, 4,* 581–582.

Steiger, J. H., & Fouladi, T. (1997). Noncentrality interval estimation and the evaluation of statistical models. In L. Harlow, S. Mulaik, & J. H. Steiger (Eds.), *What if there were no significance tests?* (pp. 222–257). Mahwah, NJ: Lawrence Erlbaum Associates, Inc.

Subkoviak, M. J., & Levin, J. R. (1977). Fallibility of measurement and the power of a statistical test. *Journal of Educational Measurement, 14,* 47–52.

Sutcliffe, J. P. (1958). Error of measurement and the sensitivity of a test of significance. *Psychometrika, 23,* 9–17.

Thompson, B., Smith, Q. W., Miller, L. M., & Thomson, W. A. (1991, January). *Stepwise methods lead to bad interpretations: Better alternatives.* Paper presented at the annual meeting of the Southwest Educational Research Association, San Antonio, TX.

Tracz, S. M., Brown, R., & Kopriva, R. (1991). Considerations, issues, and comparisons in variable selection and interpretation in multiple regression. *Multiple Linear Regression Viewpoints, 18,* 55–66.

Werts, C. E., Rock, D. A., Linn, R. L., & Jöreskog, K. G. (1976). Comparison of correlations, variances, covariances, and regression weights with or without measurement error. *Psychological Bulletin, 83,* 1007–1013.

Zuccaro, C. (1992). Mallows C_P statistic and model selection in multiple linear regression. *Journal of the Market Research Society, 34,* 163–172.

ANSWERS TO EXERCISES

1. The following LISREL–SIMPLIS program is run to analyze the theoretical regression model for predicting gross national product (GNP) from knowledge of labor, capital, and time:

```
Regression of GNP
Observed variables: GNP LABOR CAPITAL TIME
Covariance Matrix:
  4256.530
   449.016      52.984
  1535.097     139.449    1114.447
   537.482      53.291     170.024     73.747
Sample Size: 23
Equation: GNP = LABOR CAPITAL TIME
Number of Decimals = 3
Path Diagram
End of Problem
```

2. Results indicate that GNP is significantly predicted ($R^2 = .997$). The three independent variables are statistically significant, as indicated by $t > 1.96$ for each parameter estimate, so no model modification is necessary:

```
GNP = 3.819*LABOR + 0.322*CAPITAL + 3.786*TIME, Errorvar.= 12.470, R² = 0.997
     (0.216)        (0.0305)         (0.186)                  (4.046)
     17.698         10.540           20.351                    3.082
```

The F test for statistical significance, effect size, and confidence interval for the theoretical regression model is

$$F = \frac{R^2/p}{(1-R^2)/N - p - 1} = \frac{.997/3}{(1-.997)/19} = \frac{.332}{.0001} = 332.$$

The effect size is $R^2 - [p/(N-1)] = .997 - (3/22) = .86$. The 95% confidence interval is .991 to .998. The F test indicates a statistically significant R^2, the effect size is large, and the confidence interval for R^2 indicates that R^2 values will probably vary between .991 and .998 if the regression model is run with another sample of data.

3. In Amos, you must first create the special SPSS variance–covariance file *gnp.sav*, draw the Amos regression model, and then run the initial regression model estimates by

selecting **Model Fit**, and then **Calculate Estimates**. To conduct the Amos specification search, click on **Model Fit** and then **Specification Search**. Click on the dashed arrow (- - - -) and then highlight the three paths in the regression model. Click on ▶ to run all possible regression models. You can view each regression equation by selecting the regression model and then clicking on the solid monitor icon (■). The results for the regression weights are

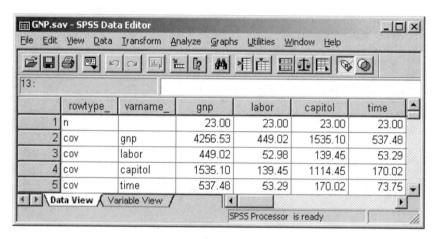

			Estimate	SE	CR	p
GNP	⟵	Labor	3.819	0.201	19.044	0.000
GNP	⟵	Capitol	0.322	0.028	11.341	0.000
GNP	⟵	Time	3.786	0.173	21.899	0.000

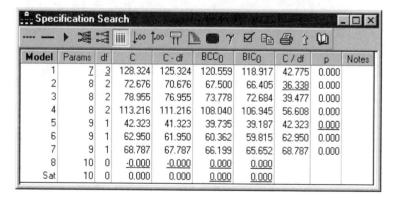

Model	Params	df	C	C - df	BCC$_0$	BIC$_0$	C / df	p	Notes
1	7	3	128.324	125.324	120.559	118.917	42.775	0.000	
2	8	2	72.676	70.676	67.500	66.405	36.338	0.000	
3	8	2	78.955	76.955	73.778	72.684	39.477	0.000	
4	8	2	113.216	111.216	108.040	106.945	56.608	0.000	
5	9	1	42.323	41.323	39.735	39.187	42.323	0.000	
6	9	1	62.950	61.950	60.362	59.815	62.950	0.000	
7	9	1	68.787	67.787	66.199	65.652	68.787	0.000	
8	10	0	-0.000	-0.000	0.000	0.000			
Sat	10	0	0.000	0.000	0.000	0.000			

Because there are three predictor variables, eight regression models were created and analyzed ($2^3 = 8$ regression models). The regression models are listed in the following order as determined by clicking on the solid monitor icon (■) and viewing which path(s) are displayed:

Model 1: Null model (no regression paths)
Model 2: Time
Model 3: Labor
Model 4: Capital
Model 5: Time and labor
Model 6: Capital and time
Model 7: Labor and capital
Model 8: Labor, capital, and time
Sat: Saturated model (all paths included in model)

An examination of the model fit criteria indicates that the best regression model is Model 8, the model with the three predictor variables, because all model fit criteria are underlined.

7

PATH MODELS

Key Concepts

Path model diagrams
Direct effects, indirect effects, and correlated independent variables
Path (structure) coefficients and standardized partial regression coefficients
Decomposition of correlations
Original and reproduced correlation coefficients
Full versus limited information function
Residual and standardized residual matrix

In this chapter we consider path models, the logical extension of multiple regression models. Although path analysis still uses models involving multiple observed variables, there may be any number of independent and dependent variables and any number of equations. Thus, as we shall see, path models require the analysis of several multiple regression equations using observed variables.

Sewall Wright is credited with the development of path analysis as a method for studying the direct and indirect effects of variables (Wright, 1921, 1934, 1960). Path analysis is not actually a method for discovering causes; rather, it tests theoretical relationships, which unfortunately has been termed *causal modeling* (a term that will not be used in this book). A specified path model might actually establish causal relationships among two variables when:

1. Temporal ordering of variables exists.
2. Covariation or correlation is present among variables.
3. Other causes are controlled for.

Obviously, a theoretical model that is tested over time (i.e., longitudinal research) and manipulates certain variables to assess the change in other variables (i.e., experimental research) more closely approaches our idea of causation. In the social sciences, the issue of causation is not as straightforward as in the physical sciences, but it has the potential to be modeled. This chapter begins with an example path model, then proceeds with sections on model specification, model identification, model estimation, model testing, and model modification.

7.1 AN EXAMPLE

We begin with a path model that will be followed throughout the chapter. McDonald and Clelland (1984) collected data on the sentiment toward unions of Southern nonunion textile laborers ($n = 173$). This example is treated in the LISREL manual (Jöreskog & Sörbom, 1993, pp. 12–15, example 3) and is included in the data files of the LISREL program and is also utilized by Bollen (1989, pp. 82–83). The model consists of five observed variables; the independent variables are the number of years worked in the textile mill (actually log of years, denoted simply as years) and worker age (age); the dependent variables are deference to managers (deference), support for labor activism (support), and sentiment toward unions (sentiment). The original variance–covariance matrix, reproduced (model-implied) variance–covariance matrix, residual matrix, and standardized residual matrix are given in Table 7.1. The path diagram of the theoretical proposed model is shown in Fig. 7.1.

TABLE 7.1
Original, Reproduced, Residual, and Standardized Residual Covariance
Matrices for the Initial Union Sentiment Model

Original matrix: Variable	Deference	Support	Sentiment	Years	Age
Deference	14.610				
Support	−5.250	11.017			
Sentiment	−8.057	11.087	31.971		
Years	−0.482	0.677	1.559	1.021	
Age	−18.857	17.861	28.250	7.139	215.662
Reproduced matrix:					
Deference	14.610				
Support	−1.562	11.017			
Sentiment	−5.045	10.210	30.534		
Years	−0.624	0.591	1.517	1.021	
Age	−18.857	17.861	25.427	7.139	215.662
Residual matrix:					
Deference	0.000				
Support	−3.688	0.000			
Sentiment	−3.012	0.877	1.437		
Years	0.142	0.086	0.042	0.000	
Age	0.000	0.000	2.823	0.000	0.000
Standardized residual matrix:					
Deference	0.000				
Support	−4.325	0.000			
Sentiment	−3.991	3.385	3.196		
Years	0.581	0.409	0.225	0.000	
Age	0.000	0.000	0.715	0.000	0.000

Path models adhere to certain common drawing conventions that are utilized in SEM models (Fig. 7.2). The observed variables are enclosed by boxes or rectangles. Lines directed from one observed variable to another observed variable denotes *direct effects*, in other words, the direct influence of one variable on another. For example, it is hypothesized that age has a direct influence on support, meaning that the age of the worker may influence an increase (or decrease) in support. A curved, double-headed line between two independent observed variables indicates *covariance*, that is, they are correlated. In this example, age and years are specified to be correlated. The rationale for such relationships is that there are influences on both of these independent variables outside of the path model. Because these influences are not studied in this path model, it is reasonable to expect that the same unmeasured variables may influence both independent variables.

Finally, each dependent variable has an error term, denoted by a circle around the error term pointing toward the proper dependent variable. Take deference, for example. Some portion of deference will be predicted

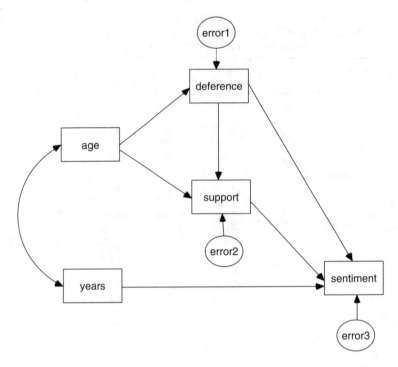

FIG. 7.1.   Union sentiment model (Amos diagram).

or explained by age and some will not. The unexplained part will become the error term, which indicates other possible influences on deference that are not contained in this model.

7.2   MODEL SPECIFICATION

Model specification is necessary in examining multiple variable relation-ships in path models, just as in the case of multiple regression. Many different relationships among a set of variables can be postulated with many different parameters being estimated. In a simple three-variable model, for example, many possible path models can be postulated on the basis of different hypothesized relationships among those three vari-ables.

For example, in Fig. 7.3a, 7.3b, and 7.3c, we see three different path models where X1 influences X2. In Model (a), X1 influences X2, which in turn influences Y. Here X2 serves as a mediator between X1 and Y. In Model (b), an additional path is drawn from X1 to Y, such that X1 has both a direct and an indirect effect upon Y. The direct effect is that

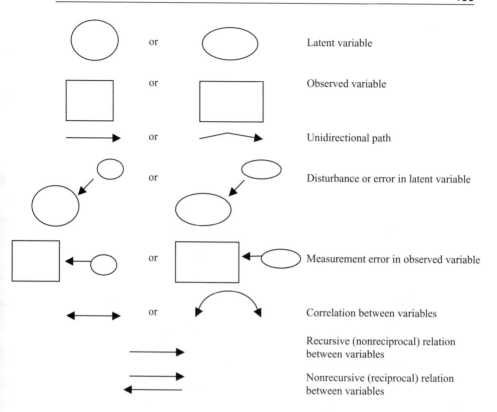

⬭	or ⬭	Latent variable
▢	or ▢	Observed variable
→	or ⌒→	Unidirectional path
	or	Disturbance or error in latent variable
	or	Measurement error in observed variable
↔	or ⌢	Correlation between variables
→		Recursive (nonreciprocal) relation between variables
⇄		Nonrecursive (reciprocal) relation between variables

FIG. 7.2. Common path diagram symbols.

X1 has a direct influence on Y (i.e., no variables intervene between X1 and Y), whereas the indirect effect is that X1 influences Y through X2, that is, X2 intervenes between X1 and Y. In Model (c), X1 influences both X2 and Y; however, X2 and Y are not related. If we were to switch X1 and X2 around, this would generate three more plausible path models.

Other path models are also possible. For example, in Fig. 7.4a and Fig. 7.4b, X1 does not influence X2. In Model (a), X1 and X2 influence Y, but are uncorrelated. In Model (b), X1 and X2 influence Y and are correlated.

How can one determine which model is correct? This is known as model specification and shows the important role that theory plays in justifying a hypothesized model. Path analysis does not provide a way to specify the model, but rather estimates the effects among the variables once the model has been specified *a priori* by the researcher on the basis of theoretical considerations. For this reason, model specification is a critical part of SEM modeling.

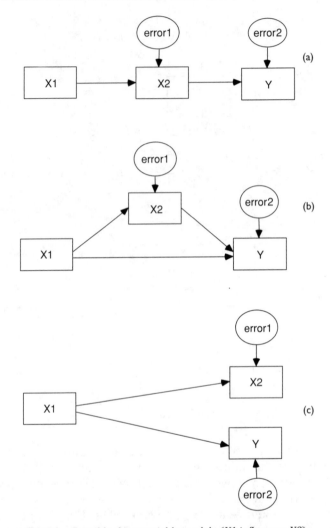

FIG. 7.3. Possible three-variable models (X1 influences X2).

Path coefficients in path models take on the values of a Pearson product–moment correlation coefficient r and/or a standardized partial regression coefficient β (Wolfle, 1977). For example, in the path model of Fig. 7.4b, the path coefficients p as depicted by arrows from X1 to Y and X2 to Y, respectively, are

$$\beta_1 = p_{Y1}$$
$$\beta_2 = p_{Y2}$$

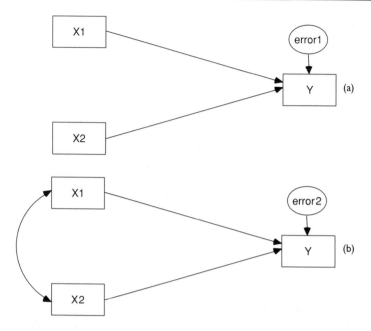

FIG. 7.4. Possible three-variable models (X1 does not influence X2).

and the curved arrow between X1 and X2 is denoted as

$$r_{X1,X2} = p_{12}.$$

The variable relationships, once specified in standard score form, become standardized partial regression coefficients. In multiple regression, a dependent variable is regressed in a single analysis on all of the independent variables. In path analysis, one or more multiple regression analyses are performed depending on the variable relationships specified in the path model. Path coefficients are therefore computed only on the basis of the particular set of independent variables that lead to the dependent variable under consideration. In the path model of Fig. 7.4b, two standardized partial regression coefficients (path coefficients) are computed, p_{Y1} and p_{Y2}. The curved arrow represents the covariance or correlation between the two independent variables p_{12} in predicting the dependent variable.

For the union sentiment model, the model specification is as follows. There are three structural equations in the model, one for each of the three dependent variables deference, support, and sentiment. In terms of variable names, the structural equations are as follows.

$$\text{deference} = \text{age} + \text{error1}$$
$$\text{support} = \text{age} + \text{deference} + \text{error2}$$
$$\text{sentiment} = \text{years} + \text{support} + \text{deference} + \text{error3}.$$

Substantive information from prior research suggested that those six paths be included in the specified model and that other possible paths (e.g., from age to sentiment) not be included. This model includes direct effects (e.g., from age to support), indirect effects (e.g., from age to support through deference) and correlated independent variables (i.e., age and years). Obviously, many possible path models could be specified for this set of observed variables.

7.3   MODEL IDENTIFICATION

Once a particular path model has been specified, then the next concern is whether the model is identified. In structural equation modeling, it is crucial that the researcher resolve the *identification problem* prior to the estimation of parameters. The general notion of identification was discussed in chapter 4. Here we consider model identification in the context of path models, and, in particular, for our union sentiment example.

As described in chapter 4, for the identification problem, we ask the following question: On the basis of the sample data contained in the sample covariance matrix S and the theoretical model implied by the population covariance matrix Σ, can a unique set of parameter estimates be found? For the union sentiment model, we would like to know if the path between age and deference is identified, as one example parameter.

In the union sentiment model, some parameters are fixed and others are free. An example of a fixed parameter is that there is no path or direct relationship between age and sentiment. An example of a free parameter is that there is a path or direct relationship between age and deference.

In determining identification, first consider the order condition. Here the number of free parameters to be estimated must be less than or equal to the number of distinct values in the matrix S. A count of the free parameters is as follows:

Six path coefficients
Three equation error variances

One correlation among the independent variables
Two independent variable variances

Thus there is a total of 12 free parameters that we wish to estimate. The number of distinct values in the matrix S is equal to

$$[p(p+1)]/2 = [5(5+1)]/2 = 15,$$

where p is the number of observed variables in the matrix. Thus the number of distinct values in the sample matrix S, 15, is indeed greater than the number of free parameters, 12. However, this is only a necessary condition and does not guarantee that the model is identified. According to the order condition, the model is also overidentified because there are more values in S than parameters to be estimated.

Although the order condition is easy to assess, other sufficient conditions are not (e.g., the rank condition). The sufficient conditions require us to algebraically determine whether each parameter in the model can be estimated from the covariance matrix S. According to the Amos, EQS, and LISREL computer programs, which check on identification through the rank test and/or information matrix, the union sentiment model is identified.

7.4 MODEL ESTIMATION

Once the identification problem has been addressed, then the next step is to estimate the parameters of the specified model(s). In this section, we consider the following topics: decomposition of the correlation matrix, parameter estimation in general, and parameter estimation of the union sentiment model.

In path analysis, the traditional method of intuitively thinking about estimation is to decompose the correlation matrix. This harkens back to the early days of path analysis in the 1960s when sociologists like Arthur S. Goldberger and Otis D. Duncan were rediscovering and further developing the procedure. The decomposition idea is that the original correlation matrix can be completely reproduced if all of the effects are accounted for in a specified path model. In other words, if all of the possible unidirectional (or recursive) paths are included in a path model, then the observed correlation matrix can be completely reproduced from the obtained standardized estimates of the model.

For example, take the model in Fig. 7.4b. Here there are two direct effects, from X1 to Y and from X2 to Y. There are also indirect effects due to the correlation between X1 and X2. In other words, X1 indirectly influences Y through X2, and also X2 indirectly affects Y through X1. The correlations among these three variables can be decomposed as follows:

$$r_{12} = \underset{\text{(CO)}}{p_{12}} \tag{1}$$

$$r_{Y1} = \underset{\text{(DE)}}{p_{Y1}} + \underset{\text{(IE)}}{p_{12}p_{Y2}} \tag{2}$$

$$r_{Y2} = \underset{\text{(DE)}}{p_{Y2}} + \underset{\text{(IE)}}{p_{12}p_{Y1}}, \tag{3}$$

where the r values are the actual observed correlations and the p values are the path coefficients (standardized estimates). Thus, in Equation (1) the correlation between X1 and X2 is simply a function of the path, or correlation relationship (CO), between X1 and X2. In equation (2), the correlation between X1 and Y is a function of (a) the direct effect (DE) of X1 on Y and (b) the indirect effect (IE) of X1 on Y through X2 [i.e., the product of the path or correlation between X1 and X2 (p_{12}) and the path or direct effect from X2 to Y (p_{Y2})]. Equation (3) is similar to Equation (2) except that X1 and X2 are reversed; there is both a direct effect and an indirect effect.

Let us illustrate how this works with an actual set of correlations. The observed correlations are as follows: $r_{12} = .224, r_{Y1} = .507$, and $r_{Y2} = .480$. The specified path model and correlation matrix were run in Amos, EQS, and LISREL; all yielded the same results. The path coefficients and the complete reproduction of the correlations are.

$$r_{12} = \underset{\text{(CO)}}{p_{12}} = .224 \tag{4}$$

$$r_{Y1} = \underset{\text{(DE)}}{p_{Y1}} + \underset{\text{(IE)}}{p_{12}p_{Y2}} = .421 + (.224)(.386) = .507 \tag{5}$$

$$r_{Y2} = \underset{\text{(DE)}}{p_{Y2}} + \underset{\text{(IE)}}{p_{12}p_{Y1}} = .386 + (.224)(.421) = .480. \tag{6}$$

Here the original correlations are completely reproduced by the model because all of the effects are accounted for, direct, indirect, and correlated. If one of the possible paths had been left out of the model (e.g., p_{12}), then the correlations would not be completely reproduced. Thus the correlation decomposition approach is a nice conceptual way of thinking about the estimation process in path analysis. For further details on the correlation decomposition approach, we highly recommend Duncan (1975).

In chapter 4 we presented the problem of estimation in general. Parameters can be estimated by different estimation procedures, such as maximum likelihood (ML), generalized least squares (GLS), and unweighted least squares (ULS), which are all unstandardized types of estimates, as well as by standardized estimates (the path coefficients previously described in this chapter are standardized estimates). In addition to different choices for estimation of the parameter estimates, *full* versus *limited* information estimation functions are invoked based on the software chosen for the analysis. *Full information* estimation computes all of the parameters (path coefficients) simultaneously, whereas *limited information* estimation computes parameters for each equation separately. The parameters (path coefficients) estimated in structural equation modeling software use full information estimation and therefore differ from parameter estimates computed in SPSS or SAS, where each regression equation in the path model is estimated separately (limited information estimation). In limited information estimation, the regression weights are determined uniquely in each separate regression equation to meet the least squares criterion of minimized residuals.

In the union sentiment example we see the estimation process at work. In order to utilize the model modification procedures discussed in section 7.6, we have slightly changed the model specification in Fig. 7.1. We remove the path from deference to support and call this the initial model. We evaluate this initial model, and hope, through the model modification process, to return to the model as originally specified in Fig. 7.1. The misspecified model was run using Amos, EQS, and LISREL with all outputs yielding the same results (EQS and LISREL computer programs are given at the end of the chapter).

The maximum likelihood estimates for the initial model are shown in the first column of Table 7.2. All of the parameter estimates are significantly different from zero, $p < .05$ (the fit of the model is discussed next in sec. 7.5). Age has a direct effect on both deference and support; deference has direct effects on support and sentiment; years has a direct effect on sentiment; and support has a direct effect on sentiment. Numerous indirect effects are also part of the path model, such as the indirect effect of deference on sentiment through support. Age and years also have a significant covariance, indicating that one or more common unmeasured variables influence both age and years.

7.5 MODEL TESTING

An important result of any path analysis is the fit of the specified model. If the fit of the path model is good, then the specified model has been

TABLE 7.2
Maximum Likelihood Estimates* and Selected Fit Indices for the Initial
and Final Union Sentiment Models

	Initial model	Final model
Paths		
Age → deference	−.09	−.09
Age → support	0.08	.06
Deference → support	—	−.28
Years → sentiment	0.86	0.86
Deference → sentiment	−.22	−.22
Support → sentiment	0.85	0.85
Equation error variances		
Deference	12.96	12.96
Support	9.54	8.49
Sentiment	26.95	19.45
Independent variables		
Variance (age)	1.02	1.02
Variance (years)	215.66	215.66
Covariance (age, years)	7.14	7.14
Selected fit indices		
χ^2	19.96	1.25
df	4	3
p value	.00	.74
RMSEA	.15	.00
SRMR	.087	.015
GFI	.96	1.00

*All estimates significantly different from zero ($p < .05$).

supported by the sample data. If the fit of the path model is not so good, then the specified model has not been supported by the sample data and the researcher typically attempts to respecify the path model to achieve a better fit (as described in sect. 7.6). As discussed in chapter 5, there is a wide variety of model fit indices available to the applied SEM researcher.

For purposes of the union sentiment example, we include a few model fit indices at the bottom of Table 7.2. For the initial path model, the χ^2 statistic, technically a measure of badness of fit, is equal to 19.96, with four degrees of freedom, and a p value less than .01. Because the p value is very small and the χ^2 value is nowhere near the number of degrees of freedom, then according to this measure of fit, the initial path model is poorly specified. The root-mean-square error of approximation (RMSEA) is equal to .15, somewhat below the acceptable level for this measure of fit, RMSEA < .05. The standardized root-mean-square residual (SRMR) is .087, also below the usual acceptable level of fit, SRMR < .05. Finally, the goodness-of-fit index (GFI) is .96 for the initial model, which is at an acceptable level for this measure of fit (criterion GFI > .95). Across this particular set of model fit indices, the conclusion is that the data-to-model fit is approaching a reasonable level, but that some model modifications might allow us to achieve a better fit between the sample variance–covariance matrix S and the reproduced (implied) variance–covariance matrix Σ, given the path model. Model modification is considered in the next section.

7.6   MODEL MODIFICATION

The final step in structural equation modeling is model modification. In other words, if the fit of the model is less than satisfactory, then the researcher typically performs a *specification search* to seek a better fitting model. As described in chapters 4 and 5, several different procedures can be used to assist in this search. One may eliminate parameters that are not significantly different from zero and/or include additional parameters to arrive at a modified model. For the elimination of parameters, the most commonly used procedures are (a) to compare the t statistic for each parameter to a tabled t value (e.g., $t > 1.96$) to determine statistical significance and (b) to use the Wald statistic (W) (similar interpretation as the t statistic).

For the inclusion of additional parameters, the most commonly used techniques are (a) the modification index (MI) (the expected value that χ^2 would decrease by if such a parameter were to be included; large values indicate potentially useful parameters), (b) the expected parameter change statistic (EPC) (the approximate value of the new parameter), and (3) the Lagrange multiplier statistic (LM) (similar interpretation as the modification index).

In addition, an examination of the residual matrix, or the more useful standardized residual matrix, often gives clues as to which original covariances or correlations are not well accounted for by the model. Recall that the residual matrix is the difference between the observed variance–covariance S and the reproduced variance–covariance matrix Σ. Large residuals indicate values not well accounted for by the model. Standardized residuals are like z scores, in that large values (e.g., greater than 1.96 or 2.58) indicate that a particular relationship is not well accounted for by the path model (Table A.1, p. 473).

For the initial union sentiment example, the original, reproduced (model-implied), residual, and standardized residual covariance matrices are given in Table 7.1. Here we see that the largest standardized residual is between deference and support (-4.325). The t and Wald statistics do not suggest the elimination of any existing parameters from the initial path model, because every parameter is statistically different from zero. With regard to the possible inclusion of new parameters, the largest modification index is for the path from deference to support (MI = 18.707). For that potential path, the estimated value, or expected parameter change (EPC), is −0.285.

Taken together, these statistics indicate that there is something mis-specified between deference and support that is not captured by the initial model. Specifically, a path is recommended from deference to support. This is precisely the path from the originally specified path model that we intentionally eliminated from the initial path model. Thus the specification search was successful here in returning us to the origi-nal model. The ML estimates and selected fit indices for the final model, where this path is now included, are shown in the second column of Table 7.2. All of the parameters included are significantly different from zero ($p < .05$), all of the fit indices now indicate an acceptable level of fit, and a second specification search did not result in any further rec-ommended changes. Thus we deem this as the final path model for the union sentiment example.

7.7 SUMMARY

This chapter presented a detailed discussion of path models. We be-gan by presenting the union sentiment path model and then followed it throughout the chapter. We moved on to model specification, first with several possible three-variable models, and then with the union senti-ment model. The next step was to consider model identification of the union sentiment model for both the order and rank conditions. Next we discussed estimation. Here we introduced the notion of correlation de-composition with a three-variable model and the difference between full versus limited estimation functions, and then considered the full infor-mation estimation results for the union sentiment model. Model testing of the altered union sentiment model was the next step, where the fit of the model was deemed not acceptable. The altered (initial) model was then modified through the addition of one path, thereby arriving at a final, best-fitting theoretical model.

We learned that path models permit theoretically meaningful rela-tionships among variables that cannot be specified in a single additive regression model. However, the issue of measurement error in observed variables is not treated in either regression or path models (Wolfle, 1979). The next chapter helps us understand how measurement error is ad-dressed in structural equation modeling.

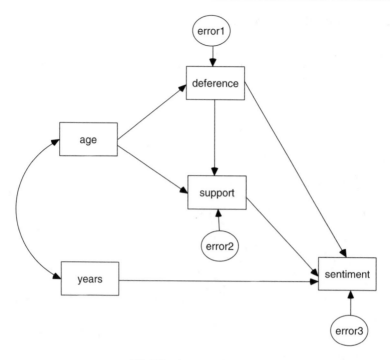

FIG. 7.5. Amos path model.

APPENDIX: COMPUTER PROGRAMS (FIG. 7.5)

EQS Path Model Program

```
/TITLE
 Union Sentiment of Textile Workers
/SPECIFICATIONS
 CASES=173; VARIABLES = 5; ME = ML;
/LABELS
 V1=Deference;V2=Support;V3=Sentiment;V4=Years;V5=Age;
/EQUATIONS
 V1 = *V5 + 1E1;
 V2 = *V1 + *V5 + 1E2;
 V3 = *V1 + *V2 + *V4 + 1E3;
/VARIANCES
 V4 TO V5=1*;E1 TO E3=1*;
/COVARIANCES
 V4,V5=1*;
/MATRIX
    14.610
    -5.250    11.017
    -8.057    11.087    31.971
    -0.482     0.677     1.559    1.021
   -18.857    17.861    28.250    7.139    215.662
/END
```

LISREL–SIMPLIS Path Model Program

```
Union Sentiment of Textile Workers
Observed Variables: Deference Support Sentiment Years Age
Covariance matrix:
    14.610
    -5.250      11.017
    -8.057      11.087      31.971
    -0.482       0.677       1.559      1.021
   -18.857      17.861      28.250      7.139     215.662
Sample Size: 173
Relationships
   Deference = Age
   Support = Age Deference
   Sentiment = Years Deference Support
Print Residuals
Options: ND=3
Path Diagram
End of problem
```

EXERCISE

Analyze the following achievement path model (Fig. 7.6) using an SEM computer software program. The path model indicates that income and ability predict aspire; and income, ability, and aspire predict achieve.

Sample size = 100

Observed variables: quantitative achievement (Ach), family income (Inc), quantitative ability (Abl), educational aspiration (Asp)

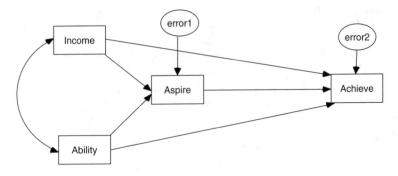

FIG. 7.6.   Achievement path model.

Variance–covariance matrix:

	Ach	Inc	Abl	Asp
Ach	25.500			
Inc	20.500	38.100		
Abl	22.480	24.200	42.750	
Asp	16.275	13.600	13.500	17.000

Regression equations:
  Asp = Inc Abl
  Ach = Inc Abl Asp

REFERENCES

Bollen, K. A. (1989). *Structural equations with latent variables*. New York: Wiley.
Duncan, O. D. (1975). *Introduction to structural equation models*. New York: Academic.
Jöreskog, K. G., & Sörbom, D. (1993). *LISREL 8: Structural equation modeling with the SIMPLIS command language*. Chicago: Scientific Software International.
McDonald, J. A., & Clelland, D. A. (1984). Textile workers and union sentiment. *Social Forces, 63*, 502–521.
Wolfle, L. M. (1977). An introduction to path analysis. *Multiple Linear Regression Viewpoints, 8*, 36–61.
Wolfle, L. M. (1979). Unmeasured variables in path analysis. *Multiple Linear Regression Viewpoints, 9*, 20–56.
Wright, S. (1921). Correlation and causation. *Journal of Agricultural Research, 20*, 557–585.
Wright, S. (1934). The method of path coefficients. *Annals of Mathematical Statistics, 5*, 161–215.
Wright, S. (1960). Path coefficients and path regression: Alternative or complementary concepts? *Biometrics, 16*, 189–202.

ANSWER TO EXERCISE

EQS Path Analysis Program

```
TITLE
 Chapter 7 Exercise
/SPECIFICATIONS
 CASES=100; VARIABLES = 4; ME = ML; MATRIX=COVARIANCE;
 ANALYSIS=COVARIANCE;
/LABELS
 V1=Achieve;V2=Income;V3=Ability;V4=Aspire;
/EQUATIONS
 V4 = 1V2 + 1V3 + E1;
 V1 = 1V2 + 1V3 + 1V4 + E2;
```

```
/VARIANCES
 E1 = 1*;
 E2 = 1*;
/COVARIANCES
 V2,V3=1*;
/MATRIX
 25.500
 20.500 38.100
 22.480 24.200 42.750
 16.275 13.600 13.500 17.000
/PRINT
 FIT=ALL;
 TABLE=EQUATION;
/END
```

EQS Computer Results

```
PARAMETER ESTIMATES APPEAR IN ORDER,
NO SPECIAL PROBLEMS WERE ENCOUNTERED DURING OPTIMIZATION.

STANDARDIZED SOLUTION:                                      R-SQUARED
 ASPIRE  = V4 = .415 V2 +  .440 V3 +               .645 E1    .584
 ACHIEVE = V1 = .231 V2 +  .244 V3 +  .556 V4 +    .387 E2    .850

CORRELATIONS AMONG INDEPENDENT VARIABLES:
 V3 -ABILITY AND V2 -INCOME                                   .600
```

8

CONFIRMATORY FACTOR MODELS

Chapter Outline

Key Concepts

Confirmatory factor analysis versus exploratory factor analysis
Latent variables (factors) and observed variables
Factor loadings and measurement errors
Correlated factors and correlated measurement errors
Reliability, Cronbach alpha versus composite

In chapter 7 we examined path models as the logical extension of multiple regression models (chap. 6) to show more meaningful theoretical relationships among our observed variables. Thus, the two previous chapters dealt exclusively with models involving observed variables. In this chapter we begin developing models involving factors or latent variables and continue latent variable modeling throughout the remainder of the book. As we see in this chapter, a major limitation of models involving only observed variables is that measurement error is not taken into account. The use of observed variables in statistics assumes that all of the measured variables are perfectly valid and reliable, which is unlikely in many applications. For example, father's educational level is not a perfect measure of a socioeconomic status factor and amount of exercise per week is not a perfect measure of a fitness factor.

The validity and reliability issues in measurement have traditionally been handled by first examining the validity and reliability of scores on instruments used in a particular context. Given an acceptable level of score validity and reliability, the scores are then used in a statistical analysis. The traditional statistical analysis of these scores (i.e., multiple regression and path analysis), however, does not adjust for measurement error. The impact of measurement error has been investigated and found to have serious consequences, for example, biased parameter estimates (Cochran, 1968; Fuller, 1987). Structural equation modeling software that accounts for the measurement error of variables was therefore developed, that is, factor analysis creates latent variables used in structural equation modeling.

Factor analysis attempts to determine which sets of observed variables share common variance–covariance characteristics that define theoretical constructs or factors (latent variables). Factor analysis presumes that some factors, which are smaller in number than the number of observed variables, are responsible for the shared variance–covariance among the observed variables. In practice, one collects data on observed variables and uses factor-analytic techniques to either *confirm* that a set of variables defines those constructs or factors or *explore* which variables relate to factors. In exploratory factor model approaches, we seek to find a model that fits the data, so we specify different alternative models, hoping to ultimately find a model that fits the data and has theoretical support. This is the primary rationale for exploratory factor analysis (EFA). In confirmatory factor model approaches, we seek to statistically test the significance of a hypothesized factor model, that is, whether the sample data confirm the model. Additional samples of data that fit the model further confirm the validity of the hypothesized model. This is the primary rationale for confirmatory factor analysis (CFA).

In CFA, the researcher specifies a certain number of factors, which factors are correlated, and which observed variables measure each factor. In EFA, the researcher explores how many factors there are, whether the factors are correlated, and which observed variables appear to best measure each factor. In CFA, the researcher has an *a priori*-specified theoretical model; in EFA, the researcher does not have such a model. In this chapter we only concern ourselves with confirmatory factor models because the focus of the book is on testing theoretical models; exploratory factor analysis is covered in depth elsewhere (Comrey & Lee, 1992; Gorsuch, 1983). This chapter begins with a classic example of a confirmatory factor model and then proceeds with sections on model specification, model identification, model estimation, model testing, and model modification.

8.1   AN EXAMPLE

We use a classic confirmatory factor model that will be followed throughout the chapter. Holzinger and Swineford (1939) collected data on 26 psychological tests from seventh- and eighth-grade children in a suburban school district of Chicago. Over the years, different subsamples of the children and different subsets of the variables of this data set have been analyzed and presented in various multivariate statistics textbooks (e.g., Harmon, 1976; Gorsuch, 1983) and SEM software program guides (e.g., Amos: Arbuckle & Wothke, 1999, example 8, *grnt_fem.sav*; EQS: Bentler & Wu, 2002, *holza.ess*; and LISREL: Jöreskog & Sörbom, 1993, example 5, *EX5A.spl* and *EX5B.spl*).

The raw data analyzed here are from Example 8 (*grnt_fem.sav*) from Amos and consist of data for 73 girls from the Grant–White School. The confirmatory factor model consists of the following six observed variables: Visual Perception, Cubes, Lozenges, Paragraph Comprehension, Sentence Completion, and Word Meaning. The first three measures were hypothesized to measure a spatial ability factor and the second three measures were believed to measure a verbal ability factor.

The Amos diagram of the proposed theoretical model is shown in Fig. 8.1. The drawing conventions utilized in Fig. 8.1 were described in chapter 7. The observed variables are enclosed by boxes or rectangles, and the factors (latent variables) are enclosed by circles or ellipses (i.e., spatial and verbal). Conceptually, a factor represents the common variation among a set of observed variables. Thus, for example, the spatial ability factor represents the common variation among the Visual Perception, Cubes, and Lozenges tasks. Lines directed from a factor to a particular observed variable denote the relationship between that factor

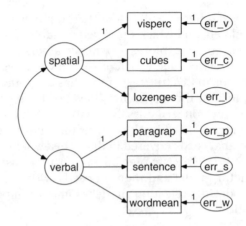

FIG. 8.1.   Confirmatory factor model (Amos diagram) (Holzinger & Swineford, 1939).

and that measure. These relationships are interpreted as factor loadings, with the square of the factor loading called the commonality estimate of the variable.

The measurement errors are enclosed by smaller ellipses and indicate that some portion of each observed variable is measuring something other than the hypothesized factor. Conceptually a measurement error represents the unique variation for a particular observed variable beyond the variation due to the relevant factor. For example, the Cubes task is largely a measure of spatial ability, but may also be assessing other characteristics such as a different common factor or unreliability. To assess measurement error, the variance of each measurement error is estimated (known as measurement error variance).

A curved, double-headed line between two factors indicates that they have shared variance or are correlated. In this example, spatial and verbal ability are specified to covary. The rationale for this particular factor correlation is that spatial ability and verbal ability are related to a more general ability factor and thus should be related. Correlated factors by definition have pattern and structure coefficients, but structure coefficients may be not be included in the confirmatory factor model for theoretical reasons (i.e., set to zero).

A curved, double-headed line between two measurement error variances indicates that they also have shared variance or are correlated. Although not shown in this example, two measurement error variances could be correlated if they shared something in common such as (a) a common method variance (i.e., the method of measurement is the same, such as the same scale of measurement, or they are both part of the same global instrument) or (b) the same measure is being used at different points in time (e.g., the Cubes task is measured at Time 1 and at Time 2).

8.2 MODEL SPECIFICATION

Model specification is a necessary first step in analyzing a confirmatory factor model, just as it was for multiple regression and path models. Many different relationships among a set of variables can be postulated with many different parameters being estimated. Thus, many different factor models can be postulated on the basis of different hypothesized relationships between the observed variables and the factors.

In our example, there are six observed variables with two different latent variables (factors) being hypothesized. Given this, many different confirmatory factor models are possible. First, each observed variable can load on either one or both factors. Thus, there could be anywhere from 6 to 12 total factor loadings. Second, the two factors may or may not be correlated. Third, there may or may not be correlations or covariances among the measurement error variances. Thus, there could be anywhere from 0 to 15 total correlated measurement error variances.

From the model in Fig. 8.1, each observed variable is hypothesized to measure only a single factor (i.e., three observed variables per factor with six factor loadings), the factors are believed to be correlated (a single factor correlation), and the measurement error variances are not related (zero correlated measurement errors). Obviously, we could have hypothesized a single factor with six observed variables or six factors each with a single observed variable. When all of this is taken into account, many different confirmatory factor models are possible with these six observed variables.

How does the researcher determine which factor model is correct? We already know that *model specification* is important in this process and shows the role that theory plays in justifying a specified model. Confirmatory factor analysis does not tell us how to specify the model, but rather estimates the parameters of the model once the model has been specified *a priori* by the researcher on the basis of theoretical knowledge. Once again, model specification is the hardest part of structural equation modeling.

For our confirmatory factor model, the model specification is diagrammed in Fig. 8.1 and contains six measurement equations in the model, one for each of the six observed variables. In terms of the variable names from Fig. 8.1, the measurement equations are as follows:

visperc = function of spatial + err_v
cubes = function of spatial + err_c
lozenges = function of spatial + err_l
paragrap = function of verbal + err_p
sentence = function of verbal + err_s
wordmean = function of verbal + err_w

Substantive theory and prior research suggest that these particular variable factor loadings should be included in the specified model (the functions being the factor loadings), and that other possible factor loadings (e.g., visperc loading on verbal) should not be included in the factor model. Our factor model includes six factor loadings and six measurement error variances, one for each observed variable, and one correlation between the factors Spatial Ability and Verbal Ability with zero correlated measurement errors.

8.3 MODEL IDENTIFICATION

Once a confirmatory factor model has been specified, the next step is to determine whether the model is identified. As stated in chapter 4, it is crucial that the researcher solve the *identification problem* prior to the estimation of parameters. We first need to revisit model identification in the context of confirmatory factor models and then specifically for our confirmatory factor model example.

In model identification (see chap. 4) we ask the following question: On the basis of the sample data contained in the sample variance–covariance matrix S, and the theoretical model implied by the population variance–covariance matrix Σ, can a unique set of parameter estimates be found? For our confirmatory factor model, we would like to know if the factor loading of Visual Perceptions on Spatial Ability, Cubes on Spatial Ability, Lozenges on Spatial Ability, Paragraph Comprehension on Verbal Ability, Sentence Completion on Verbal Ability, and Word Meaning on Verbal Ability are identified (can be estimated). In our confirmatory factor model, some parameters are fixed and others are free. An example of a *fixed parameter* is that Cubes is not allowed to load on Verbal Ability. An example of a *free parameter* is that Cubes is allowed to load on Spatial Ability.

In determining identification, we first assess the *order condition*. The number of free parameters to be estimated must be less than or equal to the number of distinct values in the matrix S. A count of the free parameters is as follows:

Six factor loadings
Six measurement error variances
Zero measurement error covariances or correlations
One correlation among the latent variables

Thus there is a total of 13 free parameters that we wish to estimate. The number of distinct values in the matrix S is equal to

$$p(p + 1)/2 = 6(6 + 1)/2 = 21,$$

where p is the number of variables in the sample variance–covariance matrix. The number of values in S, 21, is greater than the number of free parameters, 13, with the difference being the degrees of freedom for the specified model, $df = 21 - 13 = 8$. In Amos, we can easily check the order condition by clicking on the **DF** icon in the toolkit. However, this is only a necessary condition and does not guarantee that the model is identified. According to the order condition, this model is *overidentified* because there are more values in S than parameters to be estimated, that is, our degrees of freedom is positive rather than zero (*just-identified*) or negative (*underidentified*).

Although the order condition is easy to assess, other sufficient conditions are not (e.g., the rank condition). The sufficient conditions require us to algebraically determine whether each parameter in the model can be estimated from the covariance matrix S. According to Amos, EQS, and LISREL computer programs, which check on identification through the rank test and/or information matrix, the confirmatory factor model is identified.

8.4 MODEL ESTIMATION

After the identification problem has been addressed, the next step is to estimate the parameters of the specified factor model. In this section we consider the following topics: decomposition of the correlation (or variance–covariance) matrix, parameter estimation in general, and parameter estimation for the confirmatory factor model.

In factor analysis the traditional method of intuitively thinking about estimation is to decompose the correlation (or variance–covariance) matrix. The decomposition notion is that the original correlation (or variance–covariance) matrix can be completely reproduced if all of the relations among the observed variables are accounted for by the factors in a properly specified factor model. If the model is not properly specified, then the original correlation (or variance–covariance) matrix will not be completely reproduced. This would occur if (a) the number of factors were not correct, (b) the wrong factor loadings were specified, (c) the factor correlations were not correctly specified, and/or (d) the measurement error variances were not specified correctly.

In chapter 4, under model estimation, we considered the statistical aspects of estimation. We learned, for example, that parameters can be estimated by different estimation procedures, such as maximum likelihood (ML), generalized least squares (GLS), and unweighted least squares (ULS), and reported as unstandardized estimates or standardized estimates. We analyzed our confirmatory factor model using maximum likelihood estimation with standardized factor loadings to report our statistical estimates of the free parameters.

To better understand model modification in section 8.6, we have slightly changed the confirmatory factor model specified in Fig. 8.1. We forced the observed variable Lozenges to have a factor loading on the latent variable Verbal Ability instead of on the latent variable Spatial Ability. This misspecified model is shown in Fig. 8.2. We therefore use the confirmatory factor model in Fig. 8.2 as our first model and through the model modification process in section 8.6 discover the best-fitting model to be the confirmatory factor model specified in Fig. 8.1.

The misspecified model (Fig. 8.2) was run using Amos. The EQS and LISREL computer programs are given at the end of the chapter and the original sample variance–covariance matrix S is given at the top of Table 8.1 along with the reproduced matrix (model implied), residual matrix, and standardized residual matrix output from Amos for the misspecified model in Fig. 8.2.

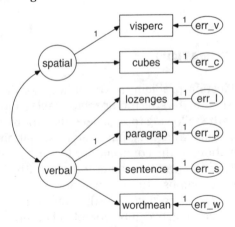

FIG. 8.2. Misspecified confirmatory factor model (Amos diagram) (Holzinger & Swineford, 1939).

TABLE 8.1

Original, Reproduced, Residual, and Standardized Residual Covariance
Matrices for the Misspecified Holzinger–Swineford Model (Amos Results)

Original matrix:

Variable	VisPerc	Cubes	Lozenges	Paragraph	Sentence	WordMean
VisPerc	47.830					
Cubes	15.138	20.547				
Lozenges	26.900	17.658	62.584			
Paragraph	8.451	3.402	9.182	12.690		
Sentence	12.820	4.092	13.411	13.042	25.547	
WordMean	13.218	6.935	24.280	22.020	29.246	69.208

Reproduced matrix:

Variable	VisPerc	Cubes	Lozenges	Paragraph	Sentence	WordMean
VisPerc	47.830					
Cubes	15.138	20.547				
Lozenges	9.343	4.031	62.584			
Paragraph	8.440	3.565	10.436	12.690		
Sentence	11.396	4.794	14.065	13.068	25.547	
WordMean	18.832	7.970	23.405	21.727	29.248	69.208

Residual matrix:

Variable	VisPerc	Cubes	Lozenges	Paragraph	Sentence	WordMean
VisPerc	0.000					
Cubes	0.000	0.000				
Lozenges	**17.557**	**13.627**	0.000			
Paragraph	0.001	−0.163	−1.254	0.000		
Sentence	1.424	−0.702	−0.654	−0.026	0.000	
WordMean	−5.614	−1.035	0.875	0.293	−0.002	0.000

Standardized residual matrix:

Variable	VisPerc	Cubes	Lozenges	Paragraph	Sentence	WordMean
VisPerc	0.000					
Cubes	0.000	0.000				
Lozenges	**2.723**	**3.251**	0.000			
Paragraph	0.000	−0.085	−0.359	0.000		
Sentence	0.333	−0.258	−0.133	−0.010	0.000	
WordMean	−0.797	−0.231	0.108	0.069	0.000	0.000

In Amos, we first draw Fig. 8.2, then select the data file and calculate
the estimates. Deleting the path from Lozenges to Verbal Ability and
redrawing the path from Lozenges to Spatial Ability creates Fig. 8.1. We
can now run the analysis to obtain estimates for the CFA model in Fig. 8.1.
The first column in Table 8.2 contains the maximum likelihood estimates
for the misspecified model (Fig. 8.2) and the second column contains the
maximum likelihood estimates for the original model (Fig. 8.1).

TABLE 8.2
Maximum Likelihood Estimates and Selected Fit Indices for the
Misspecified and Original Holzinger–Swineford Models in AMOS

	Misspecified model	Original model
Factor loadings		
Visual Perception	.866	.703
Cubes	.558	.654
Lozenges	.875	.736
Paragraph Comprehension	.830	.880
Sentence Completion	.838	.827
Word Meaning	.424	.841
Measurement error variances		
Visual Perception	11.813	23.873
Cubes	13.961	11.602
Lozenges	50.624	28.275
Paragraph Comprehension	2.943	2.834
Sentence Completion	7.841	7.967
Word Meaning	20.313	19.925
Correlation of independent variables		
Spatial, Verbal	0.453	0.487
Selected fit indices		
χ^2	26.367	7.853
df	8	8
p value	.001	.448
RMSEA	.179	.00
GFI	.905	.966

The parameter estimates are found to be significantly different from zero ($p < .05$), except for the measurement error variance of the observed variable Lozenges. The fit of the model is discussed in section 8.5. Of greatest importance is that all of the factor loadings are significantly different from zero and have the expected sign, that is, positive loadings.

8.5 MODEL TESTING

An important part of the estimation process in analyzing confirmatory factor models is to fit the sample variance–covariance data to the specified model. If the fit of the model is good, then the specified model is supported by the sample data. If the fit of the model is not so good, then the specified model is not supported by the sample data and the researcher typically has to respecify the model to achieve a better fit (see sect. 8.6). As previously in chapter 5, there is a wide variety of model fit indices available to the applied SEM researcher.

For our confirmatory factor model example, we report a few fit indices at the bottom of Table 8.2. For the misspecified model, the χ^2 statistic (technically a measure of badness of fit) is equal to 26.367, with eight degrees of freedom, and a p value less than .001. The chi-square statistic is significant, so the specified confirmatory factor model is not supported by the sample variance–covariance data. Another interpretation is that because the χ^2 value is not close to the number of degrees of freedom, the fit of the initial model is poor. Recall that the noncentrality parameter (NCP) is calculated as $\chi^2 - df$, has an expected value of 0 (NCP = 0; perfect fit), and is used in computing several of the model fit indices. A third criterion is that the root-mean-square error of approximation (RMSEA) is equal to .179, higher than the acceptable level of model fit (RMSEA < .05). Finally, the goodness-of-fit index (GFI) is .905 for the misspecified model, which is below the acceptable range of model fit (GFI > .95). Across this particular set of model fit indices, the conclusion is that the model fit is reasonable, but that some model modification might allow us to achieve a better sample variance–covariance to confirmatory factor model fit. Determining what change(s) to make to our confirmatory factor model to achieve a better fitting model is considered in the next section.

8.6   MODEL MODIFICATION

A final step in structural equation modeling is to consider changes to a specified model that has poor model fit indices, that is, model modification. This typically occurs when a researcher discovers that the fit of the specified model is less than satisfactory. The researcher typically performs a *specification search* to find a better fitting model. As discussed in chapter 4, several different procedures can be used to assist in this specification search. One may eliminate parameters that are not significantly different from zero and/or include additional parameters to arrive at a modified model. For the elimination of parameters, the most commonly used procedures are (a) to compare the t statistic for each parameter to a tabled t value (e.g., 1.96) to determine statistical significance and (b) to use the Wald statistic W (similar interpretation as the t statistic).

For the inclusion of additional parameters, the most commonly used techniques are (a) the modification index (MI) (the expected value that χ^2 would decrease by if such a parameter were to be included; large values indicate potentially useful parameters), (b) the expected parameter change statistic (EPC) (the approximate value of the new parameter), and (c) the Lagrange multiplier statistic (LM) (similar interpretation as the modification index).

In addition, an examination of the residual matrix, or the more useful standardized residual matrix, often gives clues as to which original covariances or correlations are not well accounted for by the model.

The residual matrix is the difference between the observed covariance or correlation matrix S and the reproduced covariance or correlation matrix Σ. Large residuals indicate values not well accounted for by the model. Standardized residuals are like z scores in that large values (values greater than 1.96 or 2.58) indicate that a particular relationship is not well accounted for by the model.

For the misspecified confirmatory factor model in Fig. 8.2, the original, reproduced, residual, and standardized residual covariance matrices are given in Table 8.1. Here we see that the two largest residuals are for the Lozenges observed variable (17.557 and 13.627) and the standardized residuals (2.723 and 3.251) are greater than $t = 2.58$. In Amos we requested modification indexes from **Analysis Properties**, and results indicate that the Lozenges variable should load on the Spatial Ability factor to reduce error ($MI = 14.709$) with an expected parameter change (EPC) of 20.366.

The large residuals for Lozenges, the statistically significant standardized residuals, the modification index, and the expected change values indicate that there is something wrong with the Lozenges observed variable that is not captured by the misspecified model. Specifically, the factor loading for Lozenges should be on the Spatial Ability factor rather than the Verbal Ability factor. This is precisely the factor loading from the original specified model in Fig. 8.1 that we intentionally eliminated to illustrate the model modification process. Thus, the use of several modification criteria in our specification search was successful in bringing us back to the original model in Fig. 8.1.

The ML estimates and selected model fit indices for the final model (Fig. 8.1), where the modification in the Lozenges factor loading is now included, are shown in the second column of Table 8.2. All of the parameters included are significantly different from zero ($p < .05$), and all of the fit indices now indicate an acceptable level of fit with no additional model modifications indicated. Thus we consider this to be the final best-fitting confirmatory factor model with our sample variance–covariance data. The EQS and LISREL–SIMPLIS programs are provided at the end of the chapter for this model analysis. Note that programs are slightly different in EQS, which uses a variance–covariance matrix, and LISREL–SIMPLIS, which uses a correlation matrix with standard deviations.

8.7 RELIABILITY OF A FACTOR MODEL

Another important issue in factor analysis is the reliability of a set of items that defines a construct (factor). A total score for a variable is obtained by summing the responses to a set of items. This total score from the sum of the items, or composite score, is often referred to as a scale score. The *Cronbach alpha* reliability coefficient is traditionally reported in statistics as the measure of internal consistency of responses across the set of items. Raykov (1997), however, postulated that the reliability of a composite score (scale score) when estimated under the assumption of a single common factor model is a better true indictor of internal consistency than the *Cronbach alpha* internal consistency coefficient.

EQS implements Raykov's approach (Bentler & Wu, 2002) to determining the reliability of a set of items based on a factor model (previously output in chap. 5). The Holzinger and Swineford data in the EQS system file *holza.ess* are used for the reliability analysis. In EQS, we select **File**, then **Open**, and find the *holza.ess* data set. Next, select **Build EQS** and select **Title/Specification**, and the *EQS Model Specification* dialog box appears. Simply click **OK** to proceed.

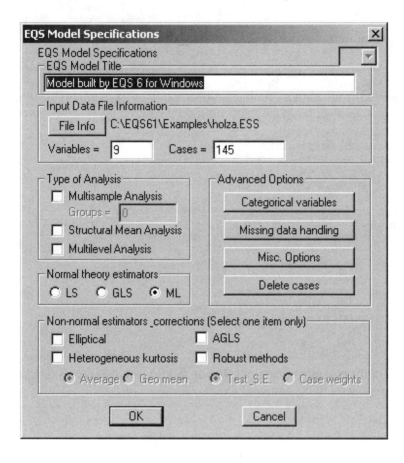

Now click on **Build EQS** again and select **Reliability** from the pull-down menu. Select the first four variables for a single common factor model and click **OK**. The *holza.eqx* model file is now ready to be run. Select **Build EQS** and click on *Run EQS*.

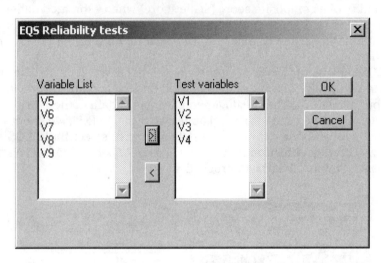

The results indicate a Cronbach alpha of .56, but a reliability coefficient of .62 when defined as a single common factor:

```
RELIABILITY COEFFICIENTS
------------------------
  CRONBACH'S ALPHA                         = .555
  RELIABILITY COEFFICIENT RHO              = .616
  GREATEST LOWER BOUND RELIABILITY                               = .653
  BENTLER'S DIMENSION-FREE LOWER BOUND RELIABILITY               = .653
  SHAPIRO'S LOWER BOUND RELIABILITY FOR A WEIGHTED COMPOSITE = .645
  WEIGHTS THAT ACHIEVE SHAPIRO'S LOWER BOUND:
      V1        V2        V3        V4
     .550      .347      .634      .419


MAXIMAL INTERNAL CONSISTENCY RELIABILITY              = .635
MAXIMAL RELIABILITY CAN BE OBTAINED BY WEIGHTING THE
VARIABLES AS FOLLOWS:
   V1        V2        V3        V4
   .085      .054      .091      .166
```

Reliability of a single common factor model can also be accomplished by running an EQS command file:

```
/TITLE
Raykov Reliability Coefficient in EQS 6 for Windows
```

```
/SPECIFICATIONS
DATA='C:\EQS61\Examples\holza.ESS';
VARIABLES=9; CASES=145;
METHOD=ML; ANALYSIS=COVARIANCE; MATRIX=RAW;
/LABELS
V1=V1; V2=V2; V3=V3; V4=V4; V5=V5;
V6=V6; V7=V7; V8=V8; V9=V9;
/RELIABILITY
SCALE=V1,V2,V3,V4;
/PRINT
FIT=ALL;
TABLE=EQUATION;
/END
```

8.8   SUMMARY

This chapter discussed confirmatory factor models using the five basic building blocks from model specification through model modification. We began by analyzing a confirmatory factor model that was misspecified (Fig. 8.2) and interpreted a few model fit criteria where the fit of the model was deemed not acceptable. We then used model modification criteria to modify the model, which yielded the confirmatory factor model in Fig. 8.1. This confirmatory factor model was deemed to be our final best-fitting model. This final best-fitting model can be further validated by testing the confirmatory factor model with other samples of data. We concluded the chapter by showing how the reliability of a set of scores can be computed for a single factor in EQS.

APPENDIX: COMPUTER PROGRAMS

EQS Confirmatory Factor Model Program

```
/TITLE
 Confirmatory Factor Model Figure 8.1
/SPECIFICATIONS
 CASES=73; VARIABLES = 6; ME = ML; ANALYSIS=Covariance;
/LABELS
 V1 = VISPERC;V2 = CUBES;V3 = LOZENGES;V4 = PARCOMP;
 V5 = SENCOMP;V6 = WORDMEAN;
/EQUATIONS
 V1 = 1*F1 + E1;
 V2 = 1*F1 + E2;
 V3 = 1*F1 + E3;
 V4 = 1*F2 + E4;
 V5 = 1*F2 + E5;
 V6 = 1*F2 + E6;
```

```
/VARIANCES
 F1 to F2 = 1.0;
 E1 TO E6=1*;
/COVARIANCES
 F1,F2=1*;
/MATRIX
    47.830
    15.138   20.547
    26.900   17.658   62.584
     8.451    3.402    9.182   12.690
    12.820    4.092   13.411   13.042   25.547
    13.218    6.935   24.280   22.020   29.246   69.208
/END
```

LISREL–SIMPLIS Confirmatory Factor Model Program

```
Confirmatory Factor Model Figure 8.1
Observed Variables:
  VISPERC CUBES LOZENGES PARCOMP SENCOMP WORDMEAN
Correlation Matrix
      1.000
      0.483   1.000
      0.492   0.492   1.000
      0.343   0.211   0.326   1.000
      0.367   0.179   0.335   0.724   1.000
      0.230   0.184   0.369   0.743   0.696   1.000
Standard deviations: 6.916 4.533 7.911 3.562 5.054 8.319
Means: 29.315 24.699 14.836 10.589 19.3014 18.014
Sample Size: 73
Latent Variables: Spatial Verbal
Relationships:
   VISPERC - LOZENGES = Spatial
   PARCOMP - WORDMEAN = Verbal
Print Residuals
Number of Decimals = 3
Path Diagram
End of problem
```

EXERCISES

1. Test the following hypothesized confirmatory factor model (Fig. 8.3) using an SEM computer software program:
       Sample size: 3094
       Observed variables:
           Academic Ability (Academic)
           Self-Concept (Concept)
           Degree Aspirations (Aspire)
           Degree (Degree)

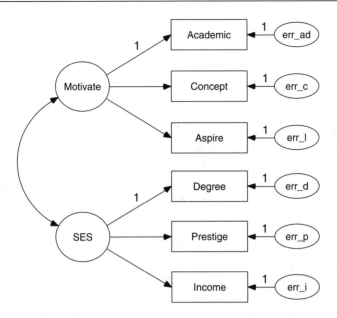

FIG. 8.3. Hypothesized CFA model as diagrammed in Amos.

TABLE 8.3
State Correlation Matrix

	Q1	Q3	Q5	Q7	Q9	Q11	Q13	Q15	Q17	Q19
Q1	1.0000									
Q3	0.4974	1.0000								
Q5	0.5289	0.7223	1.0000							
Q7	0.4867	0.5997	0.6931	1.0000						
Q9	0.4627	0.6181	0.6787	0.6549	1.0000					
Q11	0.5151	0.6829	0.7823	0.6301	0.6184	1.0000				
Q13	0.4990	0.5617	0.5948	0.6972	0.6669	0.5230	1.0000			
Q15	0.5466	0.5882	0.6630	0.6493	0.6347	0.7121	0.6176	1.0000		
Q17	0.5218	0.6794	0.7561	0.7418	0.6569	0.7106	0.6130	0.7191	1.0000	
Q19	0.4983	0.6424	0.7581	0.7641	0.7192	0.7277	0.6559	0.7864	0.7972	1.0000

State means and standard deviations

Variable	Mean	SD
Q1	5.232	1.279
Q3	5.498	1.101
Q5	5.209	1.395
Q7	4.894	1.358
Q9	5.129	1.419
Q11	5.061	1.426
Q13	5.114	1.352
Q15	4.726	1.396
Q17	4.947	1.408
Q19	5.110	1.325

TABLE 8.4
Trait Correlation Matrix

	Q2	Q4	Q6	Q8	Q10	Q12	Q14	Q16	Q18	Q20
Q2	1.0000									
Q4	0.2867	1.0000								
Q6	0.3949	0.4642	1.0000							
Q8	0.3687	0.5537	0.4315	1.0000						
Q10	0.4486	0.5861	0.5489	0.6834	1.0000					
Q12	0.3024	0.4617	0.3088	0.4535	0.5185	1.0000				
Q14	0.4184	0.5849	0.5954	0.6325	0.7179	0.5085	1.0000			
Q16	0.2188	0.3470	0.3061	0.2911	0.3348	0.2380	0.3225	1.0000		
Q18	0.3202	0.3963	0.3209	0.3874	0.4098	0.4267	0.3981	0.2262	1.0000	
Q20	0.4212	0.5227	0.3861	0.4218	0.5042	0.3424	0.5763	0.1856	0.4361	1.0000

Trait means and standard deviations

Variable	Mean	SD
Q2	5.433	0.993
Q4	5.475	0.842
Q6	4.426	1.580
Q8	4.798	1.156
Q10	4.932	1.103
Q12	5.460	1.036
Q14	5.167	0.954
Q16	4.460	1.274
Q18	5.510	1.091
Q20	5.570	0.839

Occupational Prestige (Prestige)
Income (Income)
Correlation matrix:

Academic	Concept	Aspire	Degree	Prestige	Income
1.000					
0.487	1.000				
0.236	0.206	1.000			
0.242	0.179	0.253	1.000		
0.163	0.090	0.125	0.481	1.000	
0.064	0.040	0.025	0.106	0.136	1.000

Hypothesized CFA model: The CFA model indicates that the first three observed variables measure the latent variable Academic Motivation (Motivate) and the last three observed variables measure the latent variable Socioeconomic Status (SES). Motivate and SES are correlated.

2. The State–Trait instrument has 20 questions that are supposed to comprise two factors. The State questions are the odd-numbered items (1, 3, 5, 7, 9, 11, 13, 15, 17, 19). The Trait questions are the even-numbered items (2, 4, 6, 8, 10, 12, 14, 16, 18, 20). The State–Trait instrument was administered to 263 subjects. Determine the composite reliability of each factor and then test the model fit of a two-factor confirmatory model using EQS. (See Tables 8.3–8.5.)

TABLE 8.5
State–Trait Correlation Matrix*

	Q1	Q2	Q3	Q4	Q5	Q6	Q7	Q8	Q9	Q10	Q11	Q12	Q13	Q14	Q15	Q16	Q17	Q18	Q19	Q20
Q1	1.0000																			
Q2	0.3080	1.0000																		
Q3	0.4974	0.3392	1.0000																	
Q4	0.1560	0.2867	0.2254	1.0000																
Q5	0.5289	0.3917	0.7223	0.1947	1.0000															
Q6	0.1341	0.3949	0.1715	0.4642	0.1759	1.0000														
Q7	0.4867	0.3314	0.5997	0.2816	0.6931	0.2418	1.0000													
Q8	0.1607	0.3687	0.1391	0.5537	0.1564	0.4315	0.4068	1.0000												
Q9	0.4627	0.3933	0.6181	0.2424	0.6787	0.2358	0.6549	0.3044	1.0000											
Q10	0.1925	0.4486	0.2136	0.5861	0.2103	0.5489	0.3417	0.6834	0.3178	1.0000										
Q11	0.5151	0.2884	0.6829	0.1793	0.7823	0.1747	0.6301	0.1463	0.6184	0.1676	1.0000									
Q12	0.2244	0.3024	0.1831	0.4617	0.1762	0.3088	0.2303	0.4535	0.2890	0.5185	0.2160	1.0000								
Q13	0.4990	0.4605	0.5617	0.3280	0.5948	0.2810	0.6972	0.4104	0.6669	0.3688	0.5230	0.2921	1.0000							
Q14	0.2651	0.4184	0.2218	0.5849	0.1973	0.5954	0.3584	0.6325	0.3532	0.7179	0.1775	0.5085	0.4113	1.0000						
Q15	0.5466	0.3529	0.5882	0.2737	0.6630	0.1984	0.6493	0.2519	0.6347	0.2704	0.7121	0.2247	0.6176	0.2695	1.0000					
Q16	0.1216	0.2188	0.1244	0.3470	0.1390	0.3061	0.1056	0.2911	0.1506	0.3348	0.1673	0.2380	0.1645	0.3225	0.1935	1.0000				
Q17	0.5218	0.3086	0.6794	0.1728	0.7561	0.2161	0.7418	0.1810	0.6569	0.2139	0.7106	0.0639	0.6130	0.2368	0.7191	0.1286	1.0000			
Q18	0.2186	0.3202	0.2868	0.3963	0.3261	0.3209	0.3744	0.3874	0.3222	0.4098	0.2867	0.4267	0.3358	0.3981	0.3402	0.2262	0.2812	1.0000		
Q19	0.4983	0.3493	0.6424	0.3020	0.7581	0.2054	0.7641	0.3036	0.7192	0.3160	0.7277	0.2243	0.6559	0.3023	0.7864	0.2027	0.7972	0.4391	1.0000	
Q20	0.3954	0.4212	0.3977	0.5227	0.3968	0.3861	0.4187	0.4218	0.4091	0.5042	0.3823	0.3424	0.3968	0.5763	0.3490	0.1856	0.4232	0.4361	0.4445	1.0000

*Trait means and standard deviations are the same as in the EQS program above.

REFERENCES

Arbuckle, J. L., & Wothke, W. (1999). *AMOS 4.0 user's guide*. Chicago: SPSS.

Bentler, P. M., & Wu, E. J. C. (2002). *EQS 6 for Windows user's guide*. Encino, CA: Multivariate Software.

Cochran, W. G. (1968). Errors of measurement in statistics. *Technometrics, 10*, 637–666.

Comrey, A. L., & Lee, H. B. (1992). *A first course in factor analysis*. Hillsdale, NJ: Lawrence Erlbaum Associates, Inc.

Fuller, W. A. (1987). *Measurement error models*. New York: Wiley.

Gorsuch, R. L. (1983). *Factor analysis* (2nd ed.). Hillsdale, NJ: Lawrence Erlbaum Associates, Inc.

Harmon, H. H. (1976). *Modern factor analysis* (3rd ed., rev.). Chicago: University of Chicago Press.

Holzinger, K. J., & Swineford, F. A. (1939). *A study in factor analysis: The stability of a bifactor solution*. (Supplementary Educational Monographs, No. 48). Chicago: University of Chicago, Department of Education.

Jöreskog, K. G., & Sörbom, D. (1993). *LISREL 8: Structural equation modeling with the SIMPLIS command language*. Chicago: Scientific Software International.

Raykov, T. (1997). Estimation of composite reliability for congeneric measures. *Applied Psychological Measurement, 21*, 173–184.

ANSWERS TO EXERCISES

1. We write the following LISREL–SIMPLIS program:

```
Confirmatory Factor Model Exercise Chapter 8
Observed Variables:
  Academic Concept Aspire Degree Prestige Income
Correlation Matrix
1.000
0.487  1.000
0.236  0.206  1.000
0.242  0.179  0.253  1.000
0.163  0.090  0.125  0.481  1.000
0.064  0.040  0.025  0.106  0.136  1.000
Sample Size: 3094
Latent Variables: Motivate SES
Relationships:
   Academic - Aspire = Motivate
   Degree - Income = SES
Print Residuals
Number of Decimals = 3
Path Diagram
End of problem
```

Results overall suggest a less than acceptable fit:

```
Minimum Fit Function Chi-Square = 114.252 (P = 0.0)
Degrees of Freedom = 8
Root Mean Square Error of Approximation (RMSEA) = 0.0655
Standardized RMR = 0.0377
Goodness of Fit Index (GFI) = 0.988
```

Consequently, the model modification indices were examined. The largest decrease in chi-square results from adding an error covariance between Concept and Academic (boldfaced), thus allowing us to maintain a hypothesized two-factor model.

```
        The Modification Indices Suggest to Add the
   Path to     from     Decrease in Chi-Square     New Estimate
Concept       SES              21.9                   -0.14
Aspire        SES              78.0                    0.21
Degree        Motivate         16.1                    0.31
Prestige      Motivate         18.1                   -0.22
```

```
The Modification Indices Suggest to Add an Error Covariance
   Between       and     Decrease in Chi-Square     New Estimate
Concept       Academic         78.0                    0.63
Aspire        Academic         21.9                   -0.12
Degree        Aspire           75.3                    0.13
Prestige      Concept           8.9                   -0.04
Income        Degree           18.1                   -0.10
Income        Prestige         16.1                    0.07
```

The following error covariance command line was added.

```
Let error covariance between Concept and Academic correlate
```

The results indicate further model modifications. The largest decrease in chi-square was determined to occur by adding an error covariance between Income and Prestige (boldfaced), thus maintaining our hypothesized two-factor confirmatory model. The following error covariance command line was added:

```
Let error covariance between Income and Prestige correlate
```

```
     The Modification Indices Suggest to Add the
   Path to     from     Decrease in Chi-Square     New Estimate
Degree        Motivate         20.3                    0.71
Prestige      Motivate         18.4                   -0.39
```

The Modification Indices Suggest to Add an Error Covariance

Between	and	Decrease in Chi-Square	New Estimate
Degree	Aspire	10.0	0.09
Prestige	Aspire	8.3	-0.05
Income	Degree	18.4	-0.10
Income	**Prestige**	**20.3**	**0.08**

The results indicate a more acceptable level of fit:

```
Minimum Fit Function Chi-Square = 14.407 (P = 0.0254)
Degrees of Freedom = 6
Root Mean Square Error of Approximation (RMSEA) = 0.0214
Standardized RMR = 0.0123
Goodness of Fit Index (GFI) = 0.998
```

The final LISREL–SIMPLIS program with the final CFA model (Fig. 8.4) is

```
Modified Confirmatory Factor Model - Exercise Chapter 8
Observed Variables:
Academic Concept Aspire Degree Prestige Income
Correlation Matrix
1.000
0.487  1.000
0.236  0.206  1.000
0.242  0.179  0.253  1.000
0.163  0.090  0.125  0.481  1.000
0.064  0.040  0.025  0.106  0.136  1.000
Sample Size: 3094
Latent Variables: Motivate SES
Relationships:
  Academic - Aspire = Motivate
  Degree - Income = SES
Let error covariance between Concept and Academic correlate
Let error covariance between Income and Prestige correlate
Print Residuals
Number of Decimals = 3
Path Diagram
End of problem
```

2. State and Trait reliability and confirmatory factor model results. The State Computer program and output are as follows:

```
/TITLE
 State Reliability and Confirmatory Factor Model
/SPECIFICATIONS
 VARIABLES=10; CASES=263;
 METHODS=ML;ANALYSIS=COVARIANCE;
```

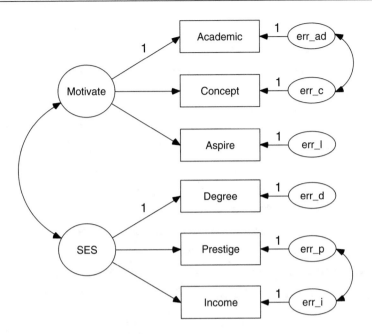

FIG. 8.4. Final CFA model as diagrammed in Amos.

```
/LABELS
 V1=Q1;V2=Q3;V3=Q5;V4=Q7;V5=Q9;V6=Q11;V7=Q13;V8=Q15;V9=Q17;V10=Q19;
/EQUATIONS
 V1  =      F1 + E1;
 V2  =  1*F1 + E2;
 V3  =  1*F1 + E3;
 V4  =  1*F1 + E4;
 V5  =  1*F1 + E5;
 V6  =  1*F1 + E6;
 V7  =  1*F1 + E7;
 V8  =  1*F1 + E8;
 V9  =  1*F1 + E9;
 V10 = 1*F1 + E10;
/VARIANCES
 F1 = 1.0;
 E1 TO E10 = *;
/MATRIX
1.0000
0.4974 1.0000
0.5289 0.7223 1.0000
0.4867 0.5997 0.6931 1.0000
0.4627 0.6181 0.6787 0.6549 1.0000
0.5151 0.6829 0.7823 0.6301 0.6184 1.0000
0.4990 0.5617 0.5948 0.6972 0.6669 0.5230 1.0000
0.5466 0.5882 0.6630 0.6493 0.6347 0.7121 0.6176 1.0000
0.5218 0.6794 0.7561 0.7418 0.6569 0.7106 0.6130 0.7191 1.0000
```

```
0.4983 0.6424 0.7581 0.7641 0.7192 0.7277 0.6559 0.7864 0.7972 1.0000
/STANDARD DEVIATIONS
 1.279 1.101 1.395 1.358 1.419 1.426 1.352 1.396 1.408 1.325
/MEANS
 5.232 5.498 5.209 4.894 5.129 5.061 5.114 4.726 4.947 5.110
/PRINT
 FIT=ALL;
/END
```

STATE RELIABILITY AND FACTOR LOADINGS

```
RELIABILITY COEFFICIENTS
------------------------
CRONBACH'S ALPHA                          = .947
RELIABILITY COEFFICIENT RHO               = .964


MAXIMUM LIKELIHOOD SOLUTION (NORMAL DISTRIBUTION THEORY)


STANDARDIZED SOLUTION:                      R-SQUARED

Q1  =V1  = .773 F1  + .635 E1              .597
Q3  =V2  = .818*F1  + .576 E2              .669
Q5  =V3  = .896*F1  + .445 E3              .802
Q7  =V4  = .865*F1  + .502 E4              .748
Q9  =V5  = .833*F1  + .553 E5              .695
Q11 =V6  = .866*F1  + .501 E6              .749
Q13 =V7  = .791*F1  + .612 E7              .625
Q15 =V8  = .865*F1  + .501 E8              .749
Q17 =V9  = .904*F1  + .428 E9              .817
Q19 =V10 = .924*F1  + .382 E10             .854
```

The Trait computer program and output are as follows:

```
/TITLE
 Trait Reliability and Confirmatory Factor Model
/SPECIFICATIONS
 VARIABLES=10; CASES=263;
 METHODS=ML;ANALYSIS=COVARIANCE;
/LABELS
 V1=Q2;V2=Q4;V3=Q6;V4=Q8;V5=Q10;V6=Q12;V7=Q14;V8=Q16;V9=Q18;V10=Q20;
/EQUATIONS
V1  =    F1  + E1;
V2  = 1*F1  + E2;
V3  = 1*F1  + E3;
V4  = 1*F1  + E4;
V5  = 1*F1  + E5;
V6  = 1*F1  + E6;
V7  = 1*F1  + E7;
V8  = 1*F1  + E8;
```

```
V9  = 1*F1  + E9;
V10 = 1*F1  + E10;
/VARIANCES
 F1 = 1.0;
 E1 TO E10 = *;
/MATRIX
1.0000
0.2867 1.0000
0.3949 0.4642 1.0000
0.3687 0.5537 0.4315 1.0000
0.4486 0.5861 0.5489 0.6834 1.0000
0.3024 0.4617 0.3088 0.4535 0.5185 1.0000
0.4184 0.5849 0.5954 0.6325 0.7179 0.5085 1.0000
0.2188 0.3470 0.3061 0.2911 0.3348 0.2380 0.3225 1.0000
0.3202 0.3963 0.3209 0.3874 0.4098 0.4267 0.3981 0.2262 1.0000
0.4212 0.5227 0.3861 0.4218 0.5042 0.3424 0.5763 0.1856 0.4361 1.0000
/STANDARD DEVIATIONS
 0.993 0.842 1.580 1.156 1.103 1.036 0.954 1.274 1.091 0.839
/MEANS
 5.433 5.475 4.426 4.798 4.932 5.460 5.167 4.460 5.510 5.570
/PRINT
 FIT=ALL;
/END
```

TRAIT RELIABILITY AND FACTOR LOADINGS

RELIABILITY COEFFICIENTS

  CRONBACH'S ALPHA   = .880
  RELIABILITY COEFFICIENT RHO   = .922

MAXIMUM LIKELIHOOD SOLUTION (NORMAL DISTRIBUTION THEORY)

```
    STANDARDIZED SOLUTION:                         R-SQUARED
        Q2  =V1  = .747 F1  + .665 E1                .558
        Q4  =V2  = .772*F1  + .636 E2                .596
        Q6  =V3  = .715*F1  + .699 E3                .511
        Q8  =V4  = .806*F1  + .592 E4                .649
        Q10 =V5  = .886*F1  + .465 E5                .784
        Q12 =V6  = .671*F1  + .741 E6                .450
        Q14 =V7  = .884*F1  + .468 E7                .781
        Q16 =V8  = .465*F1  + .885 E8                .217
        Q18 =V9  = .599*F1  + .801 E9                .358
        Q20 =V10 = .711*F1  + .703 E10               .506
```

The State–Trait computer program and output are as follows:

```
/TITLE
State Trait Confirmatory Factor Model
/SPECIFICATIONS
VARIABLES=20; CASES=263;
METHODS=ML; ANALYSIS=COVARIANCE;
/LABELS
V1=Q1;V2=Q2;V3=Q3;V4=Q4;V5=Q5;V6=Q6;V7=Q7;V8=Q8;V9=Q9;V10=Q10;V11=Q11;V12=Q12;V13=Q13;V14=Q14;V15=Q15;V16=Q16;V17=Q17;V18=Q18;V19=Q19;V20=Q20;
/EQUATIONS
V1  = 1F1 + E1;
V3  = *F1 + E3;
V5  = *F1 + E5;
V7  = *F1 + E7;
V9  = *F1 + E9;
V11 = *F1 + E11;
V13 = *F1 + E13;
V15 = *F1 + E15;
V17 = *F1 + E17;
V19 = *F1 + E19;
V2  = 1F2 + E2;
V4  = *F2 + E4;
V6  = *F2 + E6;
V8  = *F2 + E8;
V10 = *F2 + E10;
V12 = *F2 + E12;
V14 = *F2 + E14;
V16 = *F2 + E16;
V18 = *F2 + E18;
V20 = *F2 + E20;
```

```
/VARIANCES
F1 TO F2 = 1.0;
E1 TO E20 =*;
/COVARIANCES
F1,F2 = *;
/MATRIX
1.0000
0.3080  1.0000
0.4974  0.3392  1.0000
0.1560  0.2867  0.2254  1.0000
0.5289  0.3917  0.7223  0.1947  1.0000
0.1341  0.3949  0.1715  0.4642  0.1759  1.0000
0.4867  0.3314  0.5997  0.2816  0.6931  0.2418  1.0000
0.1607  0.3687  0.1391  0.5537  0.1564  0.4315  0.4068  1.0000
0.4627  0.3933  0.6181  0.2424  0.6787  0.2358  0.6549  0.3044  1.0000
0.1925  0.4486  0.2136  0.5861  0.2103  0.5489  0.3417  0.6834  0.3178  1.0000
0.5151  0.2884  0.6829  0.1793  0.7823  0.1747  0.6301  0.1463  0.6184  0.1676  1.0000
0.2244  0.3024  0.1831  0.4617  0.1762  0.3088  0.2303  0.4535  0.2890  0.5185  0.2160  1.0000
0.4990  0.4605  0.5617  0.3280  0.5948  0.2810  0.6972  0.4104  0.6669  0.3688  0.5230  0.2921  1.0000
0.2651  0.4184  0.2218  0.5849  0.1973  0.5954  0.3584  0.6325  0.3532  0.7179  0.1775  0.5085  0.4113  1.0000
0.5466  0.3529  0.5882  0.2737  0.6630  0.1984  0.6493  0.2519  0.6347  0.2704  0.7121  0.2247  0.6176  0.2695  1.0000
0.1216  0.2188  0.1244  0.3470  0.1390  0.3061  0.1056  0.2911  0.1506  0.3348  0.1673  0.2380  0.1645  0.3225  0.1935  1.0000
0.5218  0.3086  0.6794  0.1728  0.7561  0.2161  0.7418  0.1810  0.6569  0.2139  0.7106  0.0639  0.6130  0.2368  0.7191  0.1286  1.0000
0.2186  0.3202  0.2868  0.3963  0.3261  0.3209  0.3744  0.3874  0.3222  0.4098  0.2867  0.4267  0.3358  0.3981  0.3402  0.2262  0.2812  1.0000
0.4983  0.3493  0.6424  0.3020  0.7581  0.2054  0.7641  0.3036  0.7192  0.3160  0.7277  0.2243  0.6559  0.3023  0.7864  0.2027  0.7972  0.4391  1.0000
0.3954  0.4212  0.3977  0.5227  0.3968  0.3861  0.4187  0.4218  0.4091  0.5042  0.3823  0.3424  0.3968  0.5763  0.3490  0.1856  0.4232  0.4361  1.0000
/STANDARD DEVIATIONS
1.279  0.993  1.101  0.842  1.395  1.580  1.358  1.156  1.419  1.103  1.426  1.036  1.352  0.954  1.396  1.274  1.408  1.091  1.325  0.839
/MEANS
5.232  5.433  5.498  5.475  5.209  4.426  4.894  4.798  5.129  4.932  5.061  5.460  5.114  5.167  4.726  4.460  4.947  5.510  5.110  5.570
/PRINT
FIT=ALL;
/END
```

193

The Correlation among the two factors F1 and F2, is .610, and the other results are as follows:

```
MAXIMUM LIKELIHOOD SOLUTION (NORMAL DISTRIBUTION THEORY)
STANDARDIZED SOLUTION:                          R-SQUARED

Q1  =V1  = .776 F1  + .631 E1                       .602
Q2  =V2  = .754 F2  + .657 E2                       .568
Q3  =V3  = .826*F1 + .563 E3                        .683
Q4  =V4  = .782*F2 + .624 E4                        .611
Q5  =V5  = .900*F1 + .436 E5                        .810
Q6  =V6  = .724*F2 + .690 E6                        .524
Q7  =V7  = .876*F1 + .483 E7                        .767
Q8  =V8  = .813*F2 + .583 E8                        .660
Q9  =V9  = .845*F1 + .534 E9                        .715
Q10 =V10 = .887*F2 + .462 E10                       .787
Q11 =V11 = .871*F1 + .491 E11                       .758
Q12 =V12 = .683*F2 + .731 E12                       .466
Q13 =V13 = .806*F1 + .591 E13                       .650
Q14 =V14 = .887*F2 + .462 E14                       .787
Q15 =V15 = .874*F1 + .486 E15                       .764
Q16 =V16 = .478*F2 + .878 E16                       .229
Q17 =V17 = .908*F1 + .419 E17                       .824
Q18 =V18 = .624*F2 + .782 E18                       .389
Q19 =V19 = .930*F1 + .367 E19                       .865
Q20 =V20 = .736*F2 + .677 E20                       .542
```

9

DEVELOPING STRUCTURAL EQUATION MODELS. PART I

Chapter Outline

Key Concepts

Latent independent and dependent variables
Observed independent and dependent variables
Developing measurement models for latent variables
Establishing relationships between latent variables
Covariance terms
The two-step approach

Structural equation models have been developed in a number of academic disciplines to substantiate and test theory. Structural equation models have further helped to establish the relationship between latent variables or constructs, given a theoretical perspective. The structural equation modeling approach involves developing measurement models to define latent variables and then establishing relationships or structural equations among the latent variables. The focus of this chapter is on providing researchers with a better understanding of how to develop structural equation models. An attempt is made to minimize matrix and statistical notation so that the reader can better understand the structural equation modeling approach.

This chapter begins with a more extensive discussion of observed variables and latent variables and then proceeds with sections on the measurement model, the structural model, covariances, and the two/four step approach to structural equation modeling. Chapter 10 extends the development of such models by examining model specification, model identification, model estimation, model testing, and model modification.

9.1   OBSERVED VARIABLES AND LATENT VARIABLES

In structural equation modeling, as in traditional statistics, we use X and Y to denote the observed variables. We use X to refer to independent (or predictor) variables and Y to refer to dependent (or criterion) variables; this is the same in multiple regression, analysis of variance, and all general linear models. In structural equation modeling, however, we further define latent independent variables using observed variables denoted by X and latent dependent variables using observed variables denoted by Y. Latent independent and dependent variables are created with observed variables using confirmatory factor models discussed in the previous chapter.

There are two major types of variables in structural equation modeling: observed (indicator) variables and latent (construct) variables. Latent variables are not directly observable or measured, rather they are observed or measured indirectly, and hence they are inferred constructs based on what observed variables we select to define the latent variable. For example, intelligence is a latent variable and represents a psychological construct. Intelligence cannot be directly observed, for example, through visual inspection of an individual, and thus there is no single agreed-upon definition for intelligence. However, intelligence can be indirectly measured through observed or indicator variables, for example, IQ tests.

Observed or indicator variables are variables that are directly observed or measured. For example, the Wechsler Intelligence Scale for Children–Revised (WISC–R) is an instrument commonly used to

measure children's intelligence. The instrument represents one definition or measure of what we mean by intelligence. Other researchers rely
on other definitions or observed measures, and thus on other instruments, for example, the Stanford–Binet Intelligence Scale. Latent variables such as intelligence are not directly observed or measured, but
can be indirectly observed or measured by using several observed (indicator) variables, for example, IQ tests such as the WISC–R and the
Stanford–Binet Intelligence Scale.

Let us further examine the concept of latent variables as they are
used in structural equation models. Consider a basic structural equation
model in which we propose that a latent independent variable predicts
a latent dependent variable. For instance, Intelligence (latent independent variable) is believed to predict subsequent Scholastic Achievement
(latent dependent variable), which can be depicted as

$$\text{Intelligence} \longrightarrow \text{Achievement}$$

Any latent variable that is predicted by other latent variables in a structural equation model is known as a *latent dependent variable*. A latent
dependent variable therefore must have at least one arrow leading into
it from another latent variable, sometimes referred to as an *endogenous*
latent variable. Any latent variable that does not have an arrow leading
to it in a structural equation model is known as a *latent independent variable*, sometimes referred to as an *exogenous* latent variable. As shown in
the foregoing, the latent independent variable Intelligence does not have
any arrows leading to it from another latent variable. In our basic structural equation model, Intelligence is the latent independent variable with
no directed lines or arrows leading to it and Achievement is the latent dependent variable because it has an arrow leading to it from Intelligence.

Consider adding a third latent variable to our basic structural equation model, such that achievement is measured at two points in time.
This model is depicted as follows:

$$\text{Intelligence} \longrightarrow \text{Achievement}_1 \longrightarrow \text{Achievement}_2.$$

Intelligence is still a latent independent variable. Achievement_2 is clearly
a latent dependent variable because there is an arrow leading to it from
Achievement_1. However, there is an arrow leading to Achievement_1 from
Intelligence and another arrow leading from Achievement_1 to Achieve-
ment$_2$. This basic structural equation model indicates that Achievement_1
is predicted by Intelligence, but then Achievement_1 predicts Achieve-
ment$_2$. Achievement_1 is first a dependent latent variable and then an
independent latent variable. This type of structural equation model is

possible and illustrates indirect effects using latent variables. Achievement$_1$ in this basic structural equation model is a *mediating* latent variable. Our designation of a latent variable as independent or dependent is therefore determined by whether or not an arrow is drawn from one latent variable to another latent variable. If no arrows lead to a latent variable from another latent variable in the structural equation model, then it is a latent *independent* variable. If an arrow leads to a latent variable from another latent variable in the structural equation model, then it is a latent *dependent* variable.

Next we consider the concept behind the observed or indicator variables. The latent independent variables are measured by observed independent variables, traditionally denoted by X. The latent dependent variables are measured by observed dependent variables, traditionally denoted by Y. Following our example, we might choose the WISC–R and the Stanford–Binet as observed independent measures of the latent independent variable Intelligence. We can denote these observed variables as X_1 and X_2. For each of the achievement latent variables, we might choose the California Achievement Test and the Metropolitan Achievement Test as our observed dependent measures. If these measures are observed at two points in time, then we can denote the observed variables of Achievement$_1$ as Y_1 and Y_2 and those of Achievement$_2$ as Y_3 and Y_4, respectively. In our example each latent variable is measured by two observed variables.

What is the benefit of using more than one observed variable to assess a latent variable? In using a single observed variable to assess a latent variable, we assume that no measurement error is associated with the measurement of that latent variable. In other words, it is assumed that the latent variable is perfectly measured by the single observed variable, which is typically not the case. We define measurement error quite generally here to include errors due to reliability and validity problems (see chap. 8). Reliability is concerned with the ability of a measure to be consistent (e.g., internal consistency, consistency over time, and consistency using similar measures).

Would Kristen's score on the WISC–R be about the same if measured today as compared with next week? Evidence of score reliability can be shown when a measure is given to the same group of individuals at two points in time and the scores are roughly equivalent. If only a single measure of a latent variable is used and it is not very reliable, then our latent variable is not defined very well. If the reliability of a single observed measure of a latent variable is known, then it is prudent to specify or fix the value in the model. This is accomplished, for example, in LISREL–SIMPLIS by setting the error variance of the single variable. The error variance of a single variable is determined by the following formula: Error Variance of X1 $= (1 - \text{reliability coefficient})(S^2)$. If the reliability of scores for X1 is .85 with a standard deviation of 5.00, then the error variance of X1 $= (1 - .85)(5.00)^2 = .15(25) = 3.75$.

Validity is concerned with the extent to which scores accurately define the construct (e.g., content, factorial, convergent–divergent, and discriminant). Our interest in validity is related to how well we can make an inference from the scores on the latent variable, that is, how well test scores indicate what they purport to measure. Does Kristen's score on the WISC–R really measure her intelligence or something else, such as her height? Evidence of validity is indicated when two indicators of the same latent variable are substantially correlated. For example, if WISC–R and height were used as indicators of the latent variable Intelligence, we would expect them to not be correlated. If only a single measure of a latent variable is used and it is not very valid (e.g., if height is used to measure intelligence), then our latent variable is not well defined. Establishing the reliability of scores for our observed variable helps in estimating the validity coefficients (factor loadings) in our measurement model because validity is limited by the reliability of the observed variable scores, that is, the maximum validity coefficient is less than or equal to the product of the square roots of the two reliability coefficients, $\rho_{xy} \leq \sqrt{\rho_{XX'}} \sqrt{\rho_{YY'}}$.

If we selected WISC–R and height as observed indicator variables for the latent independent variable Intelligence it would certainly not be well defined and would include measurement error. The selection of only height as an observed indicator of intelligence would increase the measurement error and poorly define the construct. Consequently, in selecting observed variables to define a latent variable, we need to select observed variables that show evidence of both reliability and validity for the intended purpose of our study. Because of the inherent difficulty involved in obtaining reliable and valid measurement with a single observed variable, we strongly encourage you to consider multiple indicator variables for each latent independent and dependent variable in the structural equation model.

There are a few obvious exceptions to this recommendation, especially when research indicates that only one observed variable is available. In this case, you have no other choice than to define the latent variable using a single observed variable or use the observed variables in a MIMIC model (see chap. 13). Jöreskog and Sörbom (1993, p. 37, EX7A.SPL) provided the rationale and gave an example for setting the error variance of a single observed variable (VERBINTM) in defining the latent variable Verbint. The verbal intelligence test (VERBINTM) was a fallible (unreliable) measure of the latent variable Verbint, and therefore it was unreasonable to assume that the error variance was zero (perfectly reliable). Consequently, the reliability coefficient for VERBINTM was assumed to be $r_{xx} = .85$ rather than 1.00 (perfectly reliable, zero error variance). The assumed value of the reliability coefficient, hence designation of the error variance, will affect parameter estimates as well as standard errors. A reliability of $r_{xx} = .85$ for VERBINTM is equivalent to an error variance of 0.15 times the variance of VERBINTM (3.65^2). The assumed error variance of VERBINTM was computed as $.15(3.65^2) = 1.998$.

If we can assume a reasonable reliability value for an observed variable, then multiplying the observed variable's variance by 1 minus the reliability provides a reasonable estimate of error variance. In the LISREL–SIMPLIS program EX7B.SPL, the error variance for the single observed variable VERBINTM is accomplished by using the SET command as follows:

```
SET the error variance of VERBINTM to 1.998
```

Later in this chapter, we show how measurement error is explicitly part of any structural equation model. The basic concept, however, is that multiple observed variables used in defining a particular latent variable permit measurement error to be estimated through structural equation modeling. This provides the researcher with additional information about the measurement characteristics of the observed variables. When there is only a single observed indicator of a latent variable, then measurement error cannot be estimated through structural equation modeling. Most SEM software programs, however, permit the specification of reliabilities for single or multiple variables, whether the values are known or require our best guess. In the next two sections we discuss the two approaches that make up structural equation modeling: the measurement model and the structural model.

9.2 MEASUREMENT MODEL

As previously mentioned, the researcher specifies the measurement model to define the relationships between the latent variables and the observed variables. The measurement model is a confirmatory factor model. Using our previous example, the latent independent variable Intelligence is measured by two observed variables, the WISC–R and the Stanford–Binet Intelligence Scale. Our other latent variables Achievement$_1$ (dependent, then latent independent variable) and Achievement$_2$ (dependent latent variable) are each measured by the same two observed variables, scores on the California Achievement Test and the

Metropolitan Achievement Test, but at two different times. These observed variables yield a composite score or scale score from summing numerous individual items. In chapter 8, we pointed out that individual items on an instrument could be used to create a construct (latent variable), hence confirming the unidimensionality of the construct, while taking into account the reliability and the model fit of the factor. The use of individual items rather than the composite score as the observed variable to measure a latent variable increases the degrees of freedom in the structural model and can cause problems in model fit. Measurement characteristics at the item level might be more appropriate for exploratory data reduction methods than they are for structural equation models.

The researcher is typically interested in having the following questions answered about the observed variables: To what extent are the observed variables actually measuring the hypothesized latent variable; for example, how good is the California test as a measure of achievement? Which observed variable is the best measure of a particular latent variable; for example, is the California test a better measure of achievement than the Metropolitan test? To what extent are the observed variables actually measuring something other than the hypothesized latent variable; for example, is the California test measuring something other than achievement, such as quality of education received? These types of questions need to be addressed when creating the measurement models that define the latent variables.

In our measurement model example each latent variable is defined by two indicator variables. The relationships between the observed variables and the latent variables are indicated by factor loadings. The factor loadings provide us with information about the extent to which a given observed variable is able to measure the latent variable (a squared factor loading indicates variable communality or amount of variance shared with the factor). The factor loadings are referred to as validity coefficients because multiplying the factor loading times the observed variable score indicates how much of the observed variable score is valid (true score). The observed variable measurement error is defined as that portion of the observed variable score that is measuring something other than what the latent variable is hypothesized to measure. It serves as a measure of error variance, and hence indicates the observed variable score reliability. Measurement error could be the result of (a) an observed variable that is measuring some other latent variable, (b) unreliability, or (c) a higher order factor. For example, the California test may be measuring something besides achievement, or it may not be a very reliable measure. Thus, we would like to know how much measurement error is associated with each observed variable.

In our measurement model there are six measurement equations, one for each observed variable, which can be illustrated as follows:

$$\text{California}_1 = \text{function of Achievement}_1 + \text{error}$$

$$\text{Metropolitan}_1 = \text{function of Achievement}_1 + \text{error}$$

$$\text{California}_2 = \text{function of Achievement}_2 + \text{error}$$

$$\text{Metropolitan}_2 = \text{function of Achievement}_2 + \text{error}$$

$$\text{WISC–R} = \text{function of Intelligence} + \text{error}$$

$$\text{Stanford–Binet} = \text{function of Intelligence} + \text{error}.$$

An explicit definition of the measurement model is done in Amos by drawing the latent variables (circles or ellipses) and observed variables (squares or rectangles) and then drawing arrows from the latent variables to the observed variables. In EQS and LISREL–SIMPLIS programs this is done by specifying measurement equations. For example, in the EQS command file the measurement model equations are written in terms of "V" variables for the observed indicator variables, "F" variables for the latent variables or factors, and "E" variables for the measurement errors. The following labels are used in the EQS program to better describe these variables: $F1 = \text{Achievement}_1$, $F2 = \text{Achievement}_2$, $F3 = \text{Intelligence}$, $V1 = \text{California}_1$, $V2 = \text{Metropolitan}_1$, $V3 = \text{California}_2$, $V4 = \text{Metropolitan}_2$, $V5 = \text{WISC–R}$, and $V6 = \text{Stanford–Binet}$. The measurement model equations in EQS can be specified with a **1*** indicating to estimate a factor loading for the particular observed variable:

```
/EQUATIONS
        V1 = 1*F1 + E1;
        V2 = 1*F1 + E2;
        V3 = 1*F2 + E3;
        V4 = 1*F2 + E4;
        V5 = 1*F3 + E5;
        V6 = 1*F3 + E6;
```

In the LISREL–SIMPLIS program one can expand the variable labels in the measurement model equations using up to eight characters; the labels are case sensitive (upper and lower characters are recognized). The measurement model equations are specified using either the `Relationships:` or `Paths:` command (both methods are equivalent). For the `Relationships:` command, both the latent variables and the observed variables can be written using eight-character variable names. The observed variables are given on the left-hand side of the equation with spaces between the multiple observed variable names (`Cal1`, `Metro1`, `Cal2`, `Metro2`, `WISCR`, and `Stanford`) and the latent variables on the right-hand side of the equation (`Achieve1`, `Achieve2`, and `Intell`). The LISREL–SIMPLIS measurement equations follow (where `Achieve1` refers to Achievement$_1$, `Intell` refers to Intelligence, `Achieve2` refers to Achievement$_2$, `Cal1` refers to California$_1$, `Metro1` refers to Metropolitan$_1$, `Cal2` refers to California$_2$, `Metro2` refers to Metropolitan$_2$, `WISCR` refers to WISC–R, and `Stanford` refers to Stanford–Binet):

```
Relationships:
      Cal1 Metro1 = Achieve1
      Cal2 Metro2 = Achieve2
      WISCR Stanford = Intell
```

For the `Paths:` command, the latent variables are depicted to the left of the arrow and the observed variables to the right of the arrow with spaces between the multiple observed variable names, as in the following measurement equations:

```
Paths:
      Achieve1 → Cal1 Metro1
      Achieve2 → Cal2 Metro2
      Intell → WISCR Stanford
```

9.3 STRUCTURAL MODEL

In chapter 8 we discussed the rationale and process for specifying a measurement model to indicate whether the latent variables are measured well (are valid and reliable), given a set of observed variables. Then we specify a structural equation model to indicate how these latent variables are related. The researcher specifies the structural equation model to allow for certain relationships among the latent variables depicted by the direction of the arrows. In our example we hypothesize that intelligence and achievement are related in a specific way. We are hypothesizing that intelligence predicts later achievement. The hypothesized structural equation model can now be specified and tested to determine the extent to which these *a priori* hypothesized relationships are supported by our sample variance–covariance data. That is, are intelligence and achievement related? Can intelligence predict achievement? Could there be other latent variables that we need to consider to better predict achievement? These types of questions are addressed when specifying the structural equation model.

At this point we need to provide a more explicit definition of the structural equation model and a specific notational system for the latent variables under consideration. Let us return to our previous example, where we indicated a specific hypothesized relationship for the latent variables:

$$\text{Intelligence} \longrightarrow \text{Achievement}_1 \longrightarrow \text{Achievement}_2.$$

The hypothesized relationships for the latent variables indicate two latent dependent variables, so there will be two structural equations. The first equation should indicate that Achievement$_1$ is some function of Intelligence. The second equation should indicate that Achievement$_2$ is some function of Achievement$_1$. These two equations can be illustrated as follows:

$$\text{Achievement}_1 = \text{function of Intelligence} + \text{error}$$

$$\text{Achievement}_2 = \text{function of Achievement}_1 + \text{error}.$$

These two equations specify the estimation of two structure coefficients to indicate the magnitude (statistical significance) and direction (positive or negative) of the prediction. Each structural equation also contains a prediction error or disturbance term that indicates the portion of the latent dependent variable that is not explained or predicted by the latent independent variable in that equation. In our example there are two structure coefficients, one for Intelligence predicting Achievement$_1$ and one for Achievement$_1$ predicting Achievement$_2$. Because there are two structural equations, there will be two prediction errors or disturbances.

The EQS and LISREL–SIMPLIS command language permit an easy way to specify structural equations among the latent variables. First, in the EQS program (Bentler & Wu, 1995, 2002) the structural equations are written in terms of "F" variables for the latent variables or factors and "D" variables for the prediction errors or disturbances. The /LABEL command allows us to further describe these variables: F1 = Achievement$_1$, F2 = Achievement$_2$, and F3 = Intelligence. The EQS structural equations are specified as:

```
/EQUATIONS
    F1 = 1*F3 + D1;
    F2 = 1*F1 + D2;
```

The first structural equation indicates that F3 (Intelligence) is predicting F1 (Achievement$_1$) and the second structural equation indicates that F1 (Achievement$_1$) is predicting F2 (Achievement$_2$) (the 1* indicates that a structure coefficient should be estimated). The latent dependent variables therefore appear on the left side of the equation, whereas the other latent variables are indicated on the right side of the structural equations along with the prediction error terms.

In the LISREL–SIMPLIS program, the structural model can be denoted in terms of either `Relationships:` or `Paths:` commands (both methods are equivalent). For the `Relationships:` command, the latent variables can be written using eight-character variable names with the latent dependent variables on the left side of the equation (where `Achieve1` refers to Achievement$_1$, `Intell` refers to Intelligence, and `Achieve2` refers to Achievement$_2$):

```
Relationships:
      Achieve1 = Intell
      Achieve2 = Achieve1
```

For the `Paths:` command, these latent dependent variables are to the right of the arrow, as in the following structural equations:

```
Paths
      Intell  → Achieve1
      Achieve1 → Achieve2
```

Notice that we do not need to indicate the prediction error in LISREL–SIMPLIS structural equations for either the `Relationships:` or `Paths:` commands because these are known to exist and automatically estimated by the program. The Amos path diagrams of the measurement and structural models for our example are shown in Fig. 9.1. Amos automatically writes the computer program based on how you have drawn Fig. 9.1.

9.4   VARIANCES AND COVARIANCES

In structural equation modeling the term *covariance structure analysis* or *covariance structure modeling* is often used because the estimation of factor loadings and structure coefficients involves the decomposition of a sample variance–covariance matrix. In this section we further explore the notion of variance–covariance as it relates to observed and latent variables. There are three different variance–covariance terms that we need to define and understand. In the structural model there are two variance–covariance terms to consider. First there is a variance–covariance matrix of the latent independent variables. This consists of

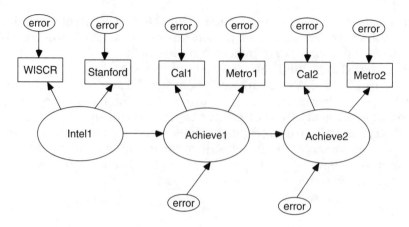

FIG. 9.1.   Achievement path model (Amos diagram).

the variances for each latent independent variable as well as the co-variances among them. Although we are interested in the variances (the amount of variance associated with the latent independent variable intelligence), the covariances may or may not be part of our theoretical model. In our model there is only one latent independent variable, so there is only one variance term and no covariance term.

If we specified two latent independent variables in a different structural equation model, for example, Intelligence and Home Background, we could include a covariance term for them. We would then be hypothesizing that Intelligence and Home Background are correlated or covary because we believe that some common unmeasured latent variable is influencing both of them. We could hypothesize that a latent variable not included in the model, such as Parenting Ability, influences both Intelligence and Home Background. In other words, Intelligence and Home Background covary, or are correlated, because of their mutual influence from Parenting Ability, which has not explicitly been included in the model (but which perhaps could be included).

In the EQS program, variances and covariances are specified using the /VARIANCES and /COVARIANCES commands, respectively. For our hypothesized structural model the /VARIANCES command would be automatically given in the output for F3 (the latent independent variable intelligence). A covariance term, if one existed, would be given in the output under /COVARIANCES for F3 and F4, the covariance between F3 and F4. In the LISREL–SIMPLIS program the variance term would automatically be given or implied in the output for the latent independent variable intelligence. A covariance term, if one existed, would also automatically be given or implied in the output. If one desired the two latent independent variables, Intelligence and Home Background, to be uncorrelated or to have a covariance of zero, then one would specify the following in the LISREL–SIMPLIS program:

```
Set the Covariance between Intell and HomeBack to 0
```

The second set of variance–covariance terms that we need to define and understand is in the covariance matrix of the structural equation prediction errors. This consists of the variances for each structural equation prediction error (the amount of unexplained variance for each structural equation) as well as covariances among them. Although we are interested in the variances, the covariances may or may not be part of our model. We could specify that two structural equation prediction errors are correlated, perhaps because some unmeasured latent variable is leading to error in both equations. An example of this might be where Parental Occupational Status (parent income) is not included as a latent variable in a model where Children's Education (in years) and Children's Occupational Status (income at age 30 years) are latent dependent variables. The structural equations for Children's Education and Children's Occupational Status would then both contain structural equation prediction error due to the omission of Parental Occupational Status. Because the same latent variable was not included in both equations, we expect that the structural equation prediction errors would be correlated. Note that our hypothesized structural model does not contain any such covariance terms.

In the EQS program, these terms are specified using the /VARIANCES and /COVARIANCES commands, respectively. In our example, the variances are specified in the program under the /VARIANCES command for D1 and D2(D1 TO D2 = 1*;), and their covariance is specified in the program under the /COVARIANCES command (D1,D2 = 1*;), although not part of our structural model and program. In the LISREL–SIMPLIS program the variance and covariance terms are automatically included in the output for each structural equation. Because the covariance terms are assumed by the program to be set to zero, one must specify in the program any covariance terms one wants estimated. A covariance term, if one existed between Achievement$_1$ and Achievement$_2$, would be specified using the following command:

```
Set the Error Covariance between Achieve1 and Achieve2 free
```

The third set of variance–covariance terms is from the measurement model. Here we need to define and understand the variances and covariances of the measurement errors. Although we are interested in the variances (the amount of measurement error variance associated with each observed variable), the covariances may or may not be part of our model. We could hypothesize that the measurement errors for two observed variables are correlated (known as *correlated measurement error*). This might be expected in our structural model where the indicators of the latent variables Achievement$_1$ and Achievement$_2$ are the same, for example, using the California Achievement Test. We might believe that the measurement error associated with the California Achievement Test at Time 1 is related to the measurement error for the California Achievement Test at Time 2.

In the EQS program these variances and covariances are specified using the /VARIANCES and /COVARIANCES commands, respectively. In our example the variances are specified in the program under the /VARIANCES command for E1 through E6 (E1 TO E6 = 1*;) and the covariances are specified in the program under the /COVARIANCES command (e.g., E4,E6 = 1*;). In the LISREL–SIMPLIS program the variance and covariance terms are automatically specified in the program for each observed variable. Once again, the covariance terms are assumed by the program to be set to zero; we must specify any covariance term of interest and allow it to become free (estimated). A covariance term, if one existed between the measurement errors for the California Achievement Test at Times 1 and 2, would be specified using the following command:

```
Set the Error Covariance between Ca11 and Ca12 free
```

In Amos, the latent variable variances and observed variable paths are set by clicking on the latent variables (circle or ellipse) or observed variable error variances (circle or ellipse) and entering a 1.0 in the dialog box.

There is one final variance–covariance term that we need to mention, and it really represents the ultimate variance–covariance for our combined measurement model and structural model. From the structure coefficient parameters we estimate in the structural model, the factor loadings in the measurement model(s), and all of the variance–covariances we generate an ultimate matrix of variance–covariances for the overall model. This variance–covariance matrix is implied by the overall model and is denoted by Σ (see chap. 15 for a representation of all of these matrices). Our goal in structural equation modeling is to estimate all of the parameters in the overall model and test the overall fit of the model to the sample variance–covariance data. In short, the parameters in our overall model create an implied variance–covariance matrix Σ from the sample variance–covariance matrix S, which contains the sample variances and covariances among our observed variables. We then interpret various model fit indices (chap. 5) to determine the level of model fit between Σ and S (closeness of the values in the variance–covariance matrix Σ implied by our hypothesized model and the sample variance–covariance matrix S given our sample data). We also examine the magnitude (statistical significance of parameter estimates) and the direction (positive or negative coefficients) to provide a meaningful interpretation of results.

9.5   TWO-STEP/FOUR-STEP APPROACH

James, Mulaik, and Brett (1982) proposed a two-step modeling approach that emphasized the analysis of the two conceptually distinct latent variable models: measurement models and structural models. Anderson and Gerbing (1988) described their approach by stating that the measurement model provides an assessment of convergent and discriminant validity and the structural model provides an assessment of predictive validity. Mulaik et al. (1989) also expanded the idea of assessing the fit of the structural equation model among latent variables (structural model) independently of assessing the fit of the observed variables to the latent variables (measurement model). Their rationale was that even with few latent variables, most parameter estimates define the relationships of the observed variables to the latent variables in the measurement model, rather than the structural equation relationships of the latent variables themselves. Mulaik and Millsap (2000) further elaborated the four-step approach discussed in chapter 5. Jöreskog and Sörbom (1993, p. 113) summarized many of their thoughts by stating, "The testing of the structural model, i.e., the testing of the initially specified theory, may be meaningless unless it is first established that the measurement model holds. If the chosen indicators for a construct do not measure that construct, the specified theory must be modified before it can be tested. Therefore, the measurement model should be tested before the structural relationships are tested."

We have found it prudent to follow their advice. In the establishment of measurement models, it is best to identify a few good indicators of each latent variable with four indicators being recommended. In our example, we intentionally used only a few indicators to define or measure the latent variables. We have also found that when selecting only a few indicator variables, it is easier to check how well each observed variable defines a latent variable, that is, to examine the factor loadings, reliabilities, and amount of latent variable variance explained. For example, rather than use individual items as indicator variables, sum the items to form a total test score (composite score or scale score). In addition, one can calculate the reliability of the composite (scale) score and even consider fixing the value of the relevant measurement error variance in the model (as described in sec. 9.1), thus reducing the need to estimate one parameter. It is only after latent variables are adequately defined (measured) that it makes sense to examine latent variable relationships in a structural equation model. We think a researcher with adequately measured latent variables is in a better position to establish a substantive, meaningful structural equation model, thus supporting theory.

9.6 SUMMARY

This chapter focused on how to develop structural equation models. We began with a more detailed look at observed and latent variables. Next we discussed measurement and structural models. We extended some of the basic concepts found in confirmatory factor models (measurement models) and regression/path models (structural models) to structural equation modeling. We then described three types of variance–covariance typically utilized in structural equation models. The chapter concluded with a discussion of the popular two-step/four-step approach to structural equation modeling. In chapter 10 we extend our discussion of the development of structural equation models by discussing model specification, model identification, model estimation, model testing, and model modification, utilizing a more complex hypothesized theoretical model.

EXERCISES

1. Diagram two indicator variables X1 and X2 of a latent variable F1.
2. Diagram two observed variables X1 and X2 that predict a third observed variable Y. X1 and X2 are correlated.
3. Diagram the latent independent variable F2 predicting the dependent latent variable F1.
4. Would you use a single indicator of a latent variable? Why or why not?

REFERENCES

Anderson, J. C., and Gerbing, D. W. (1988). Structural equation modeling in practice: A review and recommended two-step approach. *Psychological Bulletin, 103*, 411–423.
Bentler, P. M. (1995). *EQS structural equations program manual.* Encino, CA: Multivariate Software.
Bentler, P. M., & Wu, E. J. C. (1995). *EQS for Windows user's guide.* Encino, CA: Multivariate Software, Inc.
Bentler, P. M., & Wu, E. J. C. (2002). *EQS 6 for Windows user's guide.* Encino, CA: Multivariate Software, Inc.

James, L. R., Muliak, S. A., & Brett, J. M. (1982). *Causal analysis: Assumptions, models, and data*. Los Angeles, CA: Sage.

Jöreskog, K. G., & Sörbom, D. (1993). *LISREL 8: Structural equation modeling with the SIMPLIS command language*. Chicago: Scientific Software International.

Mulaik, S. A., & Millsap, R. E. (2000). Doing the four-step right. *Structural Equation Modeling, 7*, 36–73.

Mulaik, S. A., James, L. R., Alstine, J. V., Bennett, N., Lind, S., & Stilwell, C. D. (1989). Evaluation of goodness-of-fit indices for structural equation models. *Psychological Bulletin, 105*, 430–445.

ANSWERS TO EXERCISES

1. Diagram two indicator variables X1 and X2 of a latent variable F1.

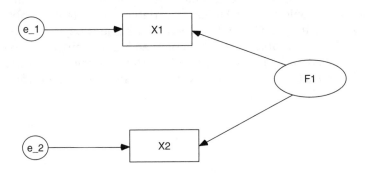

2. Diagram two observed variables X1 and X2 that predict a third observed variable Y. X1 and X2 are correlated.

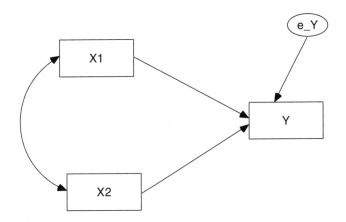

3. Diagram a latent independent variable F2 predicting the dependent latent variable F1.

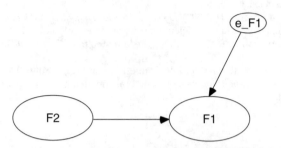

4. Would you use a single indicator of a latent variable? Why or why not?

A single indicator variable of a latent variable would not be as reliable and valid a measure for a latent variable as multiple indicator variables. The preference should be four indicator variables of a latent variable with each variable having a factor loading of .7 or higher. Single indicator variables of latent variables are not recommended, although Jöreskog and Sörbom (1993, p. 37, EX7A.SPL) provided the rationale and an example. MIMIC models (chapter 13) however do use single observed variables.

10

DEVELOPING STRUCTURAL EQUATION MODELS. PART II

———◇◆◇———

Chapter Outline

Key Concepts

Factor loadings and measurement errors
Structure coefficients and prediction errors
Variance and covariance terms
Specification search

In chapter 9 we presented the basic framework for the development of structural equation models. We focused on the measurement model, the structural model, and the different variance–covariance terms. These constitute the basic building blocks for analyzing and interpreting a structural equation model. In this chapter we extend our discussion of the development of structural equation models. We present a hypothesized theoretical structural equation model and discuss issues related to model specification, model identification, model estimation, model testing, and model modification in the context of that example.

10.1   AN EXAMPLE

We hypothesize a structural equation model based on predicting educational achievement as a latent dependent variable. The structural model is diagrammed in Fig. 10.1 with four latent variables (ellipses): two latent independent variables, home background (Home) and Ability, and two latent dependent variables, aspirations (Aspire) and achievement (Achieve).

Three of the latent variables are defined by using two indicator variables, and one latent variable, Home, is defined by using three indicator variables in the measurement models. The indicator variables are depicted using rectangles as follows: (a) for Home, family income (FamInc), father's education (FaEd), and mother's education (MoEd); (b) for Ability, verbal ability (VerbAb) and quantitative ability (QuantAb); (c) for Aspire, educational aspiration (EdAsp) and occupational aspiration (OcAsp); and (d) for Achieve, verbal achievement (VerbAch) and quantitative achievement (QuantAch).

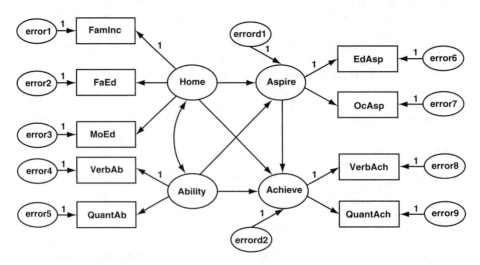

FIG. 10.1.   Structural model of educational achievement.

The measurement models for each latent variable identify which observed variables define that particular latent variable. An arrow is drawn from the latent variable to each of its observed indicator variables. For each arrow we understand that a factor loading will be computed. For example, the observed measures of family income, father's education, and mother's education define the latent variable Home, with each observed variable having a factor loading estimated. Figure 10.1 has nine arrows going from the latent variables (ellipses) to observed variables (rectangles), and thus nine factor loadings will be estimated.

In Fig. 10.1 each observed variable has a unique measurement error. This is indicated by an arrow pointing to each observed variable and indicates that some portion of each observed variable is measuring something other than the hypothesized latent variable. For example, mother's education (MoEd) is hypothesized to define Home (home background), but it may also be assessing other latent variables or be a function of unreliability. The unique measurement error is estimated for each observed variable, so there will be nine unique measurement errors estimated. Each observed variable has a factor loading and a unique measurement error that forms an equation to compute the latent variable score; for example, Home = factor loading * MoEd + measurement error.

Our diagram does not include any curved arrows for measurement errors, but this issue should be discussed. A curved arrow between two measurement errors is possible and indicates that the measurement errors are correlated. Two measurement errors could be correlated if they share something in common such as common method variance or if the same measure is being used at different points in time. For example, quantitative ability (QuantAb) and quantitative achievement (QuantAch) may have correlated measurement errors. Correlated measurement errors may also exist for father's education (FaEd) and mother's education (MoEd).

A straight arrow leading from a latent variable to a latent dependent variable designates that a structure coefficient is to be estimated. For example, it was hypothesized that Home (home background) predicts Aspire (aspirations). The structure coefficients we want to estimate in our hypothesized structural model come from a review of prior research and theory. In our hypothesized structural model there are five structure coefficients we want to estimate. Each latent dependent variable has one or more structure coefficients and a unique prediction error that go into an equation; for example, Aspire = structure coefficient * Home + structure coefficient * Ability + prediction error. The prediction error for Aspire indicates that some portion of Aspire (aspiration) is not predicted by the latent independent variables Home and Ability. There are two equations in our hypothesized structural model, so we estimate two prediction errors, one for Aspire and one for Achieve:

$$\text{Aspire} = \text{structure coefficient} * \text{Home} + \text{structure coefficient} * \text{Ability}$$
$$+ \text{prediction error}$$
$$\text{Achieve} = \text{structure coefficient} * \text{Home} + \text{structure coefficient} * \text{Ability}$$
$$+ \text{structure coefficient} * \text{Aspire} + \text{prediction error}.$$

10.2 MODEL SPECIFICATION

Model specification is usually the first step in structural equation modeling (also for regression models, path models, and confirmatory factor models). We need theory because a set of observed variables can define a multitude of different latent variables in a measurement model. In addition, many different structural equation models can be generated on the basis of different hypothesized relationships among the latent variables.

In our theoretical structural model to predict Achieve (educational achievement) we used nine observed variables and hypothesized four latent variables. Given this, many different measurement models and structural models are possible. First, each observed variable can load on one or more latent variables, so there could be nine or more possible factor loadings. Second, the two latent independent variables may or may not be correlated. Third, there may or may not be correlations or covariances among the measurement errors, suggesting there could be anywhere from zero to several possible correlated measurement errors. Fourth, different structural models could be tested, so we could have more than five or less than five structure coefficients in the different models. Finally, each structural equation has a prediction error, one for each latent dependent variable, so we could have more or less prediction errors, and the prediction errors could be correlated. How does a researcher determine which model is correct? We have already learned that model specification is complicated and we must meet certain data conditions with the observed variables (see chap. 2). Basically, SEM does not determine which model to test; rather it estimates the parameters in a model once that model has been specified *a priori* by the researcher based on theoretical knowledge. Consequently, theory plays a major role in formulating structural equation models and guides the researcher's decision on which model(s) to specify and test. Once again we are reminded that model specification is indeed the hardest part of structural equation modeling.

We used theory to formulate our measurement models and structural model in predicting Achieve (educational achievement). In the measurement models there are nine equations, one for each observed variable. From Fig. 10.1 we formed the following nine measurement equations:

$$\text{EdAsp} = \text{function of Aspire}(1) + \text{measurement error}$$

$$\text{OcAsp} = \text{function of Aspire} + \text{measurement error}$$

$$\text{VerbAch} = \text{function of Achieve}(1) + \text{measurement error}$$

$$\text{QuantAch} = \text{function of Achieve} + \text{measurement error}$$

$$\text{FamInc} = \text{function of Home}(1) + \text{measurement error}$$

$$\text{FaEd} = \text{function of Home} + \text{measurement error}$$

$$\text{MoEd} = \text{function of Home} + \text{measurement error}$$

$$\text{VerbAb} = \text{function of Ability}(1) + \text{measurement error}$$

$$\text{QuantAb} = \text{function of Ability} + \text{measurement error}.$$

Our latent variables are unobserved and have no definite scale of measurement (origin and unit of measurement are arbitrary). To define the measurement model correctly, the origin and unit of measurement for each latent variable must be defined. The origin of a latent variable is usually assumed to have a mean of 0. The unit of measurement (variance) of a latent variable can be set using two different approaches. To compare our factor loadings (interpret the parameter estimates), we need to define a common unit of measurement for the latent variables. This is accomplished by setting a single variable factor loading to 1 for each latent variable. The observed variable selected usually represents the best indicator of the latent variable and is called a *reference variable* because all other observed variables for that latent variable are interpreted in relation to its unit of measurement. Another option would be to assume that the latent variables have a standardized unit of measurement and fix the latent variable variance to 1 (Jöreskog & Sörbom, 1993, pp. 173–174).

In the EQS program (Bentler, 1995) the measurement model equations are written in terms of "V" variables for the observed indicator variables, "F" variables for the latent variables or factors, and "E" variables for the measurement errors of the observed variables. Once again, we can further describe these variables using a /LABEL command as F1 = Aspire for aspirations, F2 = Achieve for achievement, F3 = Home for home background, F4 = Ability for ability, V1 = EdAsp for educational aspiration, V2 = OcAsp for occupational aspiration, V3 = VerbAch for verbal achievement, V4 = QuantAch for quantitative achievement,

V5 = FamInc for family income, V6 = FaEd for father's education, V7 =
MoEd for mother's education, V8 = VerbAb for verbal ability, and V9 =
QuantAb for quantitative ability. This results in the following EQS mea-
surement model equations:

```
/EQUATIONS
        V1 = F1 + E1;
        V2 = 1*F1 + E2;
        V3 = F2 + E3;
        V4 = 1*F2 + E4;
        V5 = F3 + E5;
        V6 = 1*F3 + E6;
        V7 = 1*F3 + E7;
        V8 = F4 + E8;
        V9 = 1*F4 + E9;
```

*The * notation in EQS indicates the factor loadings (parameters) that one
wishes to estimate and includes a start value of 1.0.* Notice that V1 (EdAsp),
V3 (VerbAch), V5 (FamInc), and V8 (Verbab) have unstandardized factor
loadings fixed at 1.

In the LISREL–SIMPLIS command language (Jöreskog & Sörbom, 1993)
the measurement model equations are typically written using variable
names. In the `Relationships:` command, the observed variables are
specified on the left-hand side of the equation with spaces between the
multiple observed variable names and the latent variables on the right-
hand side. The LISREL–SIMPLIS measurement equations are specified
using variable names as follows:

```
Relationships:
  EdAsp         = 1*Aspire
  OcAsp         = Aspire
  VerbAch       = 1*Achieve
  QuantAch      = Achieve
  FamInc        = 1*Home
  FaEd MoEd     = Home
  VerbAb        = 1*Ability
  QuantAb       = Ability
```

The 1 notation in LISREL8–SIMPLIS indicates parameters that are fixed to
1, which is the opposite of EQS.*

In Amos we click on the paths between an observed variable and a
latent variable in the diagram and enter a 1 in the dialog box. We will see
in chapter 13 that naming these paths permits a comparison of factor
loadings between groups.

The equations for the structural model are

$$\text{Aspire} = \text{Home} + \text{Ability} + \text{prediction error}$$

$$\text{Achieve} = \text{Aspire} + \text{Home} + \text{Ability} + \text{prediction error}.$$

In EQS the structural equations are written in terms of "F" variables for the latent variables and "D" variables for the equation prediction errors. The /LABEL command allows us to further describe these variables: F1 = Aspire for aspirations, F2 = Achieve for achievement, F3 = Home for home background, and F4 = Ability for ability. The EQS structural equations are specified as follows:

```
F1 = 1*F3 + 1*F4 + D1;
F2 = 1*F1 + 1*F3 + 1*F4 + D2;
```

*The * notation in EQS indicates parameters that one wishes to estimate and includes a start value of 1.0.* The prediction errors D1 and D2 are estimated by default.

In LISREL–SIMPLIS the structural model can be specified using a Relationships: command. The latent variables can be written as eight-character variable names with either spaces or plus signs (+) between the latent variables. The prediction error terms for the two equations are assumed, so they are not included. The two structural equations are

```
Relationships:
        Aspire  = Home Ability
        Achieve = Aspire Home Ability
```

Finally, we must consider the three different types of variance–covariance terms. First we check for variances and covariances among the latent independent variables. For our model there are separate variance terms for Home and Ability and a term for the correlation between Home and Ability. All of these parameter estimates are automatically specified in the programs for both EQS and LISREL–SIMPLIS. Second, we check for variances and covariances among the prediction errors. In our model, there are separate variance terms for each of the two structural equations, that is, Aspire and Achieve, and no covariance term. These terms are also automatically specified in the programs for both EQS and LISREL–SIMPLIS. Finally, we need to check for variance and covariance terms among the measurement errors of the observed variables. In our measurement model equations there are nine variance terms for the observed variables and no covariance terms. These are also automatically specified in both software packages. Our careful attention to these details should result in our structural model being correctly specified. In Amos we have to carefully specify all of these values in the diagram, otherwise our structural equation model will not be identified!

10.3 MODEL IDENTIFICATION

Once a structural equation model has been specified the next step is to determine whether the model is identified. In chapter 4 we pointed out that the researcher must solve the *identification problem* prior to the estimation of parameters. For the identification problem we ask the following question: On the basis of the sample data contained in the sample variance–covariance matrix S and the theoretical model implied by the population variance–covariance matrix Σ, can a unique set of parameter estimates be found? For the prediction of Achieve (educational achievement) specified in our structural model we would like to know whether the factor loadings, measurement errors, structure coefficients, and prediction errors can be estimated (identified). In our model we fixed certain parameters to resolve the origin and unit of measurement problem while leaving other parameters free to be estimated. An example of a fixed parameter was setting the factor loading for FamInc (family income) on the latent independent variable Home (home background) to 1. An example of a free parameter was the factor loading for FaEd (father's education) on Home (home background) because it was not fixed, rather free to be estimated. *Note: This is done differently in EQS and LISREL programs.*

We determine model identification by first checking the order condition. The number of free parameters to be estimated must be less than or equal to the number of distinct values in the matrix S. A count of the free parameters is as follows:

Five factor loadings (with 4 other factor loadings fixed to 1)
Nine measurement error variances
Zero measurement error covariances
Two latent independent variable variances
One latent independent variable covariance
Five structure coefficients
Two equation prediction error variances
Zero equation prediction error covariances

There is a total of 24 free parameters in our structural model that we want to estimate. The number of distinct values in the matrix S is equal to $p(p+1)/2 = 9(9+1)/2 = 45$, where p is the number of observed variables in the sample variance–covariance matrix. The number of values in S, 45, is greater than the number of free parameters, 24, so the model is probably identified, so we should be able to estimate the number of parameters we want. The degrees of freedom for our structural model is the difference between the number of distinct values in the matrix S and the number of free parameters we want to estimate, $df = 45 - 24 = 21$.

In Amos we simply click on the **DF** icon in the toolkit to view this calculation. Thus, according to the order condition, the model is *overidentified*, as there are more values in S than parameters to be estimated.

However, the order condition is only a necessary condition and is no guarantee that the model is identified. Although the order condition is easy to assess, other sufficient conditions are not (e.g., the rank condition). These other sufficient conditions require us to algebraically determine whether each parameter in the model can be estimated from the sample variance–covariance matrix S. According to the Amos, EQS, and LISREL–SIMPLIS computer programs, which check on identification through the rank test and/or information matrix, the hypothesized structural model for predicting Achieve (educational achievement) is identified.

10.4   MODEL ESTIMATION

Once the identification problem has been resolved the next step is to estimate the parameters in the hypothesized structural model. Once again we can consider the traditional method of intuitively thinking about estimation by decomposing the variance–covariance (or correlation) matrix. The decomposition notion is that the original sample variance–covariance (or correlation) matrix can be completely reproduced if the relations among the observed variables are totally accounted for by the theoretical model. If the model is not properly specified, the original sample variance–covariance matrix will not be completely reproduced.

We now consider the estimation of the parameters for our hypothesized structural model in Fig. 10.1. The sample variance–covariance matrix S is shown in Table 10.1 and the standardized residual matrix is shown in Table 10.2. Our initial model was run in Amos, but EQS and

TABLE 10.1
Sample Variance–Covariance Matrix for Example Data

Variable	1	2	3	4	5	6	7	8	9
1. EdAsp	1.024								
2. OcAsp	.792	1.077							
3. VerbAch	1.027	.919	1.844						
4. QuantAch	.756	.697	1.244	1.286					
5. FamInc	.567	.537	.876	.632	.852				
6. FaEd	.445	.424	.677	.526	.518	.670			
7. MoEd	.434	.389	.635	.498	.475	.545	.716		
8. VerbAb	.580	.564	.893	.716	.546	.422	.373	.851	
9. QuantAb	.491	.499	.888	.646	.508	.389	.339	.629	.871

TABLE 10.2
Standardized Residual Matrix for Model 1

	1	2	3	4	5	6	7	8	9
1. EdAsp	.000								
2. OcAsp	.000	.000							
3. VerbAch	1.420	−.797	.000						
4. QuantAch	−.776	−.363	.000	.000					
5. FamInc	3.541	3.106	5.354	2.803	.000				
6. FaEd	−2.247	−.578	−2.631	−.863	−2.809	.000			
7. MoEd	−1.031	−1.034	−2.151	−.841	−3.240	6.338	.000		
8. VerbAb	.877	1.956	−2.276	1.314	4.590	−.903	−2.144	.000	
9. QuantAb	−2.558	.185	1.820	−.574	3.473	−1.293	−2.366	.000	.000

LISREL–SIMPLIS programs yield similar results (the EQS and LISREL–SIMPLIS computer programs are given at the end of the chapter). In Amos, first draw Fig. 10.1, select the data set for analysis, then calculate the parameter estimates.

The maximum likelihood estimates for the initial model are shown in the first column of Table 10.3. All of the parameter estimates are within the expected magnitude and direction based on previous research (Lomax, 1985). All of the parameter estimates are significantly different from zero ($p < .05$), except the structure coefficient of Home (.139) predicting Achieve (achievement). Because this structure coefficient is of substantive theoretical interest, we will not remove it from the model. ASPIRE was statistically significantly predicted, $R^2 = .613$, and ACHIEVE was statistically significantly predicted, $R^2 = .863$, by the two structural model equations, respectively:

```
ASPIRE  = F1 = .323*F3 + .515*F4 + .622 D1
ACHIEVE = F2 = .397*F1 + .139*F3 + .477*F4 + .370 D2
```

Home and Ability latent variables were correlated, $r = .728$.

10.5 MODEL TESTING

Model testing is the next crucial step in interpreting our results for the hypothesized structural model. When the model fit indices are acceptable the hypothesized structural model has been supported by the sample variance–covariance data. When the model fit indices are not acceptable we usually attempt to respecify the model by adding or deleting paths to achieve a better model-to-data fit (see sec. 10.6).

For our initial model we include several model fit indices at the bottom of Table 10.3 (see chapter 5). For the initial model the χ^2 statistic,

TABLE 10.3
Maximum Likelihood Estimates for Models 1 and 2

Estimates	Model 1	Model 2(respecified)
OcAsp factor loading	.917	.918
QuantAch factor loading	.759	.753
FaEd factor loading	1.007	.782
MoEd factor loading	.964	.720
QuantAb factor loading	.949	.949
Aspire → Achieve coefficient	.548	.526
Home → Aspire coefficient	.410	.506
Home → Achieve coefficient	.242*	.302*
Ability → Aspire coefficient	.590	.447
Ability → Achieve coefficient	.751	.685
Home variance	.532	.662
Ability variance	.663	.663
Home, Ability covariance	.432	.537
Aspire equation error variance	.335	.319
Achieve equation error variance	.225	.228
EdAsp error variance	.160	.161
OcAsp error variance	.351	.350
VerbAch error variance	.205	.193
QuantAch error variance	.342	.349
FamInc error variance	.320	.190
FaEd error variance	.130	.265
MoEd error variance	.222	.373
VerbAb error variance	.188	.188
QuantAb error variance	.274	.274
FaEd, MoEd error covariance	—	.173
Goodness-of-fit indices:		
χ^2	58.85	18.60
df	21	20
p value	.000	.548
GFI	.938	.980
AGFI	.868	.954
RMSR	.049	.015
RMSEA	.095	.000

*Estimates are not statistically significantly different from zero ($p < .05$). The χ^2 values for Model 1 and Model 2 can be checked for significance using Table A.4 in the Appendix.

a measure of badness of fit, is equal to 58.85, with 21 degrees of freedom, and a p value less than .001. Because the χ^2 value is statistically significant ($p < .001$) and is not close in value to the number of degrees of freedom (recall NCP = 0, based on $\chi^2 - df = 0$), this model fit index indicates that the initial model is unacceptable. The root-mean-square error of approximation (RMSEA) is equal to .095, also below the typical acceptable level of model fit (RMSEA < .05). The goodness-of-fit index

(GFI) is .938 for the initial model, which is below our acceptable range of model fit (GFI > .95). Finally, the adjusted goodness-of-fit index (AGFI) is .868 for this model, not an acceptable level of fit (criterion AGFI > .95). For this particular set of model fit indices we conclude that the hypothesized structural model is reasonable but that some model modification might allow us to achieve a more acceptable model-to-data fit. Model modification is discussed in the next section.

10.6 MODEL MODIFICATION

The final step in structural equation modeling is to consider model modification to achieve a better data-to-model fit. If the hypothesized structural model has model fit indices that are less than satisfactory, a researcher typically performs a *specification search* to find a better fitting model to the sample variance–covariance matrix. In chapter 4 we discussed the different procedures one can use in the specification search process. For example, the researcher might eliminate parameters that are not significantly different from zero and/or include additional parameters. To eliminate parameters, the most commonly used procedures are to (a) compare the *t* statistic for each parameter to a tabulated *t* value (e.g., $t > 1.96$) for statistical significance and (b) use the Wald (W) statistic (similar interpretation as the *t* statistic).

To include additional parameters, the most commonly used techniques are (a) select the highest modification index (MI) (the expected value that χ^2 would decrease by if such a parameter were to be included), (b) select the highest expected parameter change statistic (EPC) (the approximate value of the new parameter), and (c) use the Lagrange multiplier (LM) statistic (similar interpretation as the modification index). Amos permits identification of optional and required paths in a model, thus generating a comparison of alternative nested models in a specification search.

A researcher could also examine the residual matrix (or the more useful standardized residual matrix) to obtain clues as to which original variances and covariances are not well accounted for by the model (the residual matrix is the difference between the observed variance–covariance terms in S and the corresponding reproduced variance–covariance terms in Σ). Large standardized residuals (greater than 1.96 or 2.58) indicate that a particular variable relationship is not well accounted for in the model.

For our hypothesized structural model, the original sample variance–covariance matrix is shown in Table 10.1 and the standardized residual variance–covariance matrix is given in Table 10.2. The largest

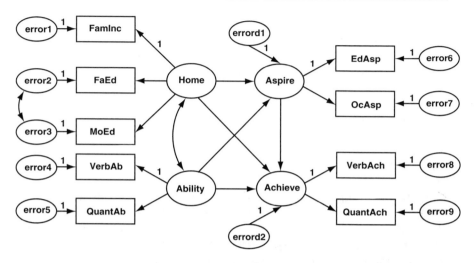

FIG. 10.2.   Respecified structural model of educational achievement.

standardized residual is for the relationship between FaEd (father's education) and MoEd (mother's education) (i.e., 6.338). Notice that the t and
Wald statistics do not suggest the elimination of any existing parameters
from the initial model because every parameter estimate except one is
statistically different from zero. When considering the addition of new
parameters in the model the largest modification index is for the measurement error covariance between FaEd (father's education) and MoEd
(mother's education) (i.e., MI = 40.176). If we were to estimate that parameter (correlation between FaEd and MoEd measurement error), the
expected change would be EPC = 0.205.

In our specification search the standardized residual and EPC values
indicated that something was wrong with how we specified the relationship between FaEd (father's education) and MoEd (mother's education)
because it was not captured by the initial model. Consequently, we de-
cided to specify a measurement error covariance (correlation) between
FaEd (father's education) and MoEd (mother's education) because upon
further reflection there should be common method variance on measures using the same scale with two different parents.

The ML estimates and selected model fit indices for the respecified
model, where the measurement error covariance modification is now
included, are shown in the second column of Table 10.3 and diagrammed
in Fig. 10.2.

All of the parameters are statistically significantly different from
zero ($p < .05$) except for the path between Home (home background)
and Achieve (achievement), but once again, for substantive theoretical

reasons, we chose to leave this relationship specified in the model. Our selected model fit indices now indicate an acceptable level of fit, and a second specification search did not result in any further recommended changes. Thus, we consider our respecified model to be our final structural model for the prediction of educational achievement. Applying this structural model to other samples of data will, we hope, provide further validation that this is a theoretically meaningful structural model.

10.7   SUMMARY

This chapter completed the basic discussion of structural equation modeling we began in chapter 9. We hypothesized a structural model to predict educational achievement and described it in further detail. We followed the recommended steps a researcher should take in the structural equation modeling process, namely model specification, model identification, model estimation, model testing, and finally model modification. We did not obtain acceptable model fit indices with our initial specified model, so we conducted a specification search. The specification search suggested adding a parameter estimate for the correlation between the measurement error terms of father's and mother's education level. The respecified model resulted in acceptable model fit indices, so this was determined to be our best data-to-model fit. In chapter 11 we provide suggestions and recommendations for how structural equation modeling studies should be reported in the literature.

APPENDIX: COMPUTER PROGRAMS

EQS Structural Equation Model Program

```
/TITLE
     Educational Achievement Example — Model 2 Respecified
/SPECIFICATIONS
     CASES=200; VARIABLES=9; ME=ML;
/LABELS
     V1=EdAsp;V2=OcAsp;V3=VerbAch;V4=QuantAch;V5=FamInc;V6=FaEd;
     V7=MoEd;V8=VerbAb;V9=QuantAb;F1=ASPIRE;F2=ACHIEVE;F3=HOME;
     F4=ABILITY;
/EQUATIONS
     V1= F1 + E1;
     V2=1*F1 + E2;
     V3= F2 + E3;
     V4=1*F2 + E4;
     V5= F3 + E5;
     V6=1*F3 + E6;
     V7=1*F3 + E7;
```

```
      V8= F4 + E8;
      V9=1*F4 + E9;
      F1=1*F3 + 1*F4 + D1;
      F2=1*F1 + 1*F3 + 1*F4 + D2;
/VARIANCES
      E1 TO E9=1*;
      D1 to D2=1*;
/COVARIANCES
   E6,E7 = *;   F3,F4 = 1*;
/MATRIX
      1.024
       .792  1.077
      1.027   .919  1.844
       .756   .697  1.244  1.286
       .567   .537   .876   .632   .852
       .445   .424   .677   .526   .518   .670
       .434   .389   .635   .498   .475   .545   .716
       .580   .564   .893   .716   .546   .422   .373   .851
       .491   .499   .888   .646   .508   .389   .339   .629   .871
/END
```

LISREL–SIMPLIS Structural Equation Model Program

```
Educational Achievement Example — Model 2 Respecified
Observed variables: EdAsp OcAsp VerbAch QuantAch FamInc FaEd
      MoEd VerbAb QuantAb
Covariance matrix:
1.024
 .792  1.077
1.027   .919  1.844
 .756   .697  1.244  1.286
 .567   .537   .876   .632   .852
 .445   .424   .677   .526   .518   .670
 .434   .389   .635   .498   .475   .545   .716
 .580   .564   .893   .716   .546   .422   .373   .851
 .491   .499   .888   .646   .508   .389   .339   .629   .871
Sample size: 200
Latent variables: ASPIRE ACHIEVE HOME ABILITY
Relationships:
   EdAsp        = 1*ASPIRE
   OcAsp        = ASPIRE
   VerbAch      = 1*ACHIEVE
   QuantAch     = ACHIEVE
   FamInc       = 1*HOME
   FaEd MoEd    = HOME
   VerbAb       = 1*ABILITY
   QuantAb      = ABILITY
   ASPIRE       = HOME ABILITY
   ACHIEVE      = ASPIRE HOME ABILITY
Let the error covariances of FaEd and MoEd correlate
Path Diagram
End of problem
```

EXERCISE

Conduct the following structural equation model analysis using an SEM software program:

Sample size = 500
Observed X variables:
    ACT score (ACT)
    College grade point average (CGPA)
    Company entry-level skills test score (ENTRY)
Observed Y variables:
    Beginning salary (SALARY)
    Current salary due to promotions (PROMO)
Latent dependent variable: Job Success (JOB)
Latent independent variable: Academic Success (ACAD)
Structural model:

```
Path:
ACAD  →  JOB
```

Variance–covariance matrix:

```
ACT       1.024
CGPA       .792  1.077
ENTRY      .567   .537  .852
SALARY     .445   .424  .518  .670
PROMO      .434   .389  .475  .545  .716
```

REFERENCES

Bentler, P. M. (1995). *EQS structural equations program manual*. Encino, CA: Multivariate Software.

Jöreskog, K. G., & Sörbom, D. (1993). *LISREL 8: Structural equation modeling with the SIMPLIS command language*. Chicago: Scientific Software International.

Lomax, R. G. (1985). A structural model of public and private schools. *Journal of Experimental Education, 53*, 216–226.

ANSWERS TO EXERCISE

Write the following LISREL–SIMPLIS program:

```
Chapter 10 Exercise
Observed variables: ACT CGPA ENTRY SALARY PROMO
Covariance matrix:
  1.024
   .792 1.077
   .567  .537 .852
   .445  .424 .518 .670
   .434  .389 .475 .545 .716
```

```
Sample size: 500
Latent variables: ACAD JOB
Relationships:
      ACT = 1*ACAD
     CGPA = ACAD
    ENTRY = ACAD
   SALARY = 1*JOB
    PROMO = JOB
      JOB = ACAD
Path Diagram
End of problem
```

The chi-square is statistically significant ($\chi^2 = 116.29$, $df = 4$, $p = .000$), so the modification indices are checked, and it is suggested to add an error covariance between the measurement error variances of CGPA and ACT:

```
The Modification Indices Suggest to Add an Error Covariance
Between    and    Decrease in Chi-Square   New Estimate
ACT        SALARY          14.0               -0.06
CGPA       ACT            113.5                0.43
ENTRY      SALARY          40.8                0.10
ENTRY      ACT             24.9               -0.15
ENTRY      CGPA            23.9               -0.14
```

The following command line is added:

Let the error covariances between CGPA and ACT correlate

The modified model is acceptable ($\chi^2 = 3.04$, $df = 3$, $p = .39$; RMSEA $= .005$; GFI $= 1.0$). JOB is statistically significantly predicted, $R^2 = .70$, by the structural equation:

```
Structural Equations

    JOB = 0.91*ACAD, Errorvar. = 0.18 ,   R² = 0.70
          (0.061)                (0.027)
          15.01                   6.59
```

11

REPORTING SEM RESEARCH

Chapter Outline

Key Concepts

Theoretical models
Model specification and identification
Model estimation and testing
Model modification and specification search
Sample matrix in SPSS or Excel

Breckler (1990) reviewed the personality and social psychology research literature and found several shortcomings of structural equation modeling, namely that model fit indices can be identical for a potentially large number of models, that assumptions of multivariate normality are required, that sample size affects results, and that cross-validation of models was infrequently addressed or mentioned. Many of the studies only reported a single model fit index. Breckler concluded that there was cause for concern in the reporting of structural equation modeling results. Raykov, Tomer, and Nesselroade (1991) proposed guidelines for reporting SEM results in the journal *Psychology and Aging*. Maxwell and Cole (1995) offered some general tips for writing methodological articles, and Hoyle and Panter (1995) published a chapter on reporting SEM research with an emphasis on describing the results and what model fit criteria to include.

The *Publication Manual of the American Psychological Association* (American Psychological Association, 2002, pp. 161, 164–167, and 185) specifically states that researchers should include the means, standard deviations, and intercorrelations of the entire set of variables so that others can replicate and confirm the analysis, as well as provide example tables and a figure(s) when reporting structural equation modeling research. Unfortunately, the guidelines do not go far enough in outlining the basic information that should be included to afford an evaluation of the research study and some fundamental points that should be addressed when conducting SEM studies. A few scholars have offered advice.

Boomsma (2000) discussed how to write a research paper when structural equation models were used in empirical research and how to decide what information should be reported. His basic premise was that all information necessary for someone else to replicate the analysis should be reported. He provided recommendations along the line of our basic steps in structural equation modeling, namely model specification, model identification, model estimation, model testing, and model modification. He found that many studies lacked a theoretical foundation for the theoretical model, gave a poor description of the model tested, provided no discussion of the psychometric properties of the variables and level of measurement, did not include sample data, and had a poor delineation or justification for the model modification process. He pointed out how difficult it can be to evaluate or judge the quality of published SEM research.

MacCallum and Austin (2000) provided an excellent survey of problems in applications of SEM, and Thompson (2000) provided guidance for conducting structural equation modeling by citing key issues and including a list of 10 commandments for good structural equation modeling behavior: (a) do not conclude that a model is the only model to fit the data, (b) test any respecified model with split-sample data or new data, (c) test multiple rival models, (d) evaluate measurement models first, then structural models, (e) evaluate models by fit, theory, and practical concerns, (f) report multiple model fit indices, (g) meet multivariate normality assumptions, (h) seek parsimonious models, (i) consider a variable scale of measurement and distribution, and (j) do not use small samples.

We further elaborate several key issues in SEM. In SEM model analyses several different types of sample matrices can be used (e.g., asymptotic variance–covariance matrix, Pearson correlation matrix, or polyserial, polychoric, or tetrachoric matrices). When to use which type of matrix depends on several factors: nonnormality, type of variables, and so on.

A second issue concerns model identification, that is, the number of distinct values in the sample variance–covariance matrix should exceed the number of free parameters estimated in the model (degrees of freedom should not be zero or negative for the model) and the rank of the matrix should yield a nonzero determinant value. A researcher must also select from various parameter estimation techniques in model estimation (e.g., unweighted least squares, maximum likelihood, or generalized least squares estimation under the assumption of multivariate normality of the sample variance–covariance data, or asymptotically distribution-free estimation using ADF or CVM techniques when multivariate normality assumption is not met). Obviously, many factors discussed in chapters 2 and 3 affect multivariate normality.

A researcher should also be aware that equivalent models and alternative models may exist in an overidentified model (more distinct values in the matrix than free parameters estimated), and we rarely are able to perfectly reproduce the sample variance–covariance matrix, given the implied theoretical model. We use model fit indices and specification searches to obtain an acceptable model-to-data fit, given alternative models. Model fit statistics should guide our search for a better fitting model. Chapter 5 outlined different model fit criteria depending on the focus of the research. Under some situations, for example, large sample sizes, the chi-square values will be inflated (statistically significant), thus erroneously implying a poor data-to-model fit. A more appropriate use of the chi-square statistic in this situation would be to compare alternative models with the same sample data (nested models). The specification search process involves finding whether a variable should be added (parameter estimated) or a variable deleted (parameter not estimated). A researcher, when modifying an initial model, should change one variable at a time (add or delete one parameter estimate) and give a theoretical justification.

Ironically, structural equation modeling requires larger sample sizes as models become more complex or require cross-validation with split samples. In traditional multivariate statistics the rule of thumb is 20 subjects per variable (20:1). The rule of thumb in structural equation modeling has changed from 100, 200, to 500 or more subjects per study depending on model complexity and cross-validation. Sample size and power are also important considerations in SEM modeling. Finally, a two-step/four-step approach is important because if measurement models do not fit the observed variables, then relationships among the latent variables in structural models are meaningless.

McDonald and Ringo Ho (2002) examined 41 of 100 articles in 13 psychological journals from 1995 to 1997. They stated that SEM researchers should give a detailed justification of the SEM model tested along with alternative models, account for identification, address nonnormality and missing data concerns, include a complete set of parameters with standard errors, correlation matrix, discrepancies, and goodness-of-fit indices.

We made many of these same suggestions in the previous chapters, and our intention in this chapter is to succinctly summarize guidelines and recommendations for researchers in reporting SEM research results. We do so by way of a theoretical model example.

11.1 AN EXAMPLE

A researcher should begin a SEM research study with the rationale and the purpose of the study, followed by a sound theoretical foundation of the measurement model(s) and the structural model. This includes a discussion of the latent variables and how they are defined in the measurement model(s). The hypothesis should involve the testing of the structural model and/or the difference between alternative models.

A SEM research study typically involves using sample data, in contrast to a methodological simulation study. The sample matrix should be described as to the type (augmented, asymptotic, covariance, or correlation), whether multivariate normality assumptions have been met, and the scale of measurement for the observed variables, and be related to an appropriate estimation technique (e.g., maximum likelihood). Multiple regression, path analysis, factor analysis, and structural equation modeling can all use data as input into a computer program (see SPSS and Microsoft Excel examples at the end of the chapter). The SEM program should include the sample matrix, means, and standard deviations of the observed variables.

A set of recommendations for data preparation includes the following (see SEM checklist in sec. 11.7):

1. Establish a sound theoretical basis for the measurement models and structural models in the study.
2. Clearly state the hypothesis for testing the structural model and/or alternative models.

3. Specify the type of correlation or variance–covariance matrix used in the computer program. Check for missing data, outliers, nonnormality, and other issues that affect correlations.
4. When using a correlation matrix, also include the means and standard deviations of the observed variables to obtain the correct estimates of standard errors for the parameter estimates (Gonzalez & Griffin, 2001).
5. Identify the estimation technique based on type of data matrix.
6. Include the computer program with the command language and data matrix. Alternatively, one could include a computer program in an appendix with the larger data matrix in a table of an article or provide a reliable website for access to the program and data.

We now present our example following these recommendations. We choose a study by Holzinger and Swineford (1939) to illustrate the first set of recommendations. The authors administered 26 psychological tests to 145 students in Chicago schools. The rationale for the study was to examine gender differences in certain psychological constructs. The purpose of our study is to determine whether boys and girls have different spatial and verbal abilities.

Theoretical support is given for a measurement model that contains two common factors, spatial and verbal (Fig. 11.1). The spatial ability factor is defined by three different tests, visual perception (visual task), spatial visualization (cube task), and spatial orientation (lozenges task), which involve spatial problems related to geometric configurations. The verbal factor is defined by three different tests, paragraph comprehension, sentence completion, and word meaning, which involve verbal problems related to language. This measurement model is to be confirmed separately for the boys and the girls. Theoretical support is given to a structural model to test gender differences between boys and girls on the correlation between the spatial and verbal factors. The null hypothesis for the structural model is that boys and girls do not differ in the correlation between spatial and verbal abilities. Consequently, we advocate a two-step approach that first confirms the reliability and validity of the measurement models before testing the structural equation model.

The correlation matrix contains Pearson product–moment correlations among the six test scores with means, standard deviations, and sample sizes listed separately for the boys ($n = 72$) and the girls ($n = 73$). These descriptive data could be placed in a table as well as included in computer programs. There are no missing data, outliers, or nonnormality indicated (skewness and kurtosis values for the variables are acceptable). Given that the multivariate normality assumption is met, the maximum likelihood estimation technique is chosen to estimate the

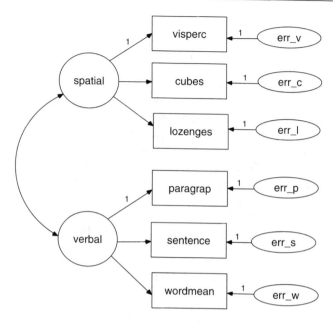

FIG. 11.1. Amos confirmatory factor model.

factor loadings and test the statistical significance of the correlation coefficient between the two common factors. All six tests yield scores considered at the interval level of measurement, and hence are treated as continuous data for analysis purposes.

Pattern and structure coefficients should be reported for most types of measurement models (Graham, Guthrie, & Thompson, 2003). The belief that a path set to zero between a measured variable and a factor has no correlation with that factor is erroneous (Bentler & Yuan, 2000). The interpretation problem resulting from not reporting structure coefficients occurs only when factors are correlated. The higher the factor correlation, the more different are the pattern and structure coefficients of the variables across the factors. Essentially, observed variables are correlated with all factors when the factors are correlated, even in CFA models where certain parameters are constrained to zero. Variables with parameters constrained to zero on a factor are intended theoretically to not measure that factor; however, factor correlation implies an indirect path or relationship. Amos structure coefficients are output as standardized estimates in the *all implied moments* matrix, which include the correlations between the observed variables and the factors. In Amos, select **View/Set** from the tool bar menu, then select **Analysis Properties** and click on *standardized estimates* and the *all implied.moments* options.

We now report the SEM program with the commands, that is, specifications for the measurement model(s) and/or structural model, and the
sample data. *In SEM, there should be no reason why the program and data
cannot be included in an article to permit replication of the model analyses.* We run a separate EQS program for the boys' and the girl's data to
obtain their factor loadings, measurement errors, and composite reliability (without the **/CONSTRAINT** command). We include the combined
EQS program here using the **/CONSTRAINT** command to test for measurement invariance (boys and girls have similar factor loadings on the
latent variables). *In SEM, a researcher should test for measurement invariance in measurement models before testing parameter estimates between
groups in a structural model.* We also use this combined program to test
whether the correlation between spatial and verbal latent variables is
the same for boys and girls (our hypothesis for the structural model).

Combined EQS Program with Constraints

```
/TITLE
  MULTIPLE GROUPS MEASUREMENT INVARIANCE-GIRLS
/SPECIFICATIONS
  CASES=73; VARIABLES=6; MATRIX=CORRELATION;
  METHOD=ML; GROUPS=2;
/LABELS
  V1=visperc;V2=cubes;V3=lozenges;V4=parcomp;V5=sencomp;V6=wordmean;
  F1=spatial;F2=verbal;
/EQUATIONS
  V1 = 1*F1 + E1;
  V2 = 1*F1 + E2;
  V3 = 1*F1 + E3;
  V4 = 1*F2 + E4;
  V5 = 1*F2 + E5;
  V6 = 1*F2 + E6;
/VARIANCES
  F1 = 1.0;
  F2 = 1.0;
  E1 TO E6 = *;
/COVARIANCES
  F1,F2 = *;
/MATRIX
      1.000
      0.483 1.000
      0.492 0.492 1.000
      0.343 0.211 0.326 1.000
      0.367 0.179 0.335 0.724 1.000
      0.230 0.184 0.369 0.743 0.696 1.000
/STANDARD DEVIATIONS
  6.916 4.533 7.911 3.562 5.054 8.319
```

```
/MEANS
 29.315 24.699 14.836 10.589 19.301 18.014
/END

/TITLE
  MULTIPLE GROUPS MEASUREMENT INVARIANCE-BOYS
/SPECIFICATIONS
  CASES=72; VARIABLES=6; MATRIX=CORRELATION;
  METHOD=ML;
/LABELS
  V1=visperc;V2=cubes;V3=lozenges;V4=parcomp;V5=sencomp;V6=wordmean;
  F1=spatial;F2=verbal;
/EQUATIONS
  V1 = 1*F1 + E1;
  V2 = 1*F1 + E2;
  V3 = 1*F1 + E3;
  V4 = 1*F2 + E4;
  V5 = 1*F2 + E5;
  V6 = 1*F2 + E6;
/VARIANCES
  F1 = 1.0;
  F2 = 1.0;
  E1 TO E6 = *;
/COVARIANCES
  F1,F2 = *;
/PRINT
 FIT=ALL;
 TABLE = EQUATION;
 EFFECT=YES;
/MATRIX
      1.000
      0.161 1.000
      0.408 0.348 1.000
      0.373 0.269 0.411 1.000
      0.254 0.143 0.276 0.705 1.000
      0.426 0.214 0.364 0.674 0.666 1.000
/STANDARD DEVIATIONS
 6.950 4.384 8.613 3.066 4.184 7.538
/MEANS
 29.847 24.903 17.111 9.306 18.389 16.542
/CONSTRAINTS
! These 6 constraints test for measurement invariance
  (1,V1 ,F1)=(2,V1,F1);
  (1,V2 ,F1)=(2,V2,F1);
  (1,V3 ,F1)=(2,V3,F1);
  (1,V4 ,F2)=(2,V4,F2);
  (1,V5 ,F2)=(2,V5,F2);
  (1,V6 ,F2)=(2,V6,F2);
! This last constraint tests our structural model
! (1,F2,F1)=(2,F2,F1);
/LMTEST
/END
```

11.2 MODEL SPECIFICATION

In the study we must clearly indicate our intent to assess two measurement models (boys and girls) and a structural model, and thus we must consider model specification issues. *Model specification* involves determining every relationship and parameter in the model that is of interest to the researcher. Moreover, the goal of the researcher is to determine, as best possible, the theoretical model that generates the sample variance–covariance matrix. If the theoretical model is misspecified, it could yield biased parameter estimates—parameter estimates that are different from what they are in the true population model, that is, specification error. We do not typically know the true population model, so bias in parameter estimates is generally attributed to the standard errors.

Figure 11.1 depicts our measurement model, and the EQS program (or LISREL–SIMPLIS or Amos diagram) further supports our measurement model by indicating which three observed variables are measures of which two latent variables. We want the factor loadings on these six observed variables to be the same for both the boys and the girls, thus supporting measurement invariance for the groups on the latent variables. We can run each program and obtain the factor loadings for the boys and girls, but then combine the programs into a single program with constraints to test whether the factor loadings are the same for the two groups, boys and girls, that is, test for measurement invariance. We therefore run three different EQS programs (LISREL–SIMPLIS, and Amos data files) to obtain reliability and validity coefficients and test for measurement invariance. *Measurement invariance should first be established before testing for between-group differences* (Cheung & Rensvold, 2002). Our hypothesis (Is the correlation between spatial and verbal the same for boys and girls?) is tested in our structural model. This is accomplished in EQS by adding a final constraint command that sets the correlation in each group equal, that is, the equality constraint tests whether correlations are the same ($H_0 : \rho_{boys} - \rho_{girls} = 0$).

A set of recommendations for model specification therefore includes the following (see SEM checklist in sec. 11.7):

1. Did you provide a rationale and purpose for your study, including why SEM rather than another statistical analysis approach was required?
2. Did you describe your latent variables, thus providing a substantive background to how they are measured?
3. Did you provide a theoretical foundation for your measurement model(s) and structural model?

4. Did you clearly state your statistical hypotheses?
5. Did you discuss the expected magnitude and direction of expected parameter estimates?
6. Did you include a figure or diagram of your measurement and structural models?
7. Have you described every parameter in the models that you want to estimate? In contrast, have you explained why other parameters are not included in the models and/or why you have included constraints or fixed certain parameters?
8. Have you tested for measurement invariance in factors before testing for between-group differences in parameters?

11.3 MODEL IDENTIFICATION

In structural equation modeling it is crucial that the researcher resolve the *identification problem* prior to the estimation of parameters in measurement models or structural models. In the identification problem we ask the following question: On the basis of the sample data contained in the sample covariance matrix S and the theoretical model implied by the population covariance matrix Σ, can a unique set of parameter estimates be found?

The sample correlation matrix contains 21 distinct variances and covariances among the six variables, so the number of distinct values is $p(p+1)/2 = 6(6+1)/2 = 21$. The measurement model specifies that we want to estimate 13 parameters, that is, 6 factor loadings, 6 corresponding measurement errors, and the correlation between the spatial and verbal latent variables. The *order condition* is therefore met because we have more distinct values in the sample correlation matrix than free parameters in the model to be estimated, that is, degrees of freedom $= 21 - 13 = 8$. We check this in Amos by clicking on the **DF** icon in the toolkit. Consequently, if the *rank condition* is met, that is, the determinant of the matrix is nonzero, we should be able to estimate our parameters in the measurement model. For the test of measurement invariance our degrees of freedom will be 22 because there are 42 distinct values from both correlation matrices minus the 20 parameters in the combined measurement model. We arrive at the final structural model degrees of freedom by subtracting 6 factor loadings, 6 measurement errors, and 7 constraints from the 42 distinct values, $42 - 19 = 23$, (see Table 11.4).

A set of recommendations for model identification includes the following (see SEM checklist in sec. 11.7):

1. Specify the number of distinct values in the sample matrix, the number of free parameters to be estimated, along with the degrees of freedom, that is, check that the order condition is satisfied.
2. Specify that the rank condition is satisified, that is, the determinant of the matrix is nonzero, and that parameters can be estimated.
3. Resolve any convergence problems by using start values, setting the admissibility check off, using a larger sample size, or using a different estimation method.
4. Resolve any non-positive definite error message resulting from correction for attenuation or Heywood cases.

11.4   MODEL ESTIMATION

In this section we specify which estimation technique we selected for estimating the parameters in our measurement models and structural model, that is, our estimates of the population parameters from sample data. We choose the maximum likelihood estimation technique because we meet the multivariate normality assumption (acceptable skewness and kurtosis), there are no missing data, no outliers, and continuous variable data. If the observed variables are interval scaled and multivariate normal, then the ML estimates, standard errors, and chi-square test are appropriate.

Our experience is that model estimation often does not work because of messy data. In chapters 2 and 3 we outlined many of the factors that can effect parameter estimation in general, and structural equation modeling specifically. Missing data, outliers, multicollinearity, and non-normality of data distributions seriously affect the estimation process and often result in fatal error messages pertaining to Heywood variables (variables with negative variance), non-positive definite matrices (determinant of matrix is zero), or failure to reach convergence (unable to compute a set of parameter estimates). SEM is a correlation research method and all of the factors that affect correlation coefficients, the general linear model (regression, path, and factor models), and statistics in general are compounded in structural equation modeling. *Do not overlook the problems caused by messy data!*

A set of recommendations for model estimation includes the following (see SEM checklist in sec. 11.7):

1. Did you edit data carefully to meet all assumptions?
2. How will you determine power and sample size for your study, given different levels of model complexity?
3. Did you specify which parameters are free, constrained, fixed, or not estimated?
4. What LM tests of parameter estimates will you consider?
5. What estimation technique is appropriate for sample data (ML and GLS multivariate normal data with small to moderate sample sizes; ADF or CVM, nonnormal, asymptotic covariance data, and WLS nonnormal with large sample sizes)?
6. Did you encounter Heywood cases (negative variance), multicollinearity, or a non-positive definite matrix?
7. How did you scale the latent variable variance?
8. Which SEM program and version did you use?
9. Did you use starting values?
10. Did you encounter any convergence problems or inadmissible solutions?

11.5 MODEL TESTING

In our study, model testing requires us to report in tables the factor loadings and communality of the variables in the measurement models for the boys and girls, along with a statement about testing for measurement invariance. These tables are in standard American Psychological Association style. Table 11.1 lists the factor loadings (pattern coefficients) for both boys and girls along with the composite reliability and measurement model fit indices. Given adequate reliability and fit, we conclude

TABLE 11.1
Measurement Model (Boys vs. Girls)

Variable	Boys ($n = 72$)		Girls ($n = 73$)	
	Loading	R^2	Loading	R^2
Visual perception	.580	.337	.703	.495
Visual spatialization	.415	.172	.654	.427
Lozenges	.708	.501	.736	.542
Paragraph comprehension	.863	.745	.879	.773
Sentence completion	.806	.650	.827	.684
Word meaning	.805	.648	.842	.709
Chi-square (df; p)	8.618 (8; .375)		7.838 (8; .449)	
Reliability rho	.808		.859	
NFI; GFI; CFI	.94; .96; .99		.96; .97; 1.00	
RMSEA (CI)	.03 (.00, .145)		.00 (.00, .135)	

TABLE 11.2
Pattern Versus Structure Coefficients in CFA Model: Boys

Variable	Spatial		Verbal	
	Pattern	Structure	Pattern	Structure
Visual perception	.580	.580	.00	.377
Cubes	.415	.415	.00	.269
Lozenges	.708	.708	.00	.460
Paragraph comprehension	.00	.560	.863	.863
Sentence completion	.00	.523	.806	.806
Word meaning	.00	.523	.805	.805

Note: For boys, $r = .649$ between spatial and verbal factors.

TABLE 11.3
Pattern Versus Structure Coefficients in CFA Model: Girls

Variable	Spatial		Verbal	
	Pattern	Structure	Pattern	Structure
Visual perception	.703	.703	.00	.343
Cubes	.654	.654	.00	.318
Lozenges	.736	.736	.00	.359
Paragraph comprehension	.00	.428	.879	.879
Sentence completion	.00	.403	.827	.827
Word meaning	.00	.410	.842	.842

Note: For girls, $r = .487$ between spatial and verbal factors.

that the sample data for the boys and girls fit the two-factor measurement model. Table 11.2 compares the pattern and structure coefficients for boys and Table 11.3 compares the pattern and structure coefficients for girls.

The pattern and structure coefficients are identical for observed variables that load on the specified factors in Fig. 11.1, as expected. Although theory supports two unidimensional factors that are correlated, we find structure coefficients for observed variables that have been constrained to zero, as expected. We do notice that the spatial factor for boys has high structure coefficients for certain observed variables (paragraph, sentence, and wordmean) that should correlate with the verbal factor. However, we conclude that the factor loadings (pattern coefficients) as specified in our measurement model are acceptable and theoretically meaningful.

Once the factor loadings and measurement model fit indices are acceptable, we can run the third program and test for measurement invariance (similar factor loadings in the measurement model for boys and girls). The model fit indices suggest that the sample data have an acceptable fit to the combined measurement model ($\chi^2 = 20.248, df = 22$, $p = .567$; NFI = .94, GFI = .957; CFI = 1.00; RMSEA = .00). The other important computer output to examine is the Lagrange multiplier (LM) test for equal factor loadings (constraints), which is as follows:

```
LAGRANGE MULTIPLIER TEST
CONSTR:  1  (1,V1,F1)-(2,V1,F1)=0;
CONSTR:  2  (1,V2,F1)-(2,V2,F1)=0;
CONSTR:  3  (1,V3,F1)-(2,V3,F1)=0;
CONSTR:  4  (1,V4,F2)-(2,V4,F2)=0;
CONSTR:  5  (1,V5,F2)-(2,V5,F2)=0;
CONSTR:  6  (1,V6,F2)-(2,V6,F2)=0;


CUMULATIVE MULTIVARIATE STATISTICS     UNIVARIATE INCREMENT
----------------------------------     ---------------------
```

STEP	PARAMETER	CHI-SQUARE	D.F.	PROBABILITY	CHI-SQUARE	PROBABILITY
1	CONSTR: 2	1.559	1	.212	1.559	.212
2	CONSTR: 5	2.119	2	.347	.559	.454
3	CONSTR: 4	2.635	3	.451	.516	.473
4	CONSTR: 6	3.252	4	.517	.618	.432
5	CONSTR: 1	3.690	5	.595	.438	.508
6	CONSTR: 3	3.729	6	.713	.039	.843

The LM test (chi-square value) for each constraint is not significant, and therefore the factor loadings are assumed the same for boys and girls. Given these findings, we are now confident that all measures of spatial and verbal abilities are operating in the same way for both groups. If the measurement invariance assumption did not hold for certain observed variables, then separate factor loadings for boys and girls would have to be set in the program for those variables that did not differ before testing between-group differences in the structural equation model parameters.

The measurement invariance assumption is met in our measurement model. Thus, we can test between group differences in the correlation between the two constructs in our structural model. We accomplish this by maintaining the equality constraints for the factor loadings and adding another constraint to specifically test a between-group difference in the correlation term in the model. The model fit indices suggest that the correlation between the groups is not statistically significant ($\chi^2 = 21.99$, $df = 23$, $p = .520$, NFI = .935, GFI = .954, CFI = 1.00, RMSEA = .00). The LM test (chi-square value) for the equality constraint to test this difference indicates a nonstatistical difference between the groups correlation coefficients ($\chi^2 = 5.383$, $p = .613$). *Having provided the SEM program and sample data along with our measurement and structural models, anyone can check our results and verify our findings.*

```
LAGRANGE MULTIPLIER TEST

CONSTR: 1  (1,V1,F1)-(2,V1,F1)=0;
CONSTR: 2  (1,V2,F1)-(2,V2,F1)=0;
CONSTR: 3  (1,V3,F1)-(2,V3,F1)=0;
CONSTR: 4  (1,V4,F2)-(2,V4,F2)=0;
CONSTR: 5  (1,V5,F2)-(2,V5,F2)=0;
CONSTR: 6  (1,V6,F2)-(2,V6,F2)=0;
CONSTR: 7  (1,F2,F1)-(2,F2,F1)=0;
```

UNIVARIATE TEST STATISTICS:

NO	CONSTRAINT	CHI-SQUARE	PROBABILITY
1	CONSTR: 1	.307	.579
2	CONSTR: 2	1.597	.206
3	CONSTR: 3	.297	.586
4	CONSTR: 4	.322	.571
5	CONSTR: 5	.584	.445
6	CONSTR: 6	.059	.807
7	CONSTR: 7	1.600	.206

		CUMULATIVE MULTIVARIATE STATISTICS			UNIVARIATE INCREMENT	
STEP	PARAMETER	CHI-SQUARE	D.F.	PROBABILITY	CHI-SQUARE	PROBABILITY
1	CONSTR: 7	1.600	1	.206	1.600	.206
2	CONSTR: 2	3.032	2	.220	1.432	.232
3	CONSTR: 5	3.520	3	.318	.489	.484
4	CONSTR: 4	4.078	4	.396	.558	.455
5	CONSTR: 6	4.722	5	.451	.644	.422
6	CONSTR: 1	5.291	6	.507	.570	.450
7	CONSTR: 3	5.383	7	.613	.091	.763

In interpreting our measurement models and structural model we established how well the data fit the models. In other words, we examined the extent to which the theoretical model was supported by the sample data. We considered model fit indices for the entire fit of the model and examined the specific LM test for the statistical significance of individual parameters in the model. Byrne (1994; chap. 8–11) provided additional examples of testing the invariance of a factor structure, measurement instrument, latent mean structure, and causal structure.

A set of recommendations for model testing includes the following (see SEM checklist in sec. 11.7):

1. Did you specify separate measurement models and structural models?
2. Did you report the correct model fit indices (single model, chi-square, GFI, NFI, RMSEA; nested model, LR test, CFI, AIC, BIC; cross-validation indices, ECVI, MECVI; and the parameter estimates, LM test, and standard errors)?
3. Did you report the composite reliability of factors?
4. Did you report pattern and structure coefficients when factors are correlated and/or when a variable measures more than one factor?
5. Did you check for measurement invariance prior to testing between-group parameter estimates in the structural model?
6. Did you tabulate the statistical significance of parameter estimates with effect sizes and confidence intervals?

11.6 MODEL MODIFICATION

Our measurement models fit the sample data well; hence no model modification is required. We also meet the measurement invariance assumption, so the constructs are assumed to be the same for both groups. We tested the between-group difference in the correlation between the spatial and verbal latent variables and found that the groups did not differ on their relationship between spatial and verbal abilities. We have therefore established reasonable support for a theoretical position that no gender differences exist in spatial and verbal abilities. However, if we had used modification indices, the Lagrange multiplier test or the Wald test to respecify the initial model, we would need to report these results and provide justification.

If the fit of an implied theoretical model is not acceptable, which is typically the case with an initial model, the next step would be to modify the model and subsequently evaluate the new, respecified model. Most of the model modification occur in the measurement models rather than the structural models. Model modification occurs more in the measurement model because that is where the main source of misspecification occurs and measurement models are the foundation for structural models.

To illustrate how model modification is done and what decisions a researcher must make, we alter our original measurement model. Figure 11.2 indicates a measurement model that does not fit the data as well as our original model in Fig. 11.1. If we had started with the measurement model in Fig. 11.2, we would have had to find out how to respecify the

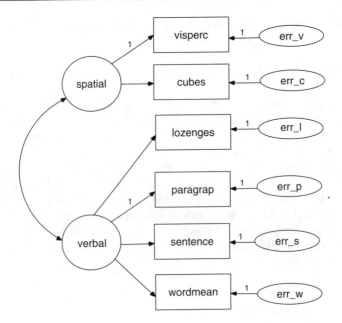

FIG. 11.2. Amos specification search, misspecified confirmatory factor model (data of Holzinger & Swineford, 1939).

measurement model to have an acceptable fit before proceeding with our test of measurement invariance and hypothesis test of the parameter estimate in the structural model.

We run the two separate EQS programs for boys and girls with a factor loading specified for the observed variable lozenges to the verbal latent variable rather than the spatial latent variable. We accomplish this by changing the /EQUATIONS command in the EQS program (boldfaced) as follows:

```
/EQUATIONS
   V1 = 1*F1 + E1;
   V2 = 1*F1 + E2;
   V3 = 1*F2 + E3;
   V4 = 1*F2 + E4;
   V5 = 1*F2 + E5;
   V6 = 1*F2 + E6;
```

We then add the /LMTEST to provide the diagnostics we need to determine whether the measurement model is correctly specified.

```
/LMTEST
```

The model fit indices for the girls indicate that the data do not fit the measurement model:

```
CHI-SQUARE = 26.345 BASED ON 8 DEGREES OF FREEDOM
PROBABILITY VALUE FOR THE CHI-SQUARE STATISTIC IS .00092

FIT INDICES
-----------

BENTLER-BONETT NORMED FIT INDEX                       =  .860
BENTLER-BONETT NON-NORMED FIT INDEX                   =  .801
COMPARATIVE FIT INDEX (CFI)                           =  .894
BOLLEN (IFI) FIT INDEX                                =  .898
MCDONALD (MFI) FIT INDEX                              =  .882
LISREL GFI FIT INDEX                                  =  .905
LISREL AGFI FIT INDEX                                 =  .751
ROOT MEAN-SQUARE RESIDUAL (RMR)                       = 5.102
STANDARDIZED RMR                                      =  .113
ROOT MEAN-SQUARE ERROR OF APPROXIMATION (RMSEA)       =  .178
```

The LM test indicates that a factor loading should have been added between spatial (F1) and the observed variable lozenges (V3), that is, the LM chi-square is statistically significant and specifies V3, F1 should be a parameter estimate. The LM test therefore indicates how to modify the measurement model so that it results in our original measurement model in Fig. 11.1.

```
LAGRANGE MULTIPLIER TEST (FOR ADDING PARAMETERS)
ORDERED UNIVARIATE TEST STATISTICS:

NO   CODE   PARAMETER   CHI-SQUARE   PROB
------------------------------------------
1    2 12   V3,F1         14.858        .000
```

The model fit indices for the boys indicate that the data do not fit the measurement model:

```
CHI-SQUARE = 16.845 BASED ON 8 DEGREES OF FREEDOM
PROBABILITY VALUE FOR THE CHI-SQUARE STATISTIC IS .03176

FIT INDICES
-----------
BENTLER-BONETT NORMED FIT INDEX                       =  .887
BENTLER-BONETT NON-NORMED FIT INDEX                   =  .877
COMPARATIVE FIT INDEX (CFI)                           =  .934
BOLLEN (IFI) FIT INDEX                                =  .938
MCDONALD (MFI) FIT INDEX                              =  .940
LISREL GFI FIT INDEX                                  =  .926
LISREL AGFI FIT INDEX                                 =  .805
ROOT MEAN-SQUARE RESIDUAL (RMR)                       = 3.418
STANDARDIZED RMR                                      =  .075
ROOT MEAN-SQUARE ERROR OF APPROXIMATION (RMSEA)       =  .125
```

The LM test for the boys also indicates that a factor loading should have been added between spatial (F1) and the observed variable lozenges (V3), that is, the LM chi-square is statistically significant and specifies V3, F1 should be a parameter estimate. The LM test for the boys also indicates how to modify the measurement model so that it will result in our original measurement model in Fig. 11.1.

```
LAGRANGE MULTIPLIER TEST (FOR ADDING PARAMETERS)
ORDERED UNIVARIATE TEST STATISTICS:

NO CODE PARAMETER CHI-SQUARE PROB
--------------------------------
1   2 12 V3,F1      9.017       .003
```

After we accept our final best fitting model, further research should undertake *model validation* by replicating the study (using multiple sample analysis), performing cross-validation (randomly splitting the sample and running the analysis on both sets of data), or bootstrapping the parameter estimates to determine the amount of bias. These model validation topics are covered in chapter 12.

Specification Searches

Amos includes another easy way to conduct model modification by doing specification searches and comparing alternative models. We illustrate this approach by first drawing Fig. 11.2 in Amos. Next, we select **File**, **Data Files**, and input either the girls or the boys SPSS MATRIX file, that is, the correlation matrix with sample size, means, and standard deviations. *To replace the girls_cor.sav data file with the boys_cor.sav data file, double click on the data file name (girls_cor.sav) and a dialog box will appear allowing you to select the other data file (boys_cor.sav).*

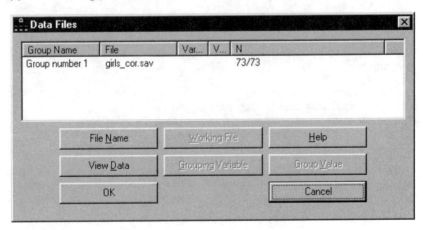

We create these special data file types in SPSS by designating special *rowtype_* and *varname_* fields in the SPSS Data Editor and entering our variable names as they appear in Fig. 11.2, as follows:

	Name	Type	Width	Decimals	Label	Values	Missing	Columns	Align	Measure
1	rowtype_	String	8	0		None	None	8	Left	Nominal
2	varname_	String	8	0		None	None	8	Left	Nominal
3	visperc	Numeric	8	3		None	None	8	Right	Scale
4	cubes	Numeric	8	3		None	None	8	Right	Scale
5	lozenges	Numeric	8	3		None	None	8	Right	Scale
6	paragrap	Numeric	8	3		None	None	8	Right	Scale
7	sentence	Numeric	8	3		None	None	8	Right	Scale
8	wordmean	Numeric	8	3		None	None	8	Right	Scale

We then enter the individual sample size, correlation coefficients, standard deviations, and means for the girls and boys data. We save these as separate files (*girls_cor.sav* and *boys_cor.sav*).

	rowtype_	varname_	visperc	cubes	lozenges	paragrap	sentence	wordmean	var	var	var
1	n		73.000	73.000	73.000	73.000	73.000	73.000			
2	corr	visperc	1.000								
3	corr	cubes	.483	1.000							
4	corr	lozenges	.492	.492	1.000						
5	corr	paragrap	.343	.211	.326	1.000					
6	corr	sentence	.367	.179	.335	.724	1.000				
7	corr	wordmean	.230	.184	.369	.743	.696	1.000			
8	stddev		6.916	4.533	7.911	3.562	5.054	8.319			
9	mean		29.315	24.699	14.836	10.589	19.301	18.014			

To run our model analysis, we select **Model Fit** from the tool bar menu and then select **Calculate Estimates** to obtain the model fit indices and parameter estimates for Fig. 11.2. Because the model fit is unacceptable, we want to conduct a specification search for better fitting models. To conduct a specification search in Amos, we once again select **Model Fit**,

	rowtype_	varname_	visperc	cubes	lozenges	paragrap	sentence	wordmean	var	var	var
1	n		72.000	72.000	72.000	72.000	72.000	72.000			
2	corr	visperc	1.000								
3	corr	cubes	.161	1.000							
4	corr	lozenges	.408	.348	1.000						
5	corr	paragrap	.373	.269	.411	1.000					
6	corr	sentence	.254	.143	.276	.705	1.000				
7	corr	wordmean	.426	.214	.364	.674	.666	1.000			
8	stddev		6.950	4.384	8.613	3.066	4.184	7.538			
9	mean		29.847	24.903	17.111	9.306	18.389	16.542			

but now select **Specification Search**. The following tool bar dialog box appears:

We use the --- icon to highlight the arrows in Figure 11.2 from verbal to lozenges and from spatial to lozenges. We then click on the ▶ icon to run the specification search.

The following specification search window appears with alternative models and model fit criteria indicating the number of parameters, degrees of freedom, chi-square (C), noncentrality parameter (NCP = $C - df$), Browne–Cudeck fit criteria, chi-square divided by degrees of freedom, and significance level (p value). Model 1 is tested with lozenges not in the CFA model. Model 2 is tested with lozenges only having a path to the spatial latent variable. Model 3 is tested with lozenges only having a path to the verbal latent variable. Model 4 is tested with lozenges having a path to both spatial and verbal latent variables. The saturated model (Sat) is a model with all paths in a CFA model; thus, it is just-identified and chi-square is always zero. The best-fitting model will have model fit indices underlined. Highlight the model of interest and click on the solid monitor icon (■) to view any of the models in a diagram. In our example, we highlight Model 2 because it has a nonsignificant chi-square and the model fit indices are underlined. We then click on the solid monitor icon and a diagram of Model 2 appears in a figure. If you want to see what the other models look like, simply highlight the model and click on the solid monitor icon. It is that easy!

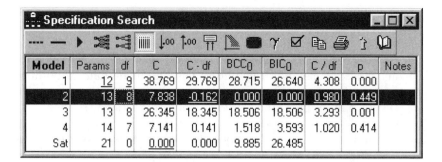

Model	Params	df	C	C - df	BCC₀	BIC₀	C / df	p	Notes
1	12	9	38.769	29.769	28.715	26.640	4.308	0.000	
2	13	8	7.838	-0.162	0.000	0.000	0.980	0.449	
3	13	8	26.345	18.345	18.506	18.506	3.293	0.001	
4	14	7	7.141	0.141	1.518	3.593	1.020	0.414	
Sat	21	0	0.000	0.000	9.885	26.485			

We could have generated many more models by drawing other paths in Fig. 11.1 and indicating them as optional paths, but they would not have been theoretically meaningful. A set of recommendations for model modification includes the following (see SEM checklist in sec. 11.7):

1. Did you clearly indicate how you modified the initial model?
2. Did you provide a theoretical justification for the respecified model?
3. Did you follow a single-step modification approach that is recommended with one parameter change at a time?
4. Did you use the LM or the Wald test in EQS rather than rely on the *t* test for parameter statistical significance?
5. Did you provide parameter estimates and model fit indices for both the initial model and the respecified model?
6. Your model is not the only model that fits the sample data, so did you check for equivalent models or theoretically justify your final model?
7. How did you evaluate and select the best model?

11.7   STRUCTURAL EQUATION MODEL CHECKLIST

Data Preparation

1. Have you adequately described the population from which the random sample data were drawn?
2. Did you report the measurement level of your variables?
3. Did you report the descriptive statistics on your variables?
4. Did you test for multivariate normality?
5. Did you create a table with correlations, means, and standard deviations?

6. Did you use LISREL normal scores because of small samples and nonnormality?
7. Is your design multilevel?
8. Do you have missing data and did you resolve this by using full information maximum likelihood estimation or data imputation methods?
9. Do you have outliers and did you resolve this by using robust statistics or deletion methods?
10. Did you resolve nonnormality of variable data by a logit or probit data transformation?
11. Did you resolve multicollinearity among variables (Mardia skewness and kurtosis coefficients)?
12. Did you resolve correlation attenuation?
13. Did you specify the type of matrix used, for example, covariance, correlation (Pearson, polychoric, polyserial), augumented moment, or asymptotic matrices?
14. How can others access your raw data and SEM program?

Model Specification

1. Did you provide a rationale and purpose for your study?
2. Did you explain why SEM rather than another statistical analysis approach was required?
3. Did you describe your latent variables, thus providing a substantive background to how they are measured?
4. Did you provide a theoretical foundation for your measurement model(s) and structural model?
5. Did you theoretically justify alternative models for comparison (e.g., nested models from simple to complex)?
6. Did you clarify whether your analysis was exploratory or confirmatory?
7. Did you use a reasonable sample size, thus power, in testing your hypothesis?
8. Did you clearly state your statistical hypotheses?
9. Did you discuss the expected magnitude and direction of expected parameter estimates?
10. Did you include a figure or diagram of your measurement and structural models?

Model Identification

1. Did you calculate the number of distinct values in your sample matrix?

2. Did you indicate the number of free parameters in your models?
3. Did you inform the reader that the order condition was satisfied?
4. Was the rank condition satisfied (nonzero matrix determinant)?

Model Estimation

1. How will you determine power and sample size for your study, given different levels of model complexity?
2. What is the ratio of chi-square to the degrees of freedom?
3. What is the ratio of sample size to number of parameters?
4. What LM tests of parameter estimates did you consider?
5. What estimation technique is appropriate for sample data (ML and GLS multivariate normal data with small to moderate sample sizes; ADF or CVM, nonnormal, asymptotic covariance data, and WLS non-normal with large sample sizes)?
6. Did you encounter Heywood cases (negative variance), multi-collinearity among latent variables, or non-positive definite matrix?
7. Did you use raw data or matrix file input?
8. How did you scale the latent variable variance?
9. Which SEM program and version did you use?
10. Did you use starting values?
11. Did you encounter any convergence problems or inadmissible solutions?
12. Did you report the R^2 values to indicate the fit of each separate equation?

Model Testing

1. Did you include your SEM program and sample data?
2. Did you provide a website for access to program and data?
3. Did you report the correct model fit indices (single model, chi-square, GFI, NFI, RMSEA; nested model, LR test, CFI, AIC, BIC; cross-validation indices, ECVI, MECVI; and the parameter estimates, LM test, and standard errors)?
4. Did you report the composite reliability of factors?
5. Did you report construct validity of factors?
6. Did you report pattern and structure coefficients when factors are correlated and/or when a variable measures more than one factor?
7. Did you specify separate measurement models and structural models?
8. Did you use single items or a composite scale score?
9. Did you check for measurement invariance prior to testing between-group parameter estimates in the structural model?

10. Did you tabulate the statistical significance of parameter estimates with effect sizes and confidence intervals?

Model Modification

1. Did you compare alternative models or equivalent models?
2. Did you clearly indicate how you modified the initial model?
3. Did you provide a theoretical justification for the respecified model?
4. Did you add or delete one path (one parameter) at a time?
5. Did you use the LM or the Wald test in EQS rather than rely on the *t* test for parameter statistical significance?
6. Did you provide parameter estimates and model fit indices for both the initial model and the respecified model?
7. Do parameter estimates have correct magnitude and direction?
8. Did you report expected change statistics?
9. Did you follow a single-step modification approach that is recommended with one parameter change at a time?
10. Your model is not the only model that fits the sample data, so did you check for equivalent models or theoretically justify your final model?
11. How did you evaluate and select the best model?

Model Validation (see chap. 12)

1. Did you replicate your SEM model analysis using another sample of data, that is, conduct a multiple-sample analysis?
2. Did you cross-validate your SEM model by splitting your original sample of data?
3. Did you use bootstrapping to determine the bias in your parameter estimates?
4. Did you report effect sizes and confidence intervals in addition to statistical significance testing?
5. Did you evaluate your results in regard to your original theoretical framework?

11.8 SUMMARY

In this chapter we showed that model fit is a subjective approach that requires substantive theory because there is no single best model (other models may be equally plausible given the sample data and/or equivalent models). In structural equation modeling the researcher follows the steps of model specification, identification, estimation, testing, and modification, so we advised the researcher to base measurement and structural equation models on *sound theory*, utilize the *two-step/four-step approach*, and establish measurement model fit and measurement invariance, before *model testing* the latent variables in the structural model. We also recommended that theoretical models need to be *replicated*, *cross-validated*, and/or *bootstrapped* to determine the stability of the parameter estimates (see chap. 12). Finally, we stated that researchers should include their SEM program, data, and graph in any article. This permits a replication of the analysis and verification of the results. We do not advocate using specification searches to find the best-fitting model without having a theoretically justified reason for respecifying the initial model. We further advocate using another sample of data to validate that the respecified model is a meaningful and substantive theoretical structural model. We finished by providing the researcher with a checklist to follow when doing structural equation modeling. This checklist follows a logical progression from data preparation through model specification, identification, estimation, testing, modification, and validation.

EXERCISES

1. Run the following LISREL–SIMPLIS program and determine whether measurement invariance holds between girls and boys.

```
Group 1: GIRLS
Model: Confirmatory Factor Model - Figure 11.1
Observed Variables:
 VISPERC CUBES LOZENGES PARCOMP SENCOMP WORDMEAN
Correlation Matrix
1.000
0.483 1.000
0.492 0.492 1.000
0.343 0.211 0.326 1.000
0.367 0.179 0.335 0.724 1.000
0.230 0.184 0.369 0.743 0.696 1.000
Means: 29.315 24.699 14.836 10.589 19.301 18.014
Standard deviations: 6.916 4.533 7.911 3.562 5.054 8.319
Sample Size: 73
Latent Variables: Spatial Verbal
Relationships:
 VISPERC - LOZENGES = Spatial
 PARCOMP - WORDMEAN = Verbal
Group 2: BOYS
Correlation Matrix
1.000
0.161 1.000
0.408 0.348 1.000
0.373 0.269 0.411 1.000
0.254 0.143 0.276 0.705 1.000
0.426 0.214 0.364 0.674 0.666 1.000
```

```
Means: 29.847 24.903 17.111 9.306 18.389 16.542
Standard deviations: 6.950 4.384 8.613 3.066 4.184 7.538
Sample Size: 72
Path Diagram
End of problem
```

2. Enter the following data in special matrix format in SPSS and save as *Fels_fem.sav*; also enter in special matrix format in EXCEL and save as *Fels_fem.xls*. Use special variable names *rowtype_* and *varname_* along with *n*, *corr*, *stddev*, and *mean* in these special data sets.

$N = 209$

Correlation matrix

Academic	1.00						
Athletic	.43	1.00					
Attract	.50	.48	1.00				
GPA	.49	.22	.32	1.00			
Height	.10	.04	−.03	.18	1.00		
Weight	.04	.02	−.16	−.10	.34	1.00	
Rating	.09	.14	.43	.15	−.16	−.27	1.00

Standard deviations	.16	.07	.49	3.49	2.91	19.32	1.01
Means		.12	.05	.42	10.34	.00	94.13	2.65

REFERENCES

American Psychological Association. (2002). *Publication manual of the American Psychological Association* (5th ed.). Washington, DC: Author.

Bentler, P. M., & Yuan, K. H. (2000). On adding a mean structure to a covariance structure model. *Educational and Psychological Measurement, 60,* 326–339.

Boomsma, A. (2000). Reporting analyses of covariance structure. *Structural Equation Modeling, 7,* 461–483.

Breckler, S. J. (1990). Applications of covariance structure modeling in psychology: Cause for concern? *Psychological Bulletin, 107,* 260–273.

Byrne, B. M. (1994). *Structural equation modeling with EQS and EQS/windows.* Thousand Oaks, Ca: Sage.

Cheung G. W., & Rensvold, R. B. (2002). Evaluating goodness-of-fit indexes for testing measurement invariance. *Structural Equation Modeling, 9,* 233–255.

Gonzalez, R., & Griffin, D. (2001). Testing parameters in structural equation modeling: Every "one" matters. *Psychological Methods, 6,* 258–269.

Graham, J. M., Guthrie, A. C., & Thompson, B. (2003). Consequences of not interpreting structure coefficients in published CFA research: A reminder. *Structural Equation Modeling, 10,* 142–153.

Holzinger, K. S., & Swineford, F. A. (1939). A study in factor analysis: The stability of a bifactor solution. *Supplementary educational monographs No. 98,* Chicago: University of Chicago, Department of Education.

Hoyle, R. H., & Panter, A. T. (1995). *Writing about structural equation models.* In R. H. Hoyle (Ed.), *Structural equation modeling: Concepts, issues, and applications* (pp. 158–176). Thousand Oaks, CA: Sage.

MacCallum, R. C., & Austin, J. T. (2000). Applications of structural equation modeling in psychological research. *Annual Review of Psychology, 51*, 201–226.

Maxwell, S. E., & Cole, D. A. (1995). Tips for writing (and reading) methodological articles. *Psychological Bulletin, 118*, 193–198.

McDonald, R. P., & Ringo Ho, M. (2002). Principles and practice in reporting structural equation analyses. *Psychological Methods, 7*, 64–82.

Raykov, T., Tomer, A., & Nesselroade, J. R. (1991). Reporting structural equation modeling results in *Psychology and Aging*: Some proposed guidelines. *Psychology and Aging, 6*, 499–533.

Thompson, B. (2000). Ten commandments of structural equation modeling. In L. Grimm & P. Yarnold (Eds.), *Reading and understanding more multivariate statistics* (pp. 261–284). Washington, DC: American Psychological Association.

ANSWERS TO EXERCISES

1a. The initial LISREL–SIMPLIS program yields a combined data set analysis with $N = 145$ to determine overall model fit. In this model all parameters are the same in both groups, that is, factor loadings, factor correlation, and error variances are set equal in both groups. We can accept the hypothesis that the same factor model holds for both boys and girls because the global chi-square value is nonsignificant. The chi-square statistics for each group and the global fit are as follows:

   Girls: goodness-of-fit statistics
       Contribution to chi-square = 12.69
       Percentage contribution to chi-square = 48.85
   Boys: goodness-of-fit statistics
       Contribution to chi-square = 13.28
       Percentage contribution to chi-square = 51.15
   Global: goodness-of-fit statistics
       Degrees of freedom = 29
       Minimum fit function chi-square = 25.97 ($p = 0.63$)

1b. To test for measurement invariance, we keep the factor loadings and factor correlation equal in both groups but permit the error variances to be freely estimated, that is, different in both groups. The following should be added to the boys program:

```
Set the error variances of VISPERC - WORDMEAN free
```

Results for this model analysis are as follows:

   Girls: goodness-of-fit statistics
       Contribution to chi-square = 10.40
       Percentage contribution to chi-square = 47.25
   Boys: goodness-of-fit statistics
       Contribution to chi-square = 11.60
       Percentage contribution to chi-square = 52.75
   Global: goodness-of-fit statistics
       Degrees of freedom = 23
       Minimum fit function chi-square = 22.00 ($p = 0.52$)

TABLE 11.4

Variable	Common factor model		Factor model (measurement invariant)	
	Spatial	Verbal	Spatial	Verbal
Visperc	.53		.53	
Cubes	.53		.54	
Lozenges	.74		.73	
Parcomp		.87		.87
Sencomp		.82		.82
Wordmean		.83		.83
Factor correlation	$r = .56$		$r = .55$	
Chi-square	$\chi^2 = 25.97$		$\chi^2 = 22.00$	
	$df = 29$		$df = 23$	
	$p = .63$		$p = .52$	

A chi-square difference between the overall model with all parameters equal and this model fit with error variance different but factor loadings and factor correlation the same for the two groups reveals that the groups are the same, hence there is measurement invariance between the boys and girls; that is, $25.97 - 22.00 = 3.97$, with $df = 29 - 23 = 6$, is nonsignificant (see Table 11.4).

2. SPSS and EXCEL matrix input using data from Amos 4.0, Example 7, pp. 173–174:

SPSS Matrix Input Example

	rowtype_	varname_	academic	athletic	attract	gpa	height	weight	rating
1	n		209.00	209.00	209.00	209.00	209.00	209.00	209.00
2	corr	academic	1.00						
3	corr	athletic	.43	1.00					
4	corr	attract	.50	.48	1.00				
5	corr	GPA	.49	.22	.32	1.00			
6	corr	height	.10	-.04	-.03	.18	1.00		
7	corr	weight	.04	.02	-.16	-.10	.34	1.00	
8	corr	rating	.09	.14	.43	.15	-.16	-.27	1.00
9	stddev		.16	.07	.49	3.49	2.91	19.32	1.01
10	mean		.12	.05	.42	10.34	.00	94.13	2.65

Fels_fem.sav - SPSS Data Editor

File Edit View Data Transform Analyze Graphs Utilities Window Help

15 : rowtype_

Data View / Variable View /

SPSS Processor is ready

Microsoft Excel Matrix Input Example

	A	B	C	D	E	F	G	H	I
1	rowtype_	varname_	academic	athletic	attract	GPA	height	weight	rating
2	n		209	209	209	209	209	209	209
3	corr	academic	1						
4	corr	athletic	0.43	1					
5	corr	attract	0.5	0.48	1				
6	corr	GPA	0.49	0.22	0.32	1			
7	corr	height	0.1	-0.04	-0.03	0.18	1		
8	corr	weight	0.04	0.02	-0.16	-0.1	0.34	1	
9	corr	rating	0.09	0.14	0.43	0.15	-0.16	-0.27	1
10	stddev		0.16	0.07	0.49	3.49	2.91	19.32	1.01
11	mean		0.12	0.05	0.42	10.34	0	94.13	2.65

12

MODEL VALIDATION

Chapter Outline

Key Concepts

Replication: model validation using multiple samples
Cross validation: split samples
Model validation indexes: ECVI, CVI, and MECVI
Simulation concepts
Bootstrap concepts
Jackknife concepts

In previous chapters we learned about the *basics* of structural equation modeling using the following steps: model specification, identification, estimation, testing, and modification. In this chapter we consider a selection of topics related to model validation. However, our discussion only scratches the surface of these approaches in structural equation modeling, so you should check out the references in this chapter for more information.

We begin by presenting a multiple-sample model that permits validation of a model using additional samples of data (replication). Then, we present the basics of how to compare generated models to a known population model (simulation), determine the stability of parameter estimates (bootstrapping), and determine the impact of outliers on parameter estimates and fit statistics (jackknifing). Ideally, a researcher should seek model validation with additional samples of data. The other methods are not as rigorous, but in the absence of replication, provide evidence of model validity, that is, the viability of the theoretical framework suggested by the measurement and/or structural models.

12.1 MULTIPLE-SAMPLE MODELS

A nice feature of structural equation modeling, although not frequently used, is the possibility of studying a theoretical model with more than one sample of data simultaneously. For example, Lomax (1985) examined a model for schooling using the High School and Beyond (HSB) database. The model included home background, academic orientation, extracurricular activity, achievement, and educational and occupational aspirations as latent variables. The research determined the extent to which the measurement and structural equation models fit both a sample of public school students and a sample of private school students and also examined whether model differences existed between the two groups. Theoretical models can also be examined across samples to determine the degree of invariance in fit indices, parameter estimates, and standard errors.

The multiple-sample approach can also be used in the analysis of quasi-experimental, experimental, cross-sectional, and/or longitudinal data. With multiple samples it is possible to (a) estimate separately the parameters for each independent sample, (b) test whether specified parameters or parameter matrices are equivalent across these groups (i.e., for any of the parameters in the measurement and/or structural equation models), and (c) test whether there are group mean differences for the indicator variables and/or for any of the structural equations.

In case (a) we can obviously use all of the previously described procedures in dealing with each group separately. The researcher can then "eyeball" the results (parameter estimates, goodness-of-fit indices, etc.) across the groups. However, statistical comparisons of the equivalence of parameters cannot be made among the groups, nor can mean differences be estimated. Case (a) is not true multiple-sample modeling because only one sample is evaluated at a time; thus, we do not consider it further.

In case (b) one can statistically determine whether certain specified parameters or parameter matrices are equivalent across the groups. For instance, one may be interested in whether the factor loadings are the same for the public and private school samples. That is, are different indicators better for the public school sample as compared with the private school sample? We refer to case b as a basic multiple-sample model.

In case (c) one can statistically determine whether there are mean differences for the indicator variables and/or the structural equations. For instance, one might be interested in whether there is a mean group difference in the structural equation for student achievement. We refer to case (c) as structured means analysis, that is, analysis of mean differences in the covariance structure.

Case (b) essentially examines the equivalence of matrices or parameter estimates across several samples taken randomly from a population. A researcher indicates the specific hypothesis to be tested, for example, equal factor loadings and factor correlation. For a measurement model, we could test whether the factor loadings are equal across the samples, or whether the factor variances and covariances are equal across the samples, or even whether the unique error variances and covariances are equal across samples. For a structural model, we could test whether the structure coefficients are equal across the samples (i.e., factor correlations). For a combined structural equation model, all parameters in the entire model are tested for equivalence across the samples. Obviously, in this instance both the covariance matrix and the coefficients are tested for equality across the samples, which leads to a more complex model requiring adequate sample size and power. We next demonstrate how to conduct multiple-sample analysis in Amos, EQS, and LISREL–SIMPLIS

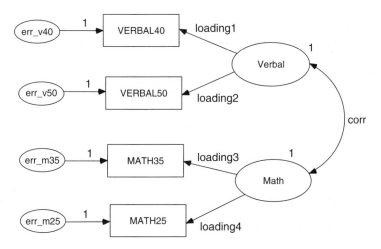

FIG. 12.1.   Path diagram for SAT verbal and math (based on Jöreskog &
Sörbom, 1996c, Example 10, p. 52).

using the example in Jöreskog and Sörbom (1996c, Example 10, p. 52)
based on two samples of data on individuals who took the Scholastic
Aptitude Test (SAT) in 1971 (Fig. 12.1).

Amos Example

The Amos approach to multiple-sample modeling requires the creation
of two separate SPSS matrix files, *sample1.sav* and *sample2.sav* (or alternatively Microsoft Excel matrix files) (*note: we use a covariance matrix
rather than a correlation matrix with standard deviations and means*).

	rowtype_	varname_	verbal40	verbal50	math35	math25
1	n		865.000	865.000	865.000	865.000
2	cov	VERBAL40	63.382	.	.	.
3	cov	VERBAL50	70.984	110.237	.	.
4	cov	MATH35	41.710	52.747	60.584	.
5	cov	MATH25	30.218	37.489	36.392	32.295

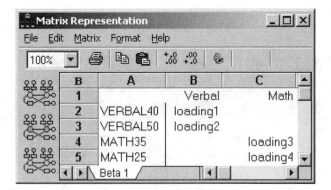

Next draw Fig. 12.1, making sure that you specify the error variances, and set both factor variances to 1.0. You need to select **View/Set** and use **Matrix Representation** to label the factor loadings. Alternatively, you can double click on a path (arrow), and an **Object Properties** dialog box will appear for you to enter a name for the path. *The labeling of the factor loadings and factor correlation is how Amos sets the factor loadings equal across the samples.*

Now, select **File**, then **Data Files**, and select the first SPSS matrix file (*sample1.sav*).

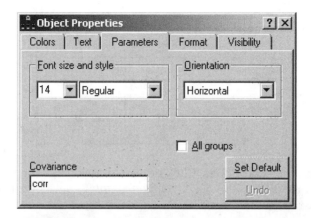

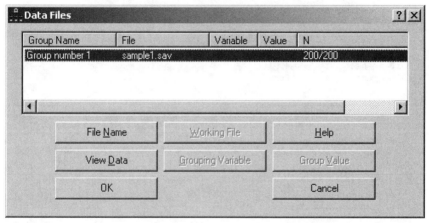

Next, double click the *Group Number 1* in the left side panel; the following dialog box appears:

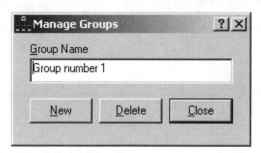

Click **New**, and the Group Number 1 changes to *Group Number 2*. Now close this dialog box.

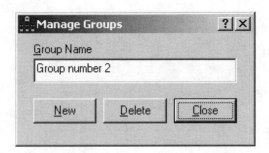

Select **File,** then **Data Files**. Click on *Group Number 2*, then *File Name*, and select the second SPSS matrix file (*sample2.cov*). Click *OK* to close the dialog box.

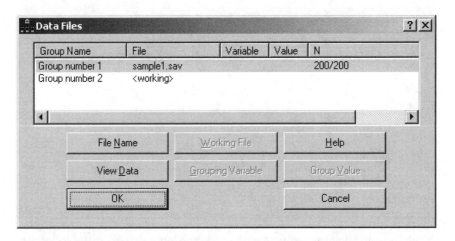

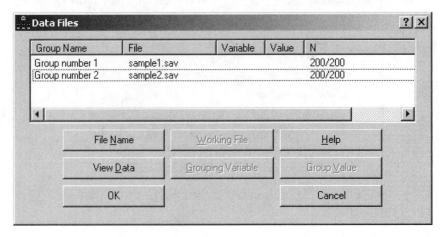

Next, Click on **View/Set**, then **Analysis Properties** to make sure you obtain *standardized estimates*, and *Squared Multiple Correlations*. To run the analysis, select **Model Fit** and then **Calculate Estimates**. The Amos computer output can be viewed by selecting **View/Set**, then **Table Output**. Click on either *Group Number 1* or *Group Number 2* to toggle between separate views of each sample computer output.

Amos Computer Output

We only present certain overall model fit results with the factor loadings (standardized regression weights), factor correlation, and squared multiple correlations for each sample. The overall chi-square value is nonsignificant, indicating that the measurement model is the same for both samples of data, that is, same factor loadings and factor correlation.

```
Global Fit

Chi-square = 10.872
Degrees of freedom = 7
Probability level = 0.144
CFI = .999
Group: Group number 1


Standardized Regression Weights
                                  Estimate

VERBAL40  ← Verbal                0.938
VERBAL50  ← Verbal                0.909
MATH35    ← Math                  0.920
MATH25    ← Math                  0.902


Correlation
                                  Estimate

Math  ⟷  Verbal                   0.767


Squared Multiple Correlations
                                  Estimate

        MATH25                    0.813
        MATH35                    0.847
        VERBAL50                  0.826
        VERBAL40                  0.879
```

```
Group: Group number 2
```

```
Standardized Regression Weights
                                        Estimate

VERBAL40  ←  Verbal                      0.897
VERBAL50  ←  Verbal                      0.944
MATH35    ←  Math                        0.931
MATH25    ←  Math                        0.884
```

```
Correlation
                                        Estimate

Math  ⟷  Verbal                          0.767
```

```
Squared Multiple Correlations
                                        Estimate

        MATH25                           0.782
        MATH35                           0.866
        VERBAL50                         0.891
        VERBAL40                         0.804
```

EQS Example

The basic EQS multiple-sample program setup includes separate programs that are "stacked" for each sample of data, but with minor modifications to the first and last programs. Certain commands have been bold-faced in the first and second individual programs of the EQS multiple-sample program setup. In the first program, the **GROUPS = 2;** subcommand indicates that comparisons are to be made across two samples of data. Notice that within each individual program the sample size can vary; however, the model specified in the **/EQUATIONS** command must be the same, that is, must use the same start values and correspond to the same number and type of variables. The variance–covariance matrices by definition are different in each of the individual programs because they represent two different samples of data. The second individual program specifies the equality of the factor loadings and the factor correlation in the model. This is accomplished by using the **/CONSTRAINTS** command and including statements indicating that the sample, observed variable, and factor of each sample are equal. In other words, the equality **(1,V1,F1)=(2,V1,F1)** tests whether the factor loading from **V1** to **F1** is the same in both samples of data. The equality statement is repeated for the other three factor loadings specified in the measurement model in the **/EQUATIONS** command. A final equality constraint is added to

test whether the factor correlation is the same in both samples of data
(1,F1,F2)=(2,F1,F2). The **/LMTEST** command requests that the Lagrange multiplier test be computed for the constraints specified in the
second program. For each constraint tested, a univariate chi-square and
associated probability value are reported, followed by multivariate cumulative chi-square and associated probability values. It is important to
examine these individual tests of equality, especially if chi-square goodness of fit indicates a lack of model fit, because it may be due to a specific
constraint in the model. A researcher could have the multiple samples of
data fit the model when a constraint is significant by fixing the value for
that parameter in the model for that particular sample of data. (*Note: The
EQS fit indices are printed only once for the multiple-sample analysis and
not for each individual program run.*) The fit indices are therefore testing
whether the specified model holds across the samples. In our example
we test whether the four factor loadings and the factor correlation are
the same in the two samples of data.

The following EQS multiple-sample program tests the equality of factor loadings and factor correlation (see /CONSTRAINTS), allowing for
different error variances in the model across both samples of data:

```
/TITLE
 SAMPLE 1
/SPECIFICATIONS
 CASES=865; VARIABLES=4; GROUPS=2;
/LABELS
 V1=VERBAL40; V2=VERBAL50; V3=MATH35; V4=MATH25;
 F1=Verbal; F2=Math;
/EQUATIONS
 V1 = 1* F1 + E1;
 V2 = 1* F1 + E2;
 V3 = 1* F2 + E3;
 V4 = 1* F2 + E4;
/VARIANCES
 F1 TO F2 = 1.0;
 E1 TO E4 = * ;
/COVARIANCES
 F1,F2 = * ;
/MATRIX
63.382
70.984 110.237
41.710 52.747 60.584
30.218 37.489 36.392 32.295
/END
/TITLE
 SAMPLE 2
/SPECIFICATIONS
CASES=900; VARIABLES=4;
```

```
/EQUATIONS
V1 = 1* F1 + E1;
V2 = 1* F1 + E2;
V3 = 1* F2 + E3;
V4 = 1* F2 + E4;
/VARIANCES
F1 TO F2 = 1.0;
E1 TO E4 = * ;
/COVARIANCES
F1,F2 = * ;
/MATRIX
67.898
72.301 107.330
40.549 55.347 63.203
28.976 38.896 39.261 35.403
/CONSTRAINTS
(1,V1,F1) = (2,V1,F1)
(1,V2,F1) = (2,V2,F1)
(1,V3,F2) = (2,V3,F2)
(1,V4,F2) = (2,V4,F2)
(1,F1,F2) = (2,F1,F2)
/LMTEST
/END
```

EQS Computer Output

The separate EQS programs produce individual standardized solutions for the factor loadings, measurement error, and R^2 values. A visual inspection of the factor loadings for the four variables across the two samples of data indicates that they appear to be similar. We also compare the R^2 values of the individual equations and notice that the R^2 values are also similar. The equality constraints we impose in the EQS program compute univariate Lagrange multiplier tests for the statistically significant difference of each factor loading across the two samples as well as the statistically significant difference in the factor correlation between the two samples.

```
MULTIPLE POPULATION ANALYSIS, INFORMATION IN GROUP 1

STANDARDIZED SOLUTION:                           R-SQUARED

VERBAL40=V1 = .938*F1 + .347 E1                     .879
VERBAL50=V2 = .909*F1 + .417 E2                     .826
MATH35   =V3 = .920*F2 + .391 E3                    .847
MATH25   =V4 = .902*F2 + .432 E4                    .813
```

MULTIPLE POPULATION ANALYSIS, INFORMATION IN GROUP 2

STANDARDIZED SOLUTION: R-SQUARED

```
V1 =V1 = .897*F1 + .443 E1              .804
V2 =V2 = .944*F1 + .330 E2              .891
V3 =V3 = .931*F2 + .366 E3              .866
V4 =V4 = .884*F2 + .467 E4              .782
```

Lagrange Multiplier Test. The univariate chi-square values for the constraints on the four factor loadings being equal are nonsignificant. These findings indicate that our measurement model has similar factor loadings across both samples of data. The chi-square value for the fifth constraint ($\chi^2 = 3.24$, $p = .072$) is also nonsignificant, indicating that the factor correlations are not different in the two samples of data. The overall chi-square and model fit indices further indicate that the measurement model fits both samples of data ($\chi^2 = 10.87$, $df = 7$, $p = .14$, and CFI $=$ .99). Given that the first sample of data is our original sample of data, the second sample of data supports our measurement model (replication).

```
LAGRANGE MULTIPLIER TEST
CONSTRAINTS FROM GROUP 2

     CONSTR: 1 (1,V1,F1) - (2,V1,F1) = 0;
     CONSTR: 2 (1,V2,F1) - (2,V2,F1) = 0;
     CONSTR: 3 (1,V3,F2) - (2,V3,F2) = 0;
     CONSTR: 4 (1,V4,F2) - (2,V4,F2) = 0;
     CONSTR: 5 (1,F1,F2) - (2,F1,F2) = 0;

UNIVARIATE TEST STATISTICS:

NO CONSTRAINT   CHI-SQUARE  PROBABILITY
--------------  ----------  --------------
1  CONSTR: 1    2.519        .113
2  CONSTR: 2    3.158        .076
3  CONSTR: 3    1.168        .280
4  CONSTR: 4     .205        .651
5  CONSTR: 5    3.240        .072

GOODNESS OF FIT SUMMARY FOR METHOD = ML
CHI-SQUARE = 10.870 BASED ON 7 DEGREES OF FREEDOM
PROBABILITY VALUE FOR THE CHI-SQUARE STATISTIC IS .14440

FIT INDICES
-----------
BENTLER-BONETT NORMED FIT INDEX     = .998
BENTLER-BONETT NON-NORMED FIT INDEX = .999
COMPARATIVE FIT INDEX (CFI)         = .999
```

LISREL–SIMPLIS Example

In LISREL-SIMPLIS, measurement and/or structural models can also be specified and tested across samples of data for model validation. The LISREL–SIMPLIS program stacks separate programs, but does not require that the observed variables, latent variables, and equations be repeated if all of the parameters in the model are assumed identical in subsequent individual programs. The second and subsequent individual programs only need to include their sample sizes and variance–covariance matrices. The computer output provides solutions for each individual program, but the global chi-square value should be reported. In a multiple-sample analysis the global chi-square is a measure of fit of all models in all groups, so individual chi-square values should not be interpreted.

LISREL generally requires running different multiple-sample program models to determine which parameters are different or similar among factor loadings, error variances, and factor correlations. In LISREL–SIMPLIS, Model A (EX10A.SPL) tests the equality of all parameters across both samples (factor loadings, error variances, and factor correlation). Model B (EX10B.SPL) allows the factor loadings to be different, but maintains equal error variances and factor correlation. Model C (EX10C.SPL) allows the factor loadings and error variances to be different, but maintains equal factor correlation across the two samples. Finally, Model D (EX10D.SPL) specifies that the factor loadings and the factor correlation are the same for both groups with the error variances different. This LISREL–SIMPLIS program yields the same overall chi-square value of model fit as the Amos and EQS programs. The LISREL–SIMPLIS (EX10D.SPL) program with the covariance matrices added for both groups is as follows:

```
Group 1: Testing Equality Of Factor Structures
Model D: Factor Loadings and Factor Correlation Invariant
Observed Variables: VERBAL40 VERBAL50 MATH35 MATH25
Covariance Matrix
63.382
70.984 110.237
41.710 52.747 60.584
30.218 37.489 36.392 32.295
Sample Size = 865
Latent Variables: Verbal Math
Relationships:
  VERBAL40 VERBAL50 = Verbal
  MATH35 MATH25 = Math
Group 2: Testing Equality Of Factor Correlations
Covariance Matrix
67.898
72.301 107.330
```

```
40.549 55.347 63.203
28.976 38.896 39.261 35.403
Sample Size = 900
Set the Error Variances of VERBAL40 - MATH25 free
Path Diagram
End of Problem
```

LISREL–SIMPLIS Computer Output

The individual programs output a chi-square value that sums to the global chi-square value ($5.48 + 5.39 = 10.87$). A percentage contribution to the global chi-square value is also indicated for the individual programs (e.g., Group 1: $5.48/10.87 = 50.40\%$; Group 2: $5.39/10.87 = 49.60\%$). The individual chi-squares for each program and the global chi-square for the overall model fit to the data are reported as follows:

```
Group 1 Goodness of Fit Statistics

Contribution to Chi-Square = 5.48
Percentage Contribution to Chi-Square = 50.40
Root Mean Square Residual (RMR) = 1.50
Standardized RMR = 0.021
Goodness of Fit Index (GFI) = 1.00


Group 2 Goodness of Fit Statistics

Contribution to Chi-Square = 5.39
Percentage Contribution to Chi-Square = 49.60
Root Mean Square Residual (RMR) = 1.23
Standardized RMR = 0.020
Goodness of Fit Index (GFI) = 1.00


Global Goodness of Fit Statistics

Degrees of Freedom = 7
Minimum Fit Function Chi-Square = 10.87 (P = 0.14)
Root Mean Square Error of Approximation (RMSEA) = 0.025
90 Percent Confidence Interval for RMSEA = (0.0 ; 0.052)
P-Value for Test of Close Fit (RMSEA < 0.05) = 0.82
Comparative Fit Index (CFI) = 1.00
```

The global chi-square and selected fit statistics indicate a good fit of the measurement model across both samples of data. The measurement model that fits across both samples of data does not allow **all** parameters to be equal across both samples of data. Error variances are typically different in a measurement model, so assuming equal factor loadings and/or factor correlation is theoretically tenable.

More complex model comparisons are possible. For example, we could test the equality of both factor loadings and factor correlations across three samples of data. Many different measurement and structural models using the multiple-sample approach are possible and illustrated in journal articles, software manuals, and books. The interested reader is referred to Jöreskog and Sörbom (1996a, 1996b, 1996c), Muthén and Muthén (1998), and Bentler and Wu (2002), as well as texts by Hayduk (1987) and Bollen (1989), for more details on running these various multiple-sample models. Other empirical examples using multiple-sample models are given by Lomax (1983, 1985), Cole and Maxwell (1985), Faulbaum (1987), and McArdle and Epstein (1987). A suggested strategy for testing models in the multiple-sample case is also given by Lomax (1983).

12.2   CROSS-VALIDATION

The replication of a study with a second set of data may be prohibitive given the time, money, or resources available. An alternative is to randomly split an original sample, assuming that the sample size is sufficient, and run the SEM analysis on one set of data while using the other in a multiple-sample analysis to compare the results. Cudeck and Browne (1983) created a split-sample cross-validation index (CVI), and Browne and Cudeck (1989, 1993) developed a single-sample expected cross-validation index (ECVI) and further explained the use of the CVI and the ECVI in structural equation modeling. Except for a constant scale factor, ECVI is similar to the AIC index (see next paragraph). Arbuckle and Wothke (1999, p. 406) also reported the MECVI, which except for a scale factor is similar to the Browne-Cudeck criterion (BCC) (see next paragraph). The BCC imposes a slightly greater penalty for model complexity than the AIC, and is a fit index developed specifically for the analysis of moment structures. These fit indices are intended for model comparisons and thus indicate "badness of fit," with simple models that fit well receiving low values and poorly fitting models receiving high values.

ECVI

Browne and Cudeck (1989) proposed a single-sample expected cross-validation index (ECVI) for comparing alternative models using only one sample of data. The alternative model that results in the *smallest* ECVI value should be the most stable in the population. The ECVI is a function of chi-square and degrees of freedom. It is computed in LISREL as ECVI $= (c/n) + 2(p/n)$, where c is the chi-square value for the overall fitted model, p is the number of independent parameters estimated, and $n = N - 1$ (sample size). Alternatively, in Amos, the ECVI is similar to the Akaike information criterion except for a scale factor: ECVI $= (1/n)$ (AIC), where $n = N - r$, with N the sample size and r the number of groups. Browne and Cudeck (1989, 1993) also provided a confidence interval for ECVI. In Amos, the 90% lower and upper limits c_L and c_U, respectively, are given by $(c_L; c_U) = [(\delta_L + d + 2q)/n; (\delta_U + d + 2q)/n]$, where δ_L is the parameter estimate for the lower limit, δ_U is the parameter estimate for the upper limit, d is the degrees of freedom, and q is the number of parameters. When sample size is small, it is important to compare the confidence intervals of the ECVI for the alternative competing models. The ECVI is also not very useful for choosing a parsimonious model when the sample size is large. In this instance we recommend one of the parsimonious model fit indices and/or the comparative fit index when comparing alternative models (see chap. 5).

Bandalos (1993), in a simulation study, further examined the use of the one-sample expected cross-validation index and found it to be quite accurate in confirmatory factor models. Other research also indicated that the one-sample expected cross-validation index yielded highly similar results to those of the two-sample approach (Benson & Bandalos, 1992; Benson & El-Zahhar, 1994; Benson, Moulin-Julian, Schwarzer, Seip, & El-Zahhar, 1992).

The ECVI is routinely printed among the fit indices reported by Amos and LISREL–SIMPLIS. We use our previous multiple-sample programs in Amos and LISREL–SIMPLIS, but this time run them separately to obtain the ECVI values. The ECVI for Sample 1 is close to zero, indicating a measurement model that is expected to cross-validate; similar findings are reported for the second sample of data. The confidence intervals around ECVI in both programs further support that ECVI probably ranges between .02 and .03 for this model. Notice that we would not interpret the ECVI in the multiple-sample model.

AMOS ECVI Output

Sample 1 ($\chi^2 = 1.3$, $df = 1$):

	Default	Saturated	Independence	Macro
Akaike information criterion (AIC)	19.255	20.000	2707.717	AIC
Browne-Cudeck criterion	19.360	20.116	2707.763	BCC
Expected cross validation index	0.022	0.023	3.134	ECVI
ECVI lower bound	0.022	0.023	2.940	ECVILO
ECVI upper bound	0.031	0.023	3.336	ECVIHI

Sample 2 ($\chi^2 = .9, df = 1$):

	Default	Saturated	Independence	Macro
Akaike information criterion (AIC)	18.922	20.000	2780.924	AIC
Browne-Cudeck criterion	19.023	20.112	2780.968	BCC
Expected cross validation index	0.021	0.022	3.093	ECVI
ECVI lower bound	0.021	0.022	2.905	ECVILO
ECVI upper bound	0.029	0.022	3.290	ECVIHI

LISREL–SIMPLIS ECVI Output

Sample 1:

```
Expected Cross-Validation Index (ECVI) = 0.021
90 Percent Confidence Interval for ECVI = (0.019; 0.028)
ECVI for Saturated Model = 0.011
ECVI for Independence Model = 3.05
```

Sample 2:

```
Expected Cross-Validation Index (ECVI) = 0.021
90 Percent Confidence Interval for ECVI = (0.021; 0.029)
ECVI for Saturated Model = 0.022
ECVI for Independence Model = 3.00
```

We report the AIC and BCC values for the Amos computer output to show the scale factor relationship to the ECVI. We have AIC $= \chi^2 + 2q = 1.3 + 2(9) = 19.3$, that is, reported as 19.255 for the first sample, where q is the number of parameters in the model. For Sample 2, AIC $= \chi^2 + 2q = .9 + 2(9) = 18.922$. For Sample 1, ECVI $= [1/(N - r)](AIC) = [1/(865 - 2)](19.255) = .022$ and for Sample 2, ECVI $= [1/(N - r)](AIC) = [1/(900 - 2)](18.922) = .021$, where N is the sample size in each group and r is the number of groups. MECVI does not apply in this model analysis, but is computed as $[1/(N - r)](BCC)$ or $[1/(865 - 2)](19.36)$ and $[1/(900 - 2)](19.023)$, respectively.

CVI

Cudeck and Browne (1983) also proposed a cross-validation index (CVI) for covariance structure analysis that incorporated splitting a sample into two subsamples. Subsample A is used as a *calibration* sample and Subsample B is used as the *validation* sample. The reproduced model-implied covariance matrix Σ_a from the calibration sample is then compared with the covariance matrix derived from Subsample B, S_b. A CVI value near zero indicates that the model cross-validates or is the same in the two subsamples. The cross-validation index is denoted as CVI $=$ $F(S_b, \Sigma_a)$. The choice among alternative models can also be based on the model that yields the smallest CVI value. One could further *double-cross-validate* by using Subsample B as the calibration sample and Subsample A as the validation sample. In this instance the cross-validation index is denoted as CVI $= F(S_a, \Sigma_b)$. If the same model holds regardless of which subsample is used as the calibration sample, greater confidence in the model validity is achieved. An obvious drawback to splitting a sample into two subsamples is that sufficient subsample sizes may not exist to provide stable parameter estimates. Obviously, this approach requires an initial large sample that can be randomly split into two subsamples of equal and sufficient size.

The CVI can be computed using LISREL–SIMPLIS command language, but requires two programs with randomly split data and the cross-validate command. In the following example, two LISREL–SIMPLIS programs are run to compute the CVI. The first program reads in the covariance matrix of the calibration sample S_a, then generates and saves the model-implied covariance matrix Σ_a. The second program uses the covariance matrix of Subsample B and then outputs the CVI value. The CVI cross-validation example involved randomly splitting an original sample of size 400 and calculating two separate covariance matrices.

```
PROGRAM ONE CALIBRATION SAMPLE
OBSERVED VARIABLES: X1 X2 X3
COVARIANCE MATRIX
5.86
3.12 3.32
35.28 23.85 622.09
LATENT VARIABLES: Factor1
RELATIONSHIPS:
 X1-X3 = Factor1
SAMPLE SIZE: 200
SAVE SIGMA IN FILE MODEL1C
END OF PROBLEM
PROGRAM TWO VALIDATION SAMPLE AND COMPUTE CVI
OBSERVED VARIABLES: X1 X2 X3
COVARIANCE MATRIX
5.74
3.47 4.36
45.65 22.58 611.63
SAMPLE SIZE: 200
CROSSVALIDATE FILE MODEL1C
END OF PROBLEM
```

As an example, let us test a single-factor measurement model with three indicator variables to see whether it cross-validates using a

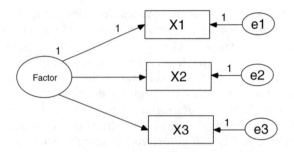

FIG. 12.2. Single–factor model.

randomly split sample of data (Fig. 12.2). The low CVI value indicates that the measurement model holds for both subsamples. The reduced computer output from the CVI cross-validation program is as follows:

```
PROGRAM ONE CALIBRATION SAMPLE
COVARIANCE MATRIX TO BE ANALYZED

              X1        X2        X3
          ------------------------
    X1   5.86
    X2   3.12      3.32
    X3  35.28     23.85    622.09

SI was written to file MODEL1C

PROGRAM TWO VALIDATION SAMPLE AND COMPUTE CVI
COVARIANCE MATRIX TO BE ANALYZED

              X1        X2        X3
          ------------------------
    X1   5.74
    X2   3.47      4.36
    X3  45.65     22.58    611.63

MATRIX SIGMA

              X1        X2        X3
          ------------------------
    X1   5.86
    X2   3.12      3.32
    X3  35.28     23.85    622.09

CROSS-VALIDATION INDEX (CVI) = 0.38
```

The ECVI and the CVI are most useful after a theoretically implied model has an acceptable model fit, that is, when a specified model yields model fit indices and parameter estimates that are meaningful with sufficient sample size and power. The number of parameters, model complexity, and sample size affect these cross-validation indices; therefore, you should not routinely discard other modeling considerations when you select the smaller ECVI of two competing models, report the CVI from two subsamples, or report the CVI across samples taken from a population. Currently, Amos and LISREL–SIMPLIS compute ECVI for single-sample expected cross-validation; however, only LISREL–SIMPLIS computes CVI for split-sample cross-validation.

12.3 SIMULATION METHODS

Monte Carlo simulation methods involve using a pseudo-random number generator and specifying known population values to produce raw data for a population correlation and/or variance–covariance matrix. Pseudo-random number generators, however, do not all perform the same, with many yielding nonrandom (nonnormal) distributions with sample sizes of less than 10,000 (Bang, Schumacker, & Schlieve, 1998). Our interest in simulation (i.e., Monte Carlo studies) is in determining the robustness of our sample statistics (parameter estimates), which we can only know when our population parameters are known. Amos, EQS, and LISREL approaches to simulation of raw data (covariance matrices) are described next.

Amos Simulation

We conduct simulation in Amos by clicking on the **Amos Basics** icon, which is a default icon next to the **Amos Graphics** icon on the desktop of your computer after installing Amos. The **Amos Basics** programming interface can be used to create SEM modeling programs or to generate raw data for population covariance matrices (**AmosRanGen** routine). Many of these applications are beyond the scope of this book, so we refer you to the extensive help routines in Amos for information about programming and only present a simple example from the *Amos Reference Guide*, namely the RandomVector Method.

When you click on the **Amos Basics** icon, a dialog box appears that permits you to enter programming commands. Simply cut and paste the program commands from the *Amos Reference Guide* example into the dialog box and save the program as *random.AmosBasic*. Before running the program you must activate an *Amos Random Number Generator* by clicking on **Edit**, then **References** to make sure there is a check mark next to *Amos Random Number Generator for Amos Basic (1.0)*. After closing this

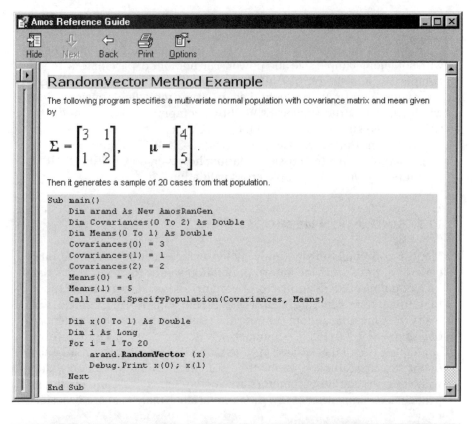

RandomVector Method Example

The following program specifies a multivariate normal population with covariance matrix and mean given by

$$\Sigma = \begin{bmatrix} 3 & 1 \\ 1 & 2 \end{bmatrix}, \qquad \mu = \begin{bmatrix} 4 \\ 5 \end{bmatrix}.$$

Then it generates a sample of 20 cases from that population.

```
Sub main()
    Dim arand As New AmosRanGen
    Dim Covariances(0 To 2) As Double
    Dim Means(0 To 1) As Double
    Covariances(0) = 3
    Covariances(1) = 1
    Covariances(2) = 2
    Means(0) = 4
    Means(1) = 5
    Call arand.SpecifyPopulation(Covariances, Means)

    Dim x(0 To 1) As Double
    Dim i As Long
    For i = 1 To 20
        arand.RandomVector (x)
        Debug.Print x(0); x(1)
    Next
End Sub
```

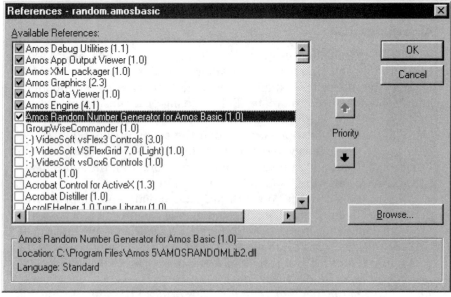

window, change the *DIM arand as New AmosRanGen* program statement to **Dim arand as New AmosRanGen2**. You are now ready to run the program by clicking on the tool bar icon, ▶, to run the Amos Basic program. Amos has other Amos Basic programs with the extension *.AmosBasic in the *Examples* folder that you can also run.

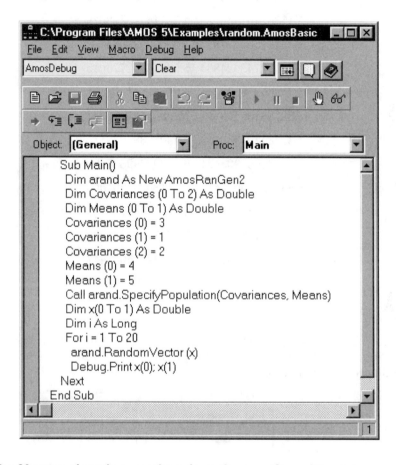

The 20 pairs of random numbers from the specific multivariate normal population are

2.08807491110152	4.40273768859142
2.97891512321393	4.87836626428366
2.20337590206091	4.0737399582424
0.607832710640209	3.00171863764663

2.08775843853259 1.93387552361059

1.06954436089037 5.0591877483715

4.50124546892443 5.8865573203892

7.4924370510332 3.44236351257712

5.11352401436258 4.53115248468029

1.8815466547482 4.39830623084162

2.52952748924864 5.54876542775015

5.74866258138715 6.89231011254506

6.22338158405298 7.26858627273002

4.37784801236089 7.4405838704911

3.88483055903421 6.70396299336409

8.45892473066417 5.34183737201003

3.90411530541254 2.82567802136742

5.38419178184952 3.77271324865089

3.98685297831289 4.19134445645447

3.10832022597992 5.25288708702007

We input this pair of 20 numbers into SPSS and compute the sample variance–covariance matrix and mean values. The sample values are similar to the population values:

$$\Sigma = \begin{bmatrix} 4.34 & .99 \\ .99 & 2.26 \end{bmatrix}, \qquad \mu = \begin{bmatrix} 3.88 \\ 4.84 \end{bmatrix}.$$

EQS Simulation

EQS provides a very easy-to-use method for conducting simulation studies, including bootstrap and jackknife output (Bentler & Wu, 2002). Simulation studies afford the opportunity to study models when data are randomly sampled from a population under known conditions. They require the specification of a population (model generated or matrix input), a sampling method (simple random sampling or resampling of input raw

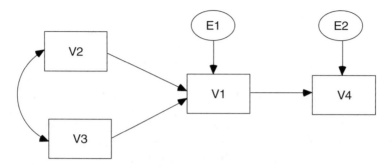

FIG. 12.3. Path model.

data), or estimation method (GLS, ML, etc.), the number of samples to be simulated, and file name(s) if we wish to save the outputted files. A basic EQS simulation program that uses a specific path model (Fig. 12.3), the maximum-likelihood estimation method, and simple random sampling that outputs five data files with the prefix SIM is as follows:

```
/TITLE
 SIMULATION EXAMPLE
/SPECIFICATIONS
 CASES=30;VARIABLES=4;METHOD=ML;
/EQUATION
 V1 = 1*V2 + 1*V3 + E1;
 V4 = 1*V1 + E2;
/SIMULATION
 SEED = 12345;
 REPLICATIONS=5;
 POPULATION=MODEL;
 DATA_PREFIX = 'SIM';
 SAVE=SEPARATE;
/OUTPUT
 LISTING;COVARIANCE MATRIX;
/END
```

In conducting simulations it is important to remember that changing the value on the REPLICATIONS subcommand increases the number of sample data sets simulated and thus can easily cause computer disk space to become exhausted. The path model specified in the /EQUA-TIONS command is analyzed for each of the five generated data sets due to the POPULATION = MODEL; subcommand, which is the program default specification. The researcher can examine the overall model fit across the five samples, as well as the path coefficients, which for our example are in the computer output listing. In addition to all program output appearing by use of the LISTING; subcommand, the /OUTPUT command can specify that only certain technical information appear in a default file named *EQSOUT.DAT*. In this example, only the covariance matrix for each data set was requested to be outputted in the file. Other choices for technical output could include, for example, parameter estimates, standard errors, residual matrix, and/or weight matrix. However, note that other specific technical information is outputted before each simulation request in the program. In our example, the covariance matrix we requested is printed after the technical information for each simulation. We know that this has been accomplished when we see the following computer output information in the listing file:

```
FOLLOWING TECHNICAL INFORMATION HAS BEEN STORED IN EQSOUT.DAT

  NOTE: COVARIANCE MATRICES IN THIS TECHNICAL OUTPUT HAVE
    BEEN ARRANGED IN THE SEQUENCE OF ALL DEPENDENT
    VARIABLES FOLLOWED BY ALL INDEPENDENT VARIABLES.
```

The five covariance matrices generated from the randomly sampled data for each simulation are follows:

Simulation 1:

3.518

1.585   1.408

 .992   .012   .881

4.133   1.623   1.088   5.479

Simulation 2:

2.414

 .554   .639

 .849   − .082   .843

2.521   .596   .898   3.950

Simulation 3:

2.225

 .709   .925

 .821   .045   .803

2.133   .472   .879   3.411

Simulation 4:

4.150

1.583   1.508

1.479   .098   1.234

3.911   1.479   1.462   4.858

Simulation 5:

2.118

 .507   .738

1.075   − .136   1.228

2.114   .600   1.232   3.093

The parameter estimates for our example were taken from the computer output listing but could have been outputted in the five simulation files along with the covariance matrices by simply changing the /OUT-PUT command to LISTING;COVARIANCE MATRIX;PARAMETER ESTI-MATES;. The path coefficients in the standardized solution for each simulation are as follows:

Simulation 1:

$V1 = .709*V2 + .558*V3 + .431 \ E1$

$V4 = .941*V1 + .339 \ E2$

Simulation 2:

$V1 = .500*V2 + .630*V3 + .594 \ E1$

$V4 = .826*V1 + .563 \ E2$

Simulation 3:

$V1 = .470*V2 + .598*V3 + .649 \ E1$

$V4 = .770*V1 + .638 \ E2$

Simulation 4:

$V1 = .605*V2 + .628*V3 + .490 \ E1$

$V4 = .865*V1 + .501 \ E2$

Simulation 5:

$V1 = .486*V2 + .703*V3 + .520 \ E1$

$V4 = .839*V1 + .544 \ E2$

Simulation programs are typically run to examine covariance matrices and/or parameter estimates to determine how much they fluctuate or change under certain conditions, for example, different sample sizes. More complex simulation programs are possible that use other optional commands. For example, a simulation using a covariance matrix could be conducted. The covariance matrix could be included in the program after the **/MATRIX** command, or read from an input data file specified as **DA='<file name>';** on the **/SPECIFICATION** command line. The simulation of a covariance matrix also requires changing the **POPULA- TION** subcommand to **POPULATION=MATRIX;**. A computer output listing file can also be named as an alternative to using the default name *EQSOUT.DAT*. This is accomplished by including in the **/OUTPUT** command the subcommand **DATA = '<file name>';**. These and other optional commands are found in the *EQS 6 for Windows user's guide* (Bentler & Wu, 2002), but we provide the program setup for modeling a covariance matrix to further illustrate the ease of performing simulations in EQS. The following EQS simulation program generates five simulations based on the input covariance matrix:

```
/TITLE
 COVARIANCE MATRIX SIMULATION EXAMPLE
/SPECIFICATIONS
 CASES=30;VARIABLES=4;METHOD=ML;
/EQUATION
 V1 = 1*V2 + 1*V3 + E1;
 V4 = 1*V1 + E2;
/SIMULATION
 SEED = 12345;
 REPLICATIONS=5;
 DATA_PREFIX = 'COV';
 SAVE=SEPARATE;
 POPULATION = MATRIX;
/MATRIX
3.518
1.585 1.408
 .992 .012 .881
4.133 1.623 1.088 5.479
/OUTPUT
 LISTING;COVARIANCE MATRIX;
/END
```

A selected amount of computer output from the listing file is as follows:

```
TITLE: SIMULATION EXAMPLE

SIMULATION DEFINITIONS

        NUMBER OF REPLICATIONS : 5
        SAMPLE DATA GENERATED FROM: MATRIX
```

```
            SAMPLE SIZE : 30
            DATA IS NORMAL ? YES
            DATA TO BE CONTAMINATED ? NO
            ORIGINAL SEED = 12345.
            DATA FILE TO BE SAVED ? YES
            IN WHICH TYPE ? SEPARATED
```

DATA GENERATED BASED ON FOLLOWING CORRELATION MATRIX

```
          V1       V2       V3       V4
    V1   1.000
    V2   0.712    1.000
    V3   0.563    0.011    1.000
    V4   0.941    0.584    0.495    1.000
```

SIMULATION IN REPLICATION 1
INPUT DATA FILE NAME IS COV001.DAT
COVARIANCE MATRIX TO BE ANALYZED:

```
          V1       V2       V3       V4
    V1   4.954
    V2   2.251    1.634
    V3   1.562    0.373    0.891
    V4   5.735    2.412    1.934    6.849
```

CHI-SQUARE = 13.280 BASED ON 3 DEGREES OF FREEDOM
PROBABILITY VALUE FOR THE CHI-SQUARE STATISTIC IS 0.00407
COMPARATIVE FIT INDEX = 0.941

STANDARDIZED SOLUTION:

```
    V1 =  .699*V2 + .622*V3 + .354 E1
    V4 =  .981*V1 + .196 E2
```

SIMULATION IN REPLICATION 2
INPUT DATA FILE NAME IS COV002.DAT
COVARIANCE MATRIX TO BE ANALYZED:

```
          V1       V2       V3       V4
    V1   2.249
    V2   0.886    0.926
    V3   0.711   -0.040    0.703
    V4   2.738    0.878    0.772    4.045
```

CHI-SQUARE = 10.071 BASED ON 3 DEGREES OF FREEDOM
PROBABILITY VALUE FOR THE CHI-SQUARE STATISTIC IS 0.01797
COMPARATIVE FIT INDEX = 0.924

STANDARDIZED SOLUTION:

```
    V1 = .631*V2 + .586*V3 + .508 E1
    V4 = .911*V1 + .413 E2
```

SIMULATION IN REPLICATION 3
INPUT DATA FILE NAME IS COV003.DAT

COVARIANCE MATRIX TO BE ANALYZED:

```
        V1        V2        V3        V4
V1    3.253
V2    1.536     1.281
V3    0.593    -0.075     0.634
V4    3.716     1.605     0.574     4.918
```

CHI-SQUARE = 8.848 BASED ON 3 DEGREES OF FREEDOM
PROBABILITY VALUE FOR THE CHI-SQUARE STATISTIC IS 0.03138
COMPARATIVE FIT INDEX = 0.945

STANDARDIZED SOLUTION:

```
V1 = .769*V2 + .464*V3 + .440 E1
V4 = .933*V1 + .360 E2
```

SIMULATION IN REPLICATION 4
INPUT DATA FILE NAME IS COV004.DAT
COVARIANCE MATRIX TO BE ANALYZED:

```
        V1        V2        V3        V4
V1    5.304
V2    2.543     2.071
V3    1.375     0.196     0.919
V4    6.074     2.563     1.509     7.756
```

CHI-SQUARE = 17.496 BASED ON 3 DEGREES OF FREEDOM
PROBABILITY VALUE FOR THE CHI-SQUARE STATISTIC IS LESS THAN 0.001
COMPARATIVE FIT INDEX = 0.892

STANDARDIZED SOLUTION:
```
V1 = .731*V2 + .554*V3 + .398 E1
V4 = .941*V1 + .337 E2
```

SIMULATION IN REPLICATION 5
INPUT DATA FILE NAME IS COV005.DAT
COVARIANCE MATRIX TO BE ANALYZED:

```
        V1        V2        V3        V4
V1    2.596
V2    0.957     1.188
V3    0.763    -0.258     0.782
V4    3.301     1.032     0.862     4.820
```

CHI-SQUARE = 20.600 BASED ON 3 DEGREES OF FREEDOM
PROBABILITY VALUE FOR THE CHI-SQUARE STATISTIC IS .00025
COMPARATIVE FIT INDEX = 0.854

STANDARDIZED SOLUTION:

```
V1 = .653*V2 + .646*V3 + .396 E1
V4 = .947*V1 + .321 E2
```

Each time you run the program, results will be different due to the different seed value. The simulation of an inputted covariance matrix permits a comparison with replicated covariance matrices under certain known conditions as well as an examination of the parameter estimates from the implied model. The variation in the covariance matrices, parameter estimates, and fit indices is readily apparent from just these five simulated replications.

PRELIS Simulation

PRELIS is considered a preprocessor for LISREL and as such screens data, creates different types of matrices, and has other useful features for data creation and data manipulation. PRELIS can easily produce several different types of data distributions (e.g., normal and nonnormal). Simply click on **File**, **New**, and then select *PRELIS* Data.

An empty PRELIS Data window will appear. Now insert the number of variables and the number of cases that you want to simulate.

First create the number of variables, which were four in the previous example. Select **Data** from the tool bar menu, then **Define Variables**. A *Define Variables* dialog box appears; click on *Insert*. An *Add Variables* dialog box appears; enter the names of the variables, for example, V1 through V4, and click *OK*. These variables now appear in the *Define Variables* dialog box; click *OK*. They now appear in the PRELIS Data window.

Next, select *Data*, then *Insert Cases*, and click *OK*.

The PRELIS Data window now has four variables and 30 cases with zeros in the cells. You are now ready to replace the zeros with numerical values by selecting **Transformation**, then **Compute**, which first prompts

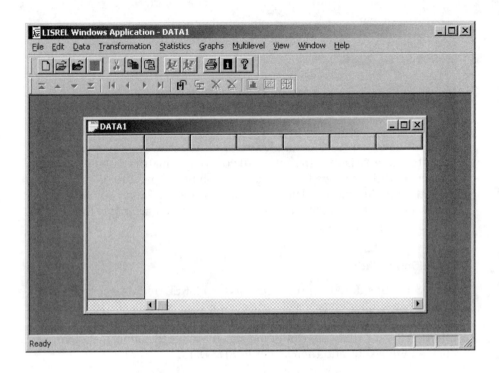

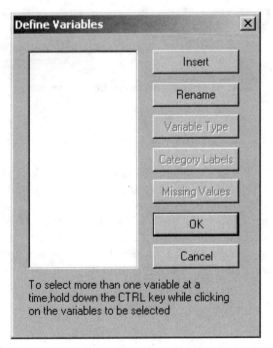

290

you to save your work as a PRELIS system file (*sample.psf*). Now carefully follow the directions and use the mouse to drag and drop and *Enter* NRAND into the equations.

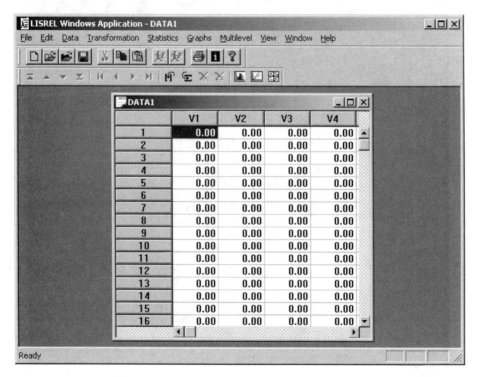

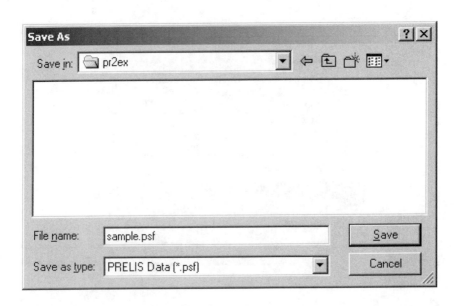

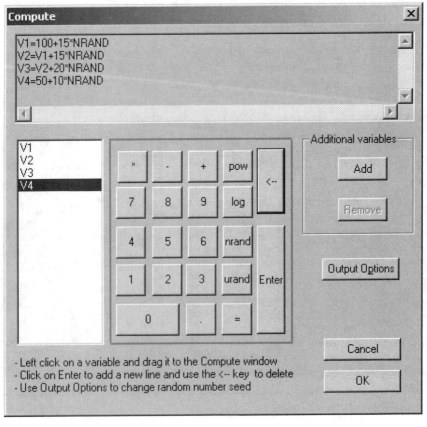

After a few minutes, you will see the computed data values in the PRELIS spreadsheet. You can now use many of the PRELIS tool bar menu features to calculate descriptive statistics or produce graphs of the variables.

```
LISREL Windows Application - sample.psf                              _□×
File  Edit  Data  Transformation  Statistics  Graphs  Multilevel  View  Window  Help
```

sample.psf				_□×
	V1	V2	V3	V4
1	92.81	50.72	26.56	43.55
2	85.77	101.72	77.33	56.88
3	100.58	119.39	136.82	43.47
4	78.61	69.20	72.00	37.83
5	96.84	92.41	107.99	60.26
6	67.73	58.90	17.28	55.95
7	89.76	94.07	117.95	48.21
8	129.05	108.85	111.22	40.63
9	98.68	98.88	94.30	70.27
10	111.99	109.42	111.54	56.68
11	91.22	50.18	38.46	44.74
12	123.93	132.13	138.90	60.98
13	114.82	112.65	81.32	50.93
14	87.47	106.25	99.84	47.69
15	101.60	91.36	74.51	55.42

Ready

Clicking on **Statistics** and then selecting **Output Options**, you can save the data in the PRELIS spreadsheet into a covariance matrix.

PRELIS also permits command files that can generate different distributions of data and either output raw data files or various types of matrices. The following PRELIS file (*raw.pr2*) creates four new variables and 200 cases; then saves the raw data in a file (*raw.dat*):

PRELIS Command File

```
Generating Raw Data Model
DA NO=200
CO ALL
NE V1=100 + 15*NRAND
NE V2= V1 + 20*NRAND
NE V3= V2 + 15*NRAND
NE V4= 50 + 10*NRAND
```

```
! XM = limit modification indices
! IX = starting seed value
OU RA=raw.dat XM IX=123
```

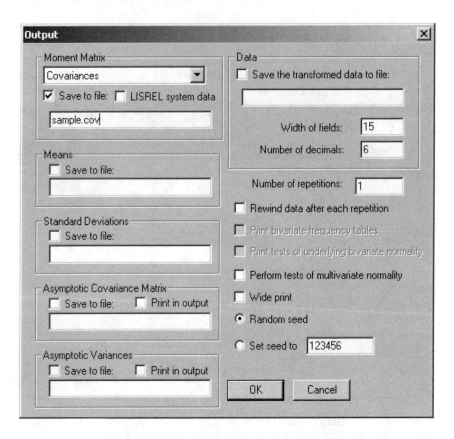

We strongly encourage you to explore the many excellent examples in the LISREL–PRELIS program. The *HELP* library is full of clear and concise documentation along with many examples that you can follow in doing your research. It also includes updates on many new features that are available. The downloaded student version contains the example data sets and library documentation.

12.4 BOOTSTRAP

The bootstrap method treats a random sample of data as a substitute for the population (pseudo population) and resamples from it a specified number of times to generate sample bootstrap estimates and standard errors. These sample bootstrap estimates and standard errors are aver-aged and used to obtain a confidence interval around the average of the bootstrap estimates. This average is termed a *bootstrap estimator*. The bootstrap estimator and associated confidence interval are used to de-termine how stable or good the sample statistic is as an estimate of the population parameter. Obviously, if the random sample initially drawn from the population is not representative, then the sample statistic and corresponding bootstrap estimator obtained from resampling will yield misleading results. The bootstrap approach is used in research when replication with additional sample data and/or cross-validation with a split sample is not possible. Fan (2003) demonstrated how the bootstrap method is implemented in various software packages and its utility with regard to correlation, regression, analysis of variance, and reliability. We present examples using Amos, EQS, and PRELIS.

AMOS Bootstrap

The bootstrap procedure in Amos (Arbuckle & Wothke, 1999, pp. 359–386) evaluates the sampling distribution of parameter estimates and as-sociated standard errors, which is helpful in determining robustness under assumptions of multivariate normality or model misspecification (Example 19), comparison of alternative models (Example 20), and com-parison of estimation methods (Example 21).

We illustrate how different estimation methods are easily compared for the model in Fig. 12.1 using the first set of individuals who took the SAT in 1971 (*sample1.sav*). We originally analyzed the model using maximum likelihood estimation, but now are interested in whether generalized least squares or unweighted least squares might work better.

In Amos, we first select **View/Set**, then **Analysis Properties**, then the *Estimation* tab, and finally select *Generalized Least Squares*. We next click on the *Bootstrap* tab, and select *Perform Bootstrap* and a series of Boot-strap outputs (Bootstrap ML, Bootstrap GLS, and Bootstrap ULS along with the 90% confidence interval, 500 bootstrap samples, and a Monte Carlo parametric bootstrap). (*Note: Boot ADF and asymptotic distribution-free estimation can only be performed with raw data.*) We can only com-pare maximum likelihood, generalized least squares, and unweighted least squares because we are inputting a sample variance–covariance matrix. To compare these other estimation methods, we will need to return to the *Estimation* tab and select a different estimation method. Consequently, we will run this analysis twice more, once for maximum likelihood and once for unweighted least squares. We must also select the **Random #** tab and enter a seed value.

We report the regression weights, bootstrap estimates, and associated standard errors for the different estimation methods selected. The regression weights and bootstrap mean estimates are very similar across all three estimation methods, that is, the bootstrap bias or difference is very small. For ML and GLS estimation methods, the bootstrap standard error estimates are very similar to the standard errors for the regression weights. We therefore interpret our results as being stable estimates of the population regression weights.

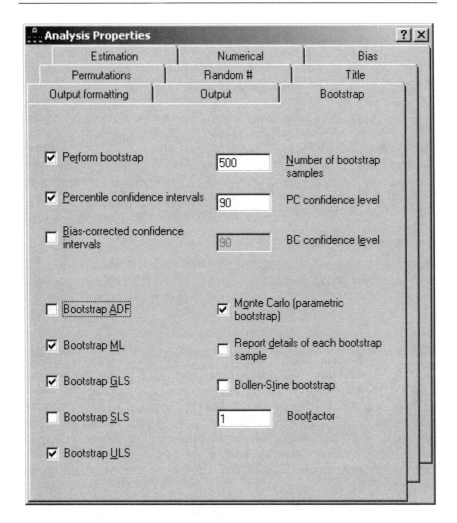

ML Estimation/Bootstrap ML

                         Bootstrap

Regression Weights	Estimate	S.E.	SE	Mean	Bias
VERBAL40 ← Verbal	7.521	0.214	0.203	7.506	−0.015
VERBAL50 ← Verbal	9.428	0.290	0.285	9.423	−0.004
MATH35 ← Math	7.106	0.215	0.205	7.103	−0.003
MATH25 ← Math	5.115	0.158	0.163	5.113	−0.002

GLS Estimation/Bootstrap GLS

			Bootstrap		
Regression Weights	Estimate	S.E.	SE	Mean	Bias
VERBAL40 ← Verbal	7.522	0.214	0.204	7.507	-0.015
VERBAL50 ← Verbal	9.429	0.290	0.285	9.425	-0.003
MATH35 ← Math	7.107	0.215	0.205	7.104	-0.003
MATH25 ← Math	5.116	0.158	0.163	5.115	-0.002

ULS Estimation/Bootstrap ULS

			Bootstrap		
Regression Weights	Estimate	S.E.	SE	Mean	Bias
VERBAL40 ← Verbal	7.512	—	-0.202	7.497	-0.015
VERBAL50 ← Verbal	9.438	—	-0.286	9.434	-0.005
MATH35 ← Math	7.125	—	-0.206	7.120	-0.004
MATH25 ← Math	5.102	—	-0.163	5.100	-0.001

EQS Bootstrap

To obtain bootstrap estimates of parameters in EQS, we use the sub-command **BOOTSTRAP = <n of cases>;**, which replaces the **POPU-LATION** subcommand in the previous EQS program. The **POPULATION** subcommand is no longer valid in this instance because the bootstrap method uses a resampling strategy given the number of cases specified. A raw data file, **DA = 'SAMPLE.DAT';**, is also specified in the following example; it contains four variables and 30 cases. The raw scores in the file are as follows:

```
50   33   14   02
64   28   56   22
65   28   46   15
67   31   56   24
63   28   51   15
46   34   14   03
69   31   51   23
62   22   45   15
59   32   48   18
46   36   10   02
```

61	30	46	14
60	27	51	16
65	30	52	20
56	25	39	11
65	30	55	18
58	27	51	19
68	32	59	23
51	33	17	05
57	28	45	13
62	34	54	23
77	38	67	22
63	33	47	16
67	33	57	25
76	30	66	21
49	25	45	17
55	35	13	02
67	30	52	23
70	32	47	14
64	32	45	15
61	28	40	13

The following bootstrap program serves to illustrate the basic EQS bootstrap program setup with raw data (*sample.dat*) for the path model in Fig. 12.3:

```
/TITLE
 BOOTSTRAP EXAMPLE
/SPECIFICATIONS
 CASES=30;VARIABLES=4;METHOD=ML; DA='SAMPLE.DAT';
/EQUATION
 V1 = 1*V2 + 1*V3 + E1;
 V4 = 1*V1 + E2;
/SIMULATION
 SEED = 12345;
 REPLICATIONS = 5;
 DATA_PREFIX = 'BOOT';
 BOOTSTRAP = 30;
 SAVE = SEPARATE;
/OUTPUT
 LISTING;
/END
```

The EQS bootstrap program can input sample data from a correlation matrix, covariance matrix, or a raw data file. We use a raw data file with 30 individual cases and four variables. Using the sample data and a maximum-likelihood estimation technique, we generate path coefficients for the path model specified in the **/EQUATION** command. The **/SIMULATION** command, using a seed number as a start value, computes five separate bootstrap estimates of the path model, based on a bootstrap sampling of 30 cases from the raw data file each time. The bootstrap samples are obviously not based on the same 30 cases, because each sample is selected at random with replacement. The bootstrap samples are outputted for each replication and saved in a separate file with the prefix Boot (e.g., **BOO001.dat to BOO005.dat**). The EQS standard computer output for all the replications is also provided because of the **LISTING;** option specified in the **/OUTPUT** command.

To compute the bootstrap estimator for a path coefficient, we first list all five bootstrap estimates for the coefficients, average them, and compute a standard deviation. The difference between this average bootstrap estimate for a given coefficient and the original sample coefficient indicates the amount of bias present. A comparison of each of these average bootstrap estimates, their standard errors, and their confidence intervals with the original sample path coefficient estimates indicates the stability or confidence in the original sample path coefficient estimates. In addition, the fit indices of the path model for each of the five replications can be compared. Notice that with 100 replications a more stable bootstrap estimator of a sample statistic is possible; however, this may require excessive disk space if we are saving the files separately, or even using the other option, which is **SAVE = CONCATE-NATE;**, to place all output into one file. In this case, the **DATA_PREFIX** command is not needed because all output is placed in the default file **EQSOUT.DAT**. However, as previously mentioned, another file name can be selected by specifying **DATA = '<file name>';** in the **/OUTPUT** command.

An abbreviated computer output listing of the bootstrap results is as follows:

```
TITLE: BOOTSTRAP EXAMPLE
SIMULATION DEFINITIONS
          BOOTSTRAP SIMULATION IS ELECTED
          NUMBER OF REPLICATIONS : 5
          SAMPLE DATA GENERATED FROM: EXIST
          SAMPLE SIZE      : 30
```

```
            ORIGINAL SEED = 12345.
            DATA FILE TO BE SAVED ? YES
            IN WHICH TYPE    ? SEPARATED
```

SIMULATION IN REPLICATION 1
INPUT DATA FILE NAME IS BOO001.DAT
COVARIANCE MATRIX TO BE ANALYZED:

```
           V1          V2          V3          V4
   V1    78.944
   V2   -14.013      12.737
   V3   145.201     -40.787     332.764
   V4    55.594     -15.870     133.523      57.689
```

STANDARDIZED SOLUTION:

```
   V1 = .176*V2 + .911*V3 + .372 E1
   V4 = .852*V1 + .524 E2
```

SIMULATION IN REPLICATION 2
INPUT DATA FILE NAME IS BOO002.DAT
COVARIANCE MATRIX TO BE ANALYZED:

```
           V1          V2          V3          V4
   V1    64.838
   V2    -4.966      11.310
   V3   117.524     -21.931     266.947
   V4    45.676      -8.862     108.680      48.547
```

STANDARDIZED SOLUTION:

```
   V1 = .192*V2 + .906*V3 + .378 E1
   V4 = .834*V1 + .552 E2
```

SIMULATION IN REPLICATION 3
INPUT DATA FILE NAME IS BOO003.DAT
COVARIANCE MATRIX TO BE ANALYZED:

```
          V1         V2          V3          V4
   V1   45.357
   V2   -1.238     10.838
   V3   80.055     -8.834     174.372
   V4   35.451     -1.683      73.076      36.257
```

STANDARDIZED SOLUTION:

```
   V1 = .130*V2 + .905*V3 + .406 E1
   V4 = .879*V1 + .477 E2
```

SIMULATION IN REPLICATION 4
INPUT DATA FILE NAME IS BOO004.DAT
COVARIANCE MATRIX TO BE ANALYZED:

	V1	V2	V3	V4
V1	57.817			
V2	9.897	13.310		
V3	91.962	10.931	177.597	
V4	34.107	6.207	73.438	36.838

STANDARDIZED SOLUTION:

V1 = .166*V2 + .900*V3 + .403 E1
V4 = .728*V1 + .686 E2

SIMULATION IN REPLICATION 5
INPUT DATA FILE NAME IS BOO005.DAT
COVARIANCE MATRIX TO BE ANALYZED:

	V1	V2	V3	V4
V1	69.454			
V2	7.937	10.171		
V3	95.707	-1.038	190.231	
V4	38.293	-0.652	78.252	40.852

STANDARDIZED SOLUTION:

V1 = .316*V2 + .835*V3 + .450 E1
V4 = .721*V1 + .693 E2

The EQS bootstrap program will produce different results each time you run it because of the seed value. The bootstrap estimates for the two path model equations, V1 = *V2 + *V3 + *E1 and V4 = *V1 + *E2, are given in Table 12.1. The five bootstrap estimates of each path coefficient and path coefficient error are compared with the original values in Table 12.1. A bootstrap estimator and standard error are also given for each path coefficient. The bootstrap estimator is simply the average over all five replications; for example, the bootstrap estimator for V2 is $(.176 + .192 + .130 + .166 + .316)/5 = .196$. The bootstrap standard error is the standard deviation of these bootstrap estimates. When reporting bootstrap estimators and standard errors, one should report confidence intervals. The 90% confidence intervals for each path coefficient are computed as follows: bootstrap estimator ± 1.645 *standard error; for example, the 90% CI for V2 is $.196 \pm 1.645 (.005) = (.188, .204)$.

The bootstrap estimators do not indicate more bias than one would normally encounter in the V2 and V3 path coefficients, that is, V2 Bias =

TABLE 12.1
Bootstrap Estimates of Path Coefficients

Sample	V2	V3	E1	V1	E2
Original	.252	.859	.446	.789	.524
Bootstrap 1	.176	.911	.372	.852	.524
Bootstrap 2	.192	.906	.378	.834	.552
Bootstrap 3	.130	.905	.406	.879	.477
Bootstrap 4	.166	.900	.403	.728	.686
Bootstrap 5	.316	.835	.450	.721	.693
Bootstrap estimator	.196	.891	.402	.803	.586
Standard error	.005	.001	.001	.005	.009

90% confidence interval
V2 (.188, .204)
V3 (.889, .893)
E1 (.400, .404)
V1 (.795, .811)
E2 (.571, .601)

$.252 - .196 = .056$ and V3 Bias $= .859 - .891 = -.032$, for the first path model equation. Similarly, the bootstrap estimate for V1 in the second path model equation does not indicate much bias, that is, V1 Bias $= .789 - .803 = -.014$. The bootstrap estimators can over- or underestimate an original path coefficient, hence the positive and negative values. Obviously, if more replications are requested, the researcher should input the data files into another statistics program and generate summary statistics on the parameter estimates, standard errors, and fit indices of interest. EQS does not readily produce the summary statistics in Table 12.1.

PRELIS Bootstrap

The LISREL–SIMPLIS software program does not provide bootstrap capabilities. However, bootstrapping can be accomplished in two different ways using PRELIS (Jöreskog & Sörbom, 1993, 1996b). Our first example demonstrates the use of the PRELIS graphical user interface. The second example uses the PRELIS command language syntax (Jöreskog & Sörbom, 1996b, pp. 185–190). In our first bootstrap example, we select **File**, then **Import External Data in Other Formats** to import the SPSS saved file *dataex7.sav*, located in the *SPSSEX* subfolder in LISREL, and save the PRELIS system file *dataex7.psf*. We now see the PRELIS spreadsheet with the raw data and the PRELIS tool bar menu with several options to choose from. We select **Statistics** from the toolbar menu and then **Bootstrapping**.

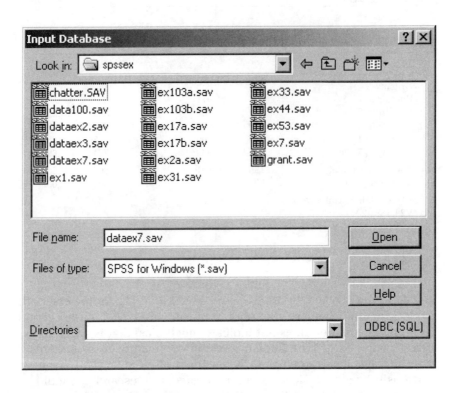

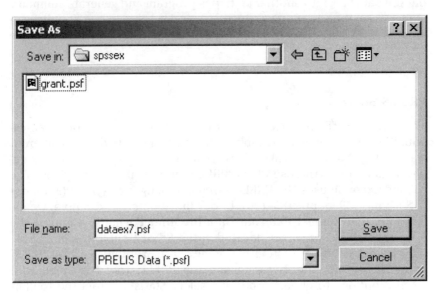

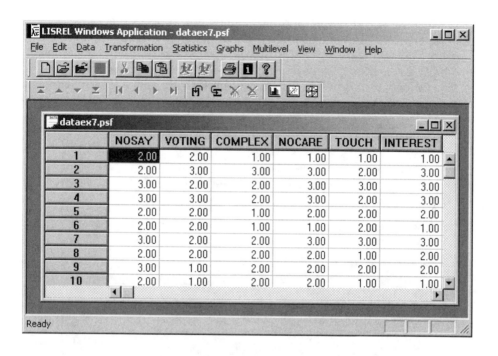

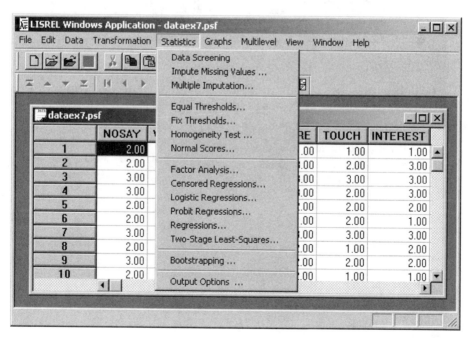

Once we select **Bootstrapping,** a dialog box appears that permits us to specify the number of bootstrap samples, bootstrap fraction, and names for saving the bootstrap matrix, means, and standard deviations. The *Syntax* button creates a PRELIS program that we can edit and save. The *Output Options* button provides other formats for saving the data.

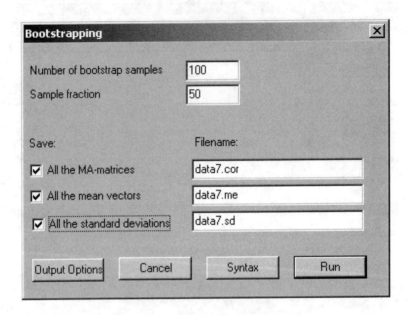

The output provides us with the PRELIS command language syntax program and descriptive statistics as follows:

```
!PRELIS SYNTAX: Can be edited
SY='C:\lisrel854\spssex\dataex7.PSF'
OU MA=KM SM=data7.cor ME=data7.me SD=data7.sd XM BS=100 SF=50
BM=data7.cor ME=data7.me SD=data7.sd


Bootstrap Correlation Matrix

             NOSAY    VOTING   COMPLEX   NOCARE   TOUCH   INTEREST
          --------------------------------------------------------------
NOSAY      1.000
VOTING     0.292    1.000
COMPLEX    0.259    0.276    1.000
NOCARE     0.462    0.263    0.442    1.000
TOUCH      0.386    0.180    0.294    0.669    1.000
INTEREST   0.408    0.239    0.368    0.710    0.640   1.000
```

```
Descriptive Statistics

Variable    Mean     St. Dev.
------------------------------
NOSAY      0.000     1.000
VOTING     0.000     1.000
COMPLEX    0.000     1.000
NOCARE     0.000     1.000
TOUCH      0.000     1.000
INTEREST   0.000     1.000
```

In our second example we use LISREL and PRELIS command language syntax in various programs to further elaborate the bootstrap method. We first run a LISREL program using the original sample data. The raw data file *efficacy.raw* is provided with LISREL and used in other examples in the *PRELIS2: User's reference guide* (Jöreskog & Sörbom, 1996b). A two-factor model is specified with six factor loadings estimated, three for each of the factors (see the MO and FR command lines). The LISREL program is written as follows:

```
Estimate factor loadings for model from file efficacy.raw
DA NI=6 NO=297 ME=GLS
RA=efficacy.raw FO;(6F2.0)
CO ALL
MO NX=6 NK=2
FR LX(1,1) LX(2,1) LX(3,1) LX(4,2) LX(5,2) LX(6,2)
OU MA=CM
```

The variance–covariance matrix to be analyzed is indicated as

```
VAR1 1.13
VAR2 0.10 1.51
VAR3 0.11 0.28 1.03
VAR4 0.41 0.11 0.27 1.40
VAR5 0.25 0.52 0.37 0.61 2.18
VAR6 0.48 0.72 0.20 0.57 1.07 2.08
```

The six factor loadings for the two-factor model specified are estimated as follows:

```
          Estimate  Standard Error
LX(1,1)    0.41        0.08
LX(2,1)    0.63        0.09
LX(3,1)    0.33        0.07
LX(4,2)    0.57        0.07
LX(5,2)    0.96        0.09
LX(6,2)    1.16        0.09
```

Then, to compute bootstrap estimates of the factor loadings for the two-factor model with three indicators per factor, the raw data file is read into a PRELIS program with the number of variables, number of cases, and estimation method specified (DA NI=6 NO=297, ME=GLS). In this example, the PRELIS program reads in a raw data file containing six variables and 297 cases with the generalized least-squares estimation method selected [RA = *efficacy.raw* FO;(6F2.0)]. The PRELIS program then generates 10 covariance matrices using the generalized least-squares estimation method. The number of bootstrap samples to be taken is specified (BS=10), and these samples are randomly drawn from the raw data file with replacement. A 100% resampling (SF=100) of the raw data file is specified. The 10 covariance matrices are output into a bootstrap save file (BM = *efficacy.cm*) for further analysis by another LISREL program. This output file is in ASCII format and can be edited. The PRELIS program is

```
Generate 10 covariance matrices from file efficacy.raw
DA NI=6 NO=297 ME=GLS
RA=efficacy.raw FO;(6F2.0)
OU MA=CM BS=10 SF=100 BM=efficacy.cm
```

The first two variance–covariance matrices output into the file *efficacy.cm* are

```
VAR 1 1.00
VAR 2 0.27 1.00
VAR 3 0.26 0.26 1.00
VAR 4 0.46 0.25 0.42 1.00
VAR 5 0.38 0.16 0.27 0.64 1.00
VAR 6 0.43 0.26 0.36 0.72 0.63 1.00


VAR 1 1.00
VAR 2 0.32 1.00
VAR 3 0.11 0.22 1.00
VAR 4 0.40 0.26 0.45 1.00
VAR 5 0.35 0.18 0.36 0.68 1.00
VAR 6 0.34 0.22 0.32 0.72 0.68 1.00
```

Notice that the diagonal values indicate variances equal to 1.0, whereas the off-diagonal values indicate the covariance terms. The manipulation of raw data (recoding variables, selecting cases, transformations) and the treatment of missing data (imputation method and/or deleting cases listwise) should be specified and handled in this program prior to bootstrap or Monte Carlo estimation. The researcher can also specify the type of matrix and estimation method desired in this PRELIS program.

The saved file `efficacy.cm` is next read by a LISREL program (CM = *efficacy.cm*) to estimate 10 sets of six factor loadings for the two-factor model. The output from this program indicates the 10 different bootstrap sampled covariance matrices read from the file, as well as parameter estimates, fit indices, and so forth (the output is no different from running 10 separate stacked programs). The LISREL program is written as

```
Estimate 10 sets of 6 factor loadings for two factor model
DA NI=6 NO=297 RP=10
CM=efficacy.cm
MO NX=6 NK=2
FR LX(1,1) LX(2,1) LX(3,1) LX(4,2) LX(5,2) LX(6,2)
OU LX=efficacy.lx
```

The LISREL program indicates that six variables and 297 cases were used to compute the 10 covariance matrices that are read in from the saved file (CM = *efficacy.cm*). The program is run 10 times (RP = 10), once for each covariance matrix saved in the file. The model specifies six variables and two factors (MO NX=6 NK=2). The parameters (factor loadings) to be estimated indicate that the first three variables define one factor and the last three variables define a second factor (see the FR command line, which indicates elements in the matrix to be free or estimated). The 10 sets of six factor loadings are computed and output in a saved file (OU LX=*efficacy.lx*).

The saved file is then read by the following PRELIS program to generate the bootstrap estimates and standard errors for the six factor loadings in the model:

```
Analyze 10 sets of 6 factor loadings from efficacy.lx file
DA NI=12
LA
'LX(1,1)' 'LX(1,2)' 'LX(2,1)' 'LX(2,2)' 'LX(3,1)' 'LX(3,2)'
'LX(4,1)' 'LX(4,2)' 'LX(5,1)' 'LX(5,2)' 'LX(6,1)' 'LX(6,2)'
RA=efficacy.lx
SD 'LX(1,2)' 'LX(2,2)' 'LX(3,2)' 'LX(4,1)' 'LX(5,1)' 'LX(6,1)'
CO ALL
OU MA=CM
```

The PRELIS program analyzes the 10 sets of six factor-loading bootstrap estimates and outputs summary statistics. Notice that we used the **SD** command to delete the other six factor loadings, which were set to zero in the two-factor model. For our example, the bootstrap estimator and standard deviation for the six factor loadings (3 factor loadings for each factor) are as follows:

UNIVARIATE SUMMARY STATISTICS FOR CONTINUOUS VARIABLES

VARIABLE	MEAN	S. D.
LX(1,1)	0.298	0.322
LX(2,1)	0.447	0.459
LX(3,1)	0.207	0.230
LX(4,2)	0.373	0.384
LX(5,2)	0.251	0.260
LX(6,2)	0.403	0.415

These values can be used to form confidence intervals around the original sample factor loading estimates to indicate how stable or good the estimates are as estimates of population values. Rather than further discuss the PRELIS and LISREL command language syntax program setups for bootstrapping and Monte Carlo experiments, we refer to the manual and excellent help examples in the software for various straightforward data set examples and output explanations. These two examples were intended only to provide a basic presentation of the bootstrap method in structural equation modeling. Lunneborg (1987) provided additional software to compute bootstrap estimates for means, correlations (bivariate, multivariate, part, and partial), regression weights, and analysis-of-variance designs, to name a few. Stine (1990) provided a basic introduction to bootstrapping methods, and Bollen and Stine (1993) gave a more in-depth discussion of bootstrapping in structural equation modeling. Mooney and Duval (1993) also provided an overview of bootstrapping methods, gave a basic algorithm and program for bootstrapping, and indicated other statistical packages that have bootstrap routines. Arbuckle and Wothke (1999) provide an exceptional set of programs for bootstrap estimation and summary statistics in Amos. We therefore refer you to these references, as well as others presented in this section, for a better coverage of the background, rationale, and appropriateness of using bootstrap techniques.

12.5 JACKKNIFE METHOD

The jackknife approach provides sample estimates of a population parameter wherein each estimate is based on $n - 1$ data points. For example, if a sample mean of 50 is based on $n = 20$ data points, then 20 additional jackknife sample means are calculated on the basis of a sample size of $n = 19$. Each sample mean, however, is based on omission of a different data point. The jackknife approach is useful in determining whether an influential data point exists that drastically changes the sample statistic.

EQS Jackknife

To obtain jackknife estimates of parameters in an EQS model, the sub-command **JACKNIFE;** replaces the **BOOTSTRAP** = <n of cases> sub-command in the program. This simulation method reuses the data file but excludes one observation on each replication. The number of replications must therefore be less than or equal to the sample size, but is typically set to the sample size for purposes of examining the influence of each data point on the sample statistic. The **SAVE** command in this instance is not applicable, although you can examine the influence of data points on the population matrices generated in each replication. The following EQS jackknife program inputs an EQS system file, *sample.ess*, saved from the raw data file *sample.dat*, which consists of four variables with spaces between the data points. The EQS program outputs 30 estimates of the path coefficients in the **/EQUATIONS** command, which represent the path model.

```
/TITLE
 JACKKNIFE PATH MODEL EXAMPLE
/SPECIFICATIONS
 CASES=30;VARIABLES=4;METHOD=ML;
 DATA_FILE = 'SAMPLE.ESS';
/EQUATION
 V1 = 1*V2 + 1*V3 + E1;
 V4 = 1*V1 + E2;
/SIMULATION
 SEED = 12345;
 REPLICATIONS=30;
 JACKNIFE;
/END
```

We are interested in examining the 30 parameter estimates for each path coefficient output by the jackknife program and comparing them to determine the influence of any individual score on the covariance matrix and hence the path model. Although not examined here, a comparison of the 30 covariance matrices and fit indices on the computer output listing would indicate potential effects on the overall model fit. The reduced computer output is not presented here; instead, only the 30 jackknife estimates for each path coefficient are compared. The results from the jackknife program are as follows:

```
TITLE: JACKKNIFE PATH MODEL EXAMPLE
SIMULATION DEFINITIONS

   JACK KNIFE SIMULATION IS ELECTED

   NUMBER OF REPLICATIONS : 30
   SAMPLE DATA GENERATED FROM: EXIST
   SAMPLE SIZE : 29
```

TABLE 12.2
Jackknife Results of Path Model

Orignal Sample
V1 = .252*V2 + .859*V3 + .446 E1   .801
V4 = .789*V1 + .615 E2   .622

30 jackknife samples
V1 = .260*V2 + .845*V3 + .467 E1   .782
V4 = .765*V1 + .644 E2   .585

V1 = .248*V2 + .859*V3 + .448 E1   .799
V4 = .790*V1 + .614 E2   .623

V1 = .264*V2 + .861*V3 + .435 E1   .811
V4 = .794*V1 + .608 E2   .630

V1 = .254*V2 + .856*V3 + .450 E1   .798
V4 = .786*V1 + .619 E2   .617

V1 = .251*V2 + .858*V3 + .448 E1   .800
V4 = .789*V1 + .614 E2   .623

V1 = .280*V2 + .833*V3 + .476 E1   .773
V4 = .754*V1 + .657 E2   .568

V1 = .251*V2 + .861*V3 + .442 E1   .804
V4 = .781*V1 + .625 E2   .609

V1 = .289*V2 + .862*V3 + .416 E1   .827
V4 = .794*V1 + .608 E2   .630

V1 = .261*V2 + .864*V3 + .431 E1   .814
V4 = .796*V1 + .605 E2   .634

V1 = .284*V2 + .827*V3 + .485 E1   .764
V4 = .746*V1 + .666 E2   .556

V1 = .251*V2 + .859*V3 + .446 E1   .801
V4 = .789*V1 + .615 E2   .622

V1 = .239*V2 + .863*V3 + .446 E1   .801
V4 = .788*V1 + .616 E2   .621

V1 = .253*V2 + .858*V3 + .448 E1   .799
V4 = .787*V1 + .617 E2   .619

V1 = .245*V2 + .860*V3 + .447 E1   .800
V4 = .787*V1 + .617 E2   .619

V1 = .253*V2 + .858*V3 + .448 E1   .800
V4 = .787*V1 + .616 E2   .620

V1 = .232*V2 + .868*V3 + .439 E1   .807
V4 = .800*V1 + .600 E2   .639

V1 = .256*V2 + .856*V3 + .449 E1   .798
V4 = .784*V1 + .621 E2   .614

V1 = .259*V2 + .847*V3 + .464 E1   .784
V4 = .770*V1 + .638 E2   .592

V1 = .241*V2 + .863*V3 + .444 E1   .803
V4 = .787*V1 + .617 E2   .619

(Continued)

TABLE 12.2
(Continued)

V1 = .276*V2 + .865*V3 + .419 E1			.824
V4 = .805*V1 + .593 E2			.648
V1 = .227*V2 + .854*V3 + .467 E1			.782
V4 = .800*V1 + .600 E2			.640
V1 = .253*V2 + .859*V3 + .445 E1			.802
V4 = .789*V1 + .614 E2			.623
V1 = .257*V2 + .857*V3 + .446 E1			.801
V4 = .789*V1 + .615 E2			.622
V1 = .263*V2 + .849*V3 + .458 E1			.790
V4 = .795*V1 + .606 E2			.633
V1 = .180*V2 + .894*V3 + .410 E1			.832
V4 = .833*V1 + .554 E2			.693
V1 = .230*V2 + .868*V3 + .440 E1			.806
V4 = .788*V1 + .615 E2			.621
V1 = .254*V2 + .858*V3 + .447 E1			.800
V4 = .784*V1 + .621 E2			.615
V1 = .242*V2 + .870*V3 + .429 E1			.816
V4 = .814*V1 + .580 E2			.663
V1 = .249*V2 + .860*V3 + .446 E1			.801
V4 = .791*V1 + .612 E2			.626
V1 = .260*V2 + .860*V3 + .438 E1			.808
V4 = .791*V1 + .612 E2			.626

The 30 jackknife results for the path model are listed in Table 12.2. We list the two equations based on 29 cases that were generated from each path model.

An examination of the path coefficients in Table 12.2 reveals a range of path coefficients (lowest, highest) from the original path coefficients in the jackknife samples, for example, V1 = .789(.746, .833), V2 = .252(.180, .289), and V3 = .859(.827, .894). An inspection of the R^2 values for both equations also indicates a range of values, $R_1^2 = .801(.764, .832)$ and $R_2^2 = .622(.556, .693)$. These results indicate how much the path coefficients and R^2 values can fluctuate given the exclusion of a single subject from the sample data. Sample 10 has the lowest R^2 values and Sample 25 has the highest R^2 values. These samples also have the lowest and highest path coefficients on V1 and V3, respectively.

Although this is a limited and simplistic example, it should serve to show how the influence of one subject's data points can affect estimates in a model. The use of the jackknife approach to determine whether influential or outlier cases are present can be assisted further in EQS by examining the univariate statistics (skewness, kurtosis) and multivariate statistics (Mardia's coefficient, normalized estimate) provided on the computer output listing. EQS computer output also lists the case numbers of those subjects with the largest multivariate kurtosis values. Obviously, a further inspection of such data is warranted with the use of the **DELETE** command to remove extreme cases in a subsequent analysis. As mentioned in chapter 2, a first step in data collection and analysis is to edit data and examine summary statistics (i.e., mean, standard deviation, skewness, and kurtosis) to avoid potential problems in structural equation modeling.

12.6   SUMMARY

In this chapter our concern was model validation. A theoretical model requires validation on additional random samples of data. We refer to this as replication and demonstrated how multiple samples can be tested against the specified theoretical model. In the absence of replication, cross-validation, simulation, bootstrap, and jackknife techniques were discussed as a means of validating a theoretical model. Our overall interest is in the accuracy and stability of parameter estimates, standard errors, and test statistics (Hu, Bentler, & Kano, 1992).

The chapter began with a look at replication involving the testing of the multiple samples of data against the theoretical model, followed by single-sample (ECVI) and split-sample (CVI) cross-validation techniques. We then introduced the basis for Monte Carlo studies, where a researcher generates simulated data for a population with known parameters. We also introduced the bootstrap method to assess the stability of our parameter estimates and standard errors, especially given different distributional assumptions. Our final topic presented the jackknife approach to assessing parameter estimate invariance where we wish to detect influential data points that affect our model results. We also noted that Amos, LISREL–SIMPLIS, and PRELIS programs at this time do not provide jackknife capabilities.

We hope that our discussion of these model validation topics in structural equation modeling has provided you with a basic overview and introduction to these methods. We encourage you to read the references provided at the end of the chapter and run some of the program setups provided in the chapter. We further hope that the basic introduction in this chapter will permit you to read the research literature. We now turn in chapters 13 and 14 to various SEM applications to demonstrate the variety of research designs and research questions that can be addressed using structural equation modeling.

EXERCISES

1. Test whether the following three variance–covariance matrices fit the theoretical path model in Fig. 12.4 using LISREL–SIMPLIS. The sample size is 80 for each sample, and the variables are entered in order as SOFED = Father's Education, SOMED = Mothers' Education, SOFOC = Father's Occupation, FAFED = Father's Education, MOMED = Mother's Education, and FAFOC = Father's Occupation.

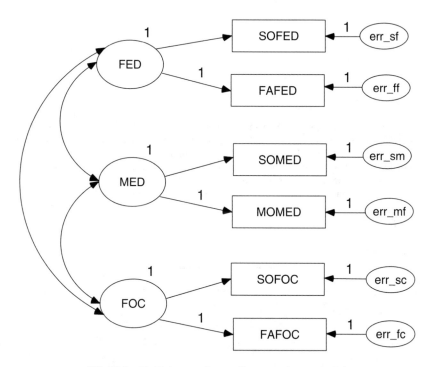

FIG. 12.4.   Multiple-samples confirmatory factor model.

```
Sample 1

5.86
3.12 3.32
35.28 23.85 622.09
4.02 2.14 29.42 5.33
2.99 2.55 19.20 3.17 4.64
35.30 26.91 465.62 31.22 23.38 546.01
```

Sample 2

8.20
3.47 4.36
45.65 22.58 611.63
6.39 3.16 44.62 7.32
3.22 3.77 23.47 3.33 4.02
45.58 22.01 548.00 40.99 21.43 585.14

Sample 3

5.74
1.35 2.49
39.24 12.73 535.30
4.94 1.65 37.36 5.39
1.67 2.32 15.71 1.85 3.06
40.11 12.94 496.86 38.09 14.91 538.76

2. For Exercise 1, run each of the samples individually in LISREL–SIMPLIS and report the single-sample expected cross-validation index (ECVI). Given a sample size of 80, would you split the sample and cross-validate the model using the CVI?
3. For Exercise 1, run the first sample of data in Amos and report the factor loadings, bootstrap estimates, and associated standard errors.
4. Jackknife the following set of data in EQS and determine whether the procedure identifies any subject that most severely affects the multiple regression prediction of GPA results, that is $Y = X1 + X2$, where $Y = $ GPA, $X1 = $ Test, and $X2 = $ IQ:

Y	X1	X2
0.8	72	114
2.2	78	117
1.6	84	117
2.6	95	120
2.7	88	117
2.1	83	123
3.1	92	118
3.0	86	114
3.2	88	114
2.6	80	115
2.7	87	114
3.0	94	112
1.6	73	115
0.9	80	111
1.9	83	112

REFERENCES

Arbuckle, J. L., & Wothke, W. (1999). *Amos 4.0 user's guide.* Chicago, IL: Smallwaters Corporation.

Bandalos, D. (1993). Factors influencing the cross-validation of confirmatory factor analysis models. *Multivariate Behavioral Research, 28,* 351–374.

Bang, J. W., Schumacker, R. E., & Schlieve, P. L. (1998). Random-number generator validity in simulation studies: An investigation of normality. *Educational and Psychological Measurement, 58,* 430–450.

Benson, J., & Bandalos, D. (1992). Second-order confirmatory factor analysis of the reactions to tests' scale with cross-validation. *Multivariate Behavioral Research, 27,* 459–487.

Benson, J., & El-Zahhar, N. (1994). Further refinement and validation of the revised test anxiety scale. *Structural Equation Modeling: A Multidisciplinary Journal, 1,* 203–221.

Benson, J., Moulin-Julian, M., Schwarzer, C., Seipp, B., & El-Zahhar, N. (1992). Cross-validation of a revised test anxiety scale using multi-national samples. In K. Hagtvet (Ed.), *Advances in test anxiety research, Vol. 7* (pp. 62–83). Lisse, Netherlands: Swets & Zeitlinger.

Bentler, P. M., & Wu, E. J. C. (2002). *EQS 6 for Windows user's guide* Encino, CA: Multivariate Software.

Bollen, K. A. (1989). *Structural equations with latent variables.* New York: Wiley.

Bollen, K. A., & Stine, R. A. (1993). Bootstrapping goodness-of-fit measures in structural equation models. In K. A. Bollen, & J. S. Long (Eds.), *Testing structural equation models* (pp. 66–110). Newbury Park, CA: Sage.

Browne, M., & Cudeck, R. (1989). Single sample cross-validation indices for covariance structures. *Multivariate Behavioral Research, 24,* 445–455.

Browne, M., & Cudeck, R. (1993). Alternative ways of assessing model fit. In K. A. Bollen & J. S. Long (Eds.), *Testing structural equation models* (pp. 136–162). Newbury Park, CA: Sage.

Cole, D. A., & Maxwell, S. E. (1985). Multitrait-multimethod comparisons across populations: A confirmatory factor analytic approach. *Multivariate Behavioral Research, 20,* 389–417.

Cudeck, R., & Browne, M. W. (1983). Cross-validation of covariance structures. *Multivariate Behavioral Research, 18,* 147–167.

Fan, X. (2003). Using commonly available software for bootstrapping in both substantive and measurement analysis. *Educational and Psychological Measurement, 63,* 24–50.

Faulbaum, F. (1987). Intergroup comparisons of latent means across waves. *Sociological Methods and Research, 15,* 317–335.

Hayduk, L. A. (1987). *Structural equation modeling with LISREL: Essentials and advances.* Baltimore: Johns Hopkins University Press.

Hu, L., Bentler, P. M., & Kano, Y. (1992). Can test statistics in covariance structure analysis be trusted? *Psychological Bulletin, 112,* 351–362.

Jöreskog, K. G., & Sörbom, D. (1993). *Bootstrapping and Monte Carlo experimenting with PRELIS2 and LISREL8.* Chicago: Scientific Software International.

Jöreskog, K. G., & Sörbom, D. (1996a). *LISREL8 user's reference guide.* Chicago: Scientific Software International.

Jöreskog, K. G., & Sörbom, D. (1996b). *PRELIS2: User's reference guide.* Chicago: Scientific Software International.

Jöreskog, K. G., & Sörbom, D. (1996c). LISREL8: *Structural equation modeling with the SIMPLIS command language.* Hillsdale, NJ: Lawrence Erlbaum Associates, Inc.

Lomax, R. G. (1983). A guide to multiple sample equation modeling. *Behavior Research Methods and Instrumentation, 15,* 580–584.

Lomax, R. G. (1985). A structural model of public and private schools. *Journal of Experimental Education, 53,* 216–226.

Lunneborg, C. E. (1987). *Bootstrap applications for the behavioral sciences, Vol. 1.* Seattle: University of Washington, Psychology Department.

McArdle, J. J., & Epstein, D. (1987). Latent growth curves within developmental structural equation models. *Child Development, 58,* 110–133.

Mooney, C. Z., & Duval, R. D. (1993). *Bootstrapping: A nonparametric approach to statistical inference.* Beverly Hills, CA: Sage.

Muthén, L., & Muthén, B. (1998). *Mplus user's guide.* Los Angeles, CA: Muthén & Muthén.

Stine, R. (1990). An introduction to bootstrap methods: Examples and ideas. In J. Fox. & J. S. Long (Eds), *Modern methods of data analysis* (pp. 325–373). Beverly Hills, CA: Sage.

ANSWERS TO EXERCISES

1. Multiple samples. LISREL–SIMPLIS program (EX11B.SPL):

```
Sample 1: Parental Socioeconomic Characteristics
Observed Variables: SOFED SOMED SOFOC FAFED MOMED FAFOC
Covariance Matrix
5.86
3.12 3.32
35.28 23.85 622.09
4.02 2.14 29.42 5.33
2.99 2.55 19.20 3.17 4.64
35.30 26.91 465.62 31.22 23.38 546.01
Sample Size: 80
Latent Variables: Fed Med Foc
SOFED = Fed
SOMED = Med
SOFOC = Foc
FAFED = 1*Fed
MOMED = 1*Med
FAFOC = 1*Foc
Set the Error Covariance between SOMED and SOFED free

Sample 2: Parental Socioeconomic Characteristics
Covariance Matrix
8.20
3.47 4.36
45.65 22.58 611.63
6.39 3.16 44.62 7.32
3.22 3.77 23.47 3.33 4.02
45.58 22.01 548.00 40.99 21.43 585.14
SOFED = Fed
SOMED = Med
SOFOC = Foc
```

```
Let the Error Variances of SOFED - SOFOC be free
Set the Error Covariance between SOMED and SOFED free

Sample 3: Parental Socioeconomic Characteristics
Covariance Matrix
5.74
1.35 2.49
39.24 12.73 535.30
4.94 1.65 37.36 5.39
1.67 2.32 15.71 1.85 3.06
40.11 12.94 496.86 38.09 14.91 538.76
SOFED = Fed
SOMED = Med
SOFOC = Foc
Let the Error Variances of SOFED - SOFOC be free
Set the Error Covariance between SOMED and SOFED equal to 0
Path Diagram
End of Problem


Global Goodness of Fit Statistics

Degrees of Freedom = 34
Minimum Fit Function Chi-Square = 52.73 (P = 0.021)

Root Mean Square Error of Approximation (RMSEA) = 0.077
90 Percent Confidence Interval for RMSEA = (0.019 ; 0.12)
P-Value for Test of Close Fit (RMSEA < 0.05) = 0.00038

Normed Fit Index (NFI) = 0.96
Comparative Fit Index (CFI) = 0.99
Critical N (CN) = 252.98
```

2. ECVI using LISREL–SIMPLIS for each sample. We would not split the sample with $n = 80$, but rather report ECVI.

```
Sample 1

Expected Cross-Validation Index (ECVI) = 0.60
90 Percent Confidence Interval for ECVI = (0.49 ; 0.80)

Sample 2

Expected Cross-Validation Index (ECVI) = 0.48
90 Percent Confidence Interval for ECVI = (0.47 ; 0.60)

Sample 3

Expected Cross-Validation Index (ECVI) = 0.47
90 Percent Confidence Interval for ECVI = (0.47 ; 0.54)
```

3. Bootstrap using Amos
   a. Create the special SPSS matrix file *chap12ex3.sav* with sample size and covariances from sample 1 in Exercise 1. Remember: Variable names must be spelled exactly as they appear in the diagram.

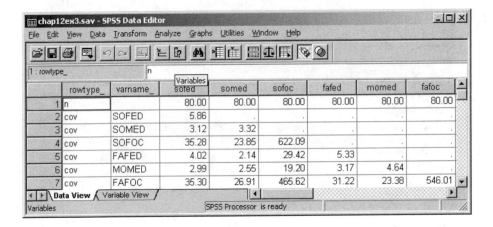

   b. Draw Fig. 12.4 including factor variances, error variances, and certain factor loadings fixed at 1.0.
   c. Select **File**, then **Data Files**; select *File Name* and pick *chap12ex3.sav* file.

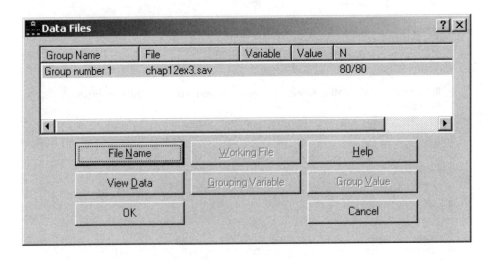

   d. Select **View/Set**, **Analysis Properties**, and pick **Standardized Estimates** and **Squared Multiple Correlations**.
   e. Select **Model Fit**, and then **Calculate Estimates**. Now select **View/Set**, then **Table Output**, and pick **standardized regression weights**.

```
Standardized Regression Weights
```

			Estimate
SOFED	←	FED	0.946
FAFED	←	FED	0.525
SOMED	←	MED	0.875
MOMED	←	MED	0.539
SOFOC	←	FOC	0.025
FAFOC	←	FOC	0.045

f. Select **View/Set**, **Analysis Properties**, pick the **Bootstrap** tab, and click on **Perform bootstrap**, enter **500**, click on **Monte Carlo**, and pick **Bootstrap ML**. Note: **Estimation** by default is ML.

g. Select **View/Set**, **Table Output**, **Standardized Regression Weights**.

```
Standardized Regression Weights Bootstrap

                Estimate   SE     SE-SE  Mean   Bias   SE-Bias
SOFED  ←  FED   0.946    0.126   0.004  0.954  0.008  0.006
FAFED  ←  FED   0.525    0.036   0.001  0.529  0.005  0.002
SOMED  ←  MED   0.875    0.110   0.003  0.879  0.003  0.005
MOMED  ←  MED   0.539    0.036   0.001  0.545  0.007  0.002
SOFOC  ←  FOC   0.025    0.446   0.014  0.047  0.023  0.020
FAFOC  ←  FOC   0.045    0.004   0.000  0.046  0.001  0.000
```

4. Jackknife using EQS:
   a. Create a file called *chap12ex4.dat* as an ASCII file with spaces between the data points.
   b. Select **File**, **New**, ESS data file, Enter 3 and 15 in the dialog box.
   c. Select **File**, **Open**, *chap12ex4.dat*, and save as *chap12ex4.ess* file type.
   d. Create EQS program, save, and run Jackknife.

```
/TITLE
 JACKKNIFE CHAPTER EXERCISE 4
/SPECIFICATIONS
 CASES=15;VARIABLES=3;METHOD=ML;
 DATA_FILE = 'chap12ex4.ESS';
/LABLE
 V1 = GPA; V2= TEST; V3=IQ;
/EQUATION
 V1 = 1*V2 + 1*V3 + E1;
/SIMULATION
 SEED = 12345;
 REPLICATIONS=10;
 JACKNIFE;
/END

EQS Original Results

GPA=V1 = .750*V2 + .034*V3 + .661 E1        .563

EQS Jackknife Results                       R-Squared
GPA=V1 = .664*V2 + .029*V3 + .747 E1        .442
GPA=V1 = .771*V2 + .005*V3 + .637 E1        .594
GPA=V1 = .768*V2 + .069*V3 + .637 E1        .594
GPA=V1 = .782*V2 + .121*V3 + .612 E1        .626
GPA=V1 = .744*V2 + .031*V3 + .668 E1        .554
GPA=V1 = .742*V2 + .070*V3 + .667 E1        .555
GPA=V1 = .725*V2 + .024*V3 + .688 E1        .526
GPA=V1 = .756*V2 + .071*V3 + .651 E1        .577
GPA=V1 = .746*V2 + .080*V3 + .661 E1        .563
GPA=V1 = .787*V2 + .039*V3 + .616 E1        .620
```

13

SEM Applications. Part I

Chapter Outline

Key Concepts

Multiple indicators and multiple causes (MIMIC models)
Testing parameter differences between groups (multiple groups)
Testing intercept and slope differences in nested groups (multilevel models)
SEM models with continuous and categorical variables (mixture models)

In previous chapters we learned about the basics of structural equation modeling. In this chapter we consider SEM models that demonstrate the variety of applications suitable for structural equation modeling. You should be aware, however, that our discussion will only introduce these SEM models. You are encouraged to explore other examples and applications reported in books (Marcoulides & Schumacker, 1996, 2001), SEM software programs (Amos, EQS, and LISREL), and the other references

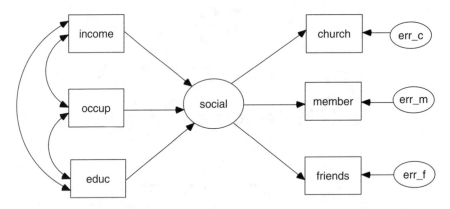

FIG. 13.1.   Multiple indicator and multiple causes model (MIMIC).

in this chapter. Our intention is to provide a basic understanding of the applications in this chapter to further your interest in the structural equation modeling approach. We use computer program examples to better illustrate particular applications.

13.1   MULTIPLE INDICATORS AND MULTIPLE CAUSES (MIMIC) MODELS

The term MIMIC refers to multiple indicators and multiple causes and defines a particular type of SEM model. The MIMIC model involves using latent variables that are predicted by observed variables. We illustrate by using an example from Jöreskog and Sörbom (1996a, Example 5.4, pp. 185–187) in which a latent variable (social participation) is defined by church attendance, memberships, and friends seen. This latent variable is predicted by the observed variables, income, occupation, and education. The MIMIC model is diagrammed in Fig. 13.1.

The latent variable, social, has arrows going out to three indicators with measurement error terms. Social has arrows pointed toward it from the three observed predictor variables, which correlate. The LISREL–SIMPLIS program that specifies the observed variables, sample size, correlation matrix with standardized variables, and the equations that reflect the MIMIC model is

```
MIMIC  Model
Observed Variables income occup educ church member friends
Sample Size 530
Correlation Matrix
```

```
1.000
 .304   1.000
 .305    .344   1.000
 .100    .156    .158   1.000
 .284    .192    .324    .360   1.000
 .176    .136    .226    .210    .265   1.000
Latent Variable social
Relationships
church = social
member = social
friends= social
social = income occup educ
Path Diagram
End of Problem
```

The model fit criteria indicate a reasonably good fit of the data to the MIMIC model:

```
Goodness of Fit Statistics

    Degrees of Freedom = 6
    Minimum Fit Function Chi-Square = 12.50 (P = 0.052)
    Normal Theory Weighted Least Squares Chi-Square = 12.02 (P = 0.061)
    Estimated Non-centrality Parameter (NCP) = 6.02
    90 Percent Confidence Interval for NCP = (0.0 ; 20.00)

    Root Mean Square Error of Approximation (RMSEA) = 0.044
    90 Percent Confidence Interval for RMSEA = (0.0 ; 0.079)
    P-Value for Test of Close Fit (RMSEA < 0.05) = 0.56

    Expected Cross-Validation Index (ECVI) = 0.079
    90 Percent Confidence Interval for ECVI = (0.068 ; 0.11)

        Normed Fit Index (NFI) = 0.97
        Goodness of Fit Index (GFI) = 0.99
```

The measurement equations in the computer output, however, reveal that church is not an important indicator variable in defining the latent variable social because no *t* value is indicated.

```
MEASUREMENT EQUATIONS

church=0.47*social, Errorvar.=0.78 , R²=0.22
                             (0.058)
                             13.61

member=0.74*social, Errorvar.=0.46 , R²=0.54
      (0.11)                  (0.075)
       6.71                    6.10

friends=0.40*social, Errorvar.=0.84 , R²=0.16
       (0.067)                 (0.058)
        6.03                    14.51
```

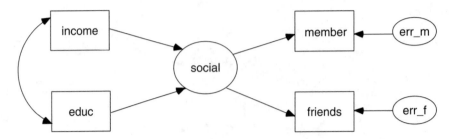

FIG. 13.2. Respecified MIMIC model.

The structural equation indicates that occup (occupation) does not statistically significantly predict social (t = parameter estimate divided by
standard error = .097/.056 = 1.73 is less than t = 1.96 at the .05 level of
significance):

```
STRUCTURAL EQUATION

social = 0.23*income + 0.097*occup + 0.33*educ, Errorvar.= 0.74 , R² = 0.26
         (0.061)        (0.056)        (0.068)                    (0.17)
          3.82           1.73           4.93                       4.35
```

We therefore respecify the model by dropping church and occup and
rerun the analysis. Figure 13.2 indicates the respecified MIMIC model.
The model fit criteria are more acceptable, indicating an almost perfect
fit of the data to the MIMIC model, because the chi-square value is close
to zero:

```
Goodness of Fit Statistics

Degrees of Freedom = 1
Minimum Fit Function Chi-Square = 0.19 (P = 0.66)

Root Mean Square Error of Approximation (RMSEA) = 0.0
90 Percent Confidence Interval for RMSEA = (0.0 ; 0.088)
P-Value for Test of Close Fit (RMSEA < 0.05) = 0.82

Normed Fit Index (NFI) = 1.00
Goodness of Fit Index (GFI) = 1.00
```

The structural equation now indicates two statistically significant predictor variables with R^2 = .36.

```
Structural Equations

social = 0.31*income + 0.42*educ, Errorvar.= 0.64, R² = 0.36
         (0.063)        (0.064)                  (0.19)
          5.01           6.65                      3.39
```

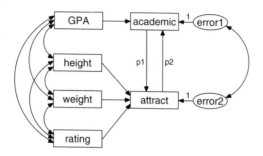

FIG. 13.3. Multiple-group model.

13.2 MULTIPLE-GROUP MODELS

Multiple-group models are set up in the same way as the multiple-sample models in chapter 12. The multiple-group model analysis must first establish the acceptance of the measurement models and measurement invariance for the groups before hypothesizing a statistically significant difference in structure coefficients between groups. We use an example from Arbuckle and Wothke (1999, Example 11a, pp. 225–233). The model examines the perceived attractiveness and perceived academic ability differences between a sample of 209 girls and a sample of 207 boys. The multiple-group model is shown in Fig. 13.3.

We are interested in testing whether boys and girls have statistically significantly different coefficients for the reciprocal paths between academic and attract.

In Amos we first draw Fig. 13.3 and then we select the two separate data files for the girls and the boys. We do this by selecting **File**, then **Data Files** to select the two data sets.

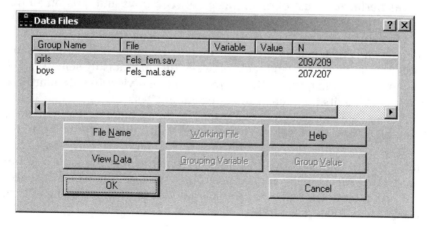

We next select **Model Fit** from the tool bar menu and **Manage Groups**, where we first add *girls* and then click on **New** and enter *boys*. These are the same steps as for the multiple-sample models.

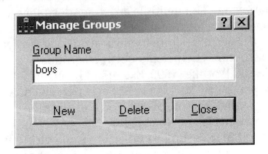

We now select **View/Set** and then **Analysis Properties**, and select the **Output** tab to indicate standardized estimates, squared multiple correlations, and critical ratios for differences. The *critical ratios for differences* performs a test of differences between boys and girls on all free parameters in the model. We are only interested in testing for the path coefficients being equal between girls and boys on attract predicting academic, and academic predicting attract, so we label each path the same in both diagrams. We can toggle between the diagrams by selecting *girls* or *boys* on the left side of the screen, and also view the standardized path coefficients for each group after our analysis.

To run the analysis, select **Model Fit**, then **Calculate Estimates**. To view all of the output, select **View/Set** and then **Table Output**. The model had an acceptable fit ($\chi^2 = 4.08$, $df = 6$, $p = .665$). We can also view a table of the critical ratios for differences and select the values in our model that we set equal across the groups. We also notice that this table has critical ratios for all of the free parameters in the model. The critical ratios are tabulated as follows:

Critical ratio	P1	P2
P1	0.000	−6.180
P2	−6.180	0.000

The P1/P1 cell value of 0.000 indicates that the path coefficient P1 (academic predicting attract) is not statistically significantly different between girls and boys. The P2/P2 cell value of 0.000 also indicates that the path coefficient P2 (attract predicting academic) is not statistically significantly different between girls and boys. The P1/P2 and P2/P1 off-diagonal cell values (−6.180) do indicate that P1 ≠ P2 in the model. We can view these path coefficients by selecting the standardized estimates on the left of the screen and toggling between the girls and boys diagrams (Figs. 13.4, 13.5, respectively).

We present the diagrams with the standardized estimates to verify the critical ratio for difference tests. We see that the path coefficient, academic predicting attract, for girls is .49 versus for boys .48, which verifies

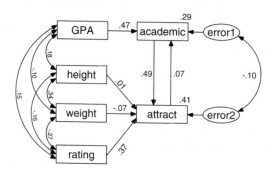

FIG. 13.4.   Standardized coefficients for girls.

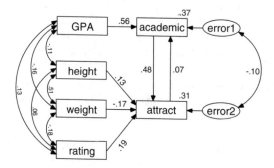

FIG. 13.5.   Standardized coefficients for boys.

the nonsignificant difference. We also see that the path coefficient, attract predicting academic, for girls is .07 versus for boys .07, which also verifies the nonsignificant difference. Finally, we see that the path coefficient P1 (.48 and .49, respectively) is statistically different from the path coefficient P2 (.07 and .07, respectively). We can hypothesize the equivalence between girls and boys of other coefficients in the model by placing the same path label in each diagram; for example, add P3 in each diagram for the path *GPA* predicting academic.

You can find multiple-group (sample) models in EQS (manual8.eqs) and LISREL–SIMPLIS (Example 10, EX10C.SPL; Example 12, EX12A.SPL) that parallel those in chapter 12. A basic difference between multiple-sample and multiple-group models is that here we are not conducting model validation (multiple-sample models), but rather hypothesizing that parameters will differ between groups (multiple-group models). In SEM we test for the statistically significant differences between the parameters of groups by setting the parameters of interest equal. In Amos this is accomplished by labeling the paths the same in the diagrams for each group. In EQS we use the **/Constraint** and **/LMTEST** commands. In LISREL–SIMPLIS we only include the **Equation** or **Relationship** command for the first group to signify that parameters are the same for all other groups. The focus of analysis is the same, although the program setups are very different.

13.3   MULTILEVEL MODELS

Multilevel models in SEM are so named because of the hierarchical nature of data in a nested research design. For example, a student's academic achievement is based in classrooms, so students are nested in classrooms, teachers are nested within schools, and schools are nested within districts. The nested research design contrasts with a crossed research design, and our interest is in the effects at different levels given the clustered nature of the data. Several textbooks introduce and present excellent multilevel examples, so we refer you to those for more information on the analysis of multilevel models in SEM (Heck & Thomas, 2000; Hox, 2002).

EQS has three methods of conducting multilevel model analysis based on a cluster variable: (a) ML (maximum likelihood using the EM algorithm), (b) MUML (Muthén ML-based estimation), and (c) HLM (hierarchical linear model).

The ML multilevel method using maximum likelihood estimation conducts two EM algorithm steps to estimate parameters and standard errors. The first is the expectation step (E), where within- and between-level covariance matrices (and/or means) are estimated itera-tively. The second is the maximization step (M), where the ML estimates and standard errors are produced if the convergence criterion was met. A simulated data set (*liang.ess*) is created in EQS for the multilevel analysis, which contains eight indicator variables for identifying two latent variables (factors) and a cluster variable, V9, that identifies the nested effect in the data. The ML multilevel model program in EQS (Bentler & Wu, 2002, p. 213) is

```
/TITLE
   EQS Multilevel Model using ML
/SPECIFICATIONS
 data='liang.ess ';
 cases=720;
 variables=9; METHOD=ML;
 matrix=raw;
 analysis=covariance;
 multilevel=ml; cluster=V9;
/MODEL
 (v1 to v4) on f1;
 (v5 to v8) on f2;
 cov (f1,f2) = *;
/END
```

This program is specially written for multilevel models because it includes **model**, **multilevel**, and **cluster** commands. The EQS ML multilevel program output lists the within and between results and a model fit statistic:

```
MULTI-LEVEL ANALYSIS: WITHIN-LEVEL
MAXIMUM LIKELIHOOD SOLUTION (NORMAL DISTRIBUTION THEORY)

STANDARDIZED SOLUTION:              R-SQUARED

V1 =V1 = .826 F1 + .564 E1    .682
V2 =V2 = .813*F1 + .582 E2    .662
V3 =V3 = .822*F1 + .570 E3    .675
V4 =V4 = .837*F1 + .547 E4    .700
V5 =V5 = .801 F2 + .598 E5    .642
V6 =V6 = .799*F2 + .602 E6    .638
V7 =V7 = .835*F2 + .550 E7    .697
V8 =V8 = .801*F2 + .599 E8    .641

CORRELATIONS AMONG INDEPENDENT VARIABLES
-----------------------------------------

F2, F1 = .439
```

```
MULTI-LEVEL ANALYSIS: BETWEEN-LEVEL
MAXIMUM LIKELIHOOD SOLUTION (NORMAL DISTRIBUTION THEORY)

STANDARDIZED SOLUTION:        R-SQUARED

V1 =V1 = .810 F1 + .586 E1      .656
V2 =V2 = .795*F1 + .606 E2      .632
V3 =V3 = .766*F1 + .643 E3      .587
V4 =V4 = .843*F1 + .538 E4      .710
V5 =V5 = .834 F2 + .551 E5      .696
V6 =V6 = .816*F2 + .578 E6      .666
V7 =V7 = .819*F2 + .574 E7      .670
V8 =V8 = .834*F2 + .552 E8      .696


CORRELATIONS AMONG INDEPENDENT VARIABLES
----------------------------------------

F2, F1 = .508
```

The model fit criterion is nonsignificant, indicating that the within and between parameter estimates do not differ significantly:

```
BENTLER-LIANG LIKELIHOOD RATIO STATISTIC = 32.796 BASED ON 38 D.F.
PROBABILITY VALUE FOR THE CHI-SQUARE STATISTIC IS .70854
```

The MUML multilevel model in EQS (p. 223) is

```
/TITLE
 EQS Multilevel model using MUML
/SPECIFICATIONS
 data='liang.ess';
 cases =720;
 variable=9; method=ml;
 matrix=raw;
 analysis=cov;
 multilevel=muml; cluster=v9;
/MODEL
 (v1 to v4) on f1;
 (v5 to v8) on f2;
 cov (f1,f2) = *;
/END
```

The MUML multilevel analysis is now indicated on the **multilevel** command instead of ML, that is, MUML instead of ML. The MUML multilevel analysis approximates ML parameter estimates and standard errors when the cluster sizes are equal and estimates means and standard deviations (**analysis = cov;** command). The EQS MUML multilevel program output is

```
MULTI-LEVEL ANALYSIS: WITHIN-LEVEL
MAXIMUM LIKELIHOOD SOLUTION (NORMAL DISTRIBUTION THEORY)

STANDARDIZED SOLUTION:        R-SQUARED

V1 =V1 = .826 F1  + .564 E1     .682
V2 =V2 = .813*F1  + .582 E2     .661
V3 =V3 = .822*F1  + .570 E3     .676
V4 =V4 = .837*F1  + .547 E4     .701
V5 =V5 = .802 F2  + .597 E5     .643
V6 =V6 = .799*F2  + .601 E6     .639
V7 =V7 = .835*F2  + .550 E7     .697
V8 =V8 = .801*F2  + .599 E8     .642


THESE EQUATIONS ARE THE BETWEEN-LEVEL MODEL

F3   =F3  = .000*V999 + .811 F11  + .585 D3   .658
F4   =F4  = .000*V999 + .789*F11  + .614 D4   .623
F5   =F5  = .000*V999 + .772*F11  + .635 D5   .596
F6   =F6  = .000*V999 + .854*F11  + .520 D6   .730
F7   =F7  = .000*V999 + .845 F12  + .534 D7   .715
F8   =F8  = .000*V999 + .822*F12  + .569 D8   .676
F9   =F9  = .000*V999 + .822*F12  + .569 D9   .676
F10  =F10 = .000*V999 + .837*F12  + .548 D10  .700


CORRELATIONS AMONG INDEPENDENT VARIABLES
----------------------------------------


F2, F1   = .439
F12, F11 = .520
```

The model fit criterion is nonsignificant, indicating that the within and between parameter estimates do not differ significantly:

```
CHI-SQUARE = 31.091 BASED ON 38 DEGREES OF FREEDOM
PROBABILITY VALUE FOR THE CHI-SQUARE STATISTIC IS .77893
```

Multilevel analyses with ML and MUML are designed to handle only two-level models. It is difficult to interpret multilevel models that have more than two nested levels. However, hierarchical linear models (HLM) have been analyzed in regression with three levels of observed variables. EQS HLM was created to analyze up to five levels using latent variables. In EQS HLM the level 1 equation is run for each cluster and the resulting parameters are saved and passed on for use in the level 2 equation. The level 2 equation therefore uses its own data as well as parameter estimates resulting from the level 1 equation. Consequently, if the level 1 equation has **n** clusters, then the level 2 equation has a sample size of **n** clusters.

The HLM multilevel model in EQS (p. 225) is similar to the ML and MUML multilevel programs, except a second data set is specified and a **/DEFINE** command is used to indicate parameters from the previous level 1 as variables to be used in the level 2 equation. The raw data sets *mlevel1.ess* and *mlevel2.ess* are used for level 1 and level 2 analysis, respectively. Parameters from variables V4, V5, and V6 are passed on to the level 2 equations. The **multilevel** command now specifies **hlm** and uses variable V1 in the level 1 data set to indicate the clusters. The EQS HLM multilevel program (*mlevel.eqs*) is

```
/Title
 Two stage multilevel example (level 1)-- an HLM approach
/Specifications
 data='mlevel1.ess'; var=6; case =250;
 multilevel=hlm; cluster=v1; analysis=moment;
 method=ml;
 matrix=raw;
/equations
 v4 = *v999 + 1f1 + e4;
 v5 = *v999 + *f1 + e5;
 v6 = *v999 + *f1 + e6;
/variance
 v999=1;
 f1 =*;
 e4 to e6 =*;
/end
/Title
 two stage model - (level 2)
/Specification
 data='mlevel2.ess'; var=3; case=50;
 method=ml;
 matrix=raw;
/DEFINE
 V4 = (V4,V999);
 V5 = (V5,V999);
 V6 = (V6,V999);
/equation
 v4 = *v2 + *v3 + e4;
 v5 = *v2 + *v3 + e5;
 v6 = *v2 + *v3 + e6;
/variance
 v2 to v3 =*;
 e4 to e6 =*;
/end
```

The EQS HLM multilevel program output is

```
TITLE: two stage model - (level 2)
```

```
MAXIMUM LIKELIHOOD SOLUTION (NORMAL DISTRIBUTION THEORY)

STANDARDIZED SOLUTION:                    R-SQUARED

V4 =V4 = -.017*V2 + .156*V3 + .988 E4    .025
V5 =V5 = -.235*V2 - .119*V3 + .965 E5    .069
V6 =V6 = -.142*V2 + .159*V3 + .977 E6    .045
```

The EQS HLM multilevel model fit criterion further indicates that this HLM two-level model does not fit well:

```
CHI-SQUARE = 87.212 BASED ON 4 DEGREES OF FREEDOM
PROBABILITY VALUE FOR THE CHI-SQUARE STATISTIC IS .00000
```

LISREL provides an extensive *HELP* library on multilevel modeling, which includes an overview of multilevel modeling, differences between OLS and multilevel random coefficient models (MRCM), latent growth curve models, testing of contrasts, analysis of two-level repeated measures data, multivariate analysis of educational data, multilevel models for categorical response variables, and examples using air traffic control data, school data, and survey data. You are encouraged to use the help library in LISREL for more information and examples using PRELIS and SIMPLIS and read about the new statistical features in LISREL (Jöreskog, Sörbom, du Toit, & du Toit, 2001).

In LISREL we use the **multilevel** tool bar menu to demonstrate *variance decomposition*, which is a basic multilevel model (equivalent to a one-way ANOVA with random effects). The multilevel null model is a preliminary first step in a multilevel analysis because it provides important information about the variability of the dependent variable. We essentially create a null model (intercept only) to serve as a baseline for comparing additional multilevel models where we add variables to test whether they significantly reduce the unexplained variability in the dependent variable (response or outcome variable).

In LISREL we begin by opening up the PRELIS system file *mouse.psf* located in the *mlevelex* folder. This is a nested data set with nine weight measurements over time on 82 mice.

The **multilevel** command now appears on the tool bar menu with linear and nonlinear model options. We select **Linear Model**, and then **Title and Options**. We specify variables for each of the options shown here, but this is accomplished by selecting **NEXT** after we enter the information for **Title and Options**. We enter the title *Mouse Data: Variance Decomposition* and then click **NEXT**. This takes us to the **Identification Variables** dialog box, where we add *iden1* to level 1 and *iden2* to level 2. The variable *iden1* ranges from 1 to 82 and identifies each unique mouse,

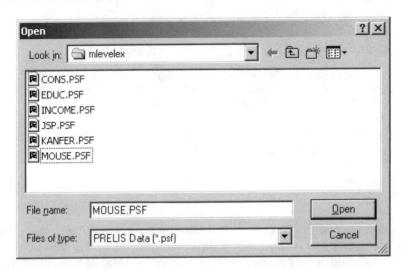

whereas *iden2* indicates the nine time measurements and ranges from 1 to 9. We again click **NEXT**. This takes us to the **Select Response and Fixed Variables** dialog box, where we add *weight* as the select response (dependent variable) and *constant* as a fixed effect to create an intercept-only (null) model. We again click **NEXT**. This takes us to the **Random Variables** dialog box, where we add *constant* to both level 1 and level 2. *Constant* is the intercept term for the response variable (*weight*) and associates an error term for the level 1 and level 2 equations. We now click **FINISH** and a PRELIS program, *mouse.pr2*, is written. The PRELIS program is executed by clicking the run **P** (**Run Prelis)** on the tool bar menu. The PRELIS computer output now indicates the results for the baseline model (intercept only).

	iden2	iden1	weight	constant	time	timesq	gender
1	1.00	1.00	15.00	1.00	1.00	1.00	1.00
2	1.00	2.00	17.00	1.00	2.00	4.00	1.00
3	1.00	3.00	23.00	1.00	3.00	9.00	1.00
4	1.00	4.00	24.00	1.00	4.00	16.00	1.00
5	1.00	5.00	26.00	1.00	5.00	25.00	1.00
6	1.00	6.00	31.00	1.00	6.00	36.00	1.00

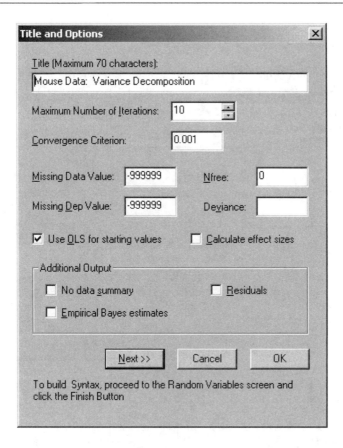

The second multilevel analysis includes adding *time* to the fixed variable list. To do so, we click on **Multilevel**, **Linear Models**, and then **Select Response and Fixed Variables**. We add *time* to the fixed variable list; we click **NEXT**, and then **FINISH**. To run the updated PRELIS file *mouse.pr2*, we click on run **P** (**Run Prelis**). We repeat this a third time to add *gender* to our fixed variables for a final multilevel analysis.

We create and run three PRELIS programs to obtain multilevel analysis results for an intercept model (Model 1), an intercept and time model (Model 2), and an intercept, time, and gender model (Model 3). The three PRELIS programs are updated each time we change the number of fixed variables. The three PRELIS programs are listed as follows, where it is easily seen that the **FIXED** command changes as we add additional variables to hypothesize better prediction in the unexplained variability of the response variable (weight).

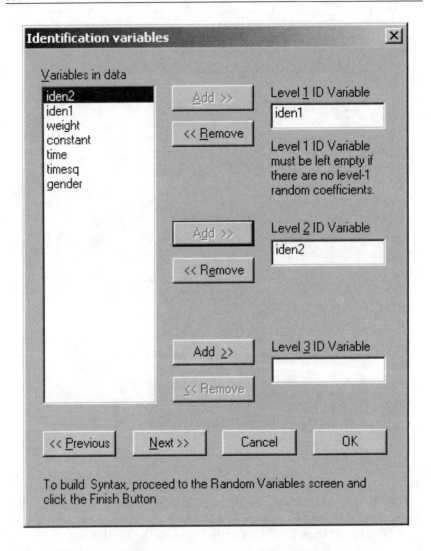

Model 1. Intercept only

```
OPTIONS OLS=YES CONVERGE=0.001000 MAXITER=10 OUTPUT=STANDARD ;
TITLE=Mouse Data: Variance Decomposition;
SY='C:\lisrel851\mlevelex\MOUSE.PSF';
ID1=iden1;
ID2=iden2;
RESPONSE=weight;
FIXED=constant;
RANDOM1=constant;
RANDOM2=constant;
```

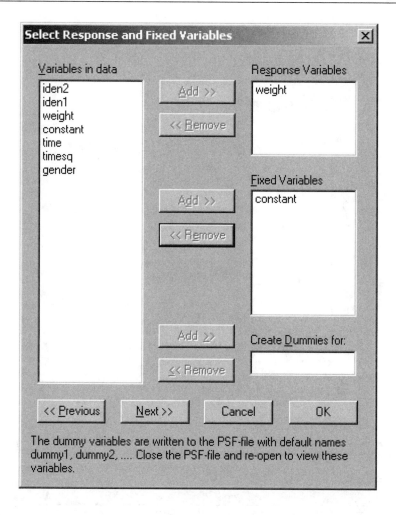

Model 2. Intercept + time

```
OPTIONS OLS=YES CONVERGE=0.001000 MAXITER=10 OUTPUT=STANDARD ;
TITLE=Mouse Data: Variance Decomposition;
SY='C:\lisrel851\mlevelex\MOUSE.PSF';
ID1=iden1;
ID2=iden2;
RESPONSE=weight;
FIXED=constant time;
RANDOM1=constant;
RANDOM2=constant;
```

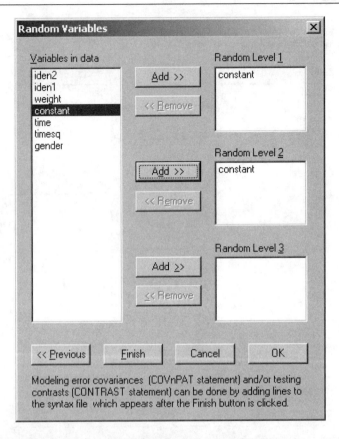

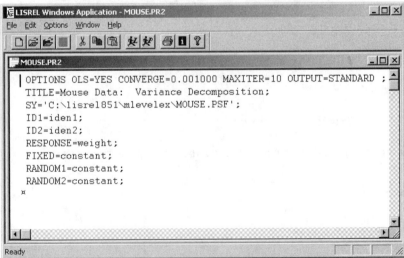

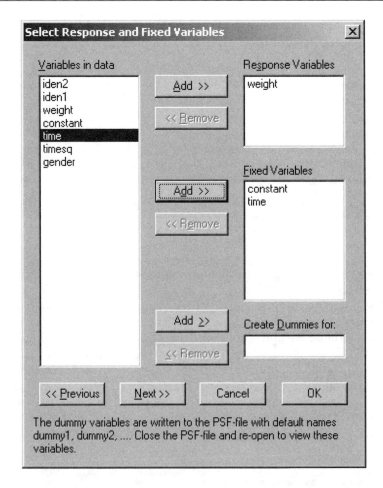

Model 3. Intercept + time + gender

```
OPTIONS OLS=YES CONVERGE=0.001000 MAXITER=10 OUTPUT=STANDARD ;
TITLE=Mouse Data: Variance Decomposition;
SY='C:\lisrel851\mlevelex\MOUSE.PSF';
ID1=iden1;
ID2=iden2;
RESPONSE=weight;
FIXED=constant time gender;
RANDOM1=constant;
RANDOM2=constant;
```

Our final analysis yields the following multilevel analysis equation:

$$Y_{ij} = \beta_0 + \beta_1 Time_{ij} + \beta_2 Gender_{ij} + u_{ij} + e_{ij}.$$

TABLE 13.1
Results for Multilevel Analysis of Mouse Weight

Multilevel model fixed factors	Model 1 intercept only	Model 2 intercept + time	Model 3 intercept + time + gender
Intercept only (B_0)	28.63 (.57)	9.09 (.60)	9.07 (.58)
Time (B_1)		4.09 (.06)	4.08 (.06)
Gender (B_2)			1.42 (.50)
Level 1 error variance (e_{ij})	130.32	16.46	16.46
Level 2 error variance (u_{ij})	11.32	20.69	18.68
Deviance ($-2LL$)	5425.49	4137.58	4129.94
Df	3	4	5
Chi-square difference ($df = 1$)		1287.97	7.64

Note. $\chi^2 = 3.84$, $df = 1$, $p = .05$ (Table A.4, p. 476).

Other multilevel models can include random effects rather than only fixed effects.

The computer outputs for the three PRELIS multilevel programs are summarized in Table 13.1 for the variance decomposition of the response variable, weight. Model 1 provides a baseline model to determine whether additional variables help in reducing the amount of variability in weight. Model 2, with time added, substantially reduces the unexplained variability in weight ($\chi^2 = 1287.91$, $df = 1$). Model 3, with gender added, also significantly reduces the amount of unexplained variability in weight ($\chi^2 = 7.64$, $df = 1$). Therefore, mouse weight variability is statistically significantly explained by time and gender fixed variables.

13.4 MIXTURE MODELS

Mixture models in SEM involve the analysis of observed variables that are categorical and continuous (Muthén & Muthén, 1998). Recall in chapter 3 we shared our concern that only continuous variables be used in a sample variance–covariance matrix (Pearson correlation matrix with means and standard deviations). EQS permits continuous and categorical models using a special **Category** command to designate which variables are categorical. In PRELIS a variable is defined as continuous by the **CO** command (by default it must have a minimum of 15 categories) or the **OR** command for ordinal variables. PRELIS outputs normal theory variance–covariance matrices (correlation between continuous variables), polychloric matrices (correlation between ordered categorical variables), polyserial matrices (correlation between continuous and

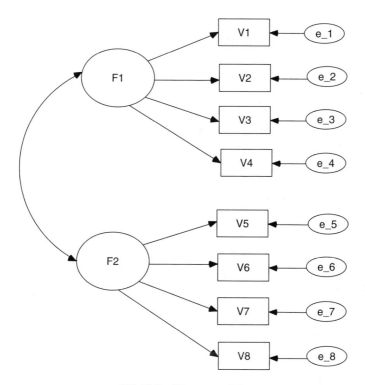

FIG. 13.6. Mixture model.

ordered categorical variables), asymptotic variance–covariance matrices (continuous and/or ordinal variables with nonnormality), and augmented moment matrices (matrices with variable means). In LISREL one uses PRELIS to create and save the appropriate variance–covariance matrix, conduct the analysis as usual, and interpret the Satorra–Bentler scaled chi-square fit statistic and/or other robust model fit measures.

In EQS we use the EQS system file *poon.ess*, which contains 200 subjects and eight variables, which define a two-factor confirmatory factor analysis (Bentler & Wu, 2002, pp. 231–235) with six continuous variables (V1–V6) and two categorical variables (V7 and V8). The model is represented in Fig. 13.6.

The EQS file structure is similar to any other EQS program with the addition of the **CATEGORY** command to indicate categorical variables and adding the *ROBUST* option to the **METHODS** command. The EQS program is

```
/TITLE
 Test Example for using Categorical Variables
/SPECIFICATIONS
 DATA='POON.ESS'; VARIABLE= 8; CASE= 200;
 METHODS=ML,ROBUST; MATRIX=RAW;
 CATEGORY=V7,V8;
 ANALYSIS = CORRELATION;
/LABELS
 V1=V1; V2=V2; V3=V3; V4=V4; V5=V5;
 V6=V6; V7=V7; V8=V8;
/EQUATIONS
 V1 = + 1*F1 + E1;
 V2 = + *F1  + E2;
 V3 = + *F1  + E3;
 V4 = + *F1  + E4;
 V5 = + 1*F2 + E5;
 V6 = + *F2  + E6;
 V7 = + *F2  + E7;
 V8 = + *F2  + E8;
/VARIANCES
 F1 TO F2 = 1;
 E1 TO E8 = *;
/COVARIANCES
 F2 , F1 = *;
/PRINT
 FIT=ALL;
 TABLE=EQUATION;
/END
```

The EQS computer output recognizes the number of categorical variables and how many ordered categories exist within each:

```
YOUR MODEL HAS SPECIFIED CATEGORICAL VARIABLES

  TOTAL NUMBER OF VARIABLES ARE 8
  NUMBER OF CONTINUOUS VARIABLES ARE 6
  NUMBER OF DISCRETE VARIABLES ARE 2

 INFORMATION ON DISCRETE VARIABLES

   V7 WITH 3 CATEGORIES
   V8 WITH 3 CATEGORIES
```

The EQS computer output next displays the polyserial and polychloric threshold estimates and standard errors along with covariance and correlation results with the other variables. These correlations are then placed in a matrix for the CFA model analysis where the Satorra–Bentler chi-square statistic is interpreted.

RESULTS OF POLYSERIAL PARTITION USING V7—3 CATEGORIES

THRESHOLDS

ESTIMATES	STD. ERR
-.5112	.0741
.4318	.0767

ESTIMATES

VARIABLE	COVARIANCE	STD. ERR
V1	.4154	.0520
V2	.4442	.0507
V3	.4957	.0493
V4	.4281	.0516
V5	.6181	.0449
V6	.6358	.0427

RESULTS OF POLYSERIAL PARTITION USING V8—3 CATEGORIES

THRESHOLDS

ESTIMATES	STD. ERR
-.4566	.0747
.4986	.0779

ESTIMATES

VARIABLE	COVARIANCE	STD. ERR
V1	.3812	.0532
V2	.2654	.0552
V3	.3558	.0539
V4	.4390	.0504
V5	.6220	.0430
V6	.6728	.0396

RESULTS OF POLYCHORIC PARTITION

AVERAGE THRESHOLDS

V7	—.5044	.4327
V8	—.4580	.4854

POLYCHORIC CORRELATION MATRIX BETWEEN DISCRETE VARIABLES

	V7	V8
V7	1.000	
V8	.583	1.000

The EQS computer output lists the following warning because a correlation matrix is used that contains variables with mixed levels of measurement, hence mixture models:

```
*** WARNING *** NORMAL THEORY STATISTICS MAY NOT BE
             MEANINGFUL DUE TO ANALYZING CORRELATION MATRIX

          V1       V2       V3       V4       V5       V6       V7       V8

V1     1.000
V2      .693    1.000
V3      .681     .627    1.000
V4      .657     .646     .657    1.000
V5      .340     .350     .399     .428    1.000
V6      .428     .350     .387     .450     .658    1.000
V7      .415     .444     .496     .428     .618     .636    1.000
V8      .381     .265     .356     .439     .622     .673     .583    1.000
```

The Satorra–Bentler scaled chi-square statistic for the robust analysis of the confirmatory factor model is nonsignificant, thus indicating a good fit to the mixture model:

```
GOODNESS OF FIT SUMMARY FOR METHOD = ROBUST

SATORRA-BENTLER SCALED CHI-SQUARE = 29.2416 ON 19 DEGREES OF FREEDOM
PROBABILITY VALUE FOR THE CHI-SQUARE STATISTIC IS .06228
```

The EQS output further warns us before printing the final robust results based on using an optimal weight matrix:

```
*** WARNING *** WITH CATEGORICAL DATA, NORMAL THEORY RESULTS WITHOUT CORRECTION
           SHOULD NOT BE TRUSTED.

MAXIMUM LIKELIHOOD SOLUTION (NORMAL DISTRIBUTION THEORY)
WITH ROBUST STATISTICS (LEE, POON, AND BENTLER OPTIMAL WEIGHT MATRIX)

STANDARDIZED SOLUTION:            R-SQUARED

V1 =V1 = .839*F1 + .545 E1        .703
V2 =V2 = .797*F1 + .605 E2        .634
V3 =V3 = .807*F1 + .590 E3        .652
V4 =V4 = .808*F1 + .589 E4        .653
V5 =V5 = .790*F2 + .613 E5        .624
V6 =V6 = .837*F2 + .548 E6        .700
V7 =V7 = .773*F2 + .634 E7        .598
V8 =V8 = .781*F2 + .625 E8        .610
CORRELATIONS AMONG INDEPENDENT VARIABLES
-----------------------------------------

(F2,F1) = .611
```

LISREL–PRELIS

We will need to save the EQS SYSTEM FILE *poon.ess* as a raw data file, *poon.dat*. In LISREL we can now write a PRELIS program that will read in the raw data file *poon.dat* and output the polyserial correlation matrix *poon.mat*. The PRELIS program only requires a few lines of code to read in a raw data file and output eight different types of matrices (Jöreskog & Sörbom, 1996b, pp. 92–93). The title of the program is *Polyserial correlation matrix*. The **DA** command specifies eight input variables (NI = 8) with 200 observations (NO = 200); missing data are identified by a zero (MI = 0) and missing data are treated listwise (TR = LI). The **RA** command identifies the raw data file (*poon.dat*). The OU command identifies the type of matrix to be computed, that is, polyserial matrix (MA = PM), and where to save the polyserial matrix (PM = poon.mat):

```
Polyserial correlation matrix
DA NI=8 NO=200 MI=0 TR=LI
RA FI=poon.dat
OU MA=PM PM=poon.mat
```

The resulting polyserial correlation matrix would be used in our LISREL mixture model analysis (note this matrix is similar to the one generated by EQS):

```
Polyserial Correlation Matrix
```

	V1	V2	V3	V4	V5	V6	V7	V8
VAR 1	1.000							
VAR 2	0.693	1.000						
VAR 3	0.681	0.627	1.000					
VAR 4	0.657	0.646	0.657	1.000				
VAR 5	0.340	0.350	0.399	0.428	1.000			
VAR 6	0.428	0.350	0.387	0.450	0.658	1.000		
VAR 7	0.413	0.444	0.500	0.431	0.620	0.637	1.000	
VAR 8	0.375	0.273	0.354	0.434	0.616	0.673	0.582	1.000

The LISREL–SIMPLIS program for the mixture model is

```
Mixture Model using Polyserial Correlation Matrix
Observed Variables: V1-V8
Correlation Matrix
1.000
0.693 1.000
0.681 0.627 1.000
0.657 0.646 0.657 1.000
0.340 0.350 0.399 0.428 1.000
0.428 0.350 0.387 0.450 0.658 1.000
0.413 0.444 0.500 0.431 0.620 0.637 1.000
0.375 0.273 0.354 0.434 0.616 0.673 0.582 1.000
```

```
Sample Size 200
Latent Variables F1 F2
Relationships
V1-V4 = F1
V5-V8 = F2
Let F1 and F2 correlate
Number of Decimals = 3
Path Diagram
End of Problem
```

The results from the LISREL–SIMPLIS analysis yield similar factor loadings and factor correlation; however, the program does not print the Satorra–Bentler scaled chi-square statistics. We need to run a LISREL syntax program to obtain the Satorra–Bentler scaled chi-square statistic.

13.5   STRUCTURED MEANS MODELS

Another important SEM application is to test group mean differences in observed or latent variables. A test for mean differences between observed variables in SEM is similar to analysis of variance and covariance. Our example, using LISREL–SIMPLIS (Jöreskog & Sörbom, 1996c, EX13B.SPL), examines the mean difference between academic and nonacademic boys in fifth and seventh grades on a latent variable, verbal ability. The path diagram is shown in Fig. 13.7, where writing and reading scores measure each latent variable at the fifth and seventh grades.

Two LISREL–SIMPLIS programs are run to test the mean difference between the latent variables Verbal5 and Verbal7. The first program

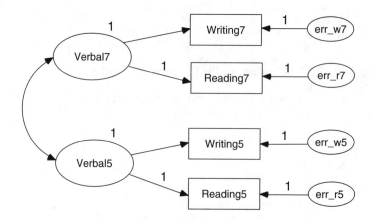

FIG. 13.7.   Path diagram for structured means: academic versus nonacademic boys.

indicates the observed variables and equations that relate to the path diagram. The coefficient **CONST** is used to designate the means in the equations for the observed variables and the latent variables, respectively. The first program also includes the sample size, covariance matrix, and means for the first group (academic boys). The second program includes the sample size, covariance matrix, and means for the second group (nonacademic boys). In addition, the second program establishes a test of the mean differences between the latent variables in the **Relationship** command:

```
Relationships:
 Verbal5 = CONST
 Verbal7 = CONST
```

The LISREL–SIMPLIS program is as follows:

```
Group ACADEMIC: Reading and Writing, Grades 5 and 7
Observed Variables: READING5 WRITING5 READING7 WRITING7
Covariance Matrix
281.349
184.219 182.821
216.739 171.699 283.289
198.376 153.201 208.837 246.069
Means 262.236 258.788 275.630 269.075
Sample Size: 373
Latent Variables: Verbal5 Verbal7
Relationships:
 READING5 = CONST + 1*Verbal5
 WRITING5 = CONST + Verbal5
 READING7 = CONST + 1*Verbal7
 WRITING7 = CONST + Verbal7

Group NONACADEMIC: Reading and Writing, Grades 5 and 7
Covariance Matrix
174.485
134.468 161.869
129.840 118.836 228.449
102.194 97.767 136.058 180.460
Means 248.675 246.896 258.546 253.349
Sample Size: 249
Relationships:
 Verbal5 = CONST
 Verbal7 = CONST
Set the Error Variances of READING5 - WRITING7 free
Set the Variances of Verbal5 - Verbal7 free
Set the Covariance between Verbal5 and Verbal7 free
Path Diagram
End of Problem
```

Our analysis must first establish that the data fit the theoretical model before testing for mean differences in the latent variable. We are therefore interested in acceptable model fit indices for each group as well as the global fit indices. The individual and global fit indices are acceptable:

Academic boys group goodness-of-fit statistics:

Contribution to chi-square $= 4.15$
Standardized RMR $= 0.025$
Goodness-of-fit index (GFI) $= 0.99$

Nonacademic boys group goodness-of-fit statistics:

Contribution to chi-square $= 5.97$
Standardized RMR $= 0.042$
Goodness-of-fit index (GFI) $= 0.99$

Global goodness-of-fit statistics:

Degrees of freedom $= 6$
Minimum fit function chi-square $= 10.11$ ($p = 0.12$)
Root-mean-square error of approximation (RMSEA) $= 0.046$
90 percent confidence interval for RMSEA $= (0.0;\ 0.095)$
p value for test of close fit (RMSEA < 0.05) $= 0.27$
Comparative fit index (CFI) $= 1.00$

The LISREL–SIMPLIS computer output reflects the structured mean equations by replacing the **CONST** term with the mean value in the measurement equations for each group:

```
Group ACADEMIC: Reading and Writing, Grades 5 and 7
LISREL Estimates (Maximum Likelihood)

Measurement Equations

READING5 = 262.37 + 1.00*Verbal5, Errorvar.= 50.15, R² = 0.81
            (0.84)                             (6.02)
           312.58                              8.34

WRITING5 = 258.67 + 0.84*Verbal5, Errorvar.= 36.48, R² = 0.81
            (0.70) (0.024)                    (4.28)
           366.96  34.35                       8.52

READING7 = 275.71 + 1.00*Verbal7, Errorvar.= 51.72, R² = 0.82
            (0.87)                             (6.62)
           317.77                              7.82
```

```
WRITING7 = 268.98 + 0.89*Verbal7, Errorvar.= 57.78, R² = 0.76
           (0.80) (0.028)                      (6.05)
           338.00  31.95                        9.55
```

Group NONACADEMIC: Reading and Writing, Grades 5 and 7
LISREL Estimates (Maximum Likelihood)

Measurement Equations

```
READING5 = 262.37 + 1.00*Verbal5, Errorvar.= 23.25, R² = 0.87
           (0.84)                              (6.23)
           312.58                              3.73

WRITING5 = 258.67 + 0.84*Verbal5, Errorvar.= 42.80, R² = 0.72
           (0.70) (0.024)                      (5.64)
           366.96  34.35                        7.59

READING7 = 275.71 + 1.00*Verbal7, Errorvar.= 65.67, R² = 0.70
           (0.87)                              (9.87)
           317.77                              6.65

WRITING7 = 268.98 + 0.89*Verbal7, Errorvar.= 67.36, R² = 0.65
           (0.80) (0.028)                      (8.74)
           338.00  31.95                        7.71
```

Our interest, however, is in the mean latent variable differences indicated by the *mean vector of independent variables*. Our interpretation is based on the knowledge that the mean latent values on Verbal5 and Verbal7 are set to 0 in the first group (academic boys), so the values reported here indicate that the second group is either greater than (positive) or less than (negative) the first group on the latent variables:

Mean Vector of Independent Variables

Verbal5	Verbal7
−13.80	−17.31
(1.18)	(1.24)
−11.71	−13.99

We see a value of −13.80 for the first latent variable, which indicates the mean difference was less than for the first group, that is, nonacademic boys scored below academic boys on verbal ability in the fifth grade. We see a value of −17.31 for the second latent variable, which indicates the mean difference was less than for the first group, that is, nonacademic boys scored below academic boys on verbal ability in the seventh grade. Overall, nonacademic boys scored below academic boys in the fifth and seventh grades, which was statistically significant, $t = -11.71$ and $t = -13.99$, respectively.

13.6   SUMMARY

In this chapter we described five very different SEM applications to demonstrate the versatility of structural equation modeling. The first application presented a SEM model that had multiple indicators of a latent variable where the latent variable was predicted by multiple observed variables. This was referred to as a *multiple indicators and multiple causes* (MIMIC) type model. The second application involved testing the difference between parameter estimates given multiple groups (e.g., different grade levels, different countries, or different schools). We referred to this as a *multiple-group model* (MG). Our third application involved nested data, which has become increasingly popular in analyzing repeated measures data, survey data, and education data because of the multilevel research design. We referred to these as *multilevel models* (ML), and we saw that ML-, MUML-, and HLM-type models are possible in EQS. In the research literature this type of model is referred to by different names, for example, hierarchical linear, random-coefficient, and variance-component modeling. The fourth application involved models that used ordinal and continuous variables. We referred to these as *mixture models*. In this application we saw that normal theory applies to continuous variables in a Pearson correlation matrix, but that other matrices can be used when ordinal and continuous variables are present in the data set. Our final application demonstrated how to test for mean differences between groups on latent variables. This extends the basic analysis of variance approach where mean differences on observed variables are tested.

The chapter presented only one example for each of the applications because a more in-depth coverage is beyond the scope of this book. The Amos, EQS, and LISREL software help libraries and examples can be searched by using keywords to find other software examples and explanations. The Amos, EQS, and LISREL user guides are also excellent references for other examples of these applications. In the next chapter we present and discuss other SEM applications.

EXERCISES

1. Find journal article examples for the SEM models covered in this chapter:
   a. Multiple indicators and multiple causes (MIMIC) models.
   b. Multiple-group models.
   c. Multilevel models.
   d. Mixture models.
   e. Structured means models.
2. Describe in your own words each of the SEM models in this chapter.

REFERENCES

Arbuckle, J. L., & Wothke, W. (1999). *Amos 4.0 user's guide*. Chicago, IL: Smallwaters.

Bentler, P. M., & Wu, E. (2002). *EQS 6 for Windows user's guide*. Encinto, CA: Multivariate Software.

Heck, R. H., & Thomas, S. L. (2000). *An introduction to multilevel modeling techniques*. Mahwah, NJ: Lawrence Erlbaum Associates, Inc.

Hox, J. (2002). *Multilevel analysis: Techniques and applications*. Mahwah, NJ: Lawrence Erlbaum Associates, Inc.

Jöreskog, K., & Sörbom, D. (1996a). *LISREL 8: User's reference guide*. Chicago, IL: Scientific Software International.

Jöreskog, K., & Sörbom, D. (1996b). *PRELIS2: User's reference guide*. Chicago, IL: Scientific Software International.

Jöreskog, K., & Sörbom, D. (1996c). *LISREL 8: Structural equation modeling with the SIMPLIS command language*. Chicago, IL: Scientific Software International.

Jöreskog, K., Sörbom, D., du Toit, S., & du Toit, M. (2001). *LISREL8: New statistical features*. Chicago, IL: Scientific Software International.

Marcoulides, G., & Schumacker, R. E. (Eds.). (1996). *Advanced structural equation modeling: Issues and techniques*. Mahwah, NJ: Lawrence Erlbaum Associates, Inc.

Marcoulides, G., & Schumacker, R. E. (Eds.). (2001). *New developments and techniques in structural equation modeling: Issues and techniques*. Mahwah, NJ: Lawrence Erlbaum Associates, Inc.

Muthén, B., & Muthén, L. (1998). *Mplus user's guide*. Los Angeles, CA: Muthén & Muthén.

14

SEM Applications. Part II

Chapter Outline

Key Concepts

Establishing reliability and validity when measuring multiple traits and
   methods
Second-order factors
Main effects and interaction effects
Types of interaction effects: continuous nonlinear, categorical, latent variable
Longitudinal data analysis using growth curve models
Dynamic models: measuring factors over time

In the previous chapter we learned about five different types of structural equation modeling applications. In this chapter we present additional applications that expand our toolkit of SEM models. Be aware that our discussion will only scratch the surface of the many exciting new developments in structural equation modeling (see, e.g., Marcoulides & Schumacker, 1996, 2001; Schumacker & Marcoulides, 1998). In addition, the newest versions of Amos, EQS, and LISREL include these capabilities with software examples and further explanations. Our intention is to provide a basic understanding of these topics to further your interest in the structural equation modeling approach. We include computer program examples to better illustrate each topic.

14.1 MULTITRAIT–MULTIMETHOD MODELS

The multitrait–multimethod model (MTMM) is used to indicate multiple traits assessed by multiple measures, for example, student achievement and student motivation (traits) assessed by teacher ratings and student self-ratings (methods). The MTMM model provides a way to determine construct validity (Campbell & Fiske, 1959). Construct validity involves providing psychometric evidence of convergent validity, discriminant validity, and trait and method effects (Cole & Maxwell, 1985; Pedhazur & Schmelkin, 1991). The multitrait–multimethod matrix conveniently displays the convergent validity coefficients, discriminant validity coefficients, and reliability coefficients along the diagonal. Reliability coefficients indicate the internal consistency of scores on the instrument, and therefore should be in the range .85 to .95 or higher. Convergent validity coefficients are correlations between measures of the same trait (construct) using different methods (instruments), and therefore should also be in the range .85 to .95 or higher. Discriminant validity coefficients are correlations between measures of different traits (constructs) using the same method (instrument), and should be much lower than the convergent validity coefficients and/or the instrument reliability coefficients. A basic two-trait/two-method model is displayed in Table 14.1 and diagrammed in Fig. 14.1.

The correlation of ratings from different methods of the same trait should be statistically significant, that is, show convergent validity (2). The convergent validity coefficients should also be greater than the correlations of ratings from different traits using the same method, that is, show discriminant validity (3), and the correlations between ratings that share neither trait nor method (−).

We analyzed a multitrait–multimethod (MTMM) model explained in Bollen (1989), where three methods (self-ratings, peer ratings, and

CHAPTER 14

TABLE 14.1
Multitrait–Multimethod Matrix

Trait	Method 1		Method 2	
	A	B	A	B
Method 1. Self				
A. Achievement	(1)			
B. Motivation	(3)	(1)		
Method 2. Teacher				
A. Achievement	(2)	—	(1)	
B. Motivation	—	(2)	(3)	(1)

Note. (1) = reliability coefficients; (2) = convergent validity coefficients; (3) = discriminant validity coefficients.

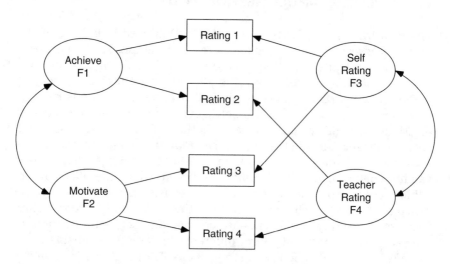

FIG. 14.1. Two-trait/two-method model.

observer ratings) were used to assess four traits of leadership in a small
group (prominence, achievement, affiliation, and leader) with a sample size of $N = 240$ subjects. In MTMM models the different methods
are uncorrelated with the different traits. We diagram the multitrait–
multimethod model in Fig. 14.2.

Bollen (1989) used LISREL matrix commands with start values and
AD=OFF (admissibility check) to obtain convergence after numerous iterations, that is, obtain parameter estimates. Multitrait–multimethod
models are difficult to analyze because they lack model identification
(initially have negative degrees of freedom) and can have convergence

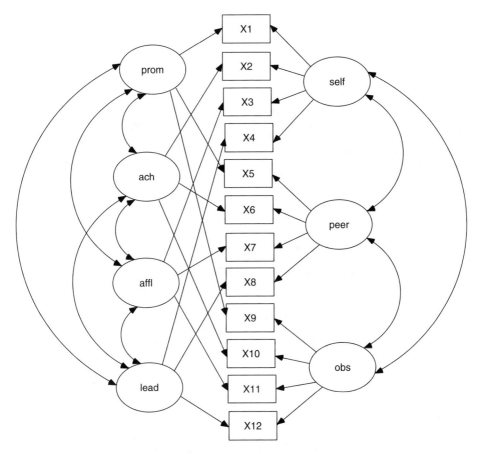

FIG. 14.2.   Multitrait–multimethod model (Bollen, 1989).

problems (non-positive definite matrix). Latent variable variances had
to be set to 1.0, factor correlations between traits and methods had to
be set to zero, otherwise the PHI matrix was non-positive definite, certain error variances had to be set equal to prevent getting negative error
variance (Heywood case), we needed permissible start values, and we
had to set AD=OFF to allow more iterations for convergence.

The LISREL–SIMPLIS program for analyzing the three sets of ratings
on the four traits as a MTMM model is

```
Multitrait-Multimethod Bollen (1989)
!Start Values Added and Admissibility Check Off
Observed Variables: X1 X2 X3 X4 X5 X6 X7 X8 X9 X10 X11 X12
```

```
Correlation Matrix
1.0
 .50 1.0
 .41   .48 1.0
 .67   .59   .40 1.0
 .45   .33   .26   .55 1.0
 .36   .32   .31   .43   .72 1.0
 .25   .21   .25   .30   .59   .72 1.0
 .46   .36   .28   .51   .85   .80   .69 1.0
 .53   .41   .34   .56   .71   .58   .43   .72 1.0
 .50   .45   .29   .52   .59   .55   .42   .63   .84 1.0
 .36   .30   .28   .37   .53   .51   .43   .57   .62   .57 1.0
 .52   .43   .31   .59   .68   .60   .46   .73   .92   .89   .63 1.0
Sample Size: 240
Latent Variables: prom ach affl lead self peer obs
Relationships:
X1 = (.2)* self + (.5)* prom
X2 = (.3)* self + (.5)* ach
X3 = (.3)* self + (.5)* affl
X4 = (.3)* self + (.5)* lead
X5 = (.3)* peer + (.5)* prom
X6 = (.2)* peer + (.5)* ach
X7 = (.2)* peer + (.5)* affl
X8 = (.2)* peer + (.5)* lead
X9 = (.2)* obs  + (.5)* prom
X10 = (.3)* obs + (.5)* ach
X11 = (.3)* obs + (.5)* affl
X12 = (.3)* obs + (.5)* lead
Set Variance of prom - obs to 1.0
Set correlation of prom and self to 0
Set correlation of ach and self to 0
Set correlation of affl and self to 0
Set correlation of lead and self to 0
Set correlation of prom and peer to 0
Set correlation of ach and peer to 0
Set correlation of affl and peer to 0
Set correlation of lead and peer to 0
Set correlation of prom and obs to 0
Set correlation of ach and obs to 0
Set correlation of affl and obs to 0
Set correlation of lead and obs to 0
Let the error variance of X10 and X12 be equal
OPTIONS: AD=OFF
LISREL OUTPUT
End of Problem
```

We tabulate the output (Table 14.2) to demonstrate the interpretation of trait and method effects. Regardless of which method is used, the assessment of affiliation (Affl) has the highest error variance (Self-ratings, error = .67; peer ratings, error = .38; observer ratings, error = .52),

TABLE 14.2
MTMM Estimates of Four Methods on Four Traits ($N = 240$)

	Traits				Methods			
	Prom	Ach	Affl	Lead	Self	Peer	Obs	Error
Prom	.22				.74			.39
Ach		.09			.72			.49
Affl			.30		.51			.67
Lead				.30	.80			.27
Prom	.46					.78		.18
Ach		.36				.79		.25
Affl			.41			.67		.38
Lead				.44		.86		.07
Prom	.43						.85	.07
Ach		−.01					.97	.05
Affl			.36				.60	.52
Lead				.33			.91	.05

and is thus the most difficult trait to assess based on the three methods used. The self-rating and peer rating methods worked best with assessing leadership (factor loading = .80 and .86, respectively). The observer rating method worked best for assessing achievement (factor loading = .97).

Although Bollen (1989, pp. 190–206) and Byrne (1998, pp. 228–229) demonstrated how to conduct a multitrait–multimethod model with a taxonomy of nested models suggested by Widaman (1985), both Marsh and Grayson (1995) and Wothke (1996) demonstrated that most attempts at running MTMM models result in unidentified models or lack convergence, and offered suggestions for other types of MTMM models, which include the correlated uniqueness model and a composite direct product model. We strongly suggest that you read Marsh and Grayson (1995) and Wothke (1996) for a discussion of these alternative MTMM models and problems with analyzing data using an MTMM model.

Correlated Uniqueness Model

We present an example of a correlated uniqueness model because it seems to have fewer convergence problems with meaningful results, and is recommended by Marsh and Grayson (1995) and Wothke (1996) as an alternative to traditional MTMM models. In correlated uniqueness models each variable is affected by one trait factor and one error term, and there are no method factors. The method effects are accounted for by the correlated error terms of each variable. The correlated error terms only occur between variables measured by the same method.

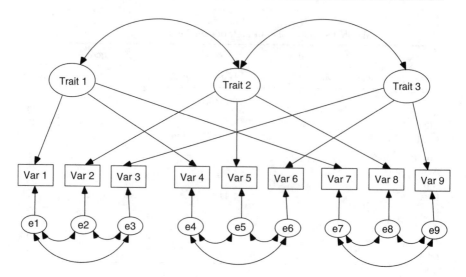

FIG. 14.3.   Correlated uniqueness model (correlated trait and error terms).

Different types of correlated uniqueness models can be analyzed (Huelsman, Furr, & Nemanick, 2003), for example, one general factor with correlated uniqueness, two correlated factors with correlated uniqueness, two correlated factors with uncorrelated uniqueness, and two uncorrelated factors with correlated uniqueness. Marsh and Grayson (1995) indicated that a significant decrease in fit between a model with correlated traits but no correlated error terms and a model with correlated traits and correlated error terms indicated the presence of method effects. Following their suggested approach, we analyze a correlated trait–correlated uniqueness (CTCU) model and a correlated trait (CT) only model. Figure 14.3 displays a CTCU model with three traits and three methods. Figure 14.4 displays the correlated CT-only model with no correlated error terms. The variables measured by the same method are grouped under each trait factor. The CTCU model in Fig. 14.3 represents the method effects through the correlated error terms of the observed variables.

We analyze the Bollen (1989) data again, but this time only using three traits (prom, ach, and affl) with three methods (self, peer, and obs). The LISREL–SIMPLIS program for the CTCU model with correlated traits and correlated error terms is

```
Correlated Traits – Correlated Uniqueness Model - Bollen (1989)
Observed Variables: Var1 Var2 Var3 Var4 Var5 Var6 Var7 Var8 Var9
```

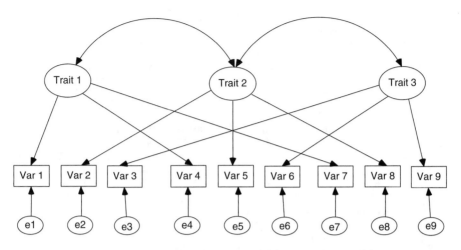

FIG. 14.4.   Correlated uniqueness model (correlated trait only).

```
Correlation Matrix
1.0
 .50 1.0
 .41   .48 1.0
 .45   .33   .26 1.0
 .36   .32   .31   .72 1.0
 .25   .21   .25   .59   .72 1.0
 .53   .41   .34   .71   .58   .43 1.0
 .50   .45   .29   .59   .55   .42   .84 1.0
 .36   .30   .28   .53   .51   .43   .62   .57 1.0
Sample Size: 240
Latent Variables: prom ach affl
Relationships:
Var1 = prom
Var2 = ach
Var3 = affl
Var4 = prom
Var5 = ach
Var6 = affl
Var7 = prom
Var8 = ach
Var9 = affl
Set Variance of prom - affl to 1.0
Let Error Covariance of Var1 — Var3 Correlate
Let Error Covariance of Var4 — Var6 Correlate
Let Error Covariance of Var7 — Var9 Correlate
Path Diagram
End of Problem
```

The results are presented in Table 14.3. Findings indicate that all three traits are statistically significantly correlated. More importantly,

TABLE 14.3
Correlated Uniqueness Model with Correlated Traits and Errors

Method	Trait	Factor loading	Uniqueness	R^2	Correlated uniqueness of error terms		
Self	Prom	.58	.67	.33	1.0		
	Ach	.48	.77	.23	.24	1.0	
	Affl	.40	.85	.16	.20	.30	1.0
Peer	Prom	.78	.40	.61	1.0		
	Ach	.68	.54	.46	.23	1.0	
	Affl	.55	.70	.30	.23	.37	1.0
Observe	Prom	.92	.16	.84	1.0		
	Ach	.84	.30	.70	.12	1.0	
	Affl	.76	.42	.58	.007	−.03	1.0

Trait correlations							
Prom	1.0						
Ach	.93	1.0					
Affl	.88	.93	1.0				

$\chi^2 = 17.38$, $p = .30$, $df = 15$; RMSEA $= .026$; $n = 240$

the observation method is the best for assessing any of the three traits, as indicated by the higher trait factor loadings and lower correlated uniqueness error terms. The data also have an acceptable fit to the CTCU model ($\chi^2 = 17.38$, $p = .30$, $df = 15$; RMSEA $= .026$).

The LISREL program was run again to estimate a CT-only model with no correlated error terms. To accomplish this we simply deleted the following command lines:

```
Let Error Covariance of Var1 — Var3 Correlate
Let Error Covariance of Var4 — Var6 Correlate
Let Error Covariance of Var7 — Var9 Correlate
```

The results are presented in Table 14.4. The trait factor loadings, uniqueness, and R^2 values are not substantially different from the previous CTCU model; however, the data are not an acceptable fit to the CT model ($\chi^2 = 270.63$, $p = .0000$, $df = 24$; RMSEA $= .21$). Comparing the previous CTCU model ($\chi^2 = 17.38$, $p = .30$) to this CT model ($\chi^2 = 270.63$, $p = .0000$) indicates a method effect. Some trait correlations in the CT model are greater than 1.0, indicating a non-positive definite matrix. The CT model modification indices also suggest the specific unique error covariances that, if added, would result in the CTCU model:

TABLE 14.4
Correlated Uniqueness Model with Correlated Traits Only

Method	Trait	Factor loading	Uniqueness	R^2
Self	Prom	.58	.66	.34
	Ach	.45	.79	.21
	Affl	.41	.83	.17
Peer	Prom	.79	.37	.63
	Ach	.72	.48	.52
	Affl	.62	.61	.39
Observe	Prom	.90	.20	.80
	Ach	.80	.35	.65
	Affl	.68	.53	.47
Trait correlations				
Prom	1.0			
Ach	1.05	1.0		
Affl	.95	1.06	1.0	

$\chi^2 = 270.63$, $p = .000$, $df = 24$; RMSEA $= .21$; $n = 240$

Note: The correlation matrix is a non-positive definite matrix because correlations are greater than 1.0.

```
The Modification Indices Suggest to Add an Error Covariance
Between  and  Decrease in Chi-Square   New Estimate
Var2    Var1    21.4                      0.22
Var3    Var1    15.4                      0.19
Var3    Var2    27.8                      0.28
Var5    Var4    30.4                      0.19
Var6    Var4    23.0                      0.17
Var6    Var5    76.3                      0.35
Var7    Var5    41.0                     -0.21
Var7    Var6    27.5                     -0.16
Var8    Var4    33.7                     -0.18
Var8    Var6    10.3                     -0.12
Var8    Var7    70.3                      0.26
```

Saris and Aalberts (2003) questioned the interpretation of the correlated uniqueness model approach in SEM. They agreed that one possible explanation for the observed correlated terms is the similarity of methods for the different traits; however, they provided other explanations for the correlated error terms. Their alternative models explained the correlated error terms based on method effects, relative answers to questions, acquiescence bias, and/or variation in response patterns when examining characteristics of survey research questions on a questionnaire. We are therefore reminded that error terms do not necessarily reflect a single unknown measure, but contain sampling error and other potentially unknown measures.

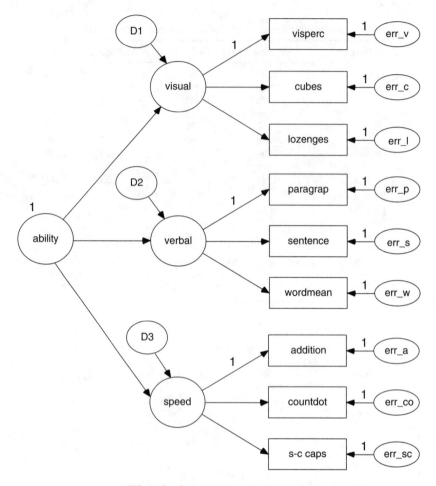

FIG. 14.5. Second-order factor model.

14.2 SECOND-ORDER FACTOR MODELS

A second-order factor model is present when first-order factors are explained by some higher order factor structure. For example, the Holzinger and Swineford data (Jöreskog & Sörbom, 1996c, Example 5) indicate nine psychological variables that identify three common factors (Visual, Verbal, and Speed). These three factors most likely indicate a second-order factor, namely Ability. We therefore hypothesize the second-order factor model in Fig. 14.5.

The LISREL–SIMPLIS program includes the Ability latent variable and sets the variance of this higher order factor to 1.0:

```
Second-Order Factor Analysis
Observed Variables
  'VIS PERC' CUBES LOZENGES 'PAR COMP' 'SEN COMP' WORDMEAN
  ADDITION COUNTDOT 'S-C CAPS'
Correlation Matrix
1.000
 .318 1.000
 .436  .419 1.000
 .335  .234  .323 1.000
 .304  .157  .283  .722 1.000
 .326  .195  .350  .714  .685 1.000
 .116  .057  .056  .203  .246  .170 1.000
 .314  .145  .229  .095  .181  .113  .585 1.000
 .489  .239  .361  .309  .345  .280  .408  .512 1.000
Sample Size 145
Latent Variables: Visual Verbal Speed Ability
Relationships:
  'VIS PERC' - LOZENGES = Visual
  'PAR COMP' - WORDMEAN = Verbal
   ADDITION - 'S-C CAPS' = Speed
Visual = Ability
Verbal = Ability
Speed  = Ability
Set variance of Ability = 1.0
Number of Decimals = 3
Wide Print
Print Residuals
Path Diagram
End of Problem
```

The *selected* LISREL–SIMPLIS model fit indices indicate that our hypothesized second-order factor model has an *unacceptable* fit (χ^2 = 49.921,
p = .00145, df = 24; RMSEA = .0866; GFI = .928). The *modified* LISREL program on CD provides model with acceptable fit indices.

```
Goodness of Fit Statistics

Degrees of Freedom = 24
Minimum Fit Function Chi-Square =52.618 (P = 0.000649)
Normal Theory Weighted Least Squares Chi-Square = 49.921 (P = 0.00145)
Estimated Non-centrality Parameter (NCP) = 25.921
90 Percent Confidence Interval for NCP = (9.429 ; 50.167)

Root Mean Square Error of Approximation (RMSEA) = 0.0866
90 Percent Confidence Interval for RMSEA = (0.0522 ; 0.120)
P-Value for Test of Close Fit (RMSEA < 0.05) = 0.0412

Root Mean Square Residual (RMR) = 0.0751
Standardized RMR = 0.0751

Expected Cross-Validation Index (ECVI) = 0.638
90 Percent Confidence Interval for ECVI = (0.524 ; 0.807)
```

```
ECVI for Saturated Model = 0.625
ECVI for Independence Model = 4.695

Normed Fit Index (NFI) = 0.920
Goodness of Fit Index (GFI) = 0.928
```

We also find that structural equations indicate the strength of relationship between the first-order factors and the second-order factor, Ability. Visual (.931) is indicated as a stronger measure of Ability, followed by Verbal (.583) and Speed (.549), with all three being statistically significant ($t > 1.96$). This model suggests that a student's ability is predominantly a function of his or her visual perception of geometric configurations with complementary verbal skills and speed in completing numerical tasks enhancing overall ability:

```
Structural Equations

Visual  = 0.931* Ability, Errorvar.= 0.133, R² = 0.867
        (0.183)                  (0.263)
         5.078                    0.507

Verbal  = 0.583* Ability, Errorvar.= 0.660 , R² = 0.340
        (0.120)                  (0.148)
         4.881                    4.449

Speed   = 0.549* Ability, Errorvar.= 0.698 , R² = 0.302
        (0.133)                  (0.205)
         4.145                    3.414
```

14.3 INTERACTION MODELS

In our previous examples we assumed that the relationships in our models are linear, that is, the relationships among all variables, observed and latent, can be represented by linear equations. Although the use of nonlinear and interaction effects is popular in regression models (Aiken & West, 1991), the inclusion of interaction hypotheses in path models has been minimal (Newman, Marchant, & Ridenour, 1993), and few examples of nonlinear factor models have been provided (Etezadi-Amoli & McDonald, 1983; McDonald, 1967). In fact, for several decades structural equation modeling had been based on linear structural relationships (LISREL). SEM models with interaction effects are now possible and better understood due to the work of many researchers including Kenny and Judd (1984), Hayduk (1987), Wong and Long (1987), Bollen (1989), Higgins and Judd (1990), Cole, Maxwell, Arvey, and Salas (1993), Mackenzie and Spreng (1992), Ping (1993, 1994, 1995), Jöreskog and Yang (1996), Schumacker and Marcoulides (1998), Algina and Moulder (2001), du Toit and du Toit (2001), Moulder and Algina (2002), and Schumacker (2002).

In structural equation modeling we can now test the main effects and interaction effects of latent variables. However, there are several types of interaction effects: product indicant, nonlinear, categorical, two-stage least squares, and latent variable using normal scores. We present examples for most of these approaches in this chapter, but some preliminary background is needed to better understand the inclusion of nonlinear and interactive effects in structural equation models, both among observed variables and among latent variables. First, consider different types of interaction effects among continuous observed variables. A nonlinear relationship could exist between two observed variables, for example, X_1 and X_2 are curvilinear. We could have a quadratic (nonlinear) term in the model, for example, $X_2 = X_1^2$. We could also have a product of two observed variables, for example, $X_3 = X_1 X_2$. The three types of interaction effects all involve *continuous* variables. We can also have interaction effects using *categorical* variables (groups) similar to analysis-of-variance or the multiple-group SEM model.

Continuous Variable Approach

Kenny and Judd (1984) developed a procedure to test the interaction between latent variables based on the products of observed variables. Their procedure allows one to include both quadratic and interaction terms among latent variables by rewriting the system of equations to include product terms among the observed variables, for example, $X_1 X_3$. For example, if F_1 is defined by the observed variables X_1 and X_2, and F_2 is defined by the observed variables X_3 and X_4, then the interaction of the latent variables, denoted as F_3, can be specified by the products of their respective observed variables: $X_1 X_3$, $X_1 X_4$, $X_2 X_3$, and $X_2 X_4$. In this approach the interaction latent variable F_3 can be represented along with the main-effect latent variables F_1 and F_2 in the structural equation $F_4 = F_1 + F_2 + F_3 + D_4$, where F_4 is the latent dependent variable and D_4 represents the error term.

Also, Kenny and Judd (1984) indicated that under certain conditions the variance of these observed-variable products can be determined using their respective factor loadings and error terms along with the variance of the latent variables. For one observed-variable product, $X_1 X_3$, this is given as $\text{var}(X_1, X_3) = \text{var}[(\lambda_{X1} F_1 + \varepsilon_{X1})(\lambda_{X3} F_2 + \varepsilon_{X3})]$, where the λ's represent the observed variable's factor loading and the ε's represent each observed variable's unique error term. The latent variable interaction effect F_3 is then specified by fixing each of the observed variable's factor loadings and error terms. For the one observed-variable product, $X_1 X_3$, the factor loading is specified as $\lambda_{X1X3} = \lambda_{X1} \lambda_{X3}$. The factor loading of the new product indicant variable is computed by simply multiplying the factor loadings of the two indicator variables. The error term is specified as $\text{var}(\varepsilon_{X1X3}) = \lambda_{X1}^2 \text{var}(F_1) \text{var}(\varepsilon_{X3}) + \lambda_{X3}^2 \text{var}(F_2) \text{var}(\varepsilon_{X1}) + \text{var}(\varepsilon_{X3}) * \text{var}(\varepsilon_{X1})$. The error term of the new product indicant variable is computed by summing the following: (a) the squared factor loading of the first indicator variable, multiplied by the variance of the first factor and the variance error term of the second indicator variable; (b) the squared factor loading of the second indicator variable, multiplied by the variance of the second factor and the variance error term of the first indicator variable; and (c) the product of the error terms of the two indicator variables. For additional information on their procedure and its limitations (i.e., the nonnormality of distributions and the use of WLS as the method of estimation to obtain proper tests of significance), the interested reader is referred to Kenny and Judd (1984), Bollen (1989), Hayduk (1987), Schumacker and Rigdon (1995), and Jöreskog and Yang (1996) for illustrative examples.

When we consider the continuous variable approach with interaction effects among latent variables, the equations are not necessarily straightforward because nonlinear constraints cannot be directly estimated in EQS and LISREL–SIMPLIS (Jöreskog & Sörbom, 1996c), and full information methods proposed by Jöreskog and Yang (1996) are difficult to apply in practice due to the complicated nonlinear constraints that must be specified and the necessity to have large samples and use asymptotic covariance matrices (see chap. 15). Ping (1993) introduced a variation of the Kenny and Judd technique that can be implemented in LISREL–SIMPLIS and EQS. The method incorporates the Anderson and Gerbing (1988) two-step approach, where the measurement parameters for the linear latent variables are estimated and then fixed in the structural model.

Basically, the measurement-model parameters are used to calculate the loadings and error variances for the observed product variables, which are then used to define the latent interaction variable. The latent interaction variable is then added to the structural model with the loadings and error variances fixed (specified) for each observed product indicant variable.

Ping (1994) outlined the technique as follows:

1. Verify indicator normality.
2. Assume that the latent variables are independent of the error terms and the error terms are independent of each other.
3. Unidimensionalize each latent variable.
4. Center the observed variables at zero by subtracting the mean of each variable from each case value for that variable.

5. Estimate loadings and error variances for the linear independent variable indicators in a measurement model.
6. Use these estimates to calculate estimates of loadings and error variances for the nonlinear latent variable indicators.
7. Fix loadings and error variances of nonlinear latent variable indicators in a structural model and then estimate the structural model.
8. Repeat Steps 6 and 7 to assess any change in measurement parameters between the two structural models.

The technique permits a difference test between the main-effects model and the interaction-effects model using the incremental fit index (IFI) and the chi-square difference test for the nested model. The degrees of freedom for the interaction structural model are reduced by the number of fixed observed product indicant variable loadings and error variances. In addition, observed product indicant variables are generally nonnormally distributed, and thus maximum-likelihood estimation (which assumes multivariate normality) and standard errors for the structural coefficients are not appropriate (Hu, Bentler, & Kano, 1992). However, interaction parameter estimates appear to be robust to departures from normality, whereas standard errors and chi-square statistics are not, and the EQS *Robust* estimator (which is less dependent on multivariate normality) is recommended. In addition, we recommend bootstrap estimates for the standard errors and chi-square statistic.

EQS Example

In our EQS interaction model example we use a set of random variables that are determined to be normally distributed and standardized (see the section Latent Variable Approach; we use **Export LISREL Data** with *raw.psf* file and save the file as *raw.dat*; then EQS reads the *raw.dat* file and saves it as *raw.ess*, an EQS system file). The EQS interaction model is shown in Fig. 14.6, where three unidimensional factors are identified with three observed indicator variables each. The latent variable F1 is a dependent latent variable and F2 and F3 are latent independent variables. We next create three EQS programs: a measurement model, a main-effects structural model, and an interaction-effects structural model. (It may also be important to check a model that has both the initial measurement model and the structural model estimates in it against the measurement model to determine whether the loadings and error variances are markedly different. This should not be the case unless unidimensional latent variables are not clearly indicated; then, the observed product variable loadings and error terms will be different depending on which model values are used).

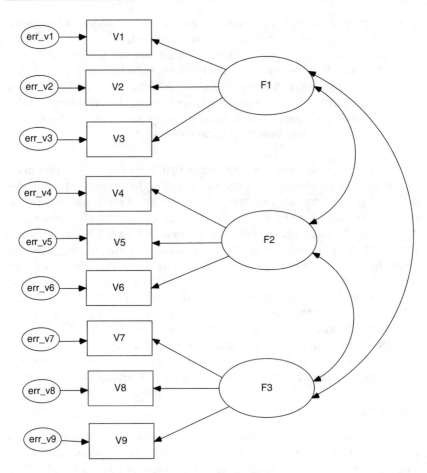

FIG. 14.6.   EQS measurement model.

The measurement model is analyzed in the following EQS program:

```
/TITLE
 MEASUREMENT MODEL
/SPECIFICATIONS
 CASES=500;VARIABLES=9;METHOD=ML;DA='RAW.ESS';
/EQUATIONS
 V1 = 1* F1 + E1;
 V2 = F1    + E2;
 V3 = F1    + E3;
 V4 = 1* F2 + E4;
 V5 = F2    + E5;
```

```
V6 = F2    + E6;
V7 = 1* F3 + E7;
V8 = F3    + E8;
V9 = F3    + E9;
/VARIANCES
 F1 TO F3 = 1.0;
 E1 TO E9 = * ;
/COVARIANCES
 F1 TO F3 =* ;
/END
```

The factor loadings for the measurement model are

```
TITLE: MEASUREMENT MODEL

MAXIMUM LIKELIHOOD SOLUTION (NORMAL DISTRIBUTION THEORY)

STANDARDIZED SOLUTION:          R-SQUARED

V1 =V1 = .442* F1 + .897 E1      .195
V2 =V2 = .851 F1 + .525 E2       .724
V3 =V3 = .848 F1 + .531 E3       .718
V4 =V4 = .638* F2 + .770 E4      .408
V5 =V5 = .912 F2 + .410 E5       .832
V6 =V6 = .769 F2 + .639 E6       .591
V7 =V7 = .698* F3 + .716 E7      .488
V8 =V8 = .847 F3 + .532 E8       .717
V9 =V9 = .735 F3 + .678 E9       .540
```

The main effects structural model, with this measurement model already specified, is indicated by simply adding F1 = *F2 + *F3 + D1; as the last statement in the /EQUATIONS command, changing the /COVARIANCES command to F2,F3 =* ;, and changing the /VARIANCE command with D1 = * ; and F2 TO F3 = 1.0; . This yields the structural coefficients for the direct effects of F2 and F3 on F1, the dependent latent variable, and permit the latent independent variables F2 and F3 to correlate (Fig. 14.7). A comparison between the factor loadings and error variances of the latent independent variables in the previous measurement model program and this structural model program should not show marked differences.

```
/TITLE
 STRUCTURAL MODEL
/SPECIFICATIONS
 CASES=500;VARIABLES=9;METHOD=ML;DA='RAW.ESS';
/EQUATIONS
 V1 = 1* F1 + E1;
 V2 = F1    + E2;
 V3 = F1    + E3;
```

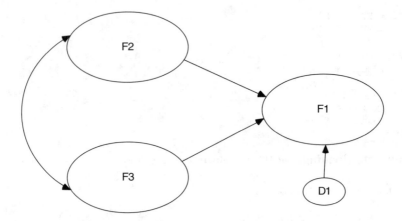

FIG. 14.7.   EQS structural model.

```
V4 = 1* F2  + E4;
V5 = F2     + E5;
V6 = F2     + E6;
V7 = 1* F3  + E7;
V8 = F3     + E8;
V9 = F3     + E9;
F1 = * F2   + * F3 + D1;
/VARIANCES
 F2 TO F3 = 1.0;
 E1 TO E9 = * ;
 D1 = * ;
/COVARIANCES
 F2,F3 =* ;
/END
```

The EQS computer output for the structural model is

```
TITLE: STRUCTURAL MODEL

MAXIMUM LIKELIHOOD SOLUTION (NORMAL DISTRIBUTION THEORY)

STANDARDIZED SOLUTION:                        R-SQUARED

V1 =V1 = .410* F1 + .912 E1                      .168
V2 =V2 = .805 F1 + .593 E2                       .648
V3 =V3 = .800 F1 + .600 E3                       .640
V4 =V4 = .638* F2 + .770 E4                      .408
V5 =V5 = .912 F2 + .410 E5                       .832
V6 =V6 = .769 F2 + .639 E6                       .591
V7 =V7 = .697* F3 + .717 E7                      .486
V8 =V8 = .847 F3 + .531 E8                       .718
V9 =V9 = .736 F3 + .677 E9                       .541
F1 =F1 = .104* F2 + .314* F3 + .933 D1           .129
```

Because the factor loadings and R^2 values are similar for the measurement model and the structural model, we use the factor loadings and error variances from the measurement model to compute the factor loadings and error terms of the product variables that define the latent interaction variable, F4. Jonsson (1998) determined that not all of the observed variables need to be multiplied and included in the interaction model. We choose three pairs of variables from the measurement model that yield high factor loadings for the three product indicant variables. The factor loadings for our product indicator variables of F4 are then computed by multiplying the factor loadings for the pair of observed variables:

$$V10 = (V3 * V5) = .848 * .912 = .773$$
$$V11 = (V6 * V9) = .769 * .735 = .565$$
$$V12 = (V2 * V8) = .851 * .847 = .721.$$

The error variance of these new product indicant variables is then computed,

$$var(\varepsilon_{X3X5}) = \lambda_{X3}^2 \, var(F_1) \, var(\varepsilon_{X5}) + \lambda_{X5}^2 \, var(F_2) \, var(\varepsilon_{X3})$$
$$+ var(\varepsilon_{X5}) * var(\varepsilon_{X3}).$$

We obtain

$$E10 = [(.848)^2(1.0)(.410)] + [(.912)^2(1.0)(.531)] + (.531 * .410)$$
$$E10 = .954$$
$$E11 = [(.769)^2(1.0)(.678)] + [(.735)^2(1.0)(.639)] + (.639 * .678)$$
$$E11 = 1.179$$
$$E12 = [(.851)^2(1.0)(.532)] + [(.847)^2(1.0)(.525)] + (.525 * .532)$$
$$E12 = 1.041.$$

We now include the original factor loadings and error terms, structure coefficients for F2 and F3, and the product indicant variable factor loadings and error terms in our final EQS interaction model program. The interaction model is diagrammed in Fig. 14.8.

The following EQS program includes the added interaction term on the /**EQUATION** command as a function of the product indicant variables

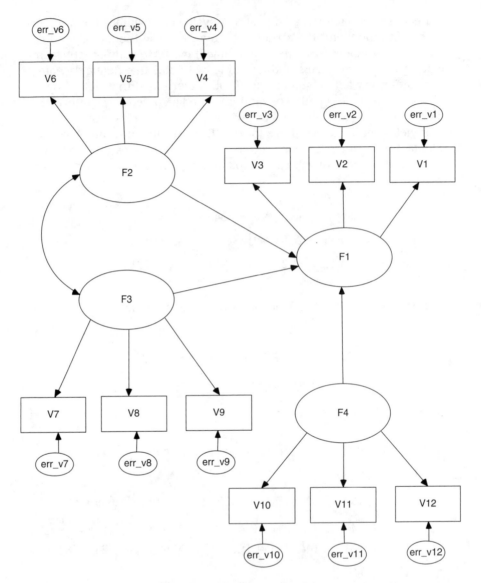

FIG. 14.8.   EQS interaction model.

in the input data file and outputs robust statistics for the parameter estimates. The *Robust* option in EQS provides the Satorra–Bentler scaled
chi-square test statistic and standard errors that are distributional free
when the normal distribution assumption is not met. **Note**: *Robust statistics can only be computed if raw data are used, so you must save the EQS*

*file raw.ess as an SPSS save file, raw.sav. Then, in SPSS compute your
product indicant variables. When you input the SPSS file raw.sav into EQS
it will automatically open as raw.ess with the three new product indicant
variables.*

```
/TITLE
 INTERACTION MODEL
/SPECIFICATIONS
 CASES=500;VARIABLES=12;METHOD=ML;DA='RAW.ESS';
/EQUATIONS
 V1  = .442F1 + .897E1;
 V2  = .851F1 + .525E2;
 V3  = .848F1 + .531E3;
 V4  = .638F2 + .770E4;
 V5  = .912F2 + .410E5;
 V6  = .769F2 + .639E6;
 V7  = .698F3 + .716E7;
 V8  = .847F3 + .532E8;
 V9  = .735F3 + .678E9;
 V10 = .773F4 + .954E10;
 V11 = .565F4 + 1.179E11;
 V12 = .721F4 + 1.041E12;
 F1  = .104F2 + .314F3 + *F4 + D1;
/VARIANCES
 F2 TO F4 = 1.0;
 D1 = * ;
/COVARIANCES
 F2 TO F4 = * ;
/END
```

The EQS computer output is

```
TITLE: INTERACTION MODEL

MAXIMUM LIKELIHOOD SOLUTION (NORMAL DISTRIBUTION THEORY)

STANDARDIZED SOLUTION:                             R-SQUARED

V1  =V1  = .445 F1 + .896 E1                          .198
V2  =V2  = .800 F1 + .600 E2                          .640
V3  =V3  = .793 F1 + .609 E3                          .629
V4  =V4  = .704 F2 + .710 E4                          .496
V5  =V5  = .860 F2 + .511 E5                          .739
V6  =V6  = .633 F2 + .774 E6                          .400
V7  =V7  = .695 F3 + .719 E7                          .483
V8  =V8  = .751 F3 + .660 E8                          .565
V9  =V9  = .574 F3 + .819 E9                          .329
V10 =V10 = .544 F4 + .839 E10                         .296
V11 =V11 = .210 F4 + .978 E11                         .044
V12 =V12 = .476 F4 + .879 E12                         .227
F1  =F1  = .105 F2 + .318 F3 - .016*F4 + .930 D1 .135
```

We want to interpret the R^2 for the main-effect model ($R^2 = .129$) versus the R^2 for the interaction model ($R^2 = .135$). We could compute the F test for this difference in R^2 values, but doubt that a .006 difference would be significant. In addition, we want to interpret the structure coefficient for our interaction latent variable, F4. We determine that it is not statistically significant and in the wrong direction, namely negative rather than positive. We therefore conclude that there is no significant interaction effect and interpret the main effects model.

Categorical-Variable Approach

In the categorical-variable approach the different samples are defined by the different levels of the interaction variable. The basic logic is that if interaction effects are present, then certain parameters should have different values in different samples. Both main effects and interaction effects can be determined by using different samples to test for differences between intercepts and slopes. We accomplish this by running two different models, main effects for group differences holding slopes constant and interaction effects for group differences with both intercepts and slopes estimated.

LISREL–SIMPLIS EXAMPLE

The following two LISREL–SIMPLIS programs analyze data for two groups: high-motivation versus low-motivation students, where group represents the categorical variable. Separate covariance matrices and means on the dependent and independent variable are input to estimate the prediction of a math score given a pretest score. The means are required; otherwise, the intercept values will be zero.

The first LISREL–SIMPLIS program includes **Equation: Math = CONST** in the low-achievement group only, which permits different intercept values to be estimated, but the slopes are set equal in the two groups:

```
Group HIGHACH: Math and Pretest Scores
Observed Variables: Math Pretest
Covariance Matrix:
181.349
84.219 182.821
Means: 82.15 78.35
Sample Size: 373
Equation: Math = CONST Pretest
Group LOWACH: Math and Pretest Scores
```

```
Covariance Matrix:
174.485
34.468 161.869
Means: 48.75 46.98
Sample Size: 249
Equation: Math = CONST
End of Problem
```

The results indicate that the slopes are equal (slope = .37) and the intercepts are different (53.26 vs. 31.43). The main-effect model for differences in intercepts with equal slopes is not an acceptable fit ($\chi^2 = 12.24$, $p = .002$, $df = 2$):

```
Math = 53.26 + 0.37* Pretest, Errorvar.= 155.07, R² = 0.14
      (3.04) (0.038)           (8.81)
       17.53   9.73            17.59


Math = 31.43 + 0.37* Pretest, Errorvar.= 155.07, R² = 0.12
      (1.95) (0.038)           (8.81)
       16.13   9.73            17.59
```

The second LISREL–SIMPLIS program uses the **Equation: Math = CONST Pretest** in both groups, thus specifying that both intercepts and slopes are being tested for group differences:

```
Group HIGHACH: Math and Pretest Scores
Observed Variables: Math Pretest
Covariance Matrix:
181.349
84.219 182.821
Means: 82.15 78.35
Sample Size: 373
Equation: Math = CONST Pretest
Group LOWACH: Math and Pretest Scores
Covariance Matrix:
174.485
34.468 161.869
Means: 48.75 46.98
Sample Size: 249
Equation: Math = CONST Pretest
End of Problem
```

The results indicate that the intercepts (46.06 vs. 38.75) and slopes (.46 vs. .21) are different in the two groups. This model with main and interaction effects present has an acceptable model fit ($\chi^2 = 1.98$, $p = .16$, $df = 1$). The main effect for group differences in math exam scores is given by the difference in the **CONST** values: $46.06 - 38.75 = 7.31$. The interaction effect is given by the difference in the slope estimates of pretest values for the two groups: $.46 - .21 = .25$.

```
High-motivation group:

Math = 46.06 + 0.46* Pretest, Errorvar.= 154.85, R² = 0.20
       (3.80) (0.048)          (8.80)
       12.13   9.65            17.59


Low-motivation group:

Math = 38.75 + 0.21* Pretest, Errorvar.= 154.85, R² = 0.045
       (3.03) (0.062)          (8.80)
       12.81   3.43            17.59
```

A categorical-variable interaction model can represent a wide variety of interaction effects, including higher order interactions, without requiring any substantial new methodological developments. This approach can also be used regardless of whether the interaction intensifies or mutes the effects of the individual variables. Because the interaction effect is represented in the difference between samples, the researcher is also able to test linear relations of variables within each sample, thus avoiding any potential complications in fitting the model. Finally, structural equation modeling programs permit parameter constraints across groups and thereby permit many different hypotheses of group differences.

The categorical approach, however, does have certain weaknesses; for example, smaller subsamples of the total sample are used. This could be a serious problem if some groups have low sample sizes that affect group parameter estimates. This reduction in sample size could also affect the results of the χ^2 difference tests. MacCallum, Roznowski, and Necowitz (1992) noted a substantial degree of instability in the fit indices in even moderately sized samples. Thus, it is possible that the categorical-variable approach may yield group samples that are too small, resulting in a χ^2 test statistic that misleads the researcher into believing that an interaction effect exists when it does not. A possible solution is to minimize the number of distinct parameters being compared in the model by fixing certain parameters to be invariant across the samples being compared.

We do **not** recommend the categorical-variable approach when hypothesizing interaction involving two continuous variables. The basic logic is that there is a loss of information when reducing a continuous variable to a categorical variable for purposes of defining a group

(Russell & Bobko, 1992). Also, where does one choose the point for dividing a continuous variable into a categorical variable to form the groups? How do we justify the arbitrary cut value, that is, mean, median, or quartile? Random-sampling error also ensures that some cases will be misclassified, violating some basic assumptions about subject membership in a particular group.

Latent Variable Approach

For our latent variable interaction example, we run a PRELIS program (Jöreskog & Sörbom, 1996b) to create nine simulated multivariate normal observed variables for 500 subjects. The raw data are saved to a PRELIS system file, *raw.psf*. The seed number is specified so that the same data can be recreated (IX = 784123). The PRELIS program is

```
Generate multivariate normal variables - SIMPLIS
DA NO=500
NE X1=NRAND; NE X2=NRAND; NE X3=NRAND
NE X4=NRAND; NE X5=NRAND; NE X6=NRAND
NE X7=NRAND; NE X8=NRAND; NE X9=NRAND
NE V1=X1
NE V2=.378*X1+.925*X2
NE V3=.320*X1+.603*X2+.890*X3
NE V4=.204*X1+.034*X2+.105*X3+.904*X4
NE V5=.076*X1+.113*X2+.203*X3+.890*X4+.925*X5
NE V6=.111*X1+.312*X2+.125*X3+.706*X4+.865*X5+.905*X6
NE V7=.310*X1+.124*X2+.310*X3+.222*X4+.126*X5+.555*X6+.897*X7
NE V8=.222*X1+.111*X2+.412*X3+.312*X4+.212*X5+.312*X6+.789*X7+.899*X8
NE V9=.321*X1+.214*X2+.124*X3+.122*X4+.234*X5+.212*X6+.690*X7+.789*X8+.907*X9
CO ALL
SD X1-X9
OU MA=CM RA=RAW.PSF XM IX=784123
```

The PRELIS univariate statistics indicate that the simulated data for the variables approximate a mean of zero and a standard deviation of one. A test of skewness and kurtosis indicates that V6 and V9 have statistically significant Z-score values for kurtosis, and V6 also has a statistically significant chi-square value for skewness and kurtosis:

```
Total Sample Size = 500

Univariate Summary Statistics for Continuous Variables

Variable Mean    St. Dev. T-Value Skewness Kurtosis
-------- -----   -------- ------  -------- --------
V1       -0.061  0.976    -1.394   0.191    0.048
V2        0.007  1.071     0.142  -0.047    0.280
V3       -0.018  1.105    -0.368   0.175    0.441
```

V4	-0.015	0.956	-0.359	-0.200	-0.158
V5	-0.013	1.351	-0.209	-0.003	0.168
V6	0.011	1.543	0.163	0.171	0.528
V7	-0.065	1.192	-1.222	-0.081	-0.350
V8	-0.041	1.491	-0.615	0.127	0.092
V9	0.005	1.595	0.075	0.058	0.514

Test of Univariate Normality for Continuous Variables

	Skewness		Kurtosis		Skewness and Kurtosis	
Variable	Z-Score	P-Value	Z-Score	P-Value	Chi-Square	P-Value
V1	1.749	0.080	0.321	0.748	3.163	0.206
V2	-0.432	0.666	1.256	0.209	1.764	0.414
V3	1.608	0.108	1.811	0.070	5.866	0.053
V4	-1.833	0.067	-0.695	0.487	3.844	0.146
V5	-0.031	0.975	0.829	0.407	0.688	0.709
V6	1.571	0.116	**2.082**	**0.037**	**6.802**	**0.033**
V7	-0.746	0.456	-1.865	0.062	4.034	0.133
V8	1.165	0.244	0.513	0.608	1.620	0.445
V9	0.531	0.595	**2.039**	**0.041**	4.438	0.109

In LISREL (Jöreskog & Sörbom, 1996a), we next select **File** and **Open**, and find the PRELIS system file *raw.psf*.

We then create our dependent latent variable and two independent latent variables and add them to the PRELIS system file *raw.psf* using the following LISREL–SIMPLIS program:

```
Computing Latent Variable Scores
Observed Variables V1-V9
Raw Data from File raw.psf
Latent Variables
eta ksi1 ksi2
Relationships
V1=1* eta
V2-V3=eta
V4=1* ksi1
V5-V6=ksi1
V7=1* ksi2
V8-V9=ksi2
PSFfile raw.psf
End of Problem
```

When we open *raw.psf* we see *latent variable scores* for the three latent variables added to the PRELIS system file.

	V1	V2	V3	V4	V5	V6	V7	V8	V9	eta	ksi1	ksi2
1	-1.09	0.38	0.20	-1.26	-2.61	-0.60	0.78	0.04	1.37	0.05	-1.24	0.13
2	-0.85	0.46	-0.17	-1.77	-0.88	-0.44	-1.72	-1.26	-1.11	-0.03	-0.45	-0.76
3	-1.08	-0.63	-0.88	-0.95	-1.76	-1.24	0.53	2.00	2.35	-0.33	-0.85	1.18
4	1.27	0.87	1.06	0.32	-1.81	-1.75	-1.70	-1.12	-3.24	0.39	-0.87	-0.79
5	-0.12	0.95	-0.11	-0.18	0.90	0.59	-0.04	0.38	1.22	0.09	0.43	0.28
6	0.45	-0.29	-0.88	-0.92	-1.79	-2.40	-1.07	-1.34	-0.12	-0.25	-0.90	-0.73
7	1.50	-0.49	-0.28	1.67	3.35	3.83	1.10	-1.20	-1.41	-0.07	1.68	-0.60
8	-1.50	0.13	-0.07	-1.99	-1.10	-0.09	-0.71	0.65	1.22	-0.05	-0.54	0.38
9	-0.60	-0.86	-1.68	0.05	-1.84	-4.29	-1.43	-2.21	-1.63	-0.57	-0.95	-1.28
10	1.15	-0.25	0.23	0.35	0.11	0.13	-0.16	1.03	2.06	0.08	0.07	0.65
11	-0.08	2.25	0.46	0.46	1.19	1.85	-1.80	-0.72	0.86	0.36	0.61	-0.38
12	-0.07	-0.25	0.49	0.91	1.93	1.28	0.77	1.77	0.53	0.12	0.95	1.00
13	-0.22	0.47	-0.06	-0.12	1.45	2.10	0.92	1.10	0.89	0.05	0.73	0.68
14	-0.37	-0.08	-1.99	-0.03	0.90	-0.49	-0.40	-0.63	1.05	-0.52	0.41	-0.27

The latent variable approach now creates the latent interaction variable by multiplying the latent variable scores for ksi1 and ksi2. This approach differs from the continuous variable approach, where pairs of observed variable scores are multiplied to create product indicator variables of a latent interaction variable. These latent variable scores are unbiased and produce the same mean and covariance matrix as the latent variables (Jöreskog, 2000). We use a PRELIS program to multiply the two independent latent variables to create an interaction latent variable (**NE** command) and add it to our PRELIS system file. The **CO** command treats the new latent interaction variable as continuous rather than ordinal data. The **RG** (regression) command estimates three structure coefficients (gamma): two main effects and one interaction effect.

The PRELIS program is

```
Estimate Gamma Coefficients in Latent Variable Interaction Model
SY=raw.psf
NE ksi12=ksi1*ksi2
CO ksi12
RG eta ON ksi1 ksi2 ksi12
OU RA=raw.psf
```

The PRELIS computer output indicates the univariate descriptive statistics for the latent variables and the structural equation for estimating the coefficients. Notice that the two latent independent variables ksi1 and ksi2 do not indicate skewness and kurtosis; however, the interaction latent variable ksi12 has a statistically significant chi-square value. Consequently, we need to be concerned about the robustness of the standard error and conduct a bootstrap estimate.

Total Sample Size = 500

Univariate Summary Statistics for Continuous Variables

Variable	Mean	St. Dev.	T-Value	Skewness	Kurtosis
V1	-0.061	0.976	-1.394	0.191	0.048
V2	0.007	1.071	0.142	-0.047	0.280
V3	-0.018	1.105	-0.368	0.175	0.441
V4	-0.015	0.956	-0.359	-0.200	-0.158
V5	-0.013	1.351	-0.209	-0.003	0.168
V6	0.011	1.543	0.163	0.171	0.528
V7	-0.065	1.192	-1.222	-0.081	-0.350
V8	-0.041	1.491	-0.615	0.127	0.092
V9	0.005	1.595	0.075	0.058	0.514
eta	0.000	0.386	0.000	0.126	0.270
ksi1	0.000	0.669	0.000	0.009	0.198
ksi2	0.000	0.873	0.000	0.111	0.053
ksi12	0.200	0.639	7.011	2.049	9.697

```
Test of Univariate Normality for Continuous Variables

                 Skewness            Kurtosis        Skewness and Kurtosis

Variable   Z-Score   P-Value   Z-Score   P-Value   Chi-Square   P-Value

V1          1.749     0.080     0.321     0.748       3.163       0.206
V2         -0.432     0.666     1.256     0.209       1.764       0.414
V3          1.608     0.108     1.811     0.070       5.866       0.053
V4         -1.833     0.067    -0.695     0.487       3.844       0.146
V5         -0.031     0.975     0.829     0.407       0.688       0.709
V6          1.571     0.116     2.082     0.037       6.802       0.033
V7         -0.746     0.456    -1.865     0.062       4.034       0.133
V8          1.165     0.244     0.513     0.608       1.620       0.445
V9          0.531     0.595     2.039     0.041       4.438       0.109
eta         1.157     0.247     1.219     0.223       2.826       0.243
ksi1        0.080     0.936     0.948     0.343       0.904       0.636
ksi2        1.024     0.306     0.343     0.731       1.166       0.558
ksi12      12.583     0.000     9.857     0.000     255.477       0.000
```

```
Estimated Equations

eta = 0.00516+0.0771* ksi1+0.155* ksi2-0.0257* ksi12+Error, R² = .173
      (0.0165)(0.0251)    (0.0192)    (0.0248)
       0.312   3.066       8.054      -1.040
```

```
Error Variance = 0.124
```

The PRELIS system file *raw.psf* now contains the latent interaction variable ksi12.

We could have created the latent interaction variable without running a PRELIS program. With the *raw.psf* PRELIS system file open, we select **Transformation** on the tool bar menu, click on **Add**, create a new variable, and then drag the variable names into an equation using the **Compute** dialog box. We instantly see ksi12.

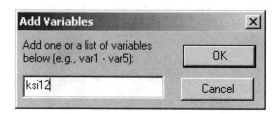

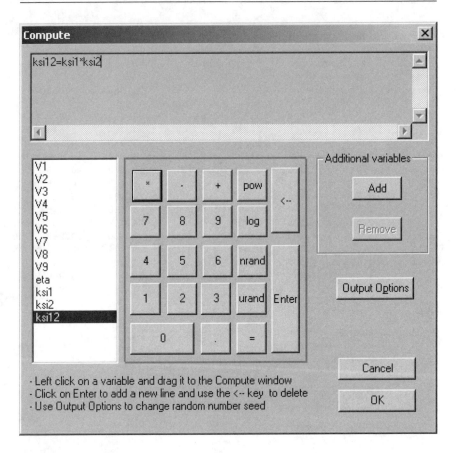

We can now run a program in LISREL–SIMPLIS to compute structure co-efficients (gamma) without an intercept term in the structural equation, and generate the diagram in Fig. 14.9.

The LISREL–SIMPLIS program with the optional LISREL OUTPUT commented out is

```
Regression Analysis on Latent Variable Scores with no Intercept
Observed Variables:
V1-V9 eta ksi1 ksi2 ksi12
Raw Data from File raw.psf
Sample Size = 500
Relationships
eta = ksi1 ksi2 ksi12
!LISREL Ouput: ND=3 Optional statement to produce matrices
Path Diagram
End of Problem
```

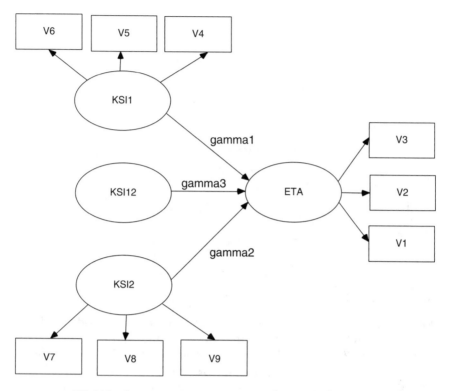

FIG. 14.9. Latent variable interaction model (Schumacker, 2002).

The LISREL–SIMPLIS computer output without the *intercept* term is

```
Regression Analysis on Latent Variable Scores with no Intercept

LISREL Estimates (Maximum Likelihood)

Structural Equations
```

$$\text{eta} = 0.077^* \text{ksi1} + 0.15^* \text{ksi2} - 0.026^* \text{ksi12}, \text{ Errorvar.} = 0.12, R^2 = 0.17$$

```
       (0.025)        (0.019)        (0.025)                    (0.0078)
        3.07           8.05          -1.04                       15.75


Covariance Matrix of Independent Variables


           ksi1        ksi2        ksi12
         --------    --------    --------
ksi1       0.45
          (0.03)
          15.75
```

```
ksi2        0.20        0.76
           (0.03)      (0.05)
            7.24       15.75

ksi12       0.03        0.02        0.41
           (0.02)      (0.03)      (0.03)
            1.79        0.84       15.75
```

```
Covariance Matrix of Latent Variables

            eta         ksi1        ksi2        ksi12
          --------    --------    --------    --------
eta         0.15
ksi1        0.06        0.45
ksi2        0.13        0.20        0.76
ksi12       0.00        0.03        0.02        0.41
```

Two-Stage Least Squares Approach

Recent developments in nonlinear structural equation modeling have focused on full information methods, for example, maximum likelihood (ML), or asymptotically distribution free methods (ADF or WLS), with a concern about estimating parameters and standard errors. We recommend bootstrap estimates of the parameters and standard errors in nonlinear models given these estimation methods because the observed and/or latent interaction variables do not meet the multivariate normality assumption. Other problems or sources of error could exist, which is why *start values* are recommended to aid convergence, that is, the initial two-stage least squares (TSLS) estimates can be replaced with user-defined start values. The TSLS estimates and their standard errors are obtained without iterations and therefore provide the researcher with clues to which parameters exceed their expected values (e.g., correlations with values greater than 1.0 in a non-positive definite matrix). TSLS estimates therefore provide useful information to determine whether the specified model is reasonable.

Bollen (1995, 1996) indicated that nonlinear SEM models can be estimated using instrumental variables in TSLS. A TSLS analysis using instrumental variables is easily run in LISREL–PRELIS (Jöreskog, Sörbom, du Toit, S., & du Toit, M., 2000, pp. 172–174) using the following **RG** command (see files KJTSLS1.PR2 and KJTSLS2.PR2):

```
Estimating Kenny-Judd Model by Bollen's TSLS
DA NI=5
```

```
LA
Y X1 X2 X3 X4
RA=KJUDD.RAW
CO ALL
NE X1X3=X1 * X3
NE X1X4=X1 * X4
NE X2X3=X2 * X3
NE X2X4=X2 * X4
RG Y ON X1 X3 X1X3 WITH X2 X4 X2X4 RES=U
OU RA=KJRES.RAW
```

The TSLS results are

```
Estimated Equations
```

$$Y = 0.936 + 0.340 * X1 + 0.399 * X3 + 0.965 * X1X3 + \text{Error}, \quad R^2 = 0.594$$
```
   (1.011) (0.115)    (0.0883)    (0.164)
    0.926   2.948      4.516       5.899
```

The latent variable score approach is also easily run using PRELIS and SIMPLIS programs (Jöreskog, Sörbom, du Toit, S., & du Toit, M., 2000, p. 173; see files KJUDD.PR2, KENJUDD.SPL, and KENJUDD.PR2). The PRELIS program KJUDD.PR2 creates the PRELIS system file KJUDD.PSF, the SIMPLIS program KENJUDD.SPL computes the latent variable scores, and the PRELIS program KENJUDD.PR2 computes the parameter estimates in the SEM interaction model. The PRELIS program for computing the PRELIS system file is

```
Computing PSF file from KJUDD.RAW
DA NI=5
LA; Y X1 X2 X3 X4
RA=KJUDD.RAW
CO ALL
OU MA=CM RA=KJUDD.PSF
```

The SIMPLIS program for computing the latent variable scores is

```
Estimating the Measurement Model in the Kenny-Judd Model
  and Latent Variable Scores
System File from File KJUDD.DSF
Latent Variables Ksi1 Ksi2
Relationships
X1=1 * Ksi1
X2=Ksi1
X3=1 * Ksi2
X4=Ksi2
PSFfile KJUDD.PSF
Path Diagram
End of Problem
```

The PRELIS program for computing the parameter estimates in the SEM interaction model is

```
Estimating Kenny-Judd Model from Latent Variable Scores
SY=KJUDD.PSF
CO ALL
NE Ksi1Ksi2 = Ksi1 * Ksi2
RG Y ON Ksi1 Ksi2 Ksi1Ksi2
OU
```

Estimated Equations

$Y = 1.082 + 0.232 * \text{Ksi1} + 0.290 * \text{Ksi2} + 0.431 * \text{Ksi1Ksi2} + \text{Error}, R^2 = 0.381$

   (0.0207)(0.0297)   (0.0218)   (0.0261) Error Variance = 0.393
    52.196   7.814   13.281   16.540

In PRELIS the **RG** command can be used to conduct univariate or multivariate regression, including ANOVA, ANCOVA, MANOVA, and MANCOVA, as well as other variations of the general multivariate linear model using a list of Y and X variables, that is, **RG** Y-Varlist ON X-Varlist.

Summary

The testing of interaction effects can present problems in structural equation modeling. First, we may have the problem of model specification. Linear models simplify the task of determining relationships to investigate and distributional assumptions to consider, but this may not be the case in latent variable interaction models. Second, discarding the linearity assumption opens up the possibility of several product indicant variable and latent variable interaction combinations, but this also serves to magnify the critical role of theory in focusing the research effort. Third, a researcher who seeks to model categorical interaction effects must also collect data that span the range of values in which interaction effects are likely to be evident in the raw data and must collect a sample size large enough to permit subsamples. Fourth, the statistical fit index and parameter standard errors are based on linearity and normality assumptions, and we may not have robust results to recognize the presence of an interaction effect unless it is substantial.

The continuous variable approach does have its good points. It is possible to check for normality of variables and to standardize them, and the approach does not require creating subsamples or forming groups where observations could be misclassified, nor does it require the researcher to categorize a variable and thereby lose information. Moreover, the continuous variable approach is parsimonious. Basically, all but one of the additional parameters involved in the interaction model are exact functions of the main-effects parameters, so the only new parameters to be estimated are the structure coefficient for the latent interaction independent variable and the prediction equation error.

The continuous variable approach also has several drawbacks. First, only a few software programs can perform the necessary nonlinear constraints, and the programming for testing interaction effects in the traditional sense is not easy. Second, if one includes too many indicator variables of the latent independent variables, this approach can become very cumbersome. For example, if one latent independent variable, Factor 1, has n_1 measures and the other latent independent variable, Factor 2, has n_2 measures, then the interaction term, Factor 1 × Factor 2, could have $n_1 \times n_2$ measures, although, as mentioned by Jonsson (1998), not all product indicant variables have to be included. If each independent latent variable has five indicator variables, then the multiplicative latent independent variable interaction would involve 25 indicators. Including the five measures for each of the two main-effect latent independent variables and two indicators of a latent dependent variable, the model would have 37 indicator variables before any other latent variable relationships were considered. Third, the functional form of the interaction needs to be specified. The simple multiplicative interaction presented here hardly covers other types of interactions, and for these other types of interactions there is little research and few examples to guide the researcher.

A fourth problem to consider is multicollinearity. It is very likely that the interaction factor will be highly correlated with the observed variables used to construct it. This multicollinearity in the measurement model causes the interaction latent independent variable to be more highly correlated with the observed variables of other main-effect latent independent variables than each set of observed variables are with their own respective main-effect latent independent variables. For multiplicative interactions between normally distributed variables, Smith and Sasaki (1979) demonstrated how multicollinearity could be eliminated by centering the observed variables (using scores expressed as deviations from their means) before computing the product variable. However, centering the variables alters the form of the interaction relationship. Smith and Sasaki noted that centering the variables turns the original multiplicative interaction into a type of consistency effect, in which interaction values take on values similar to the main-effect values when either both are above their respective means or both are below their respective means. Researchers who want to model other types of interactions may find no easy answer to the problem of multicollinearity.

A fifth concern relates to distributional problems, which are more serious than those associated with linear modeling techniques using observed variables only. If the observed variables are nonnormal, then the variance of the product variable can be very different from the values implied by the basic measurement model, and the interaction effect will perform poorly. Of course, permissible transformations, as mentioned in earlier chapters, may result in a suitable normal distribution for the observed variables. The resultant nonnormality, however, in the observed variables violates the distributional assumptions associated with the estimation methods used, for example, maximum likelihood. Furthermore, estimation methods that do not make distributional assumptions may not work for interaction models. Basically, the asymptotic weight matrix associated with the covariance matrix for an interaction model may be non-positive definite because of dependences between moments of different observed variables that are implied by the interaction model. In any case, we recommend that you bootstrap the parameter estimates and standard errors to achieve a more reasonable estimate of these values (Bollen & Stine, 1993; Jöreskog & Sörbom, 1993; Lunneborg, 1987; Mooney & Duval, 1993; Stine, 1990; Yang-Wallentin & Joreskog, 2001).

Structural equation models that include interaction effects are not prevalent in the research literature, in part because of all the concerns mentioned here. The categorical variable approach using multiple samples and constraints has been used more often. The Ping (1993) technique may provide a more plausible and user-friendly approach to modeling a continuous variable interaction effect under certain conditions. Jöreskog and Yang (1996) provided additional insights into modeling interaction effects, given the problems and concerns discussed here. Jöreskog (2000) discussed many issues related to interaction modeling and included latent variable scores in LISREL that are easy to compute and include in interaction modeling. Schumacker (2002) compared the latent variable score approach to the continuous variable approach using LISREL matrix command language and found the parameter estimates to be similar, with standard errors reasonably close. Our recommendation is to use the latent variable score approach and bootstrap the standard errors. We hope more SEM research will consider interaction hypotheses given the use of latent variable scores in LISREL–PRELIS.

14.4   LATENT GROWTH CURVE MODELS

Repeated-measures analysis of variance has been widely used with observed variables to statistically test for changes over time (Hinkle, Wiersma, & Jurs, 2003). SEM advances this basic longitudinal analysis of data to include latent variable growth over time while modeling both individual and group changes using slopes and intercepts (Byrne & Crombie, 2003; McArdle & Epstein, 1987; Stoolmiller, 1995). Latent growth curve analysis conceptually involves two different analyses. The first analysis is of the repeated measures of each individual across time, which is hypothesized to be linear or nonlinear. The second analysis involves using the individual's parameters (slope and intercept values) to determine the difference in growth from a baseline. The latent growth curve model (LGM) represents differences over time that takes into account means (intercepts) and rate of change (slopes) at the individual and group levels.

LGM permits an analysis of individual parameter differences, which is critical to any analysis of change. It not only describes an individual's growth over time (linear or nonlinear), but also detects differences in individual parameters over time. LGM using structural equation modeling can test the type of individual growth curve, use time-varying covariates, establish the type of group curve, and include interaction effects in latent growth curves (Li et al., 2001). The LGM approach, however, requires large samples, multivariate normal data, equal time intervals for all subjects, and change that occurs as a result of the time continuum (Duncan & Duncan, 1995).

We present a latent growth curve model to illustrate the modeling of slope and intercept differences over time using data from Willett and Sayer (1994). The data set contained responses from 168 adolescents over a 5-year period (ages 11–15 years) regarding tolerance toward deviant behaviors, with higher scores indicating more tolerance of such behavior. The data were transformed (i.e., $\log X$) to create equal-interval linear measures from ordinal data. The latent growth curve model is shown in Fig. 14.10.

Amos Example

Using the Amos drawing tools (Arbuckle & Wothke, 1999) we first draw Fig. 14.10. In Fig. 14.10 we see that the intercept latent variable factor loadings are set to 1.0, thus indicating the mean values for each age. The linear factor loadings (slope coefficients) are set from 0 (age 11 years) to 4 (age 15 years) to test a linear rate of growth in tolerance for deviant behavior. This linear rate of growth seems appropriate to model because the means increase from .20 at age 11 years to .45 at age 15 years. We must also designate this LGM as a structured means analysis because we use means as well as covariances. To do so, we select **View/Set**, **Analysis Properties**, select **Estimation** tab, and click on **Estimate Means and Intercepts**. We must also fix the path coefficients at 1.0 to estimate the error variances and correctly identify the LGM model.

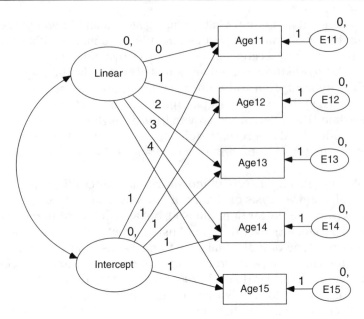

FIG. 14.10.   Amos latent growth curve model (Willet & Sayer, 1994).

After we have successfully drawn Fig. 14.10, we need to create the data set.

We create a special correlation file type using SPSS and save it as *Chap14log.sav*.

	rowtype_	varname_	age11	age12	age13	age14	age15
1	n		168.000	168.000	168.000	168.000	168.000
2	corr	age11	1.000	.	.	.	.
3	corr	age12	.161	1.000	.	.	.
4	corr	age13	.408	.348	1.000	.	.
5	corr	age14	.373	.269	.411	1.000	.
6	corr	age15	.254	.143	.276	.705	1.000
7	stddev		.178	.199	.269	.293	.296
8	mean		.201	.226	.326	.417	.446

We are now ready to run the analysis by selecting **Model Fit** on the tool bar menu and clicking on **Calculate Estimates**. We obtain our results by clicking on **View/Set** and selecting **Table Output**. The intercept values are correctly reported as the mean values for each age level and indicate a linear increase across age levels.

```
Intercepts
                 Est.      S.E.     C.R.       P
     Age11       0.201     0.014    14.845     0.000
     Age12       0.226     0.017    13.275     0.000
     Age13       0.326     0.021    15.172     0.000
     Age14       0.417     0.021    20.239     0.000
     Age15       0.446     0.023    19.088     0.000
```

There are individual differences in the slopes over time:

```
Standardized Regression Weights

                          Estimate

Age11  ←  Linear          0.000
Age12  ←  Linear          0.260
Age13  ←  Linear          0.413
Age14  ←  Linear          0.646
Age15  ←  Linear          0.759

Age11  ←  Intercept       0.603
Age12  ←  Intercept       0.478
Age13  ←  Intercept       0.380
Age14  ←  Intercept       0.396
Age15  ←  Intercept       0.349
```

```
Variances
                 Est.       S.E.      C.R.      P

     Linear      0.003      0.001     4.692     0.000
     Intercept   0.011      0.003     3.192     0.001
```

```
Squared Multiple Correlations

                       Estimate
          Age15        0.698
          Age14        0.574
          Age13        0.315
          Age12        0.296
          Age11        0.363
```

The correlation between the intercept values (group means) and the slope (linear growth) is zero, indicating that level of tolerance at age

11 years does not predict growth in tolerance across the other age groups.

```
    Covariances
                        Est.    S.E.    C.R.     P

    Intercept ⟷ Linear 0.000   0.001   -0.001   0.999
```

This LGM model indicates a linear rate of growth in adolescent tolerance for deviant behavior using the age 11 years as the baseline for assessing linear change over time. We want to graph these mean values across the age levels to graphically display the trend. We also want to interpret the correlation between the intercept and slope because a positive value indicates that high initial status at age 11 years has a greater rate of change, whereas a negative correlation indicates that high initial status at age 11 years has a lower rate of change. Our results indicate no correlation. The variance of the intercept indicates the range of individual differences in tolerance around the baseline mean at age 11 years. The mean of the slope indicates a group-level average of change from year to year. If the average slope value is zero, then no linear change has occurred. Finally, we want to assess how measurement errors across adjacent years are correlated (e.g., lagged correlation in ARIMA models). This ability to model measurement error is a unique advantage of LGM over traditional ANOVA repeated-measures designs.

EQS Example

We used the Willert and Sayer (1994) log-transformed data in our EQS example [Stoolmiller (1995) and Bentler and Wu (2002, p. 282) provided a similar LGM example using the same WISC data]. Our EQS program requires the use of a special variable V999 to indicate a CONSTANT in a structured means model (Bentler & Wu, 2002, p. 183). The LGM model is diagrammed for EQS in Fig. 14.11. The EQS program uses the **/EQUATION** command to specify the fixed 1.0 intercept values F1 and the linear growth coefficients for the slope F2. In addition, the asterisk in front of V999 for F1 and F2 indicates their intercepts (means). The EQS LGM program is

```
/TITLE
 LATENT GROWTH CURVE MODEL AND STRUCTURED MEANS -- WILLET & SAYER (1994)
/SPECIFICATIONS
 CASES=168; VARIABLES=5; ANALYSIS=MOMENT; MATRIX=CORRELATION;
 METHOD=ML; GROUPS=1;
/LABELS
 V1=AGE11;V2=AGE12;V3=AGE13;V4=AGE14;V5=AGE15;F1=INTERCEPT;F2=SLOPE;
```

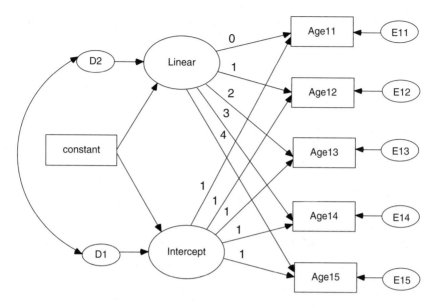

FIG. 14.11.   EQS latent growth curve model (Willet & Sayer, 1994).

```
/EQUATIONS
 V1 = 1F1 + 0F2 + E1;
 V2 = 1F1 + 1F2 + E2;
 V3 = 1F1 + 2F2 + E3;
 V4 = 1F1 + 3F2 + E4;
 V5 = 1F1 + 4F2 + E5;
 F1 = *V999 + D1;
 F2 = *V999 + D2;
/VARIANCES
 V999 = 1.0;
 E1 TO E5 = *;
 D1 TO D2 = *;
/COVARIANCES
 D1,D2 = *;
/MATRIX
 1.000
 0.3760 1.000
 0.3653 0.4788 1.000
 0.4088 0.4058 0.6742 1.000
 0.4373 0.3968 0.6024 0.7665 1.000
/STANDARD DEVIATIONS
 .1780 .1987 .2691 .2927 .2955
/MEANS
 .2008 .2263 .3255 .4168 .4460
/PRINT
 FIT=ALL;
 TABLE=EQUATION;
/END
```

The EQS computer output indicates the average values for F1 (inter-cepts) at .191 and for F2 (slopes) at .066:

```
CONSTRUCT EQUATIONS WITH STANDARD ERRORS AND TEST STATISTICS
 STATISTICS SIGNIFICANT AT THE 5% LEVEL ARE MARKED WITH @.

INTERCEP=F1 = .191*V999 + 1.000 D1
               .012
             15.521@

SLOPE =F2 = .066*V999 + 1.000 D2
             .005
           12.321@
```

The variance around the mean values for F1 and F2 are statistically significant for D1 (intercept) and D2 (slope):

```
VARIANCES OF INDEPENDENT VARIABLES
-----------------------------------

STATISTICS SIGNIFICANT AT THE 5% LEVEL ARE MARKED WITH @.

                      E                                 D
                     ---                               ---
E1 -AGE11            .019*      D1 -INTERCEP           .012*
                     .003                              .003
                    5.659@                            3.787@

E2 -AGE12            .028*      D2 -SLOPE              .003*
                     .004                              .001
                    7.962@                            4.788@

E3 -AGE13            .034*
                     .004
                    8.078@

E4 -AGE14            .025*
                     .004
                    6.735@

E5 -AGE15            .019*
                     .005
                    4.105@
```

The slope and intercept also significantly covary (see the following correlation), indicating a change in tolerance from the baseline age of 11 years:

```
COVARIANCES AMONG INDEPENDENT VARIABLES
----------------------------------------

STATISTICS SIGNIFICANT AT THE 5% LEVEL ARE MARKED WITH @.

     E                  D
     ---                ---
   D2 -SLOPE           .002*
   D1 -INTERCEP        .001
                      2.162@
```

The standardized solution is reported as

```
MAXIMUM LIKELIHOOD SOLUTION (NORMAL DISTRIBUTION THEORY)

STANDARDIZED SOLUTION:                       R-SQUARED

AGE11 =V1 = .624 F1 + .782 E1                 .389
AGE12 =V2 = .507 F1 + .245 F2 + .768 E2       .411
AGE13 =V3 = .428 F1 + .415 F2 + .714 E3       .490
AGE14 =V4 = .400 F1 + .581 F2 + .572 E4       .672
AGE15 =V5 = .359 F1 + .696 F2 + .445 E5       .802

CORRELATIONS AMONG INDEPENDENT VARIABLES
----------------------------------------

     E                  D
     ---                ---
   D2 -SLOPE           .378*
   D1 -INTERCEP
```

14.5 DYNAMIC FACTOR MODELS

A class of SEM applications that involve stationary and nonstationary latent variables across time with lagged (correlated) measurement error has been called dynamic factor analysis (Hershberger, Molenaar, & Corneal, 1996). The characteristic of these SEM applications is that the same measurement instruments are administered to the same subject on two or more occasions. The purpose of the analysis is to assess change in the latent variable between the ordered occasions due to some event or treatment. When the same measurement instruments are used over two or more occasions there is a tendency for the measurement errors to correlate (autocorrelation); for example, a specific sequence of correlated error, where error at Time 1 correlates with error at Time 2, and error at Time 2 correlates with error at Time 3, is called ARIMA modeling.

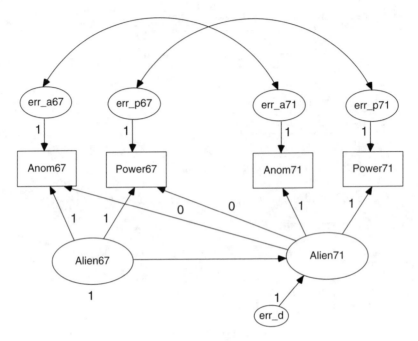

FIG. 14.12.   Dynamic factor model specified (Wheaton et al., 1977).

Amos Example

For our example we use a subset of data from Jöreskog and Sörbom (1996c, p. 30). The data contain two variables that measured anomia and powerlessness from 932 persons in two rural regions of Illinois in 1967 and 1971. These two variables defined the factor alienation. Thus, we have measures of anomia and powerlessness in 1967 and again in 1971. In Amos we first draw Fig. 14.12 to indicate the same latent variable, alienation, at two points in time, 1967 and 1971. The latent variable Alien67 has an arrow drawn to the latent variable Alien71, indicating prediction from occasion 1 to occasion 2, that is, repeated measurement of the same latent variable. Our interest in this stationary dynamic factor analysis (SDFA) is in the expected correlated measurements from using the same two measurement instruments to define a latent variable on two different occasions. We specifically correlate only the measurement errors on the same instrument across the two years in a lagged fashion, that is, err_a67 with err_a71, and err_p67 with err_p71, thus specifying an ARIMA-type model.

After drawing Fig. 14.12 we create a special variance–covariance matrix in SPSS and save it as *chap14g_cov.sav*. Because this is a covariance matrix, we use the special variable name *cov* and only include the sample size. It is important, however, to name the variables the same as those in Fig. 14.12, otherwise Amos will not recognize the data and give an error message.

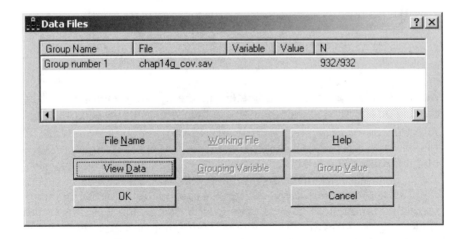

In Amos, we select **File**, and then **Data Files** to select the SPSS data file *chap14g_cov.sav*. By selecting **File Name**, we can locate the data set.

The Amos computer output indicates that attitudes toward alienation in 1967 by rural persons was a statistially significant predictor of attitudes toward alienation in 1971: The regression coefficient = .862, $R^2 = .743$.

```
Standardized Regression Weights

                              Estimate

Alien71  ← Alien67          0.862
Alien71  ← err_d            0.507
Anom67   ← Alien67          0.310
Anom71   ← Alien71          0.733
Power71  ← Alien71          0.817
Power67  ← Alien67          0.349
Anom67   ← Alien71          0.000
Power67  ← Alien71          0.000


Squared Multiple Correlations

                     Estimate
       Alien71       0.743
       Power67       0.122
       Power71       0.667
       Anom71        0.538
       Anom67        0.096
```

The lagged measurement errors on our two instruments are both positively correlated as expected, hence our use of a dynamic factor model with correlated errors is appropriately specified.

```
Correlations

                          Estimate
err_a67  ⟷  err_a71        0.415
err_p67  ⟷  err_p71        0.317
```

We can easily view these parameters in the dynamic factor model by clicking on the second path diagram in the Amos window (Fig. 14.13).

14.6 SUMMARY

In this chapter we considered multitrait–multimethod models, including correlated uniqueness models, second-order factor models, interaction models, latent growth curve models, and dynamic factor models. We showed that the traditional multitrait–multimethod model has identification and convergence problems such that Marsh and Grayson (1995) and Wothke (1996) recommended alternative approaches, namely correlated uniqueness and direct product models. We also showed that interaction models comprise many different types of models. The use of

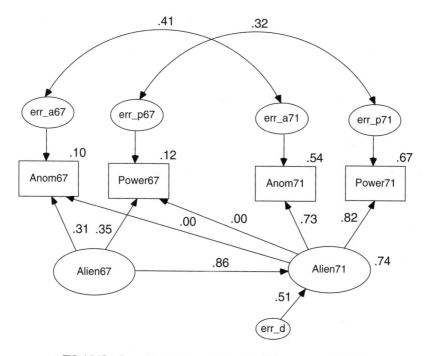

FIG. 14.13.   Dynamic factor model results (Wheaton et al., 1977).

continuous variables, categorical variables, nonlinear effects, and latent variables has intrigued scholars over the years. The current approaches that appear easiest to model are the latent variables score approach and the two-stage least squares approach. We highly recommend either of these two options. Our discussion of latent growth curve models and dynamic factor models introduced the SEM application for longitudinal data analysis.

We hope that our discussion of these SEM applications has provided you with a basic overview and introduction to these methods. We encourage you to read the references provided at the end of the chapter and run some of the program setups provided in the chapter. We further hope that the basic introduction in this chapter will permit you to read the research literature and better understand the resulting models presented, which should support various theoretical perspectives. Attempting a few basic models will help you better understand the approach; afterward, you may wish to attempt one of these SEM applications in your own research.

We now turn our attention in chapter 15 to matrix notation, and encourage you to study the introduction to matrix algebra in the Appendix.

We avoided this presentation at the beginning to permit a more meaningful exposure to the concepts, principles, and practices using Amos, EQS, and LISREL software applications. We do feel, however, that to fully understand structural equation modeling, you need to understand the eight basic matrices plus the tau and kappa matrices generated when inputting an augmented sample variance–covariance matrix.

EXERCISES

1. Find journal article examples for the SEM models covered in this chapter:
   a. Multitrait–multimethod (MTMM) models.
   b. Correlated uniqueness models.
   c. Second-order factor models.
   d. Interaction models.
   e. Latent growth curve models.
   f. Dynamic factor models.
2. Describe in your own words each of the SEM models in this chapter.

REFERENCES

Aiken, L. S., & West, S. G. (1991). *Multiple regression: Testing and interpreting interactions.* Newbury Park, CA: Sage.

Algina, J., & Moulder, B. C. (2001). A note on estimating the Jöreskog–Yang model for latent variable interaction using LISREL 8.3. *Structural Equation Modeling, 8,* 40–52.

Arbuckle, J. L., & Wothke, W. (1999). *Amos 4.0 user's guide.* Chicago, IL: Smallwaters.

Anderson, J. C., & Gerbing, D. W. (1988). Structural equation modeling in practice: A review and recommended two-step approach. *Psychological Bulletin, 103,* 411–423.

Bentler, P. M., & Wu, E. (2002). *EQS 6 for Windows user's guide.* Encinto, CA: Multivariate Software.

Bollen, K. A. (1989). *Structural equations with latent variables.* New York: Wiley.

Bollen, K. A. (1995). Structural equation models that are nonlinear in latent variables: A least squares estimator. In P. M. Marsden (Ed.), *Sociological methodology* (pp. 223–251). Cambridge, MA: Blackwell.

Bollen, K. A. (1996). An alternative two stage least squares (2SLS) estimator for latent variable equations. *Psychometrika, 61,* 109–121.

Bollen, K. A., & Stine, R. A. (1993). Bootstrapping goodness-of-fit measures in structural equation models. In K. A. Bollen & J. S. Long (Eds.), *Testing structural equation models* (pp. 66–110). Newbury Park, CA: Sage.

Byrne, B. M. (1998). *Structural equation modeling with LISREL, PRELIS, and SIMPLIS: Basic concepts, applications, and programming.* Mahwah, NJ: Lawrence Erlbaum Associates, Inc.

Byrne, B. M., & Crombie, G. (2003). Modeling and testing change: An introduction to the latent growth curve model. *Understanding Statistics, 2,* 177–203.

Campbell, D. T., & Fiske, D. W. (1959). Convergent and discriminant validation by the multitrait–multimethod matrix. *Psychological Bulletin, 56,* 81–105.

Cole, D. A., & Maxwell, S. E. (1985). Multitrait-multimethod comparisons across populations: A confirmatory factor analytic approach. *Multivariate Behavioral Research, 20*, 389–417.

Cole, D. A., Maxwell, S. E., Arvey, R., & Salas, E. (1993). Multivariate group comparisons of variable systems: MANOVA and structural equation modeling. *Psychological Bulletin, 114*, 174–184.

Duncan, T. E., & Duncan, S. C. (1995). Modeling the processes of development via latent variable growth curve methodology. *Structural Equation Modeling, 2*, 187–213.

Du Toit, M., & du Toit, S. (2001). *Interactive LISREL: User's guide.* Lincolnwood, IL: Scientific Software International.

Etezadi-Amoli, J., & McDonald, R. P. (1983). A second generation nonlinear factor analysis. *Psychometrika, 48*, 315–342.

Hayduk, L. A. (1987). *Structural equation modeling with LISREL.* Baltimore: Johns Hopkins University Press.

Hershberger, S. L., Molenaar, P. C. M., & Corneal, S. E. (1996). A hierarchy of univariate and multivariate structural times series models. In G. Marcoulides & R. E. Schumacker (Eds.), *Advanced structural equation modeling: Issues and techniques* (pp. 159–194). Mahwah, NJ: Lawrence Erlbaum Associates, Inc.

Higgins, L. F., & Judd, C. M. (1990). Estimation of non-linear models in the presence of measurement error. *Decision Sciences, 21*, 738–751.

Hinkle, D. E., Wiersma, W., & Jurs, S. G. (2003). *Applied statistics for the behavioral sciences* (5th ed.). Boston: Houghton Mifflin.

Hu, L., Bentler, P. M., & Kano, Y. (1992). Can test statistics in covariance structure analysis be trusted? *Psychological Bulletin, 112*, 351–362.

Huelsman, T. J., Furr, M. R., & Nemanick, Jr., R. C. (2003). Measurement of dispositional affect: Construct validity and convergence with a circumplex model of affect. *Educational and Psychological Measurement, 63*, 655–673.

Jonsson, F. (1998). Modeling interaction and non-linear effects: A step-by-step LISREL example. In R. E. Schumacker & G. A. Marcoulides (Eds.), *Interaction and nonlinear effects in structural equation modeling* (pp. 17–42). Mahwah, NJ: Lawrence Erlbaum Associates, Inc.

Jöreskog, K. G. (2000). *Latent variable scores and their uses.* Lincolnwood, IL: Scientific Software International.

Jöreskog, K. G., & Sörbom, D. (1993). *Bootstrapping and Monte Carlo experimenting with PRELIS2 and LISREL8.* Chicago: Scientific Software International.

Jöreskog, K. G., & Sörbom, D. (1996a). *LISREL8 user's reference guide.* Chicago: Scientific Software International.

Jöreskog, K. G., & Sörbom, D. (1996c). *LISREL8: Structural equation modeling with the SIMPLIS command language.* Chicago: Scientific Software International.

Jöreskog, K. G., & Sörbom, D. (1996b). *PRELIS2 user's reference guide.* Chicago: Scientific Software International.

Jöreskog, K. G., & Yang, F. (1996). Non-linear structural equation models: The Kenny–Judd model with interaction effects. In G. A. Marcoulides & R. E. Schumacker (Eds.), *New developments and techniques in structural equation modeling* (pp. 57–88). Mahwah, NJ: Lawrence Erlbaum Associates, Inc.

Jöreskog, K. G., Sörbom, D., du Toit, S., & du Toit, M. (2000). *LISREL8: New statistical features.* Lincolnwood, IL: Scientific Software International.

Kenny, D. A., & Judd, C. M. (1984). Estimating the non-linear and interactive effects of latent variables. *Psychological Bulletin, 96*, 201–210.

Li, F., Duncan, T. E., Duncan, S. C., Acock, A. C., Yang-Wallentin, F., & Hops, H. (2001). Interaction models in latent growth curves. In G. A. Marcoulides & R. E. Schumacker

(Eds.), *New developments and techniques in structural equation modeling* (pp. 173–201). Mahwah, NJ: Lawrence Erlbaum Associates, Inc.

Lunneborg, C. E. (1987). *Bootstrap applications for the behavioral sciences, Vol. 1.* Seattle: University of Washington, Psychology Department.

MacCallum, R. C., Roznowski, M., & Necowitz, L. B. (1992). Model modifications in covariance structure analysis: The problem of capitalization on chance. *Psychological Bulletin, 111,* 490–504.

Mackenzie, S. B., & Spreng, R. A. (1992). How does motivation moderate the impact of central and peripheral processing on brand attitudes and intentions? *Journal of Consumer Research, 18,* 519–529.

Marcoulides, G., & Schumacker, R. E. (Eds.). (1996). *Advanced structural equation modeling: Issues and techniques.* Mahwah, NJ: Lawrence Erlbaum Associates, Inc.

Marcoulides, G., & Schumacker, R. E. (Eds.). (2001). *New developments and techniques in structural equation modeling.* Mahwah, NJ: Lawrence Erlbaum Associates, Inc.

Marsh, H. W., & Grayson, D. (1995). Latent variable models of multitrait–multimethod data. In R. H. Hoyle (Ed.), *Structural equation modeling: Concepts, issues, and applications* (pp. 177–198). Thousand Oaks, CA: Sage.

McArdle, J. J., & Epstein, D. (1987). Latent growth curves within developmental structural equation models. *Child Development, 58,* 110–133.

McDonald, R. P. (1967). *Nonlinear factor analysis.* Richmond: Psychometric Society.

Mooney, C. Z., & Duval, R. D. (1993). *Bootstrapping: A nonparametric approach to statistical inference.* Beverly Hills, CA: Sage.

Moulder, B. C., & Algina, J. (2002). Comparison of methods for estimating and testing latent variable interactions. *Structural Equation Modeling, 9,* 1–19.

Newman, I., Marchant, G. J., & Ridenour, T. (1993, April). *Type VI errors in path analysis: Testing for interactions.* Paper presented at the annual meeting of the American Educational Research Association, Atlanta, GA.

Pedhazur, E. J., & Schmelkin, L. (1991). *Measurement, design, and analysis: An integrated approach.* Hillsdale, NJ: Lawrence Erlbaum Associates, Inc.

Ping, R. A., Jr. (1993). *Latent variable interaction and quadratic effect estimation: A suggested approach* (Technical Report). Dayton, OH: Wright State University.

Ping, R. A., Jr. (1994). Does satisfaction moderate the association between alternative attractiveness and exit intention in a marketing channel? *Journal of the Academy of Marketing Science, 22,* 364–371.

Ping, R. A., Jr. (1995). A parsimonious estimating technique for interaction and quadratic latent variables. *Journal of Marketing Research, 32,* 336–347.

Russell, C. J., & Bobko, P. (1992). Moderated regression analysis and Likert scales: Too coarse for comfort. *Journal of Applied Psychology, 77,* 336–342.

Saris, W. E., & Aalberts, C. (2003). Different explanations for correlated disturbance terms in MTMM studies. *Structural Equation Modeling, 10,* 193–213.

Schumacker, R. E. (2002). Latent variable interaction modeling. *Structural Equation Modeling, 9,* 40–54.

Schumacker, R. E., & Marcoulides, G. A. (1998). *Interaction and nonlinear effects in structural equation modeling.* Mahwah, NJ: Lawrence Erlbaum Associates, Inc.

Schumacker, R. E., & Rigdon, E. (1995, April). *Testing interaction effects in structural equation modeling.* Paper presented at the annual meeting of the American Educational Research Association, San Francisco.

Smith, K. W., & Sasaki, M. S. (1979). Decreasing multicollinearity: A method for models with multiplicative functions. *Sociological Methods and Research, 8,* 35–56.

Stine, R. (1990). An introduction to bootstrap methods: Examples and ideas. In J. Fox & J. S. Long (Eds.), *Modern methods of data analysis* (pp. 325–373). Beverly Hills, CA: Sage.

Stoolmiller, M. (1995). Using latent growth curves to study developmental processes. In J. M. Gottman (Ed.), *The analysis of change* (pp. 103–138). Mahwah, NJ: Lawrence Erlbaum Associates, Inc.

Wheaton, B., Muthén, B., Alwin, D. F., & Summers, G. F. (1977). Assessing reliability and stability in panel models. In D. R. Heise, (Ed.), *Sociological methodology* (pp. 84–136). San Francisco, CA: Jossey-Bass.

Widaman, K. F. (1985). Hierarchically tested covariance structure models for multitrait-multimethod data. *Applied Psychological Measurement, 9*, 1–26.

Willet, J. B., & Sayer, A. G. (1994). Using covariance structure analysis to detect correlates and predictors of individual change over time. *Psychological Bulletin, 116*, 363–381.

Wong, S. K., & Long, J. S. (1987). *Parameterizing non-linear constraints in models with latent variables.* Unpublished manuscript, Indiana University, Department of Sociology, Bloomington, IN.

Wothke, W. (1996). Models for multitrait–multimethod matrix analysis. In G. Marcoulides & R. E. Schumacker (Eds.), *Advanced structural equation modeling: Issues and techniques* (pp. 7–56). Mahwah, NJ: Lawrence Erlbaum Associates, Inc.

Yang-Wallentin, F., & Joreskog, K. G. (2001). Robust standard errors and chi-squares in interaction models. In G. Marcoulides & R. E. Schumacker (Eds.), *New developments and techniques in structural equation modeling* (pp. 159–171). Mahwah, NJ: Lawrence Erlbaum Associates, Inc.

15

MATRIX APPROACH TO STRUCTURAL EQUATION MODELING

Chapter Outline

Key Concepts

Eight matrices in SEM models
Matrix notation: measurement and structural models
Free, fixed, and constrained parameters
Structured means
Mean matrices: tau and kappa

15.1 GENERAL OVERVIEW OF MATRIX NOTATION

We have deliberately delayed presenting the matrix notation used in calculating structural equation models because we wanted to first present the basic concepts, principles, and applications of SEM. SEM models are analyzed using the eight different matrices illustrated in Fig. 15.1 (Hayduk, 1987). SEM models may use some combination of these eight matrices, but not use all of the eight matrices in a given analysis (e.g., confirmatory factor analysis).

In this chapter we consider the technical matrix notation associated with the LISREL matrix command language. As described in Jöreskog and Sörbom (1996), the structural model is written in terms of the following matrix equation:

$$\eta = B\eta + \Gamma\xi + \zeta. \tag{1}$$

The latent dependent variables are denoted by η (eta) as a vector ($m \times 1$) of m such variables. The latent independent variables are denoted by ξ (xi) as a vector ($n \times 1$) of n such variables. A matrix Φ (capital phi) contains the variances and covariances among these latent independent variables. The relationships among the latent variables are denoted by B (capital beta) and Γ (capital gamma), the elements of which are denoted by $[\beta]$ (lowercase beta) and $[\gamma]$ (lowercase gamma), respectively. B is an $m \times m$ matrix of structure coefficients that relate the latent dependent variables to one another. Γ is an $m \times n$ matrix of structure coefficients that relate the latent independent variables to the latent dependent variables. The error term ζ (zeta) in the structural model equation is a vector that contains the equation prediction errors or disturbance terms. The matrix Ψ (capital psi) contains the variances and covariances among these latent dependent prediction equation errors.

As described in Jöreskog and Sörbom (1996), the measurement models are written in terms of the following set of matrix equations:

$$Y = \Lambda_y\eta + \varepsilon \tag{2}$$

for the latent dependent variables and

$$X = \Lambda_x\xi + \delta \tag{3}$$

for the latent independent variables. The observed variables are denoted by the vector Y ($p \times 1$) for the measures of the latent dependent variables η ($m \times 1$) and by the vector X ($q \times 1$) for the measures of the latent independent variables ξ ($n \times 1$). The relationships

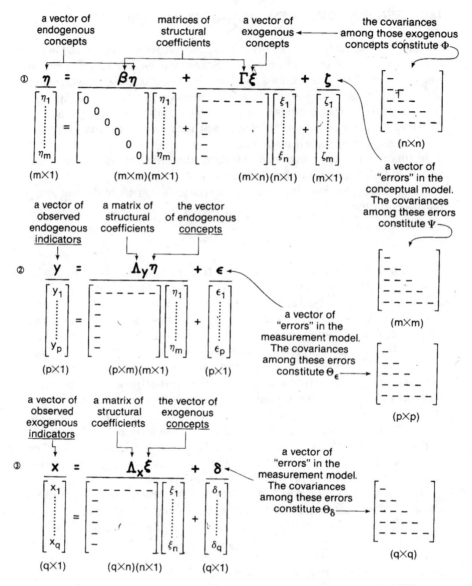

FIG. 15.1. Summary of the general structural equation model (Hayduk, 1987).

between the observed variables and the latent variables (typically referred to as *factor loadings*) are denoted by the ($p \times m$) matrix Λ_y (capital lambda sub y) for the Y's, the elements of which are denoted by $[\lambda_y]$ (lowercase lambda sub y), and by the $q \times n$ matrix Λ_x (capital lambda sub x) for the X's, the elements of which are denoted by $[\lambda_x]$ (lowercase lambda sub x). Finally, the measurement errors for the Y's are denoted by the $p \times 1$ vector ε (lowercase epsilon) and for the X's by the $q \times 1$ vector δ (lowercase delta). The theta epsilon matrix Θ_ε contains the variances and covariances among the errors for the observed dependent variables. The theta delta matrix Θ_δ contains the variances and covariances among the errors for the observed independent variables.

The summary of the general structural equation model in matrix format depicted by Hayduk (1987) is displayed in Fig. 15.1, and should be studied in great detail. The three equations diagrammed in matrix format correspond to the structural equation model [Equation (1)], the measurement model for the Y latent dependent variables [Equation (2)], and the measurement model for the X latent independent variables [Equation (3)].

Obviously, not all of the eight matrices are used in every SEM model (e.g., a confirmatory factor model). We use our examples from chapters 9 and 10 to illustrate the matrix notation for a structural equation model. In our first example in chapter 9 (see Fig. 9.1) there were two structure coefficients of interest. The first involved the influence of Intelligence on Achievement$_1$. The structure coefficient for this influence resides in the matrix Γ because it represents the relationship between the latent independent variable Intelligence and the latent dependent variable Achievement$_1$. The second structure coefficient involved the influence of Achievement$_1$ on Achievement$_2$. This coefficient resides in the matrix B, because it represents the relationship between the latent dependent variable Achievement$_1$ and the latent dependent variable Achievement$_2$. The final term in the structural model of Equation (1) is ζ (zeta), which is an $m \times 1$ vector of m equation errors or disturbances, which represents that portion of each latent dependent variable that is not explained or predicted by the model.

In LISREL notation our equations are written as $\eta_1 = \gamma_{11}\xi_1 + \zeta_1$ and $\eta_2 = \beta_{21}\eta_1 + \zeta_2$, respectively, or in the complete matrix equation as

$$\begin{bmatrix} \eta_1 \\ \eta_2 \end{bmatrix} = \begin{bmatrix} 0 & 0 \\ \beta_{21} & 0 \end{bmatrix} \begin{bmatrix} \eta_1 \\ \eta_2 \end{bmatrix} + \begin{bmatrix} \gamma_{11} \\ 0 \end{bmatrix} [\xi_1] + \begin{bmatrix} \zeta_1 \\ \zeta_2 \end{bmatrix}, \tag{1}$$

where the subscripts on β represent the rows for a latent dependent variable being predicted and columns for a latent dependent variable as the predictor, respectively. The subscripts for the γ vector represent the rows for a latent dependent variable being predicted and columns for a latent independent variable as the predictor, respectively.

The values of 0 shown in the matrix equations for B and Γ represent structure coefficients that we hypothesize to be equal to 0. For example, because we did not specify that Intelligence influenced Achievement$_2$, rather than estimate γ_{21}, we set that value to 0. Likewise, we did not specify that Achievement$_2$ influenced Achievement$_1$, so we set β_{12} to 0. Finally, notice that the diagonal values of B are also 0, that is, β_{11} and β_{22}. The diagonal values of B are always set to 0 because they indicate the extent to which a latent dependent variable influences itself. These influences are never of interest to the applied researcher. In summary, our matrix equation suggests that there are potentially four structure coefficients of interest, β_{12}, β_{21}, γ_{11}, and γ_{21}; however, our model includes only two of these coefficients. Other structural models of these same latent variables can be developed that contain different configurations of structure coefficients.

We now need to provide a more explicit definition of the measurement models in our example. We have two different measurement models in our example, one for the latent dependent variables and one for the latent independent variables. In LISREL matrix notation these equations are written for the Y's as

$$y_1 = \lambda_{y_{11}}\eta_1 + \varepsilon_1$$
$$y_2 = \lambda_{y_{21}}\eta_1 + \varepsilon_2$$
$$y_3 = \lambda_{y_{32}}\eta_2 + \varepsilon_3$$
$$y_4 = \lambda_{y_{42}}\eta_2 + \varepsilon_4$$

and for the X's as

$$x_1 = \lambda_{x_{11}}\xi_1 + \delta_1$$
$$x_2 = \lambda_{x_{21}}\xi_1 + \delta_2.$$

The factor loadings and error terms also appear in their respective error variance–covariance matrices. The complete matrix equation for the Y's are written as

$$\begin{bmatrix} y_1 \\ y_2 \\ y_3 \\ y_4 \end{bmatrix} = \begin{bmatrix} \lambda_{y_{11}} & 0 \\ \lambda_{y_{21}} & 0 \\ 0 & \lambda_{y_{32}} \\ 0 & \lambda_{y_{42}} \end{bmatrix} = \begin{bmatrix} \eta_1 \\ \eta_2 \end{bmatrix} + \begin{bmatrix} \varepsilon_1 \\ \varepsilon_2 \\ \varepsilon_3 \\ \varepsilon_4 \end{bmatrix} \qquad (2)$$

and for the X's as

$$\begin{bmatrix} x_1 \\ x_2 \end{bmatrix} = \begin{bmatrix} \lambda_{x_{11}} \\ \lambda_{x_{21}} \end{bmatrix} [\xi_1] + \begin{bmatrix} \delta_1 \\ \delta_2 \end{bmatrix}, \tag{3}$$

where the subscripts in λ_y represent the rows for an observed Y variable and the columns for a latent dependent variable and those in λ_x represent the rows for an observed X variable and the columns for a latent independent variable, respectively.

The values of 0 shown in the matrix equations for Λ_y (and theoretically for Λ_x, although not for this model) represent factor loadings that we hypothesize to be equal to 0. For example, because we did not specify that California$_1$ was an indicator of Achievement $_2$, rather than estimate λ_{y12}, we set that value to 0. Likewise, we specified that λ_{y22}, λ_{y31}, and λ_{y41} were set to 0.

There are several covariance terms that we need to define. From the structural model, there are two covariance terms to consider. First, we define Φ (capital phi) as an $n \times n$ covariance matrix of the n latent independent variables, the elements of which are denoted by $[\phi]$ (lowercase phi). The diagonal elements of Φ contain the variances of the latent independent variables. In our example model Φ contains only one element, the variance of Intelligence (denoted by ϕ_{11}).

Second, let us define Ψ (uppercase psi) as an $m \times m$ covariance matrix of the m equation errors ζ, the elements of which are denoted by $[\psi]$ (lowercase psi). The diagonal elements of Ψ contain the variances of the equation errors, that is, the amount of unexplained variance for each equation. In our example model Ψ contains two diagonal elements, one for each equation (denoted by ψ_{11} and ψ_{22}).

From the measurement model there are two additional covariance terms to be concerned with. First, we define Θ_ε (capital theta sub epsilon) as a $p \times p$ covariance matrix of the measurement errors for the Y's (i.e., ε, the elements of which are denoted by $[\theta_\varepsilon]$, lowercase theta sub epsilon). The diagonal elements of Θ_ε contain the variances of the measurement errors for the Y's. In our example model Θ_ε contains four diagonal elements, one for each Y. Second, let us define Θ_δ (capital theta sub delta) as a $q \times q$ covariance matrix of the measurement errors for the X's, that is, δ, the elements of which are denoted by $[\theta_\delta]$ (lowercase theta sub delta). The diagonal elements of Θ_δ contain the variances of the measurement errors for the X's. In our example model Θ_δ contains two diagonal elements, one for each X.

There is one more covariance term that we need to define, and it represents the ultimate covariance term. To this point we have defined eight different matrices, B, Γ, Λ_y, Λ_x, Φ, Ψ, Θ_ε, and Θ_δ. From these matrices we can generate an ultimate matrix of covariances that the overall model implies, and this matrix is denoted by Σ (sigma). Officially, Σ is a super-matrix composed of four submatrices, as follows:

$$\begin{bmatrix} \Sigma_{yy} & \Sigma_{yx} \\ \Sigma_{xy} & \Sigma_{xx} \end{bmatrix}. \tag{4}$$

This supermatrix certainly looks imposing, but it can be easily under-stood. First consider the submatrix in the upper left portion of Σ. It deals with the covariances among the Y's, and in terms of our model can be written as

$$\sum_{yy} = \left[\Lambda_y \left[(I - B)^{-1} (\Gamma \Phi \Gamma' + \Psi)(I - B')^{-1} \right] \Lambda_y' + \Theta_\varepsilon \right], \tag{5}$$

where I is an $m \times m$ identity matrix (i.e., a matrix having 1's on the di-agonal and 0's on the off-diagonal). You can see in Equation (5) that all of the matrices are involved except for those of the measurement model in the X's. That is, Equation (5) contains the matrices for the structural model and for the measurement model in the Y's.

Consider next the submatrix in the lower right portion of Σ. It deals with the covariances among the X's and in terms of our model can be written as

$$\sum_{xx} = \left[\Lambda_x \Phi \Lambda_x' + \Theta_\delta \right]. \tag{6}$$

As shown in Equation (6), the only matrices included are those that involve the X side of the model. This particular portion of the model is the same as the common factor analysis model, which you may recognize.

Finally, consider the submatrix in the lower left portion of Σ. It deals with the covariances between the X's and the Y's and in terms of our model can be written as

$$\sum_{xy} = \left[\Lambda_x \Phi \Gamma' (I - B')^{-1} \Lambda_y' \right]. \tag{7}$$

As shown in Equation (7), this portion of the model includes all of our matrices except for the error terms, that is, $\Theta_\varepsilon, \Theta_\delta$, and Ψ. The submatrix in the upper right portion of Σ is the transposed version of Equation (7) [i.e., the matrix of Equation (7) with rows and columns switched], so we need not concern ourselves with it.

15.2 FREE, FIXED, AND CONSTRAINED PARAMETERS

Let us return for a moment to our eight structural equation matrices B, Γ, Λ_x, Λ_y, Φ, Ψ, Θ_ε, and Θ_δ. In the structural equation model there are structure coefficients in matrices B and Γ. The covariances among structural equation errors are in the matrix Ψ. In the measurement models for latent independent and dependent variables there are factor loadings in the matrices Λ_x and Λ_y, respectively, for their indicator variables. The covariances of measurement errors for the latent independent and dependent variables are in the matrices Θ_δ and Θ_ε, respectively. The covariances among the latent independent variables are in the matrix Φ. Each and every element in these eight matrices, if used in a particular model, must be specified to be a free parameter, a fixed parameter, or a constrained parameter. A free parameter is a parameter that is unknown and one that you may wish to estimate. A fixed parameter is a parameter that is not free but rather is fixed to a specified value, typically either 0 or 1. A constrained parameter is a parameter that is unknown, but is constrained to be equal to one or more other parameters.

For example, consider the following matrix B:

$$B = \begin{bmatrix} 0 & \beta_{12} \\ \beta_{21} & 0 \end{bmatrix}.$$

The β's represent values in B that might be parameters of interest and thus would constitute free parameters. The 0's represent values in B that are fixed or constrained to be equal to 0. These diagonal values of B represent the influence of a latent dependent variable on itself, and by definition are always fixed to 0. If our hypothesized model included only β_{21}, then β_{12} would also be fixed to 0. For the model specified in Fig. 10.2 in chapter 10, B takes the following form:

$$B = \begin{bmatrix} 0 & 0 \\ \beta_{21} & 0 \end{bmatrix}.$$

For another example, consider the following matrix Λ_y with the factor loadings for the latent dependent variable measurement model:

$$\Lambda_y = \begin{bmatrix} \lambda_{y_{11}} & \lambda_{y_{12}} \\ \lambda_{y_{21}} & \lambda_{y_{22}} \\ \lambda_{y_{31}} & \lambda_{y_{32}} \\ \lambda_{y_{41}} & \lambda_{y_{42}} \end{bmatrix}.$$

Here the λ_y represent values in Λ_y that might be parameters of interest and would constitute free parameters. This specifies that we are allowing all of the parameters in Λ_y to be free so that each of our four indicator variables (the Y's) loads on each of our two latent dependent variables (the η's). However, to solve the identification problem for Λ_y, some constraints are usually placed on this matrix whereby some of the parameters are fixed. We might specify that the first two indicator variables are allowed only to load on the first latent dependent variable (η_1) and the latter two indicators on the second latent dependent variable (η_2). Then Λ_y appears as

$$\Lambda_y = \begin{bmatrix} \lambda_{y_{11}} & 0 \\ \lambda_{y_{21}} & 0 \\ 0 & \lambda_{y_{32}} \\ 0 & \lambda_{y_{42}} \end{bmatrix}.$$

Additional constraints in Λ_y may also be necessary for identification purposes.

For the structural equation model in chapter 10 (Fig. 10.2), the following structural equations are specified:

Aspirations = home background + ability + error

Achievement = aspirations + home background + ability + error.

The matrix equation is $\eta = B\eta + \Gamma\xi + \varsigma$ and the elements of the matrices are

$$\begin{bmatrix} \eta_1 \\ \eta_2 \end{bmatrix} = \begin{bmatrix} 0 & 0 \\ \beta_{21} & 0 \end{bmatrix} \begin{bmatrix} \eta_1 \\ \eta_2 \end{bmatrix} + \begin{bmatrix} \gamma_{11} & \gamma_{12} \\ \gamma_{21} & \gamma_{22} \end{bmatrix} \begin{bmatrix} \xi_1 \\ \xi_2 \end{bmatrix} + \begin{bmatrix} \varsigma_1 \\ \varsigma_2 \end{bmatrix}.$$

The matrix equation for the latent dependent variable measurement model is $Y = \Lambda_y \eta + \varepsilon$, and the elements of the matrices are

$$\begin{bmatrix} y_1 \\ y_2 \\ y_3 \\ y_4 \end{bmatrix} = \begin{bmatrix} 1 & 0 \\ \lambda_{y_{21}} & 0 \\ 0 & 1 \\ 0 & \lambda_{y_{42}} \end{bmatrix} \begin{bmatrix} \eta_1 \\ \eta_2 \end{bmatrix} + \begin{bmatrix} \varepsilon_1 \\ \varepsilon_2 \\ \varepsilon_3 \\ \varepsilon_4 \end{bmatrix}.$$

The matrix equation for the latent independent variable measurement model is $X = \Lambda_x \xi + \delta$ and the elements of the matrices are

$$
\begin{bmatrix} x_1 \\ x_2 \\ x_3 \\ x_4 \\ x_5 \end{bmatrix} = \begin{bmatrix} 1 & 0 \\ \lambda_{x_{21}} & 0 \\ \lambda_{x_{31}} & 0 \\ 0 & 1 \\ 0 & \lambda_{x_{52}} \end{bmatrix} \begin{bmatrix} \xi_1 \\ \xi_2 \end{bmatrix} + \begin{bmatrix} \delta_1 \\ \delta_2 \\ \delta_3 \\ \delta_4 \\ \delta_5 \end{bmatrix}.
$$

Recall that for each dependent and independent latent variable we fixed one factor loading of an observed variable to 1. This was necessary to identify the model and to fix the scale for the latent variables.

The covariance terms are written next. The covariance matrix for the latent independent variables is

$$
\Phi = \begin{bmatrix} \varphi_{11} & \\ \varphi_{21} & \varphi_{22} \end{bmatrix}.
$$

The covariance matrix for the structural equation errors is

$$
\Psi = \begin{bmatrix} \psi_{11} & \\ \psi_{21} & \psi_{22} \end{bmatrix}.
$$

The covariance matrices for the measurement errors are written as follows. For the indicators of the latent independent variables

$$
\Theta_\delta = \begin{bmatrix} \theta_{\delta_{11}} & & & & \\ 0 & \theta_{\delta_{22}} & & & \\ 0 & \theta_{\delta_{32}} & \theta_{\delta_{33}} & & \\ 0 & 0 & 0 & \theta_{\delta_{44}} & \\ 0 & 0 & 0 & 0 & \theta_{\delta_{55}} \end{bmatrix}
$$

and for the indicators of the latent dependent variables

$$
\Theta_\varepsilon = \begin{bmatrix} \theta_{\varepsilon_{11}} & & & \\ 0 & \theta_{\varepsilon_{22}} & & \\ 0 & 0 & \theta_{\varepsilon_{33}} & \\ 0 & 0 & 0 & \theta_{\varepsilon_{44}} \end{bmatrix}.
$$

Note: This matrix output is possible by including the LISREL OUTPUT command in the LISREL–SIMPLIS program for the model in chapter 10.

15.3   LISREL MODEL EXAMPLE IN MATRIX NOTATION

The LISREL matrix command language program works directly from the matrix notation previously discussed and is presented here for the example in chapter 10. The basic LISREL matrix command language program includes **TITLE**, **DATA** (DA), **INPUT**, **MODEL** (MO), and **OUTPUT** (OU) program statements. The **TITLE** lines are optional. The user's guide provides an excellent overview of the various commands and their purpose (Jöreskog & Sörbom, 1996). The **DA** statement identifies the number of input variables in the variance–covariance matrix, the **NO** statement indicates the number of observations, and **MA** identifies the kind of matrix to be *analyzed*, not the kind of matrix to be *inputted*: **MA = CM**, covariance matrix; **MA = KM**, correlation matrix based on raw scores or normal scores; **MA = MM**, matrix of moments (means) about zero; **MA = AM**, augmented moment matrix; **MA = OM**, special correlation matrix of optimal scores from PRELIS2; and **MA = PM**, correlation matrix of polychoric (ordinal variables) or polyserial (ordinal and continuous variables) correlations. The **SE** statement must be used to select and/or reorder variables used in the analysis of a model (note: *Y* variables must be listed first). An external raw score data file can be read using the **RA** statement with the **FI** and **FO** subcommands (**RA FI=raw.dat FO**). The **FO** subcommand permits the specification of how observations are to be read (for fixed, a FORMAT statement must be enclosed in parentheses; for free-field, an asterisk is placed in the first column, which appears on the line following the **RA** command). If **FI** or **UN** (logical unit number of a FORTRAN file) subcommands are not used, then the data must directly follow the **RA** command and be included in the program.

In the following LISREL matrix command language program a lower diagonal variance–covariance matrix is input, hence the use of the **CM** statement. The **SY** subcommand, which reads only the lower diagonal elements of a matrix, has been omitted because it is the default option for matrix input. The **LA** statement provides for up to eight characters for variable labels, with similar subcommand options for input and specifications as with the **RA** command for data input. A lowercase **c** permits line continuation for various commands. The **LE** command permits variable labels for the latent dependent variables, and the **LK** command permits variable labels for the latent independent variables.

The **MO** command specifies the model for LISREL analysis. The subcommands specify the number of *Y* variables (ny), number of *X* variables (nx), number of latent dependent variables (ne), and number of latent independent variables (nk). The form and mode of the eight LIS-REL parameter matrices must be specified and are further explained in the user's guide (Jöreskog & Sörbom, 1996). The **FU** parameter indicates a full nonsymmetric matrix form, and **FI** indicates a fixed matrix mode, in contrast to a free mode (FR). The **DI** statement indicates a diagonal matrix form, and the **SY** statement indicates a symmetric matrix form. It is strongly recommended that any designation of a LISREL model for analysis include the presentation of the eight matrices in matrix form. This will greatly ease the writing of the **MO** command and the identification of fixed or free parameters in the matrices on the **FR** and **VA** commands. The **VA** command assigns numerical values to the fixed parameters. The **OU** command permits the selection of various output procedures. One feature of interest on the **OU** command is the **AM** option, which provides for automatic model specification by freeing at each step the fixed or constrained parameters with the largest modification indices, although, as previously noted, this should not be the sole criterion for model respecification.

The LISREL matrix command language program used to analyze the model in Fig. 10.2 of chapter 10, using the default maximum likelihood estimation method, is as follows:

```
Respecified Model in Figure 10.2, Chapter 10
da ni=9 no=200 ma=cm
cm sy
1.024
 .792  1.077
1.027   .919  1.844
 .756   .697  1.244  1.286
 .567   .537   .876   .632   .852
 .445   .424   .677   .526   .518   .670
 .434   .389   .635   .498   .475   .545   .716
 .580   .564   .893   .716   .546   .422   .373   .851
 .491   .499   .888   .646   .508   .389   .339   .629   .871
 la
   EDASP OCASP VERBACH QUANTACH FAMINC FAED MOED VERBAB QUANTAB
mo ny=4 nx=5 ne=2 nk=2 be=fu,fi ga=fu,fi ph=sy,fi ps=di,fi    c
   ly=fu,fi lx=fu,fi td=fu,fi te=fu,fi
le
 aspire achieve
lk
 home ability
fr be(2,1) ga(1,1) ga(1,2) ga(2,1) ga(2,2)                    c
   ly(2,1) ly(4,2) lx(2,1) lx(3,1) lx(5,2)                     c
   te(1,1) te(2,2) te(3,3) te(4,4) td(1,1) td(2,2) td(3,3)     c
   td(4,4) td(5,5)                                             c
   ps(1,1) ps(2,2) ph(1,1) ph(2,2) ph(2,1) td(3,2)
```

```
va 1.0 ly(1,1) ly(3,2) lx(1,1) lx(4,2)
ou me=ml all
```

The "c" values in the LISREL program denote line continuation in program statements.

The LISREL matrix command language requires the user to specifically understand the nature, form, and mode of the eight matrices, and thereby fully comprehend the model being specified for analysis, even though all eight matrices may not be used in a particular SEM model. We present the LISREL output from this program, but do so in an edited and condensed format. We challenge you to find the various matrices we have described in this chapter in the computer output.

LISREL8 Matrix Program Output (Edited and Condensed)

```
Respecified Model in Figure 10.2, Chapter 10

                              Number of Input Variables 9
                              Number of Y - Variables   4
                              Number of X - Variables   5
                              Number of ETA - Variables 2
                              Number of KSI - Variables 2
                              Number of Observations  200
```

Covariance Matrix

	EDASP	OCASP	VERBACH	QUANTACH	FAMINC	FAED
EDASP	1.02					
OCASP	0.79	1.08				
VERBACH	1.03	0.92	1.84			
QUANTACH	0.76	0.70	1.24	1.29		
FAMINC	0.57	0.54	0.88	0.63	0.85	
FAED	0.45	0.42	0.68	0.53	0.52	0.67
MOED	0.43	0.39	0.64	0.50	0.47	0.55
VERBAB	0.58	0.56	0.89	0.72	0.55	0.42
QUANTAB	0.49	0.50	0.89	0.65	0.51	0.39

Covariance Matrix

	MOED	VERBAB	QUANTAB
MOED	0.72		
VERBAB	0.37	0.85	
QUANTAB	0.34	0.63	0.87

LISREL Estimates (Maximum Likelihood)

LAMBDA-Y

	aspire	achieve
EDASP	1.00	- -
OCASP	0.92	- -
	(0.06)	
	14.34	
VERBACH	- -	1.00
QUANTACH	- -	0.75
		(0.04)
		18.13

LAMBDA-X

	home	ability
FAMINC	1.00	- -
FAED	0.78	- -
	(0.06)	
	12.18	
MOED	0.72	- -
	(0.07)	
	10.37	
VERBAB	- -	1.00
QUANTAB	- -	0.95
		(0.07)
		14.10

BETA

	aspire	achieve
aspire	- -	- -
achieve	0.53	- -
	(0.12)	
	4.56	

GAMMA

	home	ability
aspire	0.51	0.45
	(0.15)	(0.15)
	3.29	2.96

```
achieve      0.30        0.69
            (0.16)      (0.16)
             1.87        4.27
```

Covariance Matrix of ETA and KSI

	aspire	achieve	home	ability
aspire	0.86			
achieve	1.02	1.65		
home	0.57	0.87	0.66	
ability	0.57	0.91	0.54	0.66

PHI

	home	ability
home	0.66	
	(0.09)	
	7.32	
ability	0.54	0.66
	(0.07)	(0.09)
	7.64	7.51

PSI
Note: This matrix is diagonal.

	aspire	achieve
	0.32	0.23
	(0.06)	(0.06)
	5.61	3.97

Squared Multiple Correlations for Structural Equations

aspire	achieve
0.63	0.86

Squared Multiple Correlations for Reduced Form

aspire	achieve
0.63	0.81

Reduced Form

	home	ability
aspire	0.51	0.45
	(0.15)	(0.15)
	3.29	2.96

```
achieve      0.57       0.92
            (0.17)     (0.18)
             3.26       5.20
```

THETA-EPS

	EDASP	OCASP	VERBACH	QUANTACH
	0.16	0.35	0.19	0.35
	(0.04)	(0.05)	(0.05)	(0.04)
	3.88	7.36	3.81	7.95

Squared Multiple Correlations for Y - Variables

EDASP	OCASP	VERBACH	QUANTACH
0.84	0.67	0.90	0.73

THETA-DELTA

	FAMINC	FAED	MOED	VERBAB	QUANTAB
FAMINC	0.19				
	(0.04)				
	4.74				
FAED	- -	0.27			
		(0.03)			
		7.66			
MOED	- -	0.17	0.37		
		(0.03)	(0.04)		
		5.28	8.50		
VERBAB	- -	- -	- -	0.19	
				(0.03)	
				5.41	
QUANTAB	- -	- -	- -	- -	0.27
					(0.04)
					7.20

Squared Multiple Correlations for X - Variables

FAMINC	FAED	MOED	VERBAB	QUANTAB
0.78	0.60	0.48	0.78	0.69

Goodness of Fit Statistics

Degrees of Freedom = 20
Minimum Fit Function Chi-Square = 19.17 (P = 0.51)
Normal Theory Weighted Least Squares Chi-Square = 18.60 (P = 0.55)
Estimated Non-centrality Parameter (NCP) = 0.0
90 Percent Confidence Interval for NCP = (0.0 ; 12.67)

Minimum Fit Function Value = 0.096
Population Discrepancy Function Value (F0) = 0.0
90 Percent Confidence Interval for F0 = (0.0 ; 0.064)
Root Mean Square Error of Approximation (RMSEA) = 0.0
90 Percent Confidence Interval for RMSEA = (0.0 ; 0.056)
P-Value for Test of Close Fit (RMSEA < 0.05) = 0.91

Expected Cross-Validation Index (ECVI) = 0.35
90 Percent Confidence Interval for ECVI = (0.35 ; 0.42)
ECVI for Saturated Model = 0.45
ECVI for Independence Model = 13.72

Chi-Square for Independence Model with 36 Degrees of Freedom = 2712.06
Independence AIC = 2730.06
Model AIC = 68.60
Saturated AIC = 90.00
Independence CAIC = 2768.74
Model CAIC = 176.05
Saturated CAIC = 283.42

Normed Fit Index (NFI) = 0.99
Non-Normed Fit Index (NNFI) = 1.00
Parsimony Normed Fit Index (PNFI) = 0.55
Comparative Fit Index (CFI) = 1.00
Incremental Fit Index (IFI) = 1.00
Relative Fit Index (RFI) = 0.99

Critical N (CN) = 391.00

Root Mean Square Residual (RMR) = 0.015
Standardized RMR = 0.015
Goodness of Fit Index (GFI) = 0.98
Adjusted Goodness of Fit Index (AGFI) = 0.95
Parsimony Goodness of Fit Index (PGFI) = 0.44

Fitted Covariance Matrix

	EDASP	OCASP	VERBACH	QUANTACH	FAMINC	FAED
EDASP	1.02					
OCASP	0.79	1.08				
VERBACH	1.02	0.93	1.84			
QUANTACH	0.77	0.70	1.24	1.29		
FAMINC	0.57	0.53	0.87	0.66	0.85	
FAED	0.45	0.41	0.68	0.51	0.52	0.67
MOED	0.41	0.38	0.63	0.47	0.48	0.54

VERBAB	0.57	0.52	0.91	0.69	0.54	0.42
QUANTAB	0.54	0.49	0.87	0.65	0.51	0.40

Fitted Covariance Matrix

	MOED	VERBAB	QUANTAB
	--------	--------	--------
MOED	0.72		
VERBAB	0.39	0.85	
QUANTAB	0.37	0.63	0.87

Fitted Residuals

	EDASP	OCASP	VERBACH	QUANTACH	FAMINC	FAED
	--------	--------	--------	--------	--------	--------
EDASP	0.00					
OCASP	0.00	0.00				
VERBACH	0.01	-0.01	0.00			
QUANTACH	-0.01	-0.01	0.00	0.00		
FAMINC	-0.01	0.01	0.01	-0.02	0.00	
FAED	0.00	0.01	0.00	0.01	0.00	0.00
MOED	0.02	0.01	0.01	0.03	0.00	0.00
VERBAB	0.01	0.04	-0.02	0.03	0.01	0.00
QUANTAB	-0.05	0.00	0.02	-0.01	0.00	-0.01

Fitted Residuals

	MOED	VERBAB	QUANTAB
	--------	--------	--------
MOED	0.00		
VERBAB	-0.01	0.00	
QUANTAB	-0.03	0.00	0.00

Summary Statistics for Fitted Residuals

Smallest Fitted Residual = -0.05
  Median Fitted Residual = 0.00
 Largest Fitted Residual = 0.04

 Stemleaf Plot

- 4|8
- 3|
- 2|842
- 1|4400
- 0|8865421000000000000000
  0|2469999
  1|1123
  2|0067
  3|
  4|3

Standardized Residuals

	EDASP	OCASP	VERBACH	QUANTACH	FAMINC	FAED
EDASP	- -					
OCASP	- -	- -				
VERBACH	1.26	-1.01	- -			
QUANTACH	-0.52	-0.23	- -	- -		
FAMINC	-0.64	0.45	0.55	-1.17	- -	
FAED	-0.25	0.45	-0.23	0.58	0.15	- -
MOED	0.82	0.30	0.36	0.91	-0.15	- -
VERBAB	0.88	1.93	-2.34	1.50	0.72	0.10
QUANTAB	-2.53	0.16	1.59	-0.38	-0.13	-0.50

Standardized Residuals

	MOED	VERBAB	QUANTAB
MOED	- -		
VERBAB	-0.63	- -	
QUANTAB	-1.10	- -	- -

Summary Statistics for Standardized Residuals

Smallest Standardized Residual = -2.53
 Median Standardized Residual = 0.00
 Largest Standardized Residual = 1.93

Stemleaf Plot

```
- 2|5
- 2|3
- 1|
- 1|210
- 0|6655
- 0|4322210000000000000000
  0|122344
  0|5567899
  1|3
  1|569
```

Modification Indices and Expected Change

Modification Indices for LAMBDA-Y

	aspire	achieve
EDASP	- -	0.30
OCASP	- -	0.30
VERBACH	0.32	- -
QUANTACH	0.32	- -

Expected Change for LAMBDA-Y

	aspire	achieve
EDASP	- -	0.28
OCASP	- -	-0.26
VERBACH	0.12	- -
QUANTACH	-0.09	- -

Standardized Expected Change for LAMBDA-Y

	aspire	achieve
EDASP	- -	0.36
OCASP	- -	-0.33
VERBACH	0.11	- -
QUANTACH	-0.09	- -

Modification Indices for LAMBDA-X

	home	ability
FAMINC	- -	0.40
FAED	- -	0.11
MOED	- -	0.49
VERBAB	0.63	- -
QUANTAB	0.63	- -

Expected Change for LAMBDA-X

	home	ability
FAMINC	- -	0.18
FAED	- -	0.04
MOED	- -	-0.08
VERBAB	0.16	- -
QUANTAB	-0.16	- -

Standardized Expected Change for LAMBDA-X

	home	ability
FAMINC	- -	0.15
FAED	- -	0.03
MOED	- -	-0.06
VERBAB	0.13	- -
QUANTAB	-0.13	- -

No Non-Zero Modification Indices for BETA

No Non-Zero Modification Indices for GAMMA

No Non-Zero Modification Indices for PHI

No Non-Zero Modification Indices for PSI

Modification Indices for THETA-EPS

	EDASP	OCASP	VERBACH	QUANTACH
EDASP	- -			
OCASP	- -	- -		
VERBACH	2.32	1.91	- -	
QUANTACH	0.17	0.01	- -	- -

Expected Change for THETA-EPS

	EDASP	OCASP	VERBACH	QUANTACH
EDASP	- -			
OCASP	- -	- -		
VERBACH	0.05	-0.05	- -	
QUANTACH	-0.01	0.00	- -	- -

Modification Indices for THETA-DELTA-EPS

	EDASP	OCASP	VERBACH	QUANTACH
FAMINC	0.12	0.06	0.86	2.09
FAED	0.62	0.32	0.30	0.15
MOED	1.13	0.40	0.02	0.37
VERBAB	0.51	1.13	8.44	3.03
QUANTAB	4.92	0.30	5.47	0.94

Expected Change for THETA-DELTA-EPS

	EDASP	OCASP	VERBACH	QUANTACH
FAMINC	-0.01	0.01	0.03	-0.04
FAED	-0.01	0.01	-0.01	0.01
MOED	0.02	-0.02	0.00	0.01
VERBAB	0.02	0.03	-0.09	0.05
QUANTAB	-0.06	0.02	0.07	-0.03

Modification Indices for THETA-DELTA

	FAMINC	FAED	MOED	VERBAB	QUANTAB
FAMINC	- -				
FAED	0.02	- -			
MOED	0.02	- -	- -		
VERBAB	0.15	0.14	0.36	- -	
QUANTAB	0.02	0.05	0.59	- -	- -

Expected Change for THETA-DELTA

	FAMINC	FAED	MOED	VERBAB	QUANTAB
FAMINC	- -				
FAED	0.00	- -			
MOED	0.00	- -	- -		
VERBAB	0.01	0.01	-0.01	- -	
QUANTAB	0.00	0.00	-0.02	- -	- -

Maximum Modification Index is 8.44 for Element (4, 3) of
  THETA DELTA-EPSILON

Covariances

   Y - ETA

	EDASP	OCASP	VERBACH	QUANTACH
aspire	0.86	0.79	1.02	0.77
achieve	1.02	0.93	1.65	1.24

   Y - KSI

	EDASP	OCASP	VERBACH	QUANTACH
home	0.57	0.53	0.87	0.66
ability	0.57	0.52	0.91	0.69

   X - ETA

	FAMINC	FAED	MOED	VERBAB	QUANTAB
aspire	0.57	0.45	0.41	0.57	0.54
achieve	0.87	0.68	0.63	0.91	0.87

   X - KSI

	FAMINC	FAED	MOED	VERBAB	QUANTAB
home	0.66	0.52	0.48	0.54	0.51
ability	0.54	0.42	0.39	0.66	0.63

First Order Derivatives

   LAMBDA-Y

	aspire	achieve
EDASP	0.00	-0.01
OCASP	0.00	0.01
VERBACH	-0.01	0.00
QUANTACH	0.02	0.00

```
        LAMBDA-X

                home     ability
              --------  --------
   FAMINC       0.00      -0.01
     FAED       0.00      -0.01
     MOED       0.00       0.03
   VERBAB      -0.02       0.00
  QUANTAB       0.02       0.00

        BETA

               aspire    achieve
              --------  --------
  aspire       0.00       0.00
 achieve       0.00       0.00

        GAMMA

                home     ability
              --------  --------
  aspire       0.00       0.00
 achieve       0.00       0.00

        PHI

                home     ability
              --------  --------
    home       0.00
 ability       0.00       0.00

        PSI

               aspire    achieve
              --------  --------
  aspire       0.00
 achieve       0.00       0.00

        THETA-EPS

               EDASP     OCASP    VERBACH   QUANTACH
              --------  --------  --------  --------
   EDASP       0.00
   OCASP       0.00      0.00
 VERBACH      -0.24      0.21      0.00
QUANTACH       0.07     -0.01      0.00      0.00

        THETA-DELTA-EPS

               EDASP     OCASP    VERBACH   QUANTACH
              --------  --------  --------  --------
  FAMINC       0.07     -0.04     -0.15      0.26
    FAED       0.21     -0.13      0.13     -0.09
    MOED      -0.26      0.13     -0.03     -0.13
  VERBAB      -0.15     -0.20      0.48     -0.32
 QUANTAB       0.44     -0.10     -0.38      0.17
```

THETA-DELTA

	FAMINC	FAED	MOED	VERBAB	QUANTAB
FAMINC	0.00				
FAED	-0.03	0.00			
MOED	0.03	0.00	0.00		
VERBAB	-0.08	-0.10	0.15	0.00	
QUANTAB	-0.03	-0.06	0.18	0.00	0.00

Factor Scores Regressions

ETA

	EDASP	OCASP	VERBACH	QUANTACH	FAMINC	FAED
aspire	0.50	0.21	0.10	0.04	0.04	0.02
achieve	0.12	0.05	0.52	0.22	0.07	0.03

ETA

	MOED	VERBAB	QUANTAB
aspire	0.01	0.02	0.01
achieve	0.01	0.11	0.07

KSI

	EDASP	OCASP	VERBACH	QUANTACH	FAMINC	FAED
home	0.05	0.02	0.07	0.03	0.41	0.19
ability	0.02	0.01	0.11	0.04	0.07	0.03

KSI

	MOED	VERBAB	QUANTAB
home	0.06	0.07	0.04
ability	0.01	0.37	0.24

Standardized Solution

LAMBDA-Y

	aspire	achieve
EDASP	0.93	- -
OCASP	0.85	- -
VERBACH	- -	1.29
QUANTACH	- -	0.97

LAMBDA-X

	home	ability
FAMINC	0.81	- -
FAED	0.64	- -
MOED	0.59	- -
VERBAB	- -	0.81
QUANTAB	- -	0.77

BETA

	aspire	achieve
aspire	- -	- -
achieve	0.38	- -

GAMMA

	home	ability
aspire	0.44	0.39
achieve	0.19	0.43

Correlation Matrix of ETA and KSI

	aspire	achieve	home	ability
aspire	1.00			
achieve	0.85	1.00		
home	0.76	0.83	1.00	
ability	0.75	0.87	0.81	1.00

PSI
Note: This matrix is diagonal.

	aspire	achieve
	0.37	0.14

Regression Matrix ETA on KSI (Standardized)

	home	ability
aspire	0.44	0.39
achieve	0.36	0.58

Total and Indirect Effects

Total Effects of KSI on ETA

	home	ability
aspire	0.51	0.45
	(0.15)	(0.15)
	3.29	2.96

```
achieve        0.57        0.92
              (0.17)      (0.18)
               3.26        5.20
```

Indirect Effects of KSI on ETA

	home	ability
aspire	- -	- -
achieve	0.27	0.23
	(0.10)	(0.09)
	2.63	2.62

Total Effects of ETA on ETA

	aspire	achieve
aspire	- -	- -
achieve	0.53	- -
	(0.12)	
	4.56	

Largest Eigenvalue of B*B' (Stability Index) is 0.276

Total Effects of ETA on Y

	aspire	achieve
EDASP	1.00	- -
OCASP	0.92	- -
	(0.06)	
	14.34	
VERBACH	0.53	1.00
	(0.12)	
	4.56	
QUANTACH	0.40	0.75
	(0.09)	(0.04)
	4.48	18.13

Indirect Effects of ETA on Y

	aspire	achieve
EDASP	- -	- -
OCASP	- -	- -
VERBACH	0.53	- -
	(0.12)	
	4.56	
QUANTACH	0.40	- -
	(0.09)	
	4.48	

Total Effects of KSI on Y

	home	ability
EDASP	0.51	0.45
	(0.15)	(0.15)
	3.29	2.96
OCASP	0.46	0.41
	(0.14)	(0.14)
	3.25	2.93
VERBACH	0.57	0.92
	(0.17)	(0.18)
	3.26	5.20
QUANTACH	0.43	0.69
	(0.13)	(0.14)
	3.23	5.09

Standardized Total and Indirect Effects

Standardized Total Effects of KSI on ETA

	home	ability
aspire	0.44	0.39
achieve	0.36	0.58

Standardized Indirect Effects of KSI on ETA

	home	ability
aspire	- -	- -
achieve	0.17	0.15

Standardized Total Effects of ETA on ETA

	aspire	achieve
aspire	- -	- -
achieve	0.38	- -

Standardized Total Effects of ETA on Y

	aspire	achieve
EDASP	0.93	- -
OCASP	0.85	- -
VERBACH	0.49	1.29
QUANTACH	0.37	0.97

```
           Standardized Indirect Effects of ETA on Y

                   aspire    achieve
                  --------   --------
    EDASP            - -       - -
    OCASP            - -       - -
  VERBACH           0.49       - -
 QUANTACH           0.37       - -

           Standardized Total Effects of KSI on Y

                    home     ability
                  --------   --------
    EDASP           0.41      0.36
    OCASP           0.38      0.33
  VERBACH           0.46      0.75
 QUANTACH           0.35      0.56
```

At this point we leave it up to the reader to extract the factor loadings error variances, structure coefficients, and disturbance terms from the various matrices indicated in the standardized solution. It is also helpful to determine the direct and indirect effects indicated in the model. The model fit indices indicate that the data fit the respecified theoretical model!

15.4 ADVANCED MODELS IN MATRIX NOTATION

This section presents the matrix approach to the multiple-sample model, the structured means model, and two types of interaction models in structural equation modeling. The reader is referred to the previous chapters and references in the book for further detail and explanation of these types of models.

Multiple-Sample Model

The multiple-sample model in LISREL matrix notation for the *measurement* model is written as $Y = \Lambda_y^{(g)} \eta + \varepsilon$ (for the latent dependent indicator variables) and $X = \Lambda_x^{(g)} \xi + \delta$ (for the latent independent indicator variables), where $g = 1$ to G groups and the other terms are as previously defined. The *structural* model can be written as $\eta = B^{(g)} \eta + \Gamma^{(g)} \xi + \zeta$. The four covariance matrices that you are already familiar with are written as $\Phi^{(g)}$, $\Psi^{(g)}$, $\Theta_\varepsilon^{(g)}$, and $\Theta_\delta^{(g)}$. The measurement and structural equations yield parameter estimates for each of the eight matrices for each group, $B^{(g)}$, $\Gamma^{(g)}$, $\Lambda_y^{(g)}$, $\Lambda_x^{(g)}$, $\Phi^{(g)}$, $\Psi^{(g)}$, $\Theta_\varepsilon^{(g)}$, and $\Theta_\delta^{(g)}$.

For instance, with two groups we may be interested in testing whether the factor loadings are equivalent. These hypotheses for the latent dependent variables are written as

$$\Lambda_y^{(1)} = \Lambda_y^{(2)}$$

and for the latent independent variables as

$$\Lambda_x^{(1)} = \Lambda_x^{(2)}.$$

One might also hypothesize that any of the other matrices are equivalent so that

$$\Theta_\varepsilon^{(1)} = \Theta_\varepsilon^{(2)}$$
$$\Theta_\delta^{(1)} = \Theta_\delta^{(2)}$$
$$B^{(1)} = B^{(2)}$$
$$\Gamma^{(1)} = \Gamma^{(2)}$$
$$\Phi^{(1)} = \Phi^{(2)}$$
$$\Psi^{(1)} = \Psi^{(2)}.$$

Thus, the groups can be evaluated to determine which matrices are equivalent and which are different.

Structured Means Model

The structured means model in LISREL matrix notation for the *measurement* model of the latent dependent indicator variables is written as $Y = \tau_y^{(g)} + \Lambda_y^{(g)}\eta + \varepsilon$ and for the latent independent indicator variables written as $X = \tau_x^{(g)} + \Lambda_x^{(g)}\xi + \delta$. We denote τ_y and τ_x as vectors of constant-intercept terms (means) for the indicator variables, and the other terms are as previously defined [Jöreskog and Sörbom (1996) denoted these intercept terms as τ, other publications have used υ instead]. The structural model is now written as $\eta = \alpha^{(g)} + B^{(g)}\eta + \Gamma^{(g)}\xi + \zeta$, where α is a vector of constant-intercept terms (means) for the structural equations and the other terms are as previously defined. In most SEM models the intercept terms are assumed to be zero, so the structured means model is a special application of SEM used in the analysis of variance as well as slope and intercept models. In the structured means model the intercept term is not zero and therefore is estimated.

In addition to the means of indicator variables being estimated, other latent variable means can be estimated. The mean of each latent independent variable ξ is given by κ; for example, κ_1 denotes the mean for ξ_1. The mean of each latent dependent variable is given by $(I-B)^{-1}(\alpha + \Gamma\kappa)$.

In addition to the hypotheses given previously for the simple multiple-sample model, the structured means model can also examine α, the group effects for each structural equation, and κ, the group effects for each latent independent variable. We constrain (set equal) the value for one group to be zero, so we can estimate the difference between that group and a second group, which we refer to as a *group effect*.

In the following LISREL matrix program we hypothesize that academic and nonacademic boys are different in their reading and writing ability in fifth and seventh grades. The first structured means program specifies the number of groups (NG=2), the first group's (academic boys) sample size (NO=373), the number of observed variables (NI=4), the type of matrix, that is, covariance matrix (MA = CM), and the first group's covariance matrix (CM) and means (ME). The second program only has to define the second group's (nonacademic boys) sample size (NO=249) and the second group's covariance matrix (CM) and means (ME). The means are what defines a structured means program. Special features of this program are setting TX = FR (τ matrix of observed variable means) and KA = FI (κ matrix of latent variable means). This LISREL matrix program parallels the LISREL–SIMPLIS program in chapter 13 for the structured means model, that is, adding the LISREL OUTPUT command in the LISREL–SIMPLIS program yields these same matrices and results (Fig. 15.2).

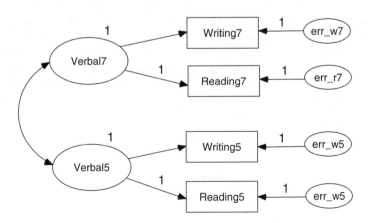

FIG. 15.2.   Structured means model.

The LISREL matrix structured means program is

```
Group: ACADEMIC
DA NI=4 NO=373 MA=CM NG=2
CM SY
281.349
184.219 182.821
216.739 171.699 283.289
198.376 153.201 208.837 246.069
ME
262.236 258.788 275.630 269.075
LA
 R5 W5 R7 W7
MO NX=4 NK=2 TX=FR KA=FI
LK
 V5 V7
FR LX(2,1),LX(4,2)
VA 1 LX(1,1),LX(3,2)
OU ND=2 AD=OFF
Group: NONACADEMIC
DA NI=4 NO=249 MA=CM
CM SY
174.485
134.468 161.869
129.840 118.836 228.449
102.194  97.767 136.058 180.460
ME
248.675 246.896 258.546 253.349
MO LX=IN TX=IN KA=FR TD=FR
LA
 R5 W5 R7 W7
OU
```

The model parameters in the first group for τ are set free (FR) and for κ are fixed (FI), so that the latent variable intercepts for the first group are fixed to 0. The estimate of the latent variable intercept in the second group (nonacademic boys) is therefore evaluated relative to 0 (academic boys intercept). The structural model is represented as $\eta_2 = \alpha_2 + \beta_2 \eta_1 + \zeta_2$ for both groups separately for the null hypothesis H_0: $\alpha_{\text{academic boys}} = \alpha_{\text{nonacademic boys}}$. The edited and condensed structured means program output is

```
Group: ACADEMIC
LISREL Estimates (Maximum Likelihood)
LAMBDA-X EQUALS LAMBDA-X IN THE FOLLOWING GROUP

        PHI

               V5             V7
            --------       --------
     V5      220.06
            (19.17)
              11.48
```

```
V7      212.11      233.59
        (17.66)     (20.50)
         12.01       11.40
```

THETA-DELTA

```
            R5          W5          R7          W7
         --------    --------    --------    --------
           50.15       36.48       51.72       57.78
          (6.02)      (4.28)      (6.62)      (6.05)
            8.34        8.52        7.82        9.55
```

Squared Multiple Correlations for X - Variables

```
            R5          W5          R7          W7
         --------    --------    --------    --------
            0.81        0.81        0.82        0.76
```

TAU-X EQUALS TAU-X IN THE FOLLOWING GROUP

Group Goodness of Fit Statistics

Contribution to Chi-Square = 4.15
Percentage Contribution to Chi-Square = 41.00
Root Mean Square Residual (RMR) = 6.07
Standardized RMR = 0.025
Goodness of Fit Index (GFI) = 0.99

Group: NONACADEMIC

LISREL Estimates (Maximum Likelihood)

LAMBDA-X

```
            KSI 1       KSI 2
         --------    --------
R5          1.00         - -

W5          0.84         - -
           (0.02)
            34.35

R7           - -        1.00

W7           - -        0.89
                       (0.03)
PHI                     31.95
```

```
            KSI 1       KSI 2
         --------    --------
KSI 1     156.34
          (16.19)
            9.66
```

```
KSI 2    126.96      153.73
         (14.22)     (18.03)
            8.93        8.53

     THETA-DELTA

              R5         W5          R7          W7
           --------   --------   --------   --------
             23.25      42.80       65.67       67.36
            (6.23)     (5.64)      (9.87)      (8.74)
              3.73       7.59        6.65        7.71
```

Squared Multiple Correlations for X - Variables

```
              R5         W5          R7          W7
           --------   --------   --------   --------
              0.87       0.72        0.70        0.65

     TAU-X

              R5         W5          R7          W7
           --------   --------   --------   --------
            262.37     258.67      275.71      268.98
            (0.84)     (0.70)      (0.87)      (0.80)
            312.58     366.96      317.77      338.00

   KAPPA

            KSI 1      KSI 2
           --------   --------
            -13.80     -17.31
            (1.18)     (1.24)
           -11.71     -13.99
```

We obtain the latent variable mean differences from the kappa matrix, where the nonacademic boys were below the academic boys in reading and writing at both the fifth grade (KSI 1) and seventh grade (KSI 2). Our model fit indices indicate an acceptable theoretical model:

```
              Global Goodness of Fit Statistics

                  Degrees of Freedom = 6
        Minimum Fit Function Chi-Square = 10.11 (P = 0.12)
Normal Theory Weighted Least Squares Chi-Square = 9.96 (P = 0.13)
           Estimated Non-centrality Parameter (NCP) = 3.96
        90 Percent Confidence Interval for NCP = (0.0 ; 16.79)

              Minimum Fit Function Value = 0.016
        Population Discrepancy Function Value (F0) = 0.0064
        90 Percent Confidence Interval for F0 = (0.0 ; 0.027)
      Root Mean Square Error of Approximation (RMSEA) = 0.046
```

```
90 Percent Confidence Interval for RMSEA = (0.0 ; 0.095)
    P-Value for Test of Close Fit (RMSEA < 0.05) = 0.27

    Expected Cross-Validation Index (ECVI) = 0.087
90 Percent Confidence Interval for ECVI = (0.068 ; 0.095)
            ECVI for Saturated Model = 0.032
          ECVI for Independence Model = 3.15
```

```
Chi-Square for Independence Model with 12 Degrees of Freedom = 1947.85
                Independence AIC = 1963.85
                    Model AIC = 53.96
                  Saturated AIC = 40.00
                Independence CAIC = 2007.31
                   Model CAIC = 173.48
                 Saturated CAIC = 148.66
```

```
              Normed Fit Index (NFI) = 0.99
          Non-Normed Fit Index (NNFI) = 1.00
     Parsimony Normed Fit Index (PNFI) = 0.50
          Comparative Fit Index (CFI) = 1.00
          Incremental Fit Index (IFI) = 1.00
             Relative Fit Index (RFI) = 0.99
```

```
                Critical N (CN) = 1031.60

          Group Goodness of Fit Statistics

          Contribution to Chi-Square = 5.97
   Percentage Contribution to Chi-Square = 59.00

        Root Mean Square Residual (RMR) = 7.69
              Standardized RMR = 0.042
          Goodness of Fit Index (GFI) = 0.99
```

Interaction Models

In chapter 14 we discussed four different types of interaction models: categorical, nonlinear, continuous observed variable, and latent variable (Schumacker & Marcoulides, 1998). In this chapter we present the LISREL matrix program using latent variables that parallels the interaction latent variable approach in chapter 14 using LISREL–SIMPLIS, except for slight differences in the standard errors. The matrix approach to latent variable interactions requires the understanding and use of nonlinear constraints, which has made it difficult for most applied researchers (Jöreskog & Yang, 1996).

The latent variable interaction approach in LISREL matrix notation for Fig. 15.3 is $\eta_1 = \gamma_1\xi_1 + \gamma_2\xi_2 + \gamma_3\xi_3 + \zeta_1$, where η_1 is the latent dependent variable, ξ_1 and ξ_2 are the main-effect latent independent variables, ξ_3 is

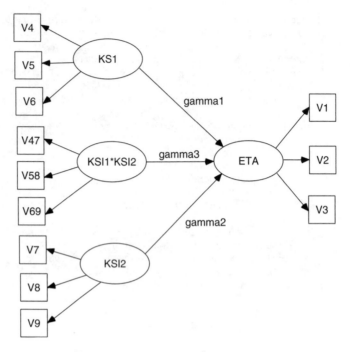

FIG. 15.3. Latent variable interaction (continuous variable approach).

the interaction effect formed by multiplying ξ_1 and ξ_2, γ_1 and γ_2 are the structure coefficients for the main-effect latent independent variables, γ_3 is the structure coefficient for the interaction-effect latent independent variable, and ζ_1 is the error term in the structural equation. Notice that the relationship between η_1 and ξ_3 is itself linear. The structure of the interaction model emerges as a logical extension of the measurement model for ξ_1 and ξ_2. The basic measurement model is $X = \Lambda \xi + \delta$, where X is a vector of observed variables, Λ is a matrix of factor loadings, and δ is a vector of measurement error terms. The covariance matrices of these common and unique factors are Φ and Θ_δ, respectively.

Kenny and Judd (1984) used simple algebraic substitution to develop their model of multiplicative interaction effects (Hayduk, 1987). Basically, given two latent independent variables, the models are $X_1 = \lambda_1 \xi_1 + \delta_1$ and $X_2 = \lambda_2 \xi_2 + \delta_2$. The interaction effect or product is $X_3 = X_1 X_2$, indicated in the model as $X_3 = \lambda_1 \lambda_2 \xi_1 \xi_2 + \lambda_1 \xi_1 \delta_2 + \lambda_2 \xi_2 \delta_1 + \delta_1 \delta_2$, or $X_3 = \lambda_3 \xi_3 + \lambda_1 \xi_4 + \lambda_2 \xi_5 + \delta_3$, where $\xi_3 = \xi_1 \xi_2$, $\xi_4 = \xi_1 \delta_2$, $\xi_5 = \xi_2 \delta_1$, $\delta_3 = \delta_1 \delta_2$, and $\lambda_3 = \lambda_1 \lambda_2$. All of these new latent variables are mutually uncorrelated and uncorrelated with all other latent variables in the model.

In order to incorporate this interaction effect into the structural equation model, we need to specify X_3 as a function of latent variables whose variances and covariances reflect these relationships. This involves specifying some model parameters as nonlinear functions of other parameters. In the LISREL program, these types of nonlinear constraints are indicated by using the VA (value), EQ (equality), and CO (constraint) commands. For example, the Kenny–Judd interaction model implies that $\sigma^2(\xi_3) = \sigma^2(\xi_1)\sigma^2(\xi_2) + \sigma(\xi_1\xi_2)^2$. This relationship using the CO command line is specified as CO PH(3,3) = PH(1,1) * PH(2,2) + PH(2,1) * * 2. Similarly, their model implies that $\sigma^2(\xi_4) = \sigma^2(\xi_1)\sigma^2(\delta_1)$, and this relationship is specified as CO PH(4,4) = PH(1,1) * TD(2,2).

We demonstrate the Kenny and Judd (1984) approach by creating a simulated data set of nine multivariate normal variables and three product indicant variables for 500 participants using a PRELIS program (*mvdata1.pr2*):

```
Generate multivariate normal variables - LISREL
DA NO=500
NE X1=NRAND; NE X2=NRAND; NE X3=NRAND
NE X4=NRAND; NE X5=NRAND; NE X6=NRAND
NE X7=NRAND; NE X8=NRAND; NE X9=NRAND
NE V1=X1
NE V2=.378*X1+.925*X2
NE V3=.320*X1+.603*X2+.890*X3
NE V4=.204*X1+.034*X2+.105*X3+.904*X4
NE V5=.076*X1+.113*X2+.203*X3+.890*X4+.925*X5
NE V6=.111*X1+.312*X2+.125*X3+.706*X4+.865*X5+.905*X6
NE V7=.310*X1+.124*X2+.310*X3+.222*X4+.126*X5+.555*X6+.897*X7
NE V8=.222*X1+.111*X2+.412*X3+.312*X4+.212*X5+.312*X6+.789*X7+.899*X8
NE V9=.321*X1+.214*X2+.124*X3+.122*X4+.234*X5+.212*X6+.690*X7+.789*X8+.907*X9
NE V47=V4*V7
NE V58=V5*V8
NE V69=V6*V9
CO ALL
SD X1-X9
OU MA=CM CM=INTERACT.CM ME=INTERACT.ME RA=INTERACT.PSF XM IX=784123
```

Although the nine observed variables were created as multivariate normal data, the product indicant variables are typically not multivariate normal. The summary statistics do indicate that the nine observed variables are univariate normal, but that the three product indicant variables have skewness and kurtosis, that is, are nonnormal (boldfaced). In LISREL, maximum likelihood estimation (ML) is the default, and appears to work well under mild violations of multivariate normality in the interaction latent variable model. We used the same random number seed as before so the data could be reproduced (IX = 784123).

PRELIS Computer Output

Univariate Summary Statistics for Continuous Variables

Variable	Mean	St. Dev.	T-Value	Skewness	Kurtosis
V1	-0.061	0.976	-1.394	0.191	0.048
V2	0.007	1.071	0.142	-0.047	0.280
V3	-0.018	1.105	-0.368	0.175	0.441
V4	-0.015	0.956	-0.359	-0.200	-0.158
V5	-0.013	1.351	-0.209	-0.003	0.168
V6	0.011	1.543	0.163	0.171	0.528
V7	-0.065	1.192	-1.222	-0.081	-0.350
V8	-0.041	1.491	-0.615	0.127	0.092
V9	0.005	1.595	0.075	0.058	0.514
V47	0.325	1.143	6.356	**0.958**	**3.861**
V58	0.670	2.179	6.877	**1.916**	**8.938**
V69	0.584	2.754	4.745	**2.304**	**15.266**

Test of Univariate Normality for Continuous Variables

	Skewness		Kurtosis		Skewness and Kurtosis	
Variable	Z-Score	P-Value	Z-Score	P-Value	Chi-Square	P-Value
V1	1.749	0.080	0.321	0.748	3.163	0.206
V2	-0.432	0.666	1.256	0.209	1.764	0.414
V3	1.608	0.108	1.811	0.070	5.866	0.053
V4	-1.833	0.067	-0.695	0.487	3.844	0.146
V5	-0.031	0.975	0.829	0.407	0.688	0.709
V6	1.571	0.116	2.082	0.037	6.802	0.033
V7	-0.746	0.456	-1.865	0.062	4.034	0.133
V8	1.165	0.244	0.513	0.608	1.620	0.445
V9	0.531	0.595	2.039	0.041	4.438	0.109
V47	7.573	0.000	7.085	0.000	**107.539**	**0.000**
V58	12.103	0.000	9.622	0.000	**239.070**	**0.000**
V69	13.428	0.000	11.101	0.000	**303.539**	**0.000**

The PRELIS program saves three files, a covariance matrix (*interact.cm*), means (*interact.me*), and a PRELIS system file (*interact.psf*). The LISREL program inputs the files with the covariance matrix and means.

The LISREL program to run the data for the model in Fig. 15.3 is

```
Fitting Model to Mean Vector and Covariance Matrix
DA NI=12 NO=500 !The three interaction variables are added prior to program
analysis
LA
V1 V2 V3 V4 V5 V6 V7 V8 V9 V47 V58 V69
```

```
CM=interact.CM
ME=interact.ME
MO NY=3 NX=9 NE=1 NK=3 TD=SY TY=FR TX=FR KA=FR
FR LY(2) LY(3) GA(1) GA(2) GA(3) LX(2,1) LX(3,1) LX(5,2) LX(6,2)
   PH(1,1)-PH(2,2)
FI PH(3,1) PH(3,2)
VA 1 LY(1) LX(1,1) LX(4,2) LX(7,3) !Should be same as SIMPLIS program for
   comparison
FI KA(1) KA(2)
CO LX(7,1)=TX(4)
CO LX(7,2)=TX(1)
CO LX(8,1)=TX(5)*LX(2,1)
CO LX(8,2)=TX(2)*LX(5,2)
CO LX(8,3)=LX(2,1)*LX(5,2)
CO LX(9,1)=TX(6)*LX(3,1)
CO LX(9,2)=TX(3)*LX(6,2)
CO LX(9,3)=LX(3,1)*LX(6,2)
CO PH(3,3)=PH(1,1)*PH(2,2)+PH(2,1)**2
CO TD(7,1)=TX(4)*TD(1,1)
CO TD(7,4)=TX(1)*TD(4,4)
CO TD(7,7)=TX(1)**2*TD(4,4)+TX(4)**2*TD(1,1)+PH(1,1)*TD(4,4)+  C
   PH(2,2)*TD(1,1)+TD(1,1)*TD(4,4)
CO TD(8,2)=TX(5)*TD(2,2)
CO TD(8,5)=TX(2)*TD(5,5)
CO TD(8,8)=TX(2)**2*TD(5,5)+TX(5)**2*TD(2,2)+LX(2,1)**2*PH(1,1)*TD(5,5)+  C
   LX(5,2)**2*PH(2,2)*TD(2,2)+TD(2,2)*TD(5,5)
CO TD(9,3)=TX(6)*TD(3,3)
CO TD(9,6)=TX(3)*TD(6,6)
CO TD(9,9)=TX(3)**2*TD(4,4)+TX(6)**2*TD(3,3)+LX(3,1)**2*PH(1,1)*TD(6,6)+  C
   LX(6,2)**2*PH(2,2)*TD(3,3)+TD(3,3)*TD(6,6)
CO KA(3)=PH(2,1)
CO TX(7)=TX(1)*TX(4)
CO TX(8)=TX(2)*TX(5)
CO TX(9)=TX(3)*TX(6)
OU AD=OFF IT=500 EP=0.001 IM=3 ND=3
```

The **CO** command (placing proper constraints in the model) is what becomes difficult to navigate in creating the matrix programs for latent variable interaction models. Discussions of different latent variable interaction models and related issues can be found in Marcoulides and Schumacker (1996, 2001) and Schumacker and Marcoulides (1998).

Given the LISREL matrix program with a latent variable interaction term, several matrices need to be specified. The structural equation with the two main-effect latent variables and the interaction-effect latent variable is

$$\eta = \alpha + \gamma_1 \xi_1 + \gamma_2 \xi_2 + \gamma_3 \xi_1 \xi_2 + \zeta.$$

The measurement model with y observed variables is defined as

$$y = T_y + \Lambda_y \eta + \varepsilon.$$

The matrices for the y-observed-variable measurement model are specified as

$$\begin{bmatrix} y_1 \\ y_2 \\ y_3 \end{bmatrix} = \begin{bmatrix} \tau_1^{(y)} \\ \tau_2^{(y)} \\ \tau_3^{(y)} \end{bmatrix} + \begin{bmatrix} 1 \\ \lambda_2^{(y)} \\ \lambda_3^{(y)} \end{bmatrix} \eta + \begin{bmatrix} \varepsilon_1 \\ \varepsilon_2 \\ \varepsilon_3 \end{bmatrix}$$

with the theta epsilon error matrix specified as:

$$\Theta_\varepsilon = \mathrm{diag}(\theta_1^\varepsilon, \theta_2^\varepsilon, \theta_3^\varepsilon).$$

The measurement model for the x observed variables, which includes both main effects and the interaction effect, is defined as

$$x = T_x + \Lambda_x \xi + \delta.$$

The matrices for the x-observed-variable measurement model are specified as

$$\begin{bmatrix} x_1 \\ x_2 \\ x_3 \\ x_4 \\ x_5 \\ x_6 \\ x_1 x_4 \\ x_2 x_5 \\ x_3 x_6 \end{bmatrix} = \begin{bmatrix} \tau_1 \\ \tau_2 \\ \tau_3 \\ \tau_4 \\ \tau_5 \\ \tau_6 \\ \tau_1 \tau_4 \\ \tau_2 \tau_5 \\ \tau_3 \tau_6 \end{bmatrix} + \begin{bmatrix} 1 & 0 & 0 \\ \lambda_2 & 0 & 0 \\ \lambda_3 & 0 & 0 \\ 0 & 1 & 0 \\ 0 & \lambda_5 & 0 \\ 0 & \lambda_6 & 0 \\ \tau_4 & \tau_1 & 1 \\ \tau_5 \lambda_2 & \tau_2 \lambda_5 & \lambda_2 \lambda_5 \\ \tau_3 \lambda_3 & \tau_3 \lambda_6 & \lambda_3 \lambda_6 \end{bmatrix} \begin{bmatrix} \xi_1 \\ \xi_2 \\ \xi_1 \xi_2 \end{bmatrix} + \begin{bmatrix} \delta_1 \\ \delta_2 \\ \delta_3 \\ \delta_4 \\ \delta_5 \\ \delta_6 \\ \delta_7 \\ \delta_8 \\ \delta_9 \end{bmatrix}$$

with errors in the theta delta matrix Θ_δ denoted as

$$
\begin{bmatrix}
\theta_1 \\
0 & \theta_2 \\
0 & 0 & \theta_3 \\
0 & 0 & 0 & \theta_4 \\
0 & 0 & 0 & 0 & \theta_5 \\
0 & 0 & 0 & 0 & 0 & \theta_6 \\
\tau_4\theta_1 & 0 & 0 & \tau_1\theta_4 & 0 & 0 & \theta_7 \\
0 & \tau_5\theta_2 & 0 & 0 & \tau_2\theta_5 & 0 & 0 & \theta_8 \\
0 & 0 & \tau_6\theta_3 & 0 & 0 & \tau_3\theta_6 & 0 & 0 & \theta_9
\end{bmatrix}.
$$

The theta delta values for the observed interaction variables are calculated as

$$
\begin{aligned}
\theta_7 &= \tau_4^2\theta_1 + \tau_1^2\theta_4 + \phi_{11}\theta_4 + \phi_{22}\theta_1 + \theta_1\theta_4 \\
\theta_8 &= \tau_5^2\theta_2 + \tau_2^2\theta_5 + \lambda_2^2\phi_{11}\theta_5 + \lambda_5^2\phi_{22}\theta_2 + \theta_2\theta_5 \\
\theta_9 &= \tau_6^2\theta_3 + \tau_3^2\theta_6 + \lambda_3^2\phi_{11}\theta_6 + \lambda_6^2\phi_{22}\theta_3 + \theta_3\theta_6.
\end{aligned}
$$

The mean vector implied by the interaction of the exogenous latent variables is defined in the following kappa mean vector matrix:

$$
\kappa =
\begin{bmatrix}
0 \\
0 \\
\phi_{21}
\end{bmatrix}
$$

with the variance–covariance of the latent independent variables (ksi1 and ksi2) defined as

$$
\Phi =
\begin{bmatrix}
\phi_{11} \\
\phi_{21} & \phi_{22} \\
0 & 0 & \phi_{11}\phi_{22} + \phi_{21}^2
\end{bmatrix}.
$$

We can now look for these matrices and their associated values in the LISREL computer output.

LISREL Computer Output

The gamma matrix contains the three structure coefficients of interest for the two main-effect latent variables $[\gamma_1 = .077(.030)$, $t = 2.60$; and $\gamma_2 = .155(.029), t = 5.378]$ and the interaction latent variable $[\gamma_3 = -.029(.029), t = -1.004]$. The gamma coefficient for the latent variable interaction effect is nonsignificant $(t = -1.004)$. We should respecify our theoretical model and test main effects only! The edited and condensed LISREL computer output is

```
LISREL Estimates (Maximum Likelihood)

     LAMBDA-Y

           ETA 1
          --------
  V1       1.000

  V2       2.080
          (0.257)
           8.097

  V3       2.532
          (0.325)
           7.788

     LAMBDA-X

           KSI 1      KSI 2      KSI 3
          --------   --------   --------
  V4       1.000       - -        - -

  V5       1.981       - -        - -
          (0.091)
          21.732

  V6       1.925       - -        - -
          (0.090)
          21.368

  V7        - -       1.000       - -

  V8        - -       1.658       - -
                     (0.072)
                     22.874

  V9        - -       1.493       - -
                     (0.069)
                     21.741
```

```
    V47      -0.070     0.013     1.000
            (0.035)   (0.028)
            -2.027     0.471


    V58      -0.094    -0.010     3.285
            (0.083)   (0.062)   (0.173)
            -1.142    -0.153    18.960


    V69       0.020    -0.049     2.875
            (0.090)   (0.067)   (0.152)
             0.226    -0.729    18.940
```

    GAMMA

```
              KSI 1     KSI 2     KSI 3
            --------  --------  --------
    ETA 1 1 0.077     0.155    -0.029
            (0.030)   (0.029)   (0.029)
             2.602     5.378    -1.004
```

            Covariance Matrix of ETA and KSI

```
              ETA 1     KSI 1     KSI 2     KSI 3
            --------  --------  --------  --------
    ETA 1     0.150
    KSI 1     0.068     0.463
    KSI 2     0.137     0.211     0.784
    KSI 3    -0.012      - -       - -      0.408
```

            Mean Vector of Eta-Variables

```
              ETA 1
            --------
             -0.006
```

    PHI

```
              KSI 1     KSI 2     KSI 3
            --------  --------  --------
    KSI 1     0.463
            (0.043)
            10.729


    KSI 2     0.211     0.784
            (0.021)   (0.069)
            10.236    11.283


    KSI 3      - -       - -      0.408
                                 (0.041)
    PSI                           9.953
```

```
        ETA 1
        --------
         0.123
        (0.029)
         4.193
```

Squared Multiple Correlations for Structural Equations

```
        ETA 1
        --------
         0.179
```

THETA-EPS

```
          V1        V2        V3
        --------  --------  --------
         0.804     0.502     0.267
        (0.053)   (0.058)   (0.074)
        15.166     8.618     3.617
```

Squared Multiple Correlations for Y - Variables

```
          V1        V2        V3
        --------  --------  --------
         0.157     0.563     0.782
```

THETA-DELTA

```
          V4        V5        V6        V7        V8        V9
        --------  --------  --------  --------  --------  --------
V4       0.458
        (0.029)
        16.044

V5        - -      0.045
                  (0.049)
                   0.931

V6        - -       - -      0.796
                            (0.065)
                            12.238

V7        - -       - -       - -      0.647
                                      (0.043)
                                      15.186

V8        - -       - -       - -       - -      0.105
                                                (0.057)
                                                 1.840
```

V9	- -	- -	- -	- -	- -	0.936 (0.070) 13.342
V47	-0.032 (0.016) -2.011	- -	- -	0.009 (0.018) 0.471	- -	- -
V58	- -	-0.002 (0.003) -0.722	- -	- -	-0.001 (0.004) -0.152	- -
V69	- -	- -	0.008 (0.037) 0.226	- -	- -	-0.031 (0.042) -0.728

THETA-DELTA

	V47	V58	V69
V47	0.957 (0.047) 20.519		
V58	- -	0.293 (0.138) 2.129	
V69	- -	- -	3.745 (0.200) 18.698

Squared Multiple Correlations for X - Variables

V4	V5	V6	V7	V8	V9
0.503	0.976	0.683	0.548	0.954	0.651

Squared Multiple Correlations for X - Variables

V47	V58	V69
0.300	0.938	0.474

TAU-Y

V1	V2	V3
-0.055 (0.044) -1.263	0.019 (0.048) 0.386	-0.004 (0.050) -0.079

TAU-X

V4	V5	V6	V7	V8	V9
0.013	-0.006	-0.033	-0.070	-0.048	0.011
(0.028)	(0.038)	(0.045)	(0.035)	(0.042)	(0.047)
0.471	-0.153	-0.729	-2.027	-1.144	0.226

TAU-X

V47	V58	V69
-0.001	0.000	0.000
(0.002)	(0.002)	(0.002)
-0.456	0.151	-0.215

KAPPA

KSI 1	KSI 2	KSI 3
- -	- -	0.211
		(0.021)
		10.236

Goodness of Fit Statistics

Degrees of Freedom = 59
Minimum Fit Function Chi-Square = 403.462 (P = 0.0)
Normal Theory Weighted Least Squares Chi-Square = 365.186 (P = 0.0)
Estimated Non-centrality Parameter (NCP) = 306.186
90 Percent Confidence Interval for NCP = (249.618 ; 370.256)

Minimum Fit Function Value = 0.809
Population Discrepancy Function Value (F0) = 0.614
90 Percent Confidence Interval for F0 = (0.500 ; 0.742)
Root Mean Square Error of Approximation (RMSEA) = 0.102
90 Percent Confidence Interval for RMSEA = (0.0921 ; 0.112)
P-Value for Test of Close Fit (RMSEA < 0.05) = 0.000

Expected Cross-Validation Index (ECVI) = 0.944
90 Percent Confidence Interval for ECVI = (0.763 ; 1.005)
ECVI for Saturated Model = 0.313
ECVI for Independence Model = 6.300

Chi-Square for Independence Model with 66 Degrees of Freedom = 3119.580
Independence AIC = 3143.580
Model AIC = 471.186
Saturated AIC = 156.000
Independence CAIC = 3206.156
Model CAIC = 747.560
Saturated CAIC = 562.739

```
      Normed Fit Index (NFI) = 0.871
  Non-Normed Fit Index (NNFI) = 0.874
Parsimony Normed Fit Index (PNFI) = 0.778
  Comparative Fit Index (CFI) = 0.887
  Incremental Fit Index (IFI) = 0.887
     Relative Fit Index (RFI) = 0.855

         Critical N (CN) = 108.807


  Root Mean Square Residual (RMR) = 0.142
        Standardized RMR = 0.0636
     Goodness of Fit Index (GFI) = 0.893
  Adjusted Goodness of Fit Index (AGFI) = 0.859
  Parsimony Goodness of Fit Index (PGFI) = 0.676
```

15.5 SUMMARY

This chapter presented the eight basic matrices used in structural equation modeling plus two new matrices, the tau and kappa matrices. We also discussed that for any structural equation model, parameters in these matrices must be free, fixed, or constrained for model identification, model estimation, and model testing. We presented the matrix notation by providing four SEM models: our theoretical model in chapter 10, a multiple-sample model, a structured means model, and an interaction model. We presented these same models in earlier chapters using LISREL–SIMPLIS, and presented them in matrix form in this chapter for comparative purposes. We firmly believe that once you master the matrix notation, you will better understand structural equation modeling.

EXERCISES

The National Science Foundation (NSF) is encouraging students to seek academic degrees and careers in science, mathematics, and engineering in the United States. Research has shown a gender difference in science, mathematics, and engineering participation. A key area of study is to investigate what factors influence these gender differences. A latent variable model is hypothesized to investigate factors that influence gender differences because previous research indicated multiple variables as characteristics of students in science, mathematics, and engineering.

A structural equation model with two exogenous variables measured by six observed variables is hypothesized to predict two endogeneous variables measured by five observed variables. The first independent latent variable, ξ_1 = Family Background, is measured by three variables: x_1 = family income, x_2 = father's education, and x_3 = mother's education. The other independent latent variable, ξ_2 = Encouragement, is identified by three variables: x_4 = personal encouragement, x_5 = institutional characteristics, and x_6 = admission status. Students' characteristics, η_1 = Students' Characteristics, is measured by three variables: y_1 = cognitive abilities, y_2 = interpersonal skills, and y_3 = motivation. The other endogenous variable, η_2 = aspirations, is measured by two variables: y_4 = occupational aspiration and y_5 = educational aspiration.

The hypothesized structural equation model represents a two-step approach: measurement model (confirmatory factor analysis) and latent variable structural model. The measurement model depicts the relationship for latent variables: ξ_1 = Family Background, ξ_2 = Encouragement, η_1 = Students' Characteristics, and η_2 = Aspirations. The structural equation model is

$$\text{Students' Characteristics} = \text{Family Background} + \text{Encouragement} + \text{Aspirations} + \text{error}$$

$$\text{Aspirations} = \text{Family Background} + \text{Encouragement} + \text{error}.$$

With this information, you should be able to do the following:

1. Diagram the structural equation model.
2. Write the measurement equations using the variable names.
3. Write the measurement equations using LISREL matrix notation.
4. Write the structural equations using the variable names.
5. Write the structural equations using LISREL matrix notation.
6. Create the matrices for the measurement model.
7. Create the matrices for the structural model.

REFERENCES

Hayduk, L. A. (1987). *Structural equation modeling with LISREL: Essentials and advances.* Baltimore: Johns Hopkins University Press.

Jöreskog, K. G., & Sörbom, D. (1996). *LISREL8 user's reference guide.* Chicago: Scientific Software International.

Jöreskog, K. G., & Yang, F. (1996). Non-linear structural equation models: The Kenny–Judd model with interaction effects. In G. A. Marcoulides & R. E. Schumacker (Eds.), *Advanced structural equation modeling: Issues and techniques* (pp. 57–88), Mahwah, NJ: Lawrence Erlbaum Associates, Inc.

Kenny, D. A., & Judd, C. M. (1984). Estimating the non-linear and interactive effects of latent variables. *Psychological Bulletin, 96,* 201–210.

Marcoulides, G., & Schumacker, R. E. (Eds.). (1996). *Advanced structural equation modeling: Issues and techniques.* Mahwah, NJ: Lawrence Erlbaum Associates, Inc.

Marcoulides, G., & Schumacker, R. E. (Eds.). (2001). *New developments and techniques in structural equation modeling.* Mahwah, NJ: Lawrence Erlbaum Associates, Inc.

Schumacker, R. E., & Marcoulides, G. A. (1998). *Interaction and nonlinear effects in structural equation modeling.* Mahwah, NJ: Lawrence Erlbaum Associates, Inc.

ANSWERS TO EXERCISES

1. The diagrammed structural model is shown as Fig. 15.4.
2. The measurement equations are as follows.

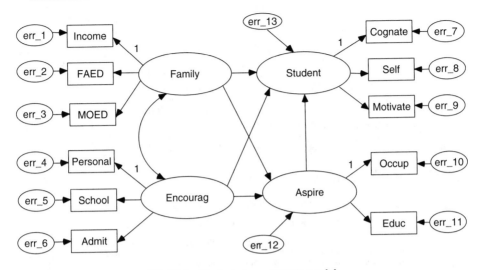

FIG. 15.4. Student characteristic model.

For the *x* variables using variable names

$$
\begin{aligned}
\text{family income} &= \text{function of Family Background} + \text{error} \\
\text{father's education} &= \text{function of Family Background} + \text{error} \\
\text{mother's education} &= \text{function of Family Background} + \text{error} \\[6pt]
\text{personal encouragement} &= \text{function of Encouragement} + \text{error} \\
\text{institutional characteristics} &= \text{function of Encouragement} + \text{error} \\
\text{admission status} &= \text{function of Encouragement} + \text{error.}
\end{aligned}
$$

The measurement equations for the *x*'s are

$$
\begin{aligned}
x_1 &= 1.0\xi_1 + \delta_1 \\
x_2 &= \lambda_{x_{21}}\xi_1 + \delta_2 \\
x_3 &= \lambda_{x_{31}}\xi_1 + \delta_3 \\[6pt]
x_4 &= 1.0\xi_2 + \delta_4 \\
x_5 &= \lambda_{x_{52}}\xi_2 + \delta_5 \\
x_6 &= \lambda_{x_{62}}\xi_2 + \delta_6.
\end{aligned}
$$

The matrix equations for the x's are

$$
\begin{bmatrix} x_1 \\ x_2 \\ x_3 \\ x_4 \\ x_5 \\ x_6 \end{bmatrix} = \begin{bmatrix} 1 & 0 \\ \lambda_{x_{21}} & 0 \\ \lambda_{x_{31}} & 0 \\ 0 & 1 \\ 0 & \lambda_{x_{52}} \\ 0 & \lambda_{x_{62}} \end{bmatrix} \begin{bmatrix} \xi_1 \\ \xi_2 \end{bmatrix} + \begin{bmatrix} \delta_1 \\ \delta_2 \\ \delta_3 \\ \delta_4 \\ \delta_5 \\ \delta_6 \end{bmatrix}.
$$

For the y variables using variable names

$$
\begin{aligned}
\text{cognitive abilities} &= \text{function of Student Characteristics} + \text{error} \\
\text{interpersonal skills} &= \text{function of Student Characteristics} + \text{error} \\
\text{motivation} &= \text{function of Student Characteristics} + \text{error} \\
\text{occupational aspirations} &= \text{function of Aspiration} + \text{error} \\
\text{educational aspirations} &= \text{function of Aspiration} + \text{error}.
\end{aligned}
$$

The measurement equations for the y's are

$$
\begin{aligned}
y_1 &= 1.0\eta_1 + \varepsilon_1 \\
y_2 &= \lambda_{y_{21}}\eta_1 + \varepsilon_2 \\
y_3 &= \lambda_{y_{31}}\eta_1 + \varepsilon_3 \\
y_4 &= 1.0\eta_2 + \varepsilon_4 \\
y_5 &= \lambda_{y_{52}}\eta_2 + \varepsilon_5.
\end{aligned}
$$

The matrix equations for the y's are

$$
\begin{bmatrix} y_1 \\ y_2 \\ y_3 \\ y_4 \\ y_5 \end{bmatrix} = \begin{bmatrix} 1 & 0 \\ \lambda_{y_{21}} & 0 \\ \lambda_{y_{31}} & 0 \\ 0 & 1 \\ 0 & \lambda_{y_{52}} \end{bmatrix} \begin{bmatrix} \eta_1 \\ \eta_2 \end{bmatrix} + \begin{bmatrix} \varepsilon_1 \\ \varepsilon_2 \\ \varepsilon_3 \\ \varepsilon_4 \\ \varepsilon_5 \end{bmatrix}.
$$

The structural equation using variable names are

$$
\begin{aligned}
\text{Students' Characteristics} &= \text{Family Background} + \text{Encouragement} \\
&\quad + \text{Aspirations} + \text{error} \\
\text{Aspirations} &= \text{Family Background} + \text{Encouragement} \\
&\quad + \text{error}.
\end{aligned}
$$

In matrix notation, the two structural equations are

$$\eta_1 = \beta_{12}\eta_2 + \gamma_{11}\xi_1 + \gamma_{12}\xi_2 + \zeta_1$$
$$\eta_2 = \gamma_{21}\xi_1 + \gamma_{22}\xi_2 + \zeta_2.$$

In matrix form, the structural equations are

$$\begin{bmatrix} \eta_1 \\ \eta_2 \end{bmatrix} = \begin{bmatrix} 0 & \beta_{12} \\ 0 & 0 \end{bmatrix} \begin{bmatrix} \eta_1 \\ \eta_2 \end{bmatrix} + \begin{bmatrix} \gamma_{11} & \gamma_{12} \\ \gamma_{21} & \gamma_{22} \end{bmatrix} \begin{bmatrix} \xi_1 \\ \xi_2 \end{bmatrix} + \begin{bmatrix} \zeta_1 \\ \zeta_2 \end{bmatrix}.$$

The matrix of the structural coefficients for the endogenous variables is

$$B = \begin{bmatrix} 0 & \beta_{12} \\ 0 & 0 \end{bmatrix}.$$

The matrix of the structural coefficients for the exogenous variables is

$$\Gamma = \begin{bmatrix} \gamma_{11} & \gamma_{12} \\ \gamma_{21} & \gamma_{22} \end{bmatrix}.$$

The matrix of the factor loadings for the endogenous variables is

$$\Lambda_y = \begin{bmatrix} 1 & 0 \\ \lambda_{y21} & 0 \\ \lambda_{y31} & 0 \\ 0 & 1 \\ 0 & \lambda_{y52} \end{bmatrix}.$$

The matrix of the factor loadings for the exogenous variables is

$$\Lambda_x = \begin{bmatrix} 1 & 0 \\ \lambda_{x21} & 0 \\ \lambda_{x31} & 0 \\ 0 & 1 \\ 0 & \lambda_{x52} \\ 0 & \lambda_{x62} \end{bmatrix}.$$

The covariance matrix for the exogenous latent variables is

$$\Phi = \begin{bmatrix} \Phi_{11} & \\ \Phi_{21} & \Phi_{22} \end{bmatrix}.$$

The covariance matrix for the equation error is

$$\Psi = \begin{bmatrix} \psi_{11} & \\ 0 & \psi_{22} \end{bmatrix}.$$

The covariance matrix for the measurement errors of the indicators of the exogenous latent variables is

$$
\Theta_\delta = \begin{bmatrix}
\delta_{11} & & & & & \\
0 & \delta_{22} & & & & \\
0 & 0 & \delta_{33} & & & \\
0 & 0 & 0 & \delta_{44} & & \\
0 & 0 & 0 & 0 & \delta_{55} & \\
0 & 0 & 0 & 0 & 0 & \delta_{66}
\end{bmatrix}.
$$

The covariance matrix for the measurement errors of the indicators of the endogenous latent variables is

$$
\Theta_\varepsilon = \begin{bmatrix}
\varepsilon_{11} & & & & \\
0 & \varepsilon_{22} & & & \\
0 & 0 & \varepsilon_{33} & & \\
0 & 0 & 0 & \varepsilon_{44} & \\
0 & 0 & 0 & 0 & \varepsilon_{55}
\end{bmatrix}.
$$

The structural equation model can be interpreted from the direct and indirect effects to yield the total effects for the model. The direct effects for Aspirations are Family Background (γ_{21}) and Encouragement (γ_{22}). The direct effect for Students' Characteristics are Family Background (γ_{11}), Encouragement (γ_{12}), and Aspirations (β_{12}). The indirect effect for Students' Characteristics is Family Background through Aspirations ($\gamma_{21}\beta_{12}$). Thus, the total effects are as follows:

$$\text{Family Background} \rightarrow \text{Aspirations} = \gamma_{21}$$
$$\text{Encouragement} \rightarrow \text{Aspirations} = \gamma_{22}$$
$$\text{Family Background} \rightarrow \text{Students' Characteristics} = \gamma_{11} + (\gamma_{21})(\beta_{12})$$
$$\text{Encouragement} \rightarrow \text{Students' Characteristics} = \gamma_{12}$$
$$\text{Aspirations} \rightarrow \text{Students' Characteristics} = \beta_{12}.$$

Appendix

Introduction to Matrix Operations

Structural equation modeling performs calculations using several different matrices. The matrix operations that perform the calculations involve addition, subtraction, multiplication, and division of elements in the different matrices (Sullins, 1973; Searle, 1982; Graybill, 1983). We present these basic matrix operations, followed by a simple multiple regression example.

MATRIX DEFINITION

A matrix is indicated by a capital letter (e.g., A, B, or R) and takes the form

$$A_{22} = \begin{bmatrix} 3 & 5 \\ 5 & 6 \end{bmatrix}.$$

The matrix can be rectangular or square and contains an array of numbers. A correlation matrix is a square matrix with the value of 1.0 in the diagonal and variable correlations in the off-diagonal. A correlation matrix is symmetrical because the correlation coefficients in the lower half of the matrix are the same as the correlation coefficients in the upper half of the matrix. We usually only report the diagonal values and the correlations in the lower half of the matrix. For example, for

$$R_{33} = \begin{bmatrix} 1.0 & .30 & .50 \\ .30 & 1.0 & .60 \\ .50 & .60 & 1.0 \end{bmatrix},$$

we report the following as the correlation matrix:

$$
\begin{matrix}
1.0 & & \\
.30 & 1.0 & \\
.50 & .60 & 1.0.
\end{matrix}
$$

Matrices have a certain number of rows and columns. The foregoing A matrix has two rows and two columns. The *order* of a matrix is its *size*, or number of rows times the number of columns. The order of the A matrix is $2 \cdot 2$, and is shown as a subscript, where the first element is the number of rows and the second element is the number of columns.

When we refer to elements in the matrix we use row and column designations to identify the location of the element in the matrix. The location of an element is given by a subscript using the row number first, followed by the column number. For example, the correlation $r = .30$ appears in the R_{21} matrix at location or row 2, column 1.

MATRIX ADDITION AND SUBTRACTION

Matrix addition adds corresponding elements in two matrices; matrix subtraction subtracts corresponding elements in two matrices. The two matrices must have the same order (number of rows and columns), so we can add $A_{32} + B_{32}$ or subtract $A_{32} - B_{32}$. In the following example matrix A elements are added to matrix B elements:

$$\begin{bmatrix} 3 & 5 & 2 \\ 1 & 6 & 0 \\ 9 & 1 & 2 \end{bmatrix} + \begin{bmatrix} 1 & -3 & 5 \\ 2 & 1 & 3 \\ 0 & 7 & -3 \end{bmatrix} = \begin{bmatrix} 4 & 2 & 7 \\ 3 & 7 & 3 \\ 9 & 8 & -1 \end{bmatrix}.$$

MATRIX MULTIPLICATION

Matrix multiplication is not as straightforward as matrix addition and subtraction. For a product of matrices we write $A \cdot B$ or AB. If A is an

$m \times n$ matrix and B is an $n \times p$ matrix, then AB is an $m \times p$ matrix of rows and columns. The number of columns in the first matrix must match the number of rows in the second matrix to be compatible and permit multiplication of the elements of the matrices. The following example illustrates how the row elements in the first matrix, A, are multiplied by the column elements in the second matrix, B, to yield the elements in the third matrix, C:

$$c_{11} = 1 \cdot 2 + 2 \cdot 1 = 2 + 2 = 4$$

$$c_{12} = 1 \cdot 4 + 2 \cdot 8 = 4 + 16 = 20$$

$$c_{13} = 1 \cdot 6 + 2 \cdot 7 = 6 + 14 = 20$$

$$c_{21} = 3 \cdot 2 + 5 \cdot 1 = 6 + 5 = 11$$

$$c_{22} = 3 \cdot 4 + 5 \cdot 8 = 12 + 40 = 52$$

$$c_{23} = 3 \cdot 6 + 5 \cdot 7 = 18 + 35 = 53$$

$$A \cdot B = \begin{bmatrix} 1 & 2 \\ 3 & 5 \end{bmatrix} \cdot \begin{bmatrix} 2 & 4 & 6 \\ 1 & 8 & 7 \end{bmatrix} = \begin{bmatrix} 4 & 20 & 20 \\ 11 & 52 & 53 \end{bmatrix}.$$

The matrix C is

$$C = \begin{bmatrix} 4 & 20 & 20 \\ 11 & 52 & 53 \end{bmatrix}.$$

It is important to note that matrix multiplication is *noncommutative*, that is, $AB \neq BA$. The order of operation in multiplying elements of the matrices is therefore very important. Matrix multiplication, however, is associative, that is, $A(BC) = (AB)C$, because the order of matrix multiplication is maintained.

A special matrix multiplication is possible when a single number is multiplied by the elements in a matrix. The single number is called a *scalar*. The scalar is simply multiplied by each of the elements in the matrix. For example,

$$D = 2 \begin{bmatrix} 3 & 4 \\ 4 & 6 \end{bmatrix} = \begin{bmatrix} 6 & 8 \\ 8 & 12 \end{bmatrix}.$$

MATRIX DIVISION

Matrix division is similar to matrix multiplication with a little twist. In regular division, we divide the numerator by the denominator. However, we can also multiply the numerator by the inverse of the denominator. For example, in regular division, 4 is divided by 2; however, we get the same result if we multiply 4 by $1/2$. Therefore, matrix division is simply A/B or $A \cdot 1/B = AB^{-1}$. The B^{-1} matrix is called the *inverse* of the B matrix.

Matrix division requires finding the inverse of a matrix, which involves computing the *determinant* of a matrix, the *matrix of minors*, and the *matrix of cofactors*. We then create a *transposed matrix* and an *inverse matrix*, which when multiplied yield an *identity matrix*. We now turn our attention to finding these values and matrices involved in matrix division.

Determinant of a Matrix

The determinant of a matrix is a unique number (not a matrix) that uses all the elements in the matrix for its calculation, and is a generalized variance for that matrix. For our illustration we compute the determinant of a 2 by 2 matrix, leaving higher order matrix determinant computations for high-speed computers. The determinant is computed by cross-multiplying the elements of the matrix:

$$A = \begin{bmatrix} a & b \\ c & d \end{bmatrix},$$

so the determinant of $A = ad - cb$.
For example, for

$$A = \begin{bmatrix} 2 & 5 \\ 3 & 6 \end{bmatrix}$$

the determinant of $A = 2 \cdot 6 - 3 \cdot 5 = -3$.

Matrix of Minors

Each element in a matrix has a *minor*. To find the minor of each element, simply draw a vertical and a horizontal line through that element to form a matrix with one less row and column. We next calculate the determinants of these minor matrices and then place them in a *matrix of minors*. The matrix of minors has the same number of rows and columns as the original matrix.

Consider the following 3 by 3 matrix:

$$A = \begin{bmatrix} 1 & 6 & -3 \\ -2 & 7 & 1 \\ 3 & -1 & 4 \end{bmatrix}.$$

We compute its *matrix of minors* as follows:

$$M_{11} = \begin{bmatrix} 7 & 1 \\ -1 & 4 \end{bmatrix} = (7)(4) - (1)(-1) = 29$$

$$M_{12} = \begin{bmatrix} -2 & 1 \\ 3 & 4 \end{bmatrix} = (-2)(4) - (1)(3) = -11$$

$$M_{13} = \begin{bmatrix} -2 & 7 \\ 3 & -1 \end{bmatrix} = (-2)(-1) - (7)(3) = -19$$

$$M_{21} = \begin{bmatrix} 6 & -3 \\ -1 & 4 \end{bmatrix} = (6)(4) - (-1)(-3) = 21$$

$$M_{22} = \begin{bmatrix} 1 & -3 \\ 3 & 4 \end{bmatrix} = (1)(4) - (-3)(3) = 13$$

$$M_{23} = \begin{bmatrix} 1 & 6 \\ 3 & -1 \end{bmatrix} = (1)(-1) - (6)(3) = -19$$

$$M_{31} = \begin{bmatrix} 6 & -3 \\ 7 & 1 \end{bmatrix} = (6)(1) - (-3)(7) = 27$$

$$M_{32} = \begin{bmatrix} 1 & -3 \\ -2 & 1 \end{bmatrix} = (1) - (-3)(-2) = -5$$

$$M_{33} = \begin{bmatrix} 1 & 6 \\ -2 & 7 \end{bmatrix} = (1)(7) - (6)(-2) = 19.$$

Thus,

$$A_{\text{Minors}} = \begin{bmatrix} 29 & -11 & -19 \\ 21 & 13 & -19 \\ 27 & -5 & 19 \end{bmatrix}.$$

Matrix of Cofactors

A *matrix of cofactors* is created by multiplying the elements of the matrix of minors by (-1) for $i + j$ elements, where i is the row number of the element and j is the column number of the element. We place these values in a new matrix, called a *matrix of cofactors*.

An easy way to remember this multiplication rule is to observe the following matrix. Start with the first row and multiply the first entry by $(+)$, the second entry by $(-)$, the third entry by $(+)$, and so on to the end of the row. For the second row start multiplying by $(-)$, then $(+)$, then $(-)$, and so on. All even rows begin with a minus sign and all odd rows begin with a plus sign.

$$
\begin{array}{ccc}
+ & - & + \\
- & + & - \\
+ & - & + \\
- & + & -
\end{array}
$$

We now multiply elements in the matrix of minors by -1 for the $i + j$ elements:

$$
A_{\text{Minors}} = \begin{bmatrix} +1 & -1 & +1 \\ -1 & +1 & -1 \\ +1 & -1 & +1 \end{bmatrix} \begin{bmatrix} 29 & -11 & -19 \\ 21 & 13 & -19 \\ 27 & -5 & 19 \end{bmatrix}
$$

to obtain the matrix of cofactors:

$$
C_{\text{Cofactors}} = \begin{bmatrix} 29 & 11 & -19 \\ -21 & 13 & 19 \\ 27 & 5 & 19 \end{bmatrix}.
$$

Determinant of a Matrix Revisited

The matrix of cofactors makes finding the determinant of any size matrix easy. We multiply elements in any row or column of our original A matrix by any one corresponding row or column in the matrix of cofactors to compute the determinant of the matrix. We can compute the determinant using any row or column, so rows with zeros make the calculation of the determinant easier. The determinant of our original 3 by 3 matrix A using the 3 by 3 matrix of cofactors is

$$
\det A = a_{11}c_{11} + a_{12}c_{12} + a_{13}c_{13}.
$$

Recall that matrix A is

$$A = \begin{bmatrix} 1 & 6 & -3 \\ -2 & 7 & 1 \\ 3 & -1 & 4 \end{bmatrix}.$$

The matrix of cofactors is

$$C_{\text{Cofactors}} = \begin{bmatrix} 29 & 11 & -19 \\ -21 & 13 & 19 \\ 27 & 5 & 19 \end{bmatrix}.$$

So, the determinant of matrix A, using the first row of both matrices, is

$$\det A = (1)(29) + (6)(11) + (-3)(-19) = 152.$$

We could have also used the second columns of both matrices and obtained the same determinant value:

$$\det A = (6)(11) + (7)(13) + (-1)(5) = 152.$$

Two of the special matrices we already mentioned also have determinants: the diagonal matrix and the triangular matrix. A *diagonal matrix* is a matrix that contains zero or nonzero elements on its main diagonal, but zeros everywhere else. A *triangular matrix* has zeros only either above or below the main diagonal. To calculate the determinants of these matrices, we only need to multiply the elements on the main diagonal. For example, the following triangular matrix K has a determinant of 96:

$$K = \begin{bmatrix} 2 & 0 & 0 & 0 \\ 4 & 1 & 0 & 0 \\ -1 & 5 & 6 & 0 \\ 3 & 9 & -2 & 8 \end{bmatrix}.$$

This is computed by multiplying the diagonal values in the matrix:

$$\det K = (2)(1)(6)(8) = 96.$$

Transpose of a Matrix

The transpose of a matrix is created by taking the *rows* of an original matrix C and placing them into corresponding *columns* of a transpose matrix C'. For example,

$$C = \begin{bmatrix} 29 & 11 & -19 \\ -21 & 13 & 19 \\ 27 & 5 & 19 \end{bmatrix}$$

$$C' = \begin{bmatrix} 29 & -21 & 27 \\ 11 & 13 & 5 \\ -19 & 19 & 19 \end{bmatrix}.$$

The *transposed matrix* of the *matrix of cofactors* is given the special term *adjoint matrix*, designated as Adj(A). The *adjoint matrix* is important because we use it to create the inverse of a matrix, our final step in matrix division operations.

Inverse of a Matrix

The general formula for finding the inverse of a matrix is one over the determinant of the matrix times the adjoint of the matrix:

$$A^{-1} = (1/\det A)\, \text{Adj}\,(A).$$

Because we already found the determinant and adjoint of A, we find the inverse of A as follows:

$$A^{-1} = \left(\frac{1}{152}\right) \begin{bmatrix} 29 & -21 & 27 \\ 11 & 13 & 5 \\ -19 & 19 & 19 \end{bmatrix} = \begin{bmatrix} .191 & -.138 & .178 \\ .072 & .086 & .033 \\ -.125 & .125 & .125 \end{bmatrix}.$$

An important property of the inverse of a matrix is that if we multiply its elements by the elements in our original matrix, we obtain an *identity matrix*. An identity matrix has 1.0 in the diagonal and zeros in the off-diagonal. The identity matrix is computed as

$$AA^{-1} = I.$$

Because we have the original matrix of A and the inverse of matrix A, we multiply elements of the matrices to obtain the *identity matrix I*:

$$AA^{-1} = \begin{bmatrix} 1 & 6 & -3 \\ -2 & 7 & 1 \\ 3 & -1 & 4 \end{bmatrix} * \begin{bmatrix} .191 & -.138 & .178 \\ .072 & .086 & .033 \\ -.125 & .125 & .125 \end{bmatrix} = \begin{bmatrix} 1 & 0 & 0 \\ 0 & 1 & 0 \\ 0 & 0 & 1 \end{bmatrix}.$$

MATRIX OPERATIONS IN STATISTICS

We now turn our attention to how the matrix operations are used to compute statistics. We only cover the calculation of the Pearson correlation and provide the matrix approach in multiple regression, leaving more complicated analyses to computer software programs.

Pearson Correlation (Variance–Covariance Matrix)

In this book we illustrated how to compute the Pearson correlation coefficient from a variance–covariance matrix. Here we demonstrate the matrix approach. An important matrix in computing correlations is the sums of squares and cross-products matrix (SSCP). We use the following pairs of scores to create the SSCP matrix:

$X1$	$X2$
5	1
4	3
6	5

The mean of X1 is 5 and the mean of X2 is 3. We use these mean values to compute deviation scores from each mean. We first create a matrix of deviation scores D:

$$D = \begin{bmatrix} 5 & 1 \\ 4 & 3 \\ 6 & 5 \end{bmatrix} - \begin{bmatrix} 5 & 3 \\ 5 & 3 \\ 5 & 3 \end{bmatrix} = \begin{bmatrix} 0 & -2 \\ -1 & 0 \\ 1 & 2 \end{bmatrix}.$$

Next, we create the transpose of matrix D, D':

$$D' = \begin{bmatrix} 0 & -1 & 1 \\ -2 & 0 & 2 \end{bmatrix}.$$

Finally, we multiply the transpose of matrix D by the matrix of deviation scores to compute the sums of squares and cross-products matrix:

$$\text{SSCP} = D' * D$$

$$\text{SSCP} = \begin{bmatrix} 0 & -1 & 1 \\ -2 & 0 & 2 \end{bmatrix} * \begin{bmatrix} 0 & -2 \\ -1 & 0 \\ 1 & 2 \end{bmatrix} = \begin{bmatrix} 2 & 2 \\ 2 & 8 \end{bmatrix}.$$

The sums of squares are along the diagonal of the matrix, and the sum of squares cross-products are on the off-diagonal. The matrix multiplications are provided as follows for the interested reader:

$$(0)(0) + (-1)(-1) + (1)(1) = 2 \quad [\text{sums of squares} = (0^2 + -1^2 + 1^2)]$$

$$(-2)(0) + (0)(-1) + (2)(1) = 2 \quad (\text{sum of squares cross product})$$

$$(0)(-2) + (-1)(0) + (1)(2) = 2 \quad (\text{sum of squares cross product})$$

$$(-2)(-2) + (0)(0) + (2)(2) = 8 \quad [\text{sums of squares} = (-2^2 + 0^2 + 2^2)]$$

$$\text{SSCP} = \begin{bmatrix} 2 & 2 \\ 2 & 8 \end{bmatrix} \quad \text{sum of squares in diagonal of matrix.}$$

Variance–Covariance Matrix

Structural equation modeling uses a sample variance–covariance matrix in its calculations. The SSCP matrix is used to create the variance–covariance matrix S:

$$S = \frac{\text{SSCP}}{n - 1}.$$

In matrix notation this becomes one half times the matrix elements:

$$S = \frac{1}{2} * \begin{bmatrix} 2 & 2 \\ 2 & 8 \end{bmatrix} = \begin{bmatrix} 1 & 1 \\ 1 & 4 \end{bmatrix} \quad \begin{array}{l} \text{covariance terms in the} \\ \text{off-diagonal of matrix} \\ \text{variance of variables in diagonal of} \\ \text{matrix.} \end{array}$$

We can now calculate the Pearson correlation coefficient using the basic formula of covariance divided by the square root of the product of the variances:

$$r = \frac{\text{CovarianceX1X2}}{\sqrt{\text{VarianceX1*VarianceX2}}} = \frac{1}{\sqrt{1*4}} = \frac{1}{2} = .50.$$

Multiple Regression

The multiple linear regression equation with two predictor variables is

$$y = \beta_0 + \beta_1 x_1 + \beta_2 x_2 + e_i,$$

where y is the dependent variable, x_1 and x_2 are the two predictor variables, β_0 is the regression constant or y intercept, β_1 and β_2 are the regression weights to be estimated, and e is the error of prediction.

Given the following data, we can use matrix algebra to estimate the regression weights:

y	x_1	x_2
3	2	1
2	3	5
4	5	3
5	7	6
8	8	7

We model each subject's y score as a linear function of the betas:

$$y_1 = 3 = 1\beta_0 + 2\beta_1 + 1\beta_2 + e_1$$
$$y_2 = 2 = 1\beta_0 + 3\beta_1 + 5\beta_2 + e_2$$
$$y_3 = 4 = 1\beta_0 + 5\beta_1 + 3\beta_2 + e_3$$
$$y_4 = 5 = 1\beta_0 + 7\beta_1 + 6\beta_2 + e_4$$
$$y_5 = 8 = 1\beta_0 + 8\beta_1 + 7\beta_2 + e_5.$$

This series of equations can be expressed as a single matrix equation:

$$y = X\beta + e$$

$$y = \begin{bmatrix} 3 \\ 2 \\ 4 \\ 5 \\ 8 \end{bmatrix} = \begin{bmatrix} 1 & 2 & 1 \\ 1 & 3 & 5 \\ 1 & 5 & 3 \\ 1 & 7 & 6 \\ 1 & 8 & 7 \end{bmatrix} \begin{bmatrix} \beta_0 \\ \beta_1 \\ \beta_2 \end{bmatrix} + \begin{bmatrix} e_1 \\ e_2 \\ e_3 \\ e_4 \\ e_5 \end{bmatrix}.$$

The first column of matrix X is made up of 1's, which compute the regression constant. In matrix form, the multiple linear regression equation is $y = X\beta + e$.

Using calculus, we translate this matrix to solve for the regression weights:

$$\hat{\beta} = (X'X)^{-1}X'y.$$

The matrix equation is

$$
\hat{\beta} = \left\{ \begin{bmatrix} 1 & 1 & 1 & 1 & 1 \\ 2 & 3 & 5 & 7 & 8 \\ 1 & 5 & 3 & 6 & 7 \end{bmatrix} \begin{bmatrix} 1 & 2 & 1 \\ 1 & 3 & 5 \\ 1 & 5 & 3 \\ 1 & 7 & 6 \\ 1 & 8 & 7 \end{bmatrix} \right\} * \begin{bmatrix} 1 & 1 & 1 & 1 & 1 \\ 2 & 3 & 5 & 7 & 8 \\ 1 & 5 & 3 & 6 & 7 \end{bmatrix} \begin{bmatrix} 3 \\ 2 \\ 4 \\ 5 \\ 8 \end{bmatrix}
$$

with the columns labeled X', X, X', y.

We first compute $X'X$ and then compute $X'y$:

$$
X'X = \begin{bmatrix} 5 & 25 & 22 \\ 25 & 151 & 130 \\ 22 & 130 & 120 \end{bmatrix} \quad \text{and} \quad X'y = \begin{bmatrix} 22 \\ 131 \\ 111 \end{bmatrix}.
$$

Next we create the inverse of $X'X$, where 1016 is the determinant of $X'X$:

$$
X'X = \frac{1}{1016} \begin{bmatrix} 1220 & -140 & -72 \\ -140 & 116 & -100 \\ -72 & -100 & 130 \end{bmatrix}.
$$

Finally, we solve for the X_1 and X_2 regression weights:

$$
\hat{\beta} = \frac{1}{1016} \begin{bmatrix} 1220 & -140 & -72 \\ -140 & 116 & -100 \\ -72 & -100 & 130 \end{bmatrix} \begin{bmatrix} 22 \\ 131 \\ 111 \end{bmatrix} = \begin{bmatrix} .50 \\ 1 \\ -.25 \end{bmatrix}.
$$

The multiple regression equation is

$$
\hat{y}_i = .50 + 1X_1 - .25X_2.
$$

We use the multiple regression equation to compute predicted scores and then compare the predicted values to the original y values to compute the error of prediction values e. For example, the first y score was 3 with $X_1 = 2$ and $X_2 = 1$. We substitute the X_1 and X_2 values in the regression equation and compute a predicted y score of 2.25. The error of prediction is computed as $y -$ this predicted y score, or $3 - 2.25 = .75$. These computations are as follows and are repeated for the remaining y values:

$$
\hat{y}_1 = .50 + 1(2) - .25(1)
$$
$$
\hat{y}_1 = 2.25
$$

$$\hat{e}_1 = 3 - 2.25 = .75$$
$$\hat{y}_2 = .50 + 1(3) - .25(5)$$
$$\hat{y}_2 = 2.25$$
$$\hat{e}_2 = 2 - 2.25 = -.25$$

$$\hat{y}_3 = .50 + 1(5) - .25(3)$$
$$\hat{y}_3 = 4.75$$
$$\hat{e}_3 = 4 - 4.75 = -.75$$

$$\hat{y}_4 = .50 + 1(7) - .25(6)$$
$$\hat{y}_4 = 6.00$$
$$\hat{e}_4 = 5 - 6 = -1.00$$

$$\hat{y}_5 = .50 + 1(8) - .25(7)$$
$$\hat{y}_5 = 6.75$$
$$\hat{e}_5 = 8 - 6.75 = 1.25.$$

We can now place the y values, X values, regression weights, and error terms back into the matrices to yield a complete solution for the y values. Notice that the error term vector should sum to zero (0.0). Also notice that each y value is uniquely composed of an intercept term (.50), a regression weight (1.0) times an X_1 value, a regression weight (−.25) times an X_2 value, and a residual error; for example, the first y value of 3 is $.5 + 1.0(2) - .25(1) + .75$. We have

$$
\begin{bmatrix} 3 \\ 2 \\ 4 \\ 5 \\ 8 \end{bmatrix} = .5 + 1.0 \begin{bmatrix} 2 \\ 3 \\ 5 \\ 7 \\ 8 \end{bmatrix} - .25 \begin{bmatrix} 1 \\ 5 \\ 3 \\ 6 \\ 7 \end{bmatrix} + \begin{bmatrix} .75 \\ -.25 \\ -.75 \\ -1.00 \\ 1.25 \end{bmatrix}.
$$

REFERENCES

Graybill, F. A. (1983). *Matrices with applications in statistics* (2nd Ed), Belmont, CA: Wadsworth.

Searle, S. R. (1982). *Matrix algebra useful for statistics*. New York: Wiley.

Sullins, W. L. (1973). *Matrix algebra for statistical applications*. Danville, IL: Interstate.

ABOUT THE AUTHORS

RANDALL E. SCHUMACKER received his Ph.D. in educational psychology from Southern Illinois University. He is currently professor of educational research at the University of North Texas, where he teaches courses in structural equation modeling, quantitative research methodology, statistical simulation, and measurement. His research focuses are varied, including best model selection methods, robust statistics, teacher accountability, and measurement issues related to ability estimation, mixed-item formats, and reliability. He has published in several journals including *Academic Medicine, Educational and Psychological Measurement, Journal of Applied Measurement, Journal of Educational and Behavioral Statistics, Journal of Research Methodology, Multiple Linear Regression Viewpoints,* and *Structural Equation Modeling.* He has served on the editorial boards of numerous journals and is a member of the American Educational Research Association and American Psychological Association–Division 5, and is past president of the Southwest Educational Research Association, and emeritus editor of the journal *Structural Equation Modeling.* He can be contacted at University of North Texas, College of Education, P.O. Box 311335, Denton, TX 76203-1335, or by e-mail at rschumacker@unt.edu.

RICHARD G. LOMAX received his Ph.D. in educational research methodology from the University of Pittsburgh. He is currently professor of education and applied statistics at the University of Alabama, where he teaches courses in quantitative research methodology. His research primarily focuses on models of literacy acquisition, multivariate statistics, and assessment. He has published in such diverse journals as *Parenting: Science and Practice; Understanding Statistics: Statistical Issues in*

Psychology, Education, and the Social Sciences; Violence Against Women; Journal of Early Adolescence; and *The Journal of Negro Education.* He has served on the editorial boards of numerous journals, and is a member of the American Educational Research Association, the American Statistical Association, and the National Reading Conference. He can be contacted at the University of Alabama, College of Education, Box 870231, Tuscaloosa, AL 35406, or by e-mail at rlomax@bamaed.ua.edu.

APPENDIX
STATISTICAL TABLES

———◇◆◇———

Appendix Outline

Tables were copied from Randall E. Schumacker and Allen Akers, *Understanding Statistical Concepts Using S-PLUS*, Mahwah, NJ: Lawrence Erlbaum Associates, Publishers, Inc., 2001.

TABLE A.1
Areas Under the Normal Curve (z-scores)

z	.00	.01	.02	.03	.04	.05	.06	.07	.08	.09
					Second decimal place in z					
.0	.0000	.0040	.0080	.0120	.0160	.0199	.0239	.0279	.0319	.0359
.1	.0398	.0438	.0478	.0517	.0557	.0596	.0636	.0675	.0714	.0753
.2	.0793	.0832	.0871	.0910	.0948	.0987	.1026	.1064	.1103	.1141
.3	.1179	.1217	.1255	.1293	.1331	.1368	.1406	.1443	.1480	.1517
.4	.1554	.1591	.1628	.1664	.1700	.1736	.1772	.1808	.1844	.1879
.5	.1915	.1950	.1985	.2019	.2054	.2088	.2123	.2157	.2190	.2224
.6	.2257	.2291	.2324	.2357	.2389	.2422	.2454	.2486	.2517	.2549
.7	.2580	.2611	.2642	.2673	.2704	.2734	.2764	.2794	.2823	.2852
.8	.2881	.2910	.2939	.2967	.2995	.3023	.3051	.3078	.3106	.3133
.9	.3159	.3186	.3212	.3238	.3264	.3289	.3315	.3340	.3365	.3389
1.0	.3413	.3438	.3461	.3485	.3508	.3531	.3554	.3577	.3599	.3621
1.1	.3643	.3665	.3686	.3708	.3729	.3749	.3770	.3790	.3810	.3830
1.2	.3849	.3869	.3888	.3907	.3925	.3944	.3962	.3980	.3997	.4015
1.3	.4032	.4049	.4066	.4082	.4099	.4115	.4131	.4147	.4162	.4177
1.4	.4192	.4207	.4222	.4236	.4251	.4265	.4279	.4292	.4306	.4319
1.5	.4332	.4345	.4357	.4793	.4382	.4394	.4406	.4418	.4429	.4441
1.6	.4452	.4463	.4474	.4484	.4495	.4505	.4515	.4525	.4535	.4545
1.7	.4554	.4564	.4573	.4582	.4591	.4599	.4608	.4616	.4625	.4633
1.8	.4641	.4649	.4656	.4664	.4671	.4678	.4686	.4693	.4699	.4706
1.9	.4713	.4719	.4726	.4732	.4738	.4744	.4750	.4756	.4761	.4767
2.0	.4772	.4778	.4783	.4788	.4793	.4798	.4803	.4808	.4812	.4817
2.1	.4821	.4826	.4830	.4834	.4838	.4842	.4846	.4850	.4854	.4857
2.2	.4861	.4826	.4868	.4871	.4875	.4878	.4881	.4884	.4887	.4890
2.3	.4893	.4896	.4898	.4901	.4904	.4906	.4909	.4911	.4913	.4916
2.4	.4918	.4920	.4922	.4925	.4927	.4929	.4931	.4932	.4934	.4936
2.5	.4938	.4940	.4941	.4943	.4945	.4946	.4948	.4949	.4951	.4952
2.6	.4953	.4955	.4956	.4957	.4959	.4960	.4961	.4962	.4963	.4964
2.7	.4965	.4966	.4967	.4968	.4969	.4970	.4971	.4972	.4973	.4974
2.8	.4974	.4975	.4976	.4977	.4977	.4978	.4979	.4979	.4980	.4981
2.9	.4981	.4982	.4982	.4983	.4984	.4984	.4985	.4985	.4986	.4986
3.0	.4987	.4987	.4987	.4988	.4988	.4989	.4989	.4989	.4990	.4990
3.1	.4990	.4991	.4991	.4991	.4992	.4922	.4992	.4992	.4993	.4993
3.2	.4993	.4993	.4994	.4994	.4994	.4994	.4994	.4995	.4995	.4995
3.3	.4995	.4995	.4995	.4996	.4996	.4996	.4996	.4996	.4996	.4997
3.4	.4997	.4997	.4997	.4997	.4997	.4997	.4997	.4997	.4997	.4998
3.5	.4998									
4.0	.49997									
4.5	.499997									
5.0	.4999997									

TABLE A.2
Distribution of t for Given Probability Levels

	Level of significance for one-tailed test					
	.10	.05	.025	.01	.005	.0005
	Level of significance for two-tailed test					
df	.20	.10	.05	.02	.01	.001
1	3.078	6.314	12.706	31.821	63.657	636.619
2	1.886	2.920	4.303	6.965	9.925	31.598
3	1.638	2.353	3.182	4.541	5.841	12.941
4	1.533	2.132	2.776	3.747	4.604	8.610
5	1.476	2.015	2.571	3.365	4.032	6.859
6	1.440	1.943	2.447	3.143	3.707	5.959
7	1.415	1.895	2.365	2.998	3.499	5.405
8	1.397	1.860	2.306	2.896	3.355	5.041
9	1.383	1.833	2.262	2.821	3.250	4.781
10	1.372	1.812	2.228	2.764	3.169	4.587
11	1.363	1.796	2.201	2.718	3.106	4.437
12	1.356	1.782	2.179	2.681	3.055	4.318
13	1.350	1.771	2.160	2.650	3.012	4.221
14	1.345	1.761	2.145	2.624	2.977	4.140
15	1.341	1.753	2.131	2.602	2.947	4.073
16	1.337	1.746	2.120	2.583	2.921	4.015
17	1.333	1.740	2.110	2.567	2.898	3.965
18	1.330	1.734	2.101	2.552	2.878	3.992
19	1.328	1.729	2.093	2.539	2.861	3.883
20	1.325	1.725	2.086	2.528	2.845	3.850
21	1.323	1.721	2.080	2.518	2.831	3.819
22	1.321	1.717	2.074	2.508	2.819	3.792
23	1.319	1.714	2.069	2.500	2.807	3.767
24	1.318	1.711	2.064	2.492	2.797	3.745
25	1.316	1.708	2.060	2.485	2.787	3.725
26	1.315	1.706	2.056	2.479	2.779	3.707
27	1.314	1.703	2.052	2.473	2.771	3.690
28	1.313	1.701	2.048	2.467	2.763	3.674
29	1.311	1.699	2.045	2.462	2.756	3.659
30	1.310	1.697	2.042	2.457	2.750	3.646
40	1.303	1.684	2.021	2.423	2.704	3.551
60	1.296	1.671	2.000	2.390	2.660	3.460
120	1.289	1.658	1.980	2.358	2.617	3.373
∞	1.282	1.645	1.960	2.326	2.576	3.291

TABLE A.3
Distribution of r for Given Probability Levels

	Level of significance for one-tailed test			
	.05	.025	.01	.005
	Level of significance for two-tailed test			
df	.10	.05	.02	.01
1	.988	.997	.9995	.9999
2	.900	.950	.980	.990
3	.805	.878	.934	.959
4	.729	.811	.882	.917
5	.669	.754	.833	.874
6	.622	.707	.789	.834
7	.582	.666	.750	.798
8	.540	.632	.716	.765
9	.521	.602	.685	.735
10	.497	.576	.658	.708
11	.576	.553	.634	.684
12	.458	.532	.612	.661
13	.441	.514	.592	.641
14	.426	.497	.574	.623
15	.412	.482	.558	.606
16	.400	.468	.542	.590
17	.389	.456	.528	.575
18	.378	.444	.516	.561
19	.369	.433	.503	.549
20	.360	.423	.492	.537
21	.352	.413	.482	.526
22	.344	.404	.472	.515
23	.337	.396	.462	.505
24	.330	.388	.453	.496
25	.323	.381	.445	.487
26	.317	.374	.437	.479
27	.311	.367	.430	.471
28	.306	.361	.423	.463
29	.301	.355	.416	.486
30	.296	.349	.409	.449
35	.275	.325	.381	.418
40	.257	.304	.358	.393
45	.243	.288	.338	.372
50	.231	.273	.322	.354
60	.211	.250	.295	.325
70	.195	.232	.274	.303
80	.183	.217	.256	.283
90	.173	.205	.242	.267
100	.164	.195	.230	.254

TABLE A.4

Distribution of Chi-Square for Given Probability Levels

Probability

df	.99	.98	.95	.90	.80	.70	.50	.30	.20	.10	.05	.02	.01	.001
1	.00016	.00663	.00393	.0158	.0642	.148	.455	1.074	1.642	2.706	3.841	5.412	6.635	10.827
2	.0201	.0404	.103	.211	.446	.713	1.386	2.408	3.219	4.605	5.991	7.824	9.210	13.815
3	.115	.185	.352	.584	1.005	1.424	2.366	3.665	4.642	6.251	7.815	9.837	11.345	16.266
4	.297	.429	.711	1.064	1.649	2.195	3.357	4.878	5.989	7.779	9.488	11.668	13.277	18.467
5	.554	.752	1.145	1.610	2.343	3.000	4.351	6.064	7.289	9.236	11.070	13.388	15.086	20.515
6	.872	1.134	1.635	2.204	3.070	3.828	5.348	7.231	8.558	10.645	12.592	15.033	16.812	22.457
7	1.239	1.564	2.167	2.833	3.822	4.671	6.346	8.383	9.803	12.017	14.067	16.622	18.475	24.322
8	1.646	2.032	2.733	3.490	4.594	5.527	7.344	9.524	11.030	13.362	15.507	18.168	20.090	26.125
9	2.088	2.532	3.325	4.168	5.380	6.393	8.343	10.656	12.242	14.684	16.919	19.679	21.666	27.877
10	2.558	3.059	3.940	4.865	6.179	7.267	9.342	11.781	13.442	15.987	18.307	21.161	23.209	29.588
11	3.053	3.609	4.575	5.578	6.989	8.148	10.341	12.899	14.631	17.275	19.675	22.618	24.725	31.264
12	3.571	4.178	5.226	6.304	7.807	9.034	11.340	14.011	15.812	18.549	21.026	24.054	26.217	32.909
13	4.107	4.765	5.892	7.042	8.634	9.926	12.340	15.119	16.985	19.812	22.362	25.472	27.688	34.528
14	4.660	5.368	6.571	7.790	9.467	10.821	13.339	16.222	18.151	21.064	23.685	26.873	29.141	36.123
15	5.229	5.985	7.261	8.547	10.307	11.721	14.339	17.322	19.311	22.307	24.996	28.259	30.578	37.697
16	5.812	6.614	7.962	9.312	11.152	12.624	15.338	18.418	20.465	23.542	26.296	29.633	32.000	39.252
17	6.408	7.255	8.672	10.085	12.002	13.531	16.338	19.511	21.615	24.769	27.587	30.995	33.409	40.790
18	7.015	7.906	9.390	10.865	12.857	14.440	17.338	20.601	22.760	25.989	28.869	32.346	34.805	42.312
19	7.633	8.567	10.117	11.651	13.716	15.352	18.338	21.689	23.900	27.204	30.144	33.687	36.191	43.820
20	8.260	9.237	10.851	12.443	14.578	16.266	19.337	22.775	25.038	28.412	31.410	35.020	37.566	45.315
21	8.897	9.915	11.591	13.240	15.445	17.182	20.337	23.858	26.171	29.615	32.671	36.343	38.932	46.797
22	9.542	10.600	12.338	14.041	16.314	18.101	21.337	24.939	27.301	30.813	33.924	37.659	40.289	48.268
23	10.196	11.293	13.091	14.848	17.187	19.021	22.337	26.018	28.429	32.007	35.172	38.968	41.638	49.728

df													
24	10.856	11.992	13.848	15.659	18.062	19.943	23.337	27.096	29.553	33.196	36.415	40.270	42.980	51.179
25	11.524	12.697	14.611	16.473	18.940	20.867	24.337	28.172	30.675	34.382	37.652	41.566	44.314	52.620
26	12.198	13.409	15.379	17.292	19.820	21.792	25.336	29.246	31.795	35.563	38.885	42.856	45.642	54.052
27	12.879	14.125	16.151	18.114	20.703	22.719	26.336	30.319	32.912	36.741	40.113	44.140	46.963	55.476
28	13.565	14.847	16.928	18.939	21.588	23.647	27.336	31.391	34.027	37.916	41.337	45.419	48.278	56.893
29	14.256	15.574	17.708	19.768	22.475	24.577	28.336	32.461	35.139	39.087	42.557	46.693	49.588	58.302
30	14.953	16.306	18.493	20.599	23.364	25.508	29.336	33.530	36.250	40.256	43.773	47.962	50.892	59.703
32	16.362	17.783	20.072	22.271	25.148	27.373	31.336	35.665	38.466	42.585	46.194	50.487	53.486	62.487
34	17.789	19.275	21.664	23.952	26.938	29.242	33.336	37.795	40.676	44.903	48.602	52.995	56.061	65.247
36	19.233	20.783	23.269	25.643	28.735	31.115	35.336	39.922	42.879	47.212	50.999	55.489	58.619	67.985
38	20.691	22.304	24.884	27.343	30.537	32.992	37.335	42.045	45.076	49.513	53.384	57.969	61.162	70.703
40	22.164	23.838	26.509	29.051	32.345	34.872	39.335	44.165	47.269	51.805	55.759	60.436	63.691	73.402
42	23.650	25.383	28.144	30.765	34.147	36.755	41.335	46.282	49.456	54.090	58.124	62.892	66.206	76.084
44	25.148	26.939	29.787	32.487	35.974	38.641	43.335	48.396	51.639	56.369	60.481	65.337	68.710	78.750
46	26.657	28.504	31.439	34.215	37.795	40.529	45.335	50.507	53.818	58.641	62.830	67.771	71.201	81.400
48	28.177	30.080	33.098	35.949	39.621	42.420	47.335	52.616	55.993	60.907	65.171	70.197	73.683	84.037
50	29.707	31.664	34.764	37.689	41.449	44.313	49.335	54.723	58.164	63.167	67.505	72.613	76.154	86.661
52	31.246	33.256	36.437	39.433	43.281	46.209	51.335	56.827	60.332	65.422	69.832	75.021	78.616	89.272
54	32.793	34.856	38.116	41.183	45.117	48.106	53.335	58.930	62.496	67.673	72.153	77.422	81.069	91.872
56	34.350	36.464	39.801	42.937	46.955	50.005	55.335	61.031	64.658	69.919	74.468	79.815	83.513	94.461
58	35.913	38.078	41.492	44.696	48.797	51.906	57.335	63.129	66.816	72.160	76.778	82.201	85.950	97.039
60	37.485	39.699	43.188	46.459	50.641	53.809	59.335	65.227	68.972	74.397	79.082	84.580	88.379	99.607
62	39.063	41.327	44.889	48.226	52.487	55.714	61.335	67.322	71.125	76.630	81.381	86.953	90.802	102.166
64	40.649	42.960	46.595	49.996	54.336	57.620	63.335	69.416	73.276	78.860	83.675	89.320	93.217	104.716
66	42.240	44.599	48.305	51.770	56.188	59.527	65.335	71.508	75.424	81.085	85.965	91.681	95.626	107.258
68	43.838	46.244	50.020	53.548	58.042	61.436	67.335	73.600	77.571	83.308	88.250	94.037	98.028	109.791
70	45.442	47.893	51.739	55.329	59.898	63.346	69.335	75.689	79.715	85.527	90.531	96.388	100.425	112.317

Note: For larger values of *df*, the expression $\sqrt{(X^2)^2} - \sqrt{2df} - 1$ may be used as a normal deviate with unit variance, remembering that the probability for X^2 corresponds with that of a single tail of the normal curve.

TABLE A.5

The Distribution of F for Given Probability Levels (.05 Level)

df1 df2	1	2	3	4	5	6	7	8	9	10	12	15	20	24	30	40	60	120	∞
1	161.4	199.5	215.7	224.6	230.2	234.0	236.8	238.9	240.5	241.9	243.9	245.9	248.0	249.1	250.1	251.1	252.2	253.3	254.3
2	18.51	19.00	19.16	19.25	19.30	19.33	19.35	19.37	19.38	19.49	19.41	19.43	19.45	19.45	19.46	19.47	19.48	19.49	19.50
3	10.13	9.55	9.28	9.12	9.01	8.94	8.89	8.85	8.81	8.79	8.74	8.70	8.66	8.64	8.62	8.59	8.57	8.55	8.53
4	7.71	6.94	6.59	6.39	6.26	6.15	6.09	6.04	6.00	5.96	5.91	5.86	5.80	5.77	5.75	5.72	5.69	5.66	5.63
5	6.61	5.79	5.41	5.19	5.05	4.95	4.88	4.82	4.77	4.74	4.68	4.62	4.56	4.53	4.50	4.46	4.43	4.40	4.36
6	5.99	5.14	4.76	4.53	4.39	4.28	4.21	4.15	4.10	4.06	4.00	3.94	3.87	3.84	3.81	3.77	3.74	3.70	3.67
7	5.59	4.74	4.35	4.12	3.97	3.87	3.79	3.73	3.68	3.64	3.57	3.51	3.44	3.41	3.38	3.34	3.30	3.27	3.23
8	5.32	4.46	4.07	3.84	3.69	3.58	3.50	3.44	3.39	3.35	3.28	3.22	3.15	3.12	3.08	3.04	3.01	2.97	2.93
9	5.12	4.26	3.86	3.63	3.48	3.37	3.29	3.23	3.18	3.14	3.07	3.01	2.94	2.90	2.86	2.83	2.79	2.75	2.71
10	4.96	4.10	3.71	3.48	3.33	3.22	3.14	3.07	3.02	2.98	2.91	2.85	2.77	2.74	2.70	2.66	2.62	2.58	2.54
11	4.84	3.98	3.59	3.36	3.20	3.09	3.01	2.95	2.90	2.85	2.79	2.72	2.65	2.61	2.57	2.53	2.49	2.45	2.40
12	4.75	3.89	3.49	3.26	3.11	3.00	2.91	2.85	2.80	2.75	2.69	2.62	2.54	2.51	2.47	2.43	2.38	2.34	2.30
13	4.67	3.81	3.41	3.18	3.03	2.92	2.83	2.77	2.71	2.67	2.60	2.53	2.46	2.42	2.38	2.34	2.30	2.25	2.21
14	4.60	3.74	3.34	3.11	2.96	2.85	2.76	2.70	2.65	2.60	2.53	2.46	2.39	2.35	2.31	2.27	2.22	2.18	2.13
15	4.54	3.68	3.29	3.06	2.90	2.79	2.71	2.64	2.59	2.54	2.48	2.40	2.33	2.29	2.25	2.20	2.16	2.11	2.07
16	4.49	3.63	3.24	3.01	2.85	2.74	2.66	2.59	2.54	2.49	2.42	2.35	2.28	2.24	2.19	2.1	2.11	2.06	2.01
17	4.45	3.59	3.20	2.96	2.81	2.70	2.61	2.55	2.49	2.45	2.38	2.31	2.23	2.19	2.15	2.10	2.06	2.01	1.96

18	4.41	3.55	3.16	2.93	2.77	2.66	2.58	2.51	2.46	2.41	2.34	2.27	2.19	2.15	2.11	2.06	2.02	1.97	1.92
19	4.38	3.52	3.13	2.90	2.74	2.63	2.54	2.48	2.42	2.38	2.31	2.23	2.16	2.11	2.07	2.03	1.98	1.93	1.88
20	4.35	3.49	3.10	2.87	2.71	2.60	2.51	2.45	2.39	2.35	2.28	2.20	2.12	2.08	2.04	1.99	1.95	1.90	1.84
21	4.32	3.47	3.07	2.84	2.68	2.57	2.49	2.42	2.37	2.32	2.25	2.18	2.10	2.05	2.01	1.96	1.92	1.87	1.81
22	4.30	3.44	3.05	2.82	2.66	2.55	2.46	2.40	2.34	2.30	2.23	2.15	2.07	2.03	1.98	1.94	1.89	1.84	1.78
23	4.28	3.42	3.03	2.80	2.64	2.53	2.44	2.37	2.32	2.27	2.20	2.13	2.05	2.01	1.96	1.91	1.86	1.81	1.76
24	4.26	3.40	3.01	2.78	2.62	2.51	2.42	2.36	2.30	2.25	2.18	2.11	2.03	1.98	1.94	1.89	1.84	1.79	1.73
25	4.24	3.39	2.99	2.76	2.60	2.49	2.40	2.34	2.28	2.24	2.16	2.09	2.01	1.96	1.92	1.87	1.82	1.77	1.71
26	4.23	3.37	2.98	2.74	2.59	2.47	2.39	2.32	2.27	2.22	2.15	2.07	1.99	1.95	1.90	1.85	1.80	1.75	1.69
27	4.21	3.35	2.96	2.73	2.57	2.46	2.37	2.31	2.25	2.20	2.13	2.06	1.97	1.93	1.88	1.84	1.79	1.73	1.67
28	4.20	3.34	2.95	2.71	2.56	2.45	2.36	2.29	2.24	2.19	2.12	2.04	1.96	1.91	1.87	1.82	1.77	1.71	1.65
29	4.18	3.33	2.93	2.70	2.55	2.43	2.35	2.28	2.22	2.18	2.10	2.03	1.94	1.90	1.85	1.81	1.75	1.70	1.64
30	4.17	3.32	2.92	2.69	2.53	2.42	2.33	2.27	2.21	2.16	2.09	2.01	1.93	1.89	1.84	1.79	1.74	1.68	1.62
40	4.08	3.23	2.84	2.61	2.45	2.34	2.25	2.18	2.12	2.08	2.00	1.92	1.84	1.79	1.74	1.69	1.64	1.58	1.51
60	4.00	3.15	2.76	2.53	2.37	2.25	2.17	2.10	2.04	1.99	1.92	1.84	1.75	1.70	1.65	1.59	1.53	1.47	1.39
120	3.92	3.07	2.68	2.45	2.29	2.17	2.09	2.02	1.96	1.91	1.83	1.75	1.66	1.61	1.55	1.50	1.43	1.35	1.25
∞	3.84	3.00	2.60	2.37	2.21	2.10	2.01	1.94	1.88	1.83	1.75	1.67	1.57	1.52	1.46	1.39	1.32	1.22	1.00

TABLE A.5
Distribution of F for Given Probability Levels (.01 Level)

df1 / df2	1	2	3	4	5	6	7	8	9	10	12	15	20	24	30	40	60	120	∞
1	4052	4999.5	5403	5625	5764	5859	5928	5982	6022	6056	6106	6157	6209	6235	6261	6287	6313	6339	6366
2	98.5	99.00	99.17	99.25	99.30	99.33	99.36	99.37	99.39	99.40	99.42	99.43	99.45	99.46	99.47	99.47	99.48	99.49	99.50
3	34.12	30.82	29.46	28.71	28.24	27.91	27.67	27.49	27.25	27.23	27.05	26.87	26.69	26.60	26.50	26.41	26.32	26.22	26.13
4	21.20	18.00	16.69	15.98	15.52	15.21	14.98	14.80	14.66	14.55	14.37	14.20	14.02	13.93	13.84	13.75	13.65	13.56	13.46
5	16.26	13.27	12.06	11.39	10.97	10.67	10.46	10.29	10.16	10.05	9.89	9.72	9.55	9.47	9.38	9.29	9.20	9.11	9.02
6	13.75	10.92	9.78	9.15	8.75	8.47	8.26	8.10	7.98	7.87	7.72	7.56	7.40	7.31	7.23	7.14	7.06	6.97	6.88
7	12.25	9.55	8.45	7.85	7.46	7.19	6.99	6.84	6.72	6.62	6.47	6.31	6.16	6.07	5.99	5.91	5.82	5.74	5.65
8	11.26	8.65	7.59	7.01	6.63	6.37	6.18	6.03	5.91	5.81	5.67	5.52	5.36	5.28	5.20	5.12	5.03	4.95	4.86
9	10.56	8.02	6.99	6.42	6.06	5.80	5.61	5.47	5.35	5.26	5.11	4.96	4.81	4.73	4.65	4.57	4.48	4.40	4.31
10	10.04	7.56	6.55	5.99	5.64	5.39	5.20	5.06	4.94	4.85	4.71	4.56	4.41	4.33	4.25	4.17	4.08	4.00	3.91
11	9.65	7.21	6.22	5.67	5.32	5.07	4.89	4.74	4.63	4.54	4.40	4.25	4.10	4.02	3.94	3.86	3.78	3.69	3.60
12	9.33	6.93	5.95	5.41	5.06	4.82	4.64	4.50	4.39	4.30	4.16	4.01	3.86	3.78	3.70	3.62	3.54	3.45	3.36
13	9.07	6.70	5.74	5.21	4.86	4.62	4.44	4.30	4.19	4.10	3.96	3.82	3.66	3.59	3.51	3.43	3.34	3.25	3.17
14	8.86	6.51	5.56	5.04	4.69	4.46	4.28	4.14	4.03	3.94	3.80	3.66	3.51	3.43	3.35	3.27	3.18	3.09	3.00
15	8.68	6.36	5.42	4.89	4.56	4.32	4.14	4.00	3.89	3.80	3.67	3.52	3.37	3.29	3.21	3.13	3.05	2.96	2.87
16	8.53	6.23	5.29	4.77	4.44	4.20	4.03	3.89	3.78	3.69	3.55	3.41	3.26	3.18	3.10	3.02	2.93	2.84	2.75

17	8.40	6.11	5.18	4.67	4.34	4.10	3.93	3.79	3.68	3.59	3.46	3.31	3.16	3.08	3.00	2.92	2.83	2.75	2.65
18	8.29	6.01	5.09	4.58	4.25	4.01	3.84	3.71	3.60	3.51	3.37	3.23	3.08	3.00	2.92	2.84	2.75	2.66	2.57
19	8.18	5.93	5.01	4.50	4.17	3.94	3.77	3.63	3.52	3.43	3.30	3.15	3.00	2.92	2.84	2.76	2.67	2.58	2.49
20	8.10	5.85	4.94	4.43	4.10	3.87	3.70	3.56	3.46	3.37	3.23	3.09	2.94	2.86	2.78	2.69	2.61	2.52	2.42
21	8.02	5.78	4.87	4.37	4.04	3.81	3.64	3.51	3.40	3.31	3.17	3.03	2.88	2.80	2.72	2.64	2.55	2.46	2.36
22	7.95	5.72	4.82	4.31	3.9	3.76	3.59	3.45	3.35	3.26	3.12	2.98	2.83	2.75	2.67	2.58	2.50	2.40	2.31
23	7.88	5.66	4.76	4.26	3.94	3.71	3.54	3.41	3.30	3.21	3.07	2.93	2.78	2.70	2.62	2.54	2.45	2.35	2.26
24	7.82	5.61	4.72	4.22	3.90	3.67	3.50	3.36	3.26	3.17	3.03	2.89	2.74	2.66	2.58	2.49	2.40	2.31	2.21
25	7.77	5.57	4.68	4.18	3.85	3.63	3.46	3.32	3.22	3.13	2.99	2.85	2.70	2.62	2.54	2.45	2.36	2.27	2.17
26	7.72	5.53	4.64	4.14	3.82	3.59	3.42	3.29	3.18	3.09	2.96	2.81	2.66	2.58	2.50	2.42	2.33	2.23	2.13
27	7.68	5.49	4.60	4.11	3.78	3.56	3.39	3.26	3.15	3.06	2.93	2.78	2.63	2.55	2.47	2.38	2.29	2.20	2.10
28	7.64	5.45	4.57	4.07	3.75	3.53	3.36	3.23	3.12	3.03	2.90	2.75	2.60	2.52	2.44	2.35	2.26	2.17	2.06
29	7.60	5.42	4.54	4.04	3.73	3.50	3.33	3.20	3.09	3.00	2.87	2.73	2.57	2.49	2.41	2.33	2.23	2.14	2.03
30	7.56	5.39	4.51	4.02	3.70	3.47	3.30	3.17	3.07	2.98	2.84	2.70	2.55	2.47	2.39	2.30	2.21	2.11	2.01
40	7.31	5.18	4.31	3.83	3.51	3.29	3.12	2.99	2.89	2.80	2.66	2.52	2.37	2.29	2.20	2.11	2.02	1.92	1.80
60	7.08	4.98	4.13	3.65	3.34	3.12	2.95	2.82	2.72	2.63	2.50	2.35	2.20	2.12	2.03	1.94	1.84	1.73	1.60
120	6.85	4.79	3.95	3.48	3.17	2.96	2.79	2.66	2.56	2.47	2.34	2.19	2.03	1.95	1.86	1.76	1.66	1.53	1.38
∞	6.63	4.61	3.78	3.32	3.02	2.80	2.64	2.51	2.41	2.32	2.18	2.04	1.88	1.79	1.70	1.59	1.47	1.32	1.00

AUTHOR INDEX

Numbers in *italics* indicate pages with complete bibliographic information.

SUBJECT INDEX

487